THOMAS AQUINAS O

MW00785733

The *Summa theologiae* is Thomas Aquinas' undisputed masterwork, and it includes his thoughts on the elemental forces in human life. Feelings such as love, hatred, pleasure, pain, hope, and despair were described by Aquinas as "passions," representing the different ways in which happiness could be affected. But what causes the passions? What impact do they have on the person who suffers them? Can they be shaped and reshaped in order to promote human flourishing? The aim of this book is to provide a better understanding of Aquinas' account of the passions. It identifies the Aristotelian influences that lie at the heart of the *Summa Theologiae*, and it enters into a dialogue with contemporary thinking about the nature of emotion. The study argues that Aquinas' work is still important today, and shows why for Aquinas both the understanding and the attainment of happiness require prolonged reflection on the passions.

ROBERT MINER is Associate Professor of Philosophy at Baylor University.

THOMAS AQUINAS ON THE PASSIONS

A *Study of* Summa Theologiae *1a2ae* 22–48

ROBERT MINER

CAMBRIDGE
UNIVERSITY PRESS

CAMBRIDGE UNIVERSITY PRESS
Cambridge, New York, Melbourne, Madrid, Cape Town, Singapore,
São Paulo, Delhi, Dubai, Tokyo, Mexico City

Cambridge University Press
The Edinburgh Building, Cambridge CB2 8RU, UK

Published in the United States of America by Cambridge University Press, New York

www.cambridge.org
Information on this title: www.cambridge.org/9780521187596

© Robert Miner 2009

First published 2009
First paperback edition 2010

A catalogue record for this publication is available from the British Library

Library of Congress Cataloguing in Publication data
Miner, Robert.
Thomas Aquinas on the passions : a study of Summa Theologiae : 1a2ae 22–48 / Robert Miner.
p. cm.
Includes bibliographical references and index.
ISBN 978-0-521-89748-8 (hardback)
1. Thomas, Aquinas, Saint, 1225?–1274. Summa theologica.
2. Emotions–Religious aspects–Christianity. I. Title.

BX1749.T6M56 2009
128′.37–dc22

2008049145

ISBN 978-0-521-89748-8 Hardback
ISBN 978-0-521-18759-6 Paperback

Contents

Figures

Tables

Acknowledgments

I am pleased to thank the National Endowment for the Humanities for awarding me a 2005 Summer Stipend. I am also grateful to Baylor University for a sabbatical in spring 2005. The generosity of both institutions was instrumental to progress in research.

Learning about the passions comes not only from reading, but also from conversing with friends. Discussions with David and Elizabeth Corey have been a constant source of inspiration and renewal. I am glad to acknowledge a special debt to Margaret Watkins, who read the entire manuscript and whose insights have improved the whole. Thanks are also due to the decanal side of the Honors College, Thomas Hibbs and Alden Smith, and to my colleagues in Great Texts: Scott Moore, Barry Harvey, Peter Candler, Phillip Donnelly, Michael Foley, Doug Henry, Sarah-Jane Murray, Amy Vail, and William Weaver.

Over and above my colleagues at Baylor, I wish to thank the exceptionally inquisitive students in the Honors College. Teaching them has contributed much to my understanding of Thomas Aquinas and *sacra doctrina*. Their willingness to read an initially forbidding author, and to respond to him in unpredictable and creative ways, has taught me much.

Various forms of support in and around Baylor have been provided by the following individuals: Michele Anderson, Katharine Boswell, Anne-Marie Bowery, Darin Davis, Paulette Edwards, Jeff Fish, Doris Kelly, Bob Kruschwitz, Mark Long, Luis Noble, Anna Shaw, Haley Stewart, Daniel Stewart, and Amanda Weppler. Beyond Waco, I wish to thank Michael Barrett, David Burrell, Kerry Cronin, Rebecca DeYoung, Greg MacIsaac, Sean McCrossin, Paul McNellis, Giuseppe Mazzotta, Christian Moevs, Kevin Ormand, David Solomon, Lou Solomon, John Stroup, Ronald Tacelli, Jason Taylor, and John von Heyking. Special acknowledgment is due to Mark Jordan. I am profoundly grateful for his encouragement over the years to read and teach Thomas Aquinas.

Editorial guidance of a particularly valuable kind was provided by Kate Brett of Cambridge University Press. I appreciate her early and unstinting support for the project. I am also grateful to Nicholas Healy and Robert Pasnau, who read the manuscript for the Press. Both made insightful comments and suggestions that led to substantive improvements and the avoidance of any number of mistakes. The errors that remain are the ones I cannot bear to abandon.

Most of all, I am grateful for the constant support of my parents, Mary Miner and Bob Miner. Thanks also to Christopher Miner, Meredith Miner, Morgan Miner, Laura Lusk, Brad Lusk, Tammy Miner, and Jeanette Moseley.

Finally, but in no sense as an afterthought, I should like to acknowledge the blessing of my children: Anne, Sebastian, Sophia, Emma, Maria, Louisa, and Lily. All seven have provided occasions for insights into all the passions, but especially love, *prima radix omnium passionum.*

A note on the texts

References to *ST* 1a2ae cite the question, article, and portion of article (e.g. 35.3.co).

References to other parts of *ST* are the same, except that an initial part number is prefixed (e.g. 1.78.4.co).

References to *InDA*, *InNE*, *InMet*, and *InPh* cite the book number of the Aristotelian text, followed by numerals referring to the *lectio* and the paragraph divisions as they appear in Alarcón's editions.

Unless indicated otherwise, I am working with the Latin texts as established by Enrique Alarcón, whose electronic version of Aquinas' *opera omnia*, published at www.corpusthomisticum.org, is the most complete, accurate, and up-to-date edition that currently exists. Alarcón has taken over where Roberto Busa left off. Readers of Aquinas everywhere are indebted to both men.

All translations of Aquinas' texts are my own. Latin nouns that appear in the text have generally been converted to their nominative forms, unless they appear within a clause with their grammatically correct cases.

The following titles of Aquinas' texts are cited by these abbreviations:

InDA	*Sententia libri De anima*
InMet	*Sententia libri Metaphysicae*
InNE	*Sententia libri Ethicorum*
InPh	*In libros Physicorum*
QDA	*Questiones disputae de anima*
QDM	*Questiones disputatae de malo*
QDV	*Quaestiones disputate de veritate*
ST	*Summa theologiae*

1a = first part; 1a2ae = first part of second part, etc.; pr. = prologue; arg. N = Nth argument or "objection"; sc = argument *sed contra*; co = body of article; ad Nm = reply to the Nth argument.

PL and *PG* refer to J.-P. Migne, *Patrologia latina* and *Patrologia graeca* (see Bibliography).

Introduction

WHY READ THOMAS AQUINAS ON THE PASSIONS?

Five of the greatest modern thinkers – Descartes, Hobbes, Spinoza, Hume, and Rousseau – take the passions as a primary theme in their major works. This is required, it seems, by the task of developing a new mechanistic account of human nature that is compatible with the mechanism of the new science and the new politics. But to what conception of the passions are these thinkers responding? What account of the passions do the architects of modernity judge it necessary to criticize and replace? Directly or indirectly, modern thinkers are responding to the non-mechanistic, teleological conception of the passions articulated by Thomas Aquinas in Questions 22–48 of the 1a2ae of the *Summa theologiae*, the so-called "Treatise on the Passions."[1] Today we speak more frequently of "the emotions" than of the passions. But contemporary discourses about the emotions, which strongly emphasize their role as the springs of many (if not all) of our actions, descend directly from the fundamental psychological innovations of the seventeenth century (see Rosenkrantz 2005, p. 214). Consequently, Aquinas' work on the passions constitutes no small part of the background against which both early modern discussions of the passions and recent talk about the emotions must be understood.

The above constitutes one answer to the question: Why study Aquinas on the passions? The answer may satisfy those who sense that the concept of "the emotions" taken for granted by many recent philosophers and psychologists has a history, and cannot be understood apart from that

---

[1] Here and elsewhere, I occasionally acquiesce in the practice of referring to 1-2. 22–48 as the "Treatise on the Passions." I hasten to add that I am using "treatise" under erasure, since Thomas does not, strictly speaking, write treatises. Jordan (1994) observes: "The *Summa* is not built out of treatises, but out of clusters of Questions caught up into larger and larger rhythms of investigation" (p. 471).

history. (For one provocative genealogy, see Thomas Dixon's *From Passions to Emotions: The Creation of a Secular Psychological Category* [2003].) But what about those who are convinced that modern neuroscience has uncovered the essential mechanisms of the emotions, and that historical investigation has little to contribute to genuine understanding of the emotions, regardless of its capacity to illuminate pre-scientific thought? It is unlikely that members of this class would be persuaded to read Aquinas, or even Hume, unless they were convinced by a very different argument for the importance of thinking about the passions in a manner that is not dictated by the latest advances in neuroscience. A recent book by Robert Roberts offers one such argument. Modern scientific thinking illuminates the physical substructure of the emotions, often in novel and compelling ways. But information about the physical substructure of emotions does little, if anything, to clarify how, when, why, and by whom humans become angry, jealous, sad, or embarrassed. Roberts makes an analogy to the distinction between the human experience of music and its acoustical substructure. "Physically speaking, music is nothing but temporally extended and divided sequenced mixtures of air vibrations of various frequencies and amplitudes or, alternatively, mixtures of atmospheric compression wave trains of varying wavelengths and amplitudes" (2003, pp. 52–3). A competent physicist can give an exact acoustical account of a piece of music, delineating its mathematical substructure in precise terms. Such an account, while useful for any number of purposes, is not the same as understanding a piece of music as a musician understands it. Musicians "hear and speak of melodies, harmonies and counterpoint, rhythms, themes and their development, musical structure, dynamics, evocation and musical meanings, phrases, cadences, dissonances and resolutions of dissonances, and much more. It is only incidentally and occasionally that they hear and speak of frequencies, amplitudes, and wavelengths" (p. 53). Similarly, a purely neurological explanation of emotions, no matter how advanced and accurate, cannot substitute for, or compete with, an account given "in terms of the person's concerns, beliefs, thoughts, perceptions, personal history, present situation, and other factors" (p. 53).

If Roberts is right about this – and I think he is – it follows that contemporary neuroscience is not an alternative to an account of the form given by Aquinas, that is, one that analyzes the passions in terms of their human significance rather than their physiological mechanisms. This argument eliminates one motive that a contemporary reader might have for avoiding Aquinas. Yet it does little to show that Aquinas merits particular attention. For Roberts, the demonstration that neuroscientific accounts of emotion are necessarily limited in scope is a way of clearing the ground for "conceptual analysis" of the emotions. As Roberts understands it, conceptual analysis is primarily a matter of attending to experienced emotional phenomena, making appropriate distinctions and generalizations. It proceeds from "observations that ordinary emotional subjects can make simply by being intelligent and observant human beings" (2003, p. 59). For this enterprise, sustained engagement with the history of philosophy is, at best, ancillary. At one point in his book, Roberts notices a proposal by Martha Nussbaum about the Stoic account of emotion, but avoids prolonged discussion on the ground that he is "concerned more with substantive questions than those of historical scholarship" (2003, p. 83).

This neat divide between "substantive questions" and "historical scholarship" is questionable. It assumes a single, stable category of "the emotions" on which the analyst can go to work, without much attention to the concept's history. Though he interestingly argues that the particular things divided by Paul Griffiths ("affect programs," "higher cognitive emotions," and "emotional pretenses") are interrelated, Roberts assumes the prior existence of "the emotions" as a stable category, invulnerable to historical change, which others can attempt to "fracture." But what if one was never persuaded that "the emotions" are either historically or transcendentally basic? Suppose one takes the more plausible view that "the emotions" are a descendant from seventeenth-century discourses on passions, which in turn are constituted as reactions to medieval conceptions of the *passiones*. In that case, it appears that Roberts and others who take "the emotions" for granted exemplify what Amélie Rorty calls "the historical innocence of most philosophical analyses of the emotions" (1984, p. 522).

Such innocence leads contemporary practitioners of conceptual analysis to assume not only the existence of an unchanging subject-matter designated by "the emotions," but also the essential value of their own discussions. Both assumptions are questionable. Rorty finds the historical innocence of conceptual analysis of the emotions to carry certain consequences. "To put it bluntly," she writes,

current philosophical debates about the passions and emotions seem to stand even further away from the phenomena they are meant to illuminate than philosophical discussions normally do. We seem to be engaged in ill-formed and unresolvable polemical debates. What is even more puzzling is that the very questions we address seem, on the face of it, bizarre and factious, guaranteed to generate arbitrary and factitious discussions. Officially we are preoccupied with determining whether emotions can be evaluated for their rationality; or whether they are voluntary; or whether they can be "reduced" to cognitions; or whether they are interruptions of behavior that is normally purposeful. But in fact we know better: when we are really thinking, rather than making pronouncements, we know that we evaluate the appropriateness of emotions by criteria that are much richer than those of logical consistency: we are interested in determining whether they are inadequate or excessive, crude or subtle; whether they are harmoniously balanced with one another; whether we admire the character traits they reveal and the motives that usually accompany them. And when we are careful, we usually also distinguish passions, emotions, affects, sentiments. (1984, pp. 521–2)

This passage suggests at least two more reasons to read Aquinas on the passions. First, it is not clear how to "distinguish passions, emotions, affects, sentiments." Aquinas speaks frequently of *passiones* and occasionally of *affectiones*, but never of "emotions." What is the difference? If "the emotions" emerge only as the end product of a long history that involves multiple transformations of the concepts of *pathe*, *passiones*, and passions (see Rorty 1984, p. 545), one must first know what the passions are. Reading Aquinas on the *passiones* is one way to accomplish this goal. (It should be clear the practice of translating *passiones* by "emotions," rather than "passions," is misleading, since it necessarily obscures the question about the relation between passions and emotions.)

Second, one may share Rorty's sense that despite their technical sophistication, most current discussions of the emotions lack existential interest.[2] One may discover sources of relief from this condition in the history of philosophy. Of contemporary philosophical writers on the emotions, the one who has most illuminated the path toward such relief is Martha Nussbaum. What makes Nussbaum's writing so powerful is not primarily her powers of analysis, but her ability to draw upon primary texts in the history of philosophy. Precisely because of her deep engagement with such texts, along with her willingness to test their insights with "real-life" examples, Nussbaum's work escapes Rorty's charge of sterility and irrelevance. Nussbaum draws liberally from Plato and Aristotle, more heavily from the Stoics, a little from Dante, and not at all from Aquinas. In this work, I wish to draw upon Aquinas, keeping Nussbaum's work in mind as an exemplary reminder that subtle exegesis of historical texts can

[2] See, for instance, Roberts 2003: "the defining proposition for romantic love as an emotion is: *She (he) is mine and I am hers (his); she (he) is uniquely wonderful and sexually attractive; we belong together forever*" (pp. 291–2; italics in original).

have both intellectual power and human relevance.[3] Aquinas' view of the passions, I will show, incorporates elements of the Stoic philosophy, whose appreciation Nussbaum urges. Moreover, it has two key advantages over Stoicism. First, Aquinas understands, no less acutely than the Stoics, the central place of intentional apprehension in the activation of the passions. Yet he does not simply identify the passions with judgments, as the Stoics do. Second, whereas Nussbaum has to work very hard to combine the insights of Stoicism with the position that the emotions play an important role in human life and ought not to be eliminated, Aquinas' awareness of Augustine's adjudication of the debates between the Peripatetics and the Stoics enables him to articulate the same position naturally and without strain.

Why should one read Aquinas on the passions? I have given several reasons: to avoid scientistic (not scientific) reductionism, to escape historical innocence, to grasp the problematic relation between "passion" and "emotion," to think about the passions without severing the connection to life. I have not mentioned the most obvious reason – to improve our grasp of Aquinas' thought. One might suppose that students of Aquinas, or at least his ethics, would not require a commentary on the "Treatise on the Passions." Yet the surprising truth is that Questions 22–48 of the 1a2ae of the *Summa theologiae* are among the most neglected in his corpus. Nothing is more commonplace for readers of Aquinas, and especially of what has come to be known as his "moral theology," than to pay close attention to the Questions on happiness, virtue, and natural law in the 1a2ae. For many of the same readers, nothing is more habitual than to skim through, or skip entirely, the "Treatise on the Passions." This neglect has not gone entirely unnoticed. Servais Pinckaers observes that the twenty-seven Questions containing 132 Articles on the passions comprise "une oeuvre unique, classique . . . et trop négligée" (1990, p. 379). Pinckaers's observation raises a simple question: Why are Questions 22–48 of the 1a2ae so strangely neglected?[4]

One might propose an answer in terms drawn from Aquinas himself. Ethics is the study of human actions, their ends, and their principles. The passions, as Thomas himself says, are not properly human actions – that is,

[3] Some thoughtful comparisons between Nussbaum and Aquinas may be found in Leget 2003. Solomon 2002 offers an insightful review of Nussbaum's *Upheavals of Thought*, commenting that "it is the literary and historical dimensions that make the book a special contribution to the now burgeoning literature on the emotions" (p. 898).
[4] See Amis 1954, pp. 14–15.

free acts of the will – but acts that human beings have in common with
other animals. However intriguing Thomas's analysis of the non-rational
side of humanity, it has no direct relevance to moral matters, understood as the study of properly human action. D. M. Prümmer, in
his *Manuale Theologiae Moralis*, treats the passions under the heading
De hostibus voluntarii, as "obstacles to the voluntary character of human
actions" (quoted in Pinckaers 1990, p. 380). In treating the passions
thus, Prümmer undoubtedly took himself to proceed *ad mentem sancti
Thomae*.

  Is this a genuinely Thomist approach to the passions? As Pinckaers has
shown with consummate elegance, the "manualist" adaptations of what is
taken to be Thomist moral theology are not so much faithful translations
as grotesque distortions of Aquinas' thinking, usually with a pronounced
"Kantian" flavor. Pinckaers contrasts the ancient conception of ethics as a
response to the question of happiness with the manuals that "gravely
make ethics revolve around the question of obligations" (1990, p. 380).
Thomas begins the 1a2ae with an inquiry into happiness, considered as the
ultimate end for human beings. Ethics is, above all, the study of what
human beings need to know in order to attain happiness. Anything
belonging to the consideration of moral matters in general that constitutes
the 1a2ae is meant to serve this end.

  Nothing could be more alien to Aquinas than the habit of ignoring the
passions because they are (allegedly) irrelevant to morals. Just as modern
readers of Aquinas' doctrines about being and knowing have often
approached these doctrines with questions of essentially Kantian proven-
ance, and thus distorted his thinking, so many students of the *pars moralis*
of the *ST* have similarly misconstrued his notions about ethics. The error
is not limited to readers of fifty years ago who would focus on natural law
as though it were a sufficient guide to rational morality. It includes more
recent scholars who see the importance of virtue for Aquinas' conception
of ethics, but proceed as though virtue were perfectly intelligible without a
prior grasp of the passions.

  Does understanding the virtues require a prolonged study of the
passions? An affirmative answer to this question is not self-evident. What
is clear, however, is that Aquinas does not suppose that the virtues can
be approached without a thorough grounding in the passions. There is
nothing accidental about the architecture of either the *ST* as a whole, or
the 1a2ae in particular. The 1a2ae treats the end of human life and what is
necessary to attain that end. Questions 1–5 treat the end; Questions 6–48
treat the acts required to attain the end; Questions 49–114 treat the

principia, interior and exterior, of those acts. Within the consideration of the acts, the main division is between "acts of the will" (Questions 6–21) and the "acts in common with animals" that Aquinas identifies as the passions (Questions 22–48). Why does Aquinas accord twice as many Questions to the acts in common with animals as he does to distinctively human acts?[5] The question is sharpened when one remembers that in the *ST* Aquinas does not devote space to idle Questions. As the Prologue of that work reminds us, he writes with pedagogical concerns in mind. He wants to avoid the multiplication of useless questions, articles, and arguments, as well as the frequent repetition that brings weariness and confusion to the souls of students. Why, then, should a consideration of moral matters *in universali* include so many Questions on the passions, prior to the treatment of the virtues?

By the time Aquinas comes to write the *ST*, he is convinced that knowing the passions is fundamental for understanding the rational creature's quest for beatitude. But why? We should know about the passions, one might think, because they are powerful forces that impede reason and thereby frustrate the attempts of human beings to live wisely and happily. But Aquinas does not take this line. In his judgment, what kills the progress of the rational creature toward the end is not passion but sin. One may persist – Thomas treats the passions at length because protection against sin requires a knowledge of its causes. Passion can indeed be a cause of sin. But it is not *only* a cause of sin. Moreover, it is neither the unique nor the most potent cause of sin. No reasoning that terminates in a solely negative justification for treating the passions at length can be reconciled with Thomas's thought.

To understand why Aquinas privileges the passions as he does in the *ST*, the reader must grasp what he teaches about the passions in that text. That is, she must encounter the *ST*'s actual teaching. Such an encounter makes any number of demands on the reader. It requires some knowledge of Aquinas' *auctoritates*: not only Aristotle and Augustine, but also Dionysius and Damascene, Scripture and Cicero. It requires attention to the four Questions about the passions in general. Finally, and most importantly, it requires a careful reading of the twenty-three Questions that treat of the particular passions.

---

[5] Uffenheimer-Lippens (2003) accurately observes that the Questions on the passions comprise nearly a quarter of the 1a2ae (p. 530). Pinckaers (1990) makes a similar observation, noting that the Questions on the passions outnumber those on happiness and human acts, as well as those on the virtues and the gifts, or law and grace.

The aim of this book is to facilitate an encounter with Thomas Aquinas' teaching on the passions, as we have it in its most detailed elaboration.[6] But what does it mean to grasp any particular teaching of the *ST*? Is it adequate to select isolated passages that appear to offer definitions of the passions, or to focus mainly on passages that seem relevant to contemporary concerns? While such methods may yield some insights, they are not sufficient for an integral reading. In order to perceive what Aquinas is up to in the *ST*, the reader must adopt a different approach. She must attend closely to each Question in the Treatise, following the steps of its articulation. Initially, I was convinced that the natural correlate of close reading was article-by-article exposition of each Question. I still have sympathy with this approach, especially when the goal is to set forth a detailed and comprehensive reading of the text that avoids doing violence to its form. But since contemporary readers will inevitably find some questions more pressing than others, and since there is no reason to believe that the priorities of such readers will correspond to Aquinas' own, I have not strictly adhered to an *articulatim* approach.[7] Instead, I have adopted the following procedure. In Part 1 of the book, I treat topics in a logical sequence that contemporary readers should find intelligible. I ask about the sensitive appetite in general, proceed to a consideration of its acts (i.e. the passions), inquire into the various things that arouse these acts, and conclude with a consideration of Aquinas' thought on the relation between the passions and morality. Here I follow Aquinas' order in a broad sense. The initial delineation of the sensitive appetite focuses on the Ia *pars*; the analysis of the other topics switches to Aquinas' consideration of the passions in general, which comprises Questions 22–5 of the Ia2ae. Since recent commentary on the passions tends almost exclusively

---

[6] The *ST* is not the only work in which Aquinas addresses the passions. Other texts include the *Scriptum* on Peter Lombard's *Sentences* (bk. 3, dist. 26), the *Quaestiones disputatae de veritate* (Questions 25 and 26), the *Quaestiones disputatae de malo*, and the *expositio* of Aristotle's *Nicomachean Ethics*. In this book, I am not concerned to provide comprehensive readings of these texts; I attend to them only as they are useful for illuminating the teaching of the *ST*.

[7] On this point I am grateful to Robert Pasnau, who convinced me that strict adherence to the *articulatim* approach might limit the audience of this book to the small class of readers who are seeking a literal commentary on 1-2.22–48. Some may still judge that Parts 2 and 3 preserve too much of this approach. But in light of the intrinsic relation between what Aquinas thinks about a particular passion, and the rhetorical form of his treatment, I think the benefits of this procedure far outweigh the liabilities. On the dangers of abstracting the "teachings" of a thinker from the forms of the texts in which those teachings are conveyed, see Jordan 1992b.

to emphasize these questions, the proportion of dialogue with other interpreters of Aquinas' thought and contemporary thinkers who write about "the emotions" is relatively high in the four chapters that comprise Part 1.

Parts 2 and 3 adopt a different approach. I begin Part 2 with an argument for the proposition that in order to achieve any serious understanding of Aquinas' thinking about the passions, Questions 26–48 must be privileged. Part 2 focuses on the "concupiscible" passions treated in Questions 26–39; Part 3 examines the "irascible" passions that Aquinas discusses in Questions 40–8. In both parts, I take the view that grasping what Aquinas thinks about any particular passion, and why he thinks it, requires careful attention to the form and mode of treatment – that is, to the distribution of Questions corresponding to any particular passion, and to the organization of Articles within any given Question. Though not every Question and every Article receives equal emphasis, my basic procedure in these two parts is to follow the thread that informs the individual Questions and Articles devoted to the particular passions. This means that Parts 2 and 3 have a different character from Part 1. Some readers who find Part 1 philosophically interesting may wonder about the importance of Parts 2 and 3. Conversely, those who find Parts 2 and 3 to the point may have reservations about the mode of approach characteristic of Part 1. My hope is that readers will find each part beneficial, recognizing that a treatment of the passions "in general" will naturally have a different character from a serial examination of particular passions. (Some such difference, I think, informs Aquinas' own treatment.)

If Part 1 interacts with a range of contemporary writers, Parts 2 and 3 engage in a sustained dialogue with one commentator in particular, Santiago Ramírez. Ramírez's *De passionibus animae*, the transcript of a series of lectures he gave in Latin during the middle of the last century, is one of the few recent commentaries on the whole of the Treatise. In forming my own interpretations, I have found Ramírez's treatment quite helpful, notwithstanding my disagreement with many of his specific claims. I have especially benefited from his persistent attempts to ferret out the *ordo articulorum* ("order of articles") that comprises the spine of any given Question in the *ST*. Ramírez's attempts in this area typically propose an *ordo articulorum* that coincides with a logical distinction familiar to Thomas (e.g. "per se causes" vs. "per accidens causes"). Eschmann observes that "a strictly 'logical' scheme, such as that of Ramírez, is simply too narrow for the rich and abundant

Thomistic text" (1997, p. 41).[8] He acknowledges, however, that Ramírez is
"very keen and not infrequently successful in analyzing the logic of Saint
Thomas's proceedings" (p. 58). I think that Eschmann is right on both
counts.

Umberto Galeazzi observes that any present inquiry into Aquinas'
thinking on the passions is "inevitably conditioned" by our relation to
"modern and contemporary thought" (2004, p. 548). This is true, I think,
yet it remains a worthwhile goal to attempt to understand Aquinas as he
understood himself, for reasons not merely antiquarian in character. In
asserting the contemporary relevance of Aquinas, I do not mean to suggest
that he already says everything that one would want to know about the
passions. Some students of Aquinas, impressed by the power of his
thought, the amplitude of his interests, and his personal sanctity, suppose
that the answer to any significant question is somehow contained within
his texts, either implicitly or explicitly. Since I am myself impressed with
Aquinas on all three counts, I understand the temptation to make this
supposition. But it should be resisted. Aquinas is simply not in a position
to address some questions of contemporary interest. What is the precise
relation between the distinguishable forms of fear that are manifested in
specific autonomic responses and the reactions in various regions of the
brain, especially the amygdala? Pressing Aquinas on such questions is not
a profitable use of his texts. Modern neuroscience has much to tell us
about the passions that Aquinas was unable to know.[9] Yet it remains
possible that Aquinas offers a conceptual framework in which the findings
of modern neuroscience may be integrated. Despite our distance from the
Middle Ages, we have plenty of reasons to encounter Aquinas' account
of the passions, an analysis "précise, détaillée, bien articulée et reliée
à l'ensemble, un petit chef-d'oeuvre à la manière des édifices du temps"
(Pinckaers 1990, p. 381).

---

[8] On the tendency to assimilate Thomas's textual structures to a quasi-mathematical order, the
following warning of Pascal remains apposite: "Je sais un peu ce que c'est, et combien peu de
gens l'entendent. Nulle science humaine ne le peut garder. Saint Thomas ne l'a pas gardé.
La mathématique le garde, mais elle est inutile en sa profondeur" (1976, §61, p. 63; see also
Pascal 1966, §694, p. 246).

[9] Here Kenny (2004) strikes the right balance. One may admit that some of Aquinas' views have been
"superannuated by the progress of science," while proceeding to acknowledge (as Kenny does a
paragraph later) that "Aquinas was an intellectual giant, and those of us who try to interpret him to
a twenty-first century audience are like Lilliputians trying to tie him down with our own conceptual
netting" (p. 462).

PART I

The passions in general

CHAPTER I

The sensitive appetite

To understand the passions, one must know "where" the passions are located in a human being. This requires Aquinas to identify the "seat" or "subject" of the passions. Thomas identifies the subject of the passions as the "sensitive appetite." When Aquinas speaks of the sensitive appetite, he supposes its place in a more comprehensive teaching about the soul and its powers. Setting the "vegetative" and "locomotive" powers of the soul aside, we may focus on what Aquinas means by the core notion of "appetite" (§1.1). Though "appetite" does have a univocal meaning, it is irreducibly differentiated into three types–natural, rational, and sensitive. Aquinas gives a preliminary explanation of sensitive appetite by situating it "between" natural appetite (§1.2) and rational appetite (§1.3). Why does Thomas hold that the primary object of appetite is good, and that there is no appetite for evil as such? Aquinas's teaching on the priority of good over evil provides the first clue for understanding why he orders the passions in the manner that he does (§1.4).

1.1 THE APPETITIVE POWER IN GENERAL

Aristotle defines soul as "the first actuality of a physical body potentially having life" (*De anima* 2.1, 412a28) and "the what-it-is-to-be for a body of this sort" (412b12). He proceeds to identify three types of soul in human beings: intellectual, sensitive, and vegetative. After discussing the soul's essence and its types, Aristotle moves to isolate the *dunameis* of the soul – a term variously rendered as "capacities," "faculties," or "powers" (*potentiae*). Three of its powers correspond exactly to the three types. There is the rational power, the sensitive power, and the vegetative power. Beyond the capacities for reasoning, sensing, and growing, Aristotle determines that the soul is the origin (*arche*) of movement from place to place, and the principle of desire (*orexis*). Therefore, in addition to the intellectual, sensitive, and vegetative powers, Aristotle attributes to the soul a "locomotive" and an "appetitive" power.

Table 1.1 *Types of soul, activities, modes of living*

Type of soul	Activities	Mode of living
Rational	Thinking, sensing, growing, moving about, desiring	Mode of rational animals
Sensitive (i)	Sensing, growing, moving about, desiring	Mode of animals with locomotion
Sensitive (ii)	Sensing, growing, desiring	Mode of immobile animals
Vegetative	Growing	Mode of plants

In the 1a *pars* of the *ST*, Aquinas makes this doctrine his own. In Question 78, he defends the Aristotelian enumeration of the five kinds of powers of the soul, observing that three of these kinds are simply referred to as "souls" (rational, sensitive, vegetative) and four are called "modes of living." Aquinas adds that of the "three souls," the operation of rational soul "so far surpasses bodily nature that it is not even exercised by any bodily organ" (1.78.1.co). This distinguishes rational soul from sensitive and vegetative soul, neither of which can function without a bodily organ.

If each type of soul has its own distinctive operation, why does Aquinas identify four (rather than three) modes of living? The apparent anomaly arises from the fact that some animals move and others do not. Since all animals take in nutrients, grow, and sense, all animals have vegetative and sensitive soul. Yet not every animal can move from place to place; there are "immobile animals" like shellfish. Thus while every animal has both vegetative and sensitive soul, not every animal has the power of local motion. This necessitates a distinction between two "modes of living" among animals (see table 1.1). As the table indicates, the higher includes the lower. Animals with rational soul (i.e. human beings) also possess sensitive and vegetative soul, and thus the modes of living proper to the lower animals. Similarly, animals with sensitive soul possess both their own mode of living and the mode of living proper to vegetative soul.

Because both desiring and moving about are activities shared by animals with different types of soul, neither act picks out a specific type of soul. There is no "locomotive soul" or "appetitive soul." Nor does either act correspond to a particular mode of living: "appetite does not constitute a grade of living things, because in whatever there is sense, there is also appetite, as said in *De anima* 2.3" (78.1 ad 2m). Yet desiring and locomotion do name acts of which some organisms are capable and others are not. It turns out that organisms with the capacity for sensation, and only these organisms, have the capacity for desiring, the "appetitive power." Neither Aristotle nor Aquinas takes this to be an accident. They infer that the appetitive power essentially depends upon the power of apprehension.

In light of this dependence, why is sensitive appetite a distinct power from sensitive apprehension? Why not hold that appetition is one of many acts attributable to the apprehensive power? Aquinas suggests two reasons for distinguishing sensitive apprehension and sensitive appetite as powers. First, he observes that sensitive appetite is related to sensitive apprehension as moved is related to mover. Without a prior apprehension, it is simply inert. Aquinas expresses this by describing the sensitive appetite as a "passive" power. Before it can be in act, it must be acted upon. Hence the sensitive appetite is "naturally moved by the thing apprehended, whence the apprehended appetible is a 'mover that is not moved,' whereas the appetite is a 'mover moved,' as is said in *De anima* (3.10, 433b16) and *Metaphysics* (12.7, 1072a26)" (1.80.2.co). Second, the act of an apprehensive power is not the same as the act of an appetitive power. "The operation of the apprehensive power is completed in the fact that the things apprehended are in the person who apprehends, while the operation of the appetitive power is completed in the fact that the person desiring (*appetens*) is inclined towards the appetible thing" (*in rem appetibilem*) (1.81.1.co). Apprehension brings the thing to us, as it were, through its sensible or intelligible species. Appetite, by contrast, moves us toward the thing itself, and not merely its species. This contrast between apprehension and appetite receives striking elaboration in 1a2ae, where it will ground the claim that "love is more unitive than cognition" (28.3 ad 3m).

"Appetite follows apprehension" (79.2 ad 2m). The dependence of appetite on apprehension is crucial for Aquinas' teaching on the passions. The difference between two forms of perception, rational apprehension and sensitive apprehension, generates a corresponding distinction between two appetites, rational appetite and sensitive appetite. Rational appetite, or "the will" (*voluntas*), follows rational apprehension; sensitive appetite follows sensitive apprehension. Or so it appears: I will show (§1.3) the multiple ways in which Aquinas complicates this apparently simple doctrine. Though appetite requires apprehension as a precondition, it is a distinct power of the soul. What does Aquinas mean by appetite? Before considering the sensitive appetite in detail, it is helpful to examine his general notion of appetite.

The Latin term *appetitus* has resonances that the English word "appetite" lacks. *Appetitus* is a compound of *ad,* "towards," and *petere,* to "aim at" or "desire."[1] In its main signification, the term denotes a "reaching toward something."[2] This is precisely the point from which Thomas begins his own reflection on appetite. Early in the 1a *pars,* Aquinas defines appetite as "a kind of motion toward a thing" (1.5.4.co). The qualifying *quidam* should not be neglected.[3] Thomas refrains from saying that an appetite is simply or literally a motion. In its most basic sense, *appetitus* is a reaching forth, a stretching toward some kind of object.

What has appetite in this sense? A short and only partly misleading answer: everything that exists, with the exception of God.[4] Because God is pure act, he never reaches for or stretches toward something that would complete his being. He is always already complete. Everything other than God, however, is radically incomplete, and therefore seeks its completion, consciously or not. In its most general sense, *appetitus* names the universal tendency of anything to seek what completes it. Because no form (except for God who is "pure form, or better pure act") (1.3.7.co) is complete by its own nature, every creature has an inclination toward what completes its form. Possessing a body, sense, reason, or will determines the kinds of appetite that a creature can have, but it has no bearing on whether it has appetite as such. What causes a creature to have an appetite is nothing less than the fact of creaturehood itself. Within anything that contains a distinction between what it is (its *essentia*) and the grounding act by which it is (its *esse*), there is some difference between potency and act. In its most fundamental sense, *appetitus* denotes the disposition of the creature's potency toward actualization.

As the term implies, *appetitus* is essentially appetite toward something, i.e. its "term" (*terminus*). Appetite is the natural inclination of a form to some term that completes that form. Because attainment of the term

---

[1] Ramírez (1973) notes this clearly: "appetere = petere seu pergere ad aliud, hoc est, ad aliud moveri" (p. 88).

[2] Stump (2003) notices that "it is not easy to provide a satisfactory translation of 'appetitus,' especially in a single word: 'desire,' 'tendency,' 'inclination,' 'attraction' are all more or less unsatisfactory possibilities" (p. 496n40). Vogler (2002) makes this observation: "*Appetite* is, roughly, what characterizes an agent as a pursuer or seeker. There is no contemporary equivalent for 'appetite' in widespread use."

[3] Though commentators often fail to notice it, Thomas frequently signals to the reader that his use of the language of motion is metaphorical. To take another example from the 1a2ae: "passio quidam motus est" (23.2.co). For more on what Aquinas means by describing passions as motions, see §2.3.

[4] In its most proper sense, as a stretching forth or reaching out to what an agent wants but lacks, *appetitus* does not apply to God. But if *appetitus* is taken in a secondary sense, as delighting in what is already possessed, then appetite may legitimately be attributed to God (cf. 1.19.1 ad 2m).

completes a being, at least with respect to the relevant form, and because any being naturally desires its own completion, the term of appetite is rightly identified with what is "desirable" and therefore good (1.5.6.co). Notice the order: goodness is understood in terms of desirability; desirability is understood in terms of completion; completion is understood in terms of potency and act. This is precisely the order that Thomas follows in Questions 3–5 of the 1a *pars*. As he says in the first Article of Question 5:

The nature (*ratio*) of good consists in this, that it is something desirable (*appetibile*), whence the Philosopher says in chapter 1 of the *Ethics* that "good is what all things desire" (*appetunt*). Now it is clear that something is desirable according as it is complete (*perfectum*), for all things desire their own completion (*perfectionem*). But to the degree that something is complete (*perfectum*), it is to that extent in act. (1.5.1.co)

In what does *appetitus* terminate? In one sense, there are as many terms as there are appetites. Beneath the multiplicity of material terms, however, stands a threefold structure. Any term of an appetite is sought as either useful (*utile*), intrinsically good (*honestum*), or pleasant (*delectabile*). This threefold division of "formal aspects" (*rationes*) under which anything is desired bears a close correspondence to the three kinds of friendship identified by Aristotle (friendship based on utility, pleasure, or virtue).[5] Aquinas also finds the threefold division of good to inform the distinction that Aristotle makes at the beginning of the *Ethics* between three kinds of lives: the pleasurable, the civic, and the contemplative (see *Nicomachean Ethics*, 1095b15–20). In his commentary on the *Ethics*, Aquinas writes:

Because man is most of all moved toward the ultimate end, it is necessary that the [three] lives are diversified according to the diversity of the ultimate end. Now the end has the aspect of good. Now the good is divided into three – the useful (*utile*), the pleasurable (*delectabile*), and the befitting (*honestum*). Two of these, the pleasurable and befitting, have the aspect of an end, because both are desirable on account of themselves. The befitting is said to be the good according to reason, which has a certain pleasure joined to it. Whence the pleasurable, which is divided against the befitting, is the pleasurable according to the senses. Now reason is both speculative and practical. Therefore the life is called sensual (*voluptuosa*), which places the end in the pleasure of the senses. The life, however, is called civic (*civilis*), which places the end in the good of practical reason, e.g. in the exercise of virtuous deeds. But the life called contemplative (*contemplativa*)

---

[5] See Aristotle, *Nicomachean Ethics* 8.3, 1156a6–1156b32. Later writers will pick up the threefold division. One example is Ambrose, whose use of the division at *De officiis* 1.9 Aquinas cites (but does not explain) at 1.5.6.sc.

is that which places its end in the good of speculative reason, viz. in the contemplation of truth. (*InNE* 1.5.4–5)

Noting this passage, Candace Vogler confesses that she finds it "very hard to follow the link Aquinas makes between the sensual, the public, and the virtuous lives and the threefold division" (2002, p. 258n7). Her difficulty may lie in her misdescription of the lives. Though "sensual" and "public" are acceptable renderings of *voluptuosa* and *civilis*, the third life is not the "virtuous." It is the "contemplative" (*contemplativa*). Vogler thinks that Aquinas identifies the public life with the *utile* because it privileges honor, and thereby makes happiness a function of others. "I suppose that there is a sense in which this makes all of what one does in one's public capacity a mere *means* to attaining a good reputation, but, again, it's a stretch" (2002, p. 259n7). This is not at all what Thomas has in mind. Aquinas connects the *vita civilis* to the formal aspect of the *utile*, not because honor is an external good that comes from others (though that is true), but for a quite different reason. Aquinas is prepared to acknowledge that in its best form, the public life will place the last end not in honor, but in virtue, where *virtus* names that which enables the noble exercise of practical reason. Such a life is nevertheless linked to the *utile*, because it is not ultimate. It is ordered toward something else that transcends the public sphere. This "something else" is the end of the *vita contemplativa*, the contemplation of truth for its own sake. This good – the good of speculative reason as distinguished from practical reason – corresponds most closely to the *bonum honestum*. Aquinas does not, of course, deny that considerations belonging to the *bonum honestum* may be applied by the practical intellect for public benefit. He does not propose any stark alienation between the *bonum honestum* and the public life. But in this passage, his point is to suggest that the relation between the *vita civilis* and the *vita contemplativa* mirrors the relation between the instrumental and the final, the *utile* and *honestum*.[6]

Though Vogler has misunderstood the sense of the passage from the *Ethics* commentary, I agree that the passage is not the best source for understanding the "threefold division." It is more profitable, I think, to examine the division's appearance early in the Ia *pars*. The relation between the three "formal aspects" (*rationes*) under which anything is desired is not univocal but analogical. Aquinas writes:

---

[6] This consideration is also required to make sense of the different kinds of prudence that Aquinas distinguishes at 61.4. See Miner 2000, pp. 412–13.

Good is not divided into these three as something univocal to be predicated equally of them all, but as something analogical to be predicated of them according to priority and posteriority. Hence it is predicated chiefly of the *honestum*, then of the *delectabile*, and lastly of the *utile*. (1.5.6 ad 3m)

In the most proper sense, "good" names what absolutely completes or perfects a form. Only what is simply final, desired for its own sake – the *bonum honestum* – satisfies this condition. Pleasant things are rightly called "good" by analogy, because they too are desired for their own sake. Yet they fall short of the *bonum honestum*, because they are not fully perfective. The rest they bring to the appetite is not permanent. Furthest from the proper notion of good is *bonum utile*. It is a term of the appetite, but only "relatively" (*secundum quid*). The useful good, Thomas claims, terminates the appetite's movement "as a means by which something tends to another" (1.5.6.co).

In the widest sense of the term, appetite is a being's inclination, according to its form, toward some good. Whatever the good may be materially, it can be sought only as useful, pleasurable, or simply befitting. Are these three formalities exhaustive? Drawing upon Aquinas explicitly, Vogler writes:

It's hard to see where we would look for *more* concluding points for intentional action. We have: the conclusion is in the future and doing this is a way of getting there (the useful). We have: the conclusion is attaining this very end, which expresses or is otherwise rooted in more enduring, patterning features of my life (the befitting). We have: the point in doing this is to savor the doing of the present action (the pleasant) . . . Formally, the different kinds of practical considerations have different *temporal* relations to what you do. It is hard to see what has been left out. (2002, pp. 42–3)

Aquinas' threefold differentiation of good underlies the core notion of appetite. It also generates the fundamental distinction between the concupiscible and irascible powers of the sensitive appetite (§2.4). But before attending to the sensitive appetite's two powers, it is important to see how Aquinas describes the sensitive appetite itself. He does so by setting it off from two other forms of appetite, rational and natural appetite.

1.2 SENSITIVE VS. NATURAL APPETITE

In light of appetite's dependence upon apprehension, it might appear that beings without sensation lack appetite. But plants, according to Aquinas, do not lack appetite. Like any other creature marked by the real distinction between act and potency, they have a natural desire for their own flourishing. But if plants do not have an apprehensive power, as Aquinas expressly says, then how can their appetite depend upon apprehension? Aquinas answers: the apprehension need not belong to the plant itself. Beings that have natural forms but lack the capacity for apprehension are directed toward an end as apprehended by God. This is what it means to say that they do not move themselves, but are "moved by another." Aquinas' favorite example is that of an arrow moving toward its target. Its act is directed not by its own apprehension, but by that of the archer (cf. 1.2.co). The name for the appetite that belongs to a thing by its nature, without depending upon the apprehensive power of that thing, is "natural appetite."

Strictly speaking, the *appetitus naturalis* is not an exception to the claim "appetition follows apprehension," since it is utterly dependent upon the divine apprehension. Not only inanimate things, but anything that has a natural form, has what Aquinas understands by natural appetite. This corresponds to what Aquinas in Question 26 of the Treatise will call "natural love" or a "connaturality" of something for its own fulfillment. The simplest case is that of a thing that possesses only natural love, such as a heavy body whose "connaturality" is its *gravitas*, its natural tendency to move downward unless acted upon by some countervailing motion. But all created things have a natural appetite. Thomas writes:

Natural love is not only in the powers of the vegetative soul, but in all the soul's powers, and even in all the parts of the body, and in all things universally because, as Dionysius says (*Div. Nom.* iv), "The beautiful and the good are lovable to all things," since anything whatever has a *connaturalitas* toward that which is suitable to itself (*sibi conveniens*) according to its nature. (26.1 ad 3m)

The most famous characterization of natural appetite in human beings may appear in the 1a2ae's treatment of natural law. "In man there is first of all an inclination to good according to nature, in which he shares with all substances, so far as any substance desires (*appetit*) the preservation of its own being, according to its nature" (94.2.co).

I have focused on natural appetite in order to isolate two basic features of the sensitive appetite. Unlike natural appetite, sensitive appetite is (1) present only in a being with sensation and (2) essentially caused by and dependent upon the apprehensive powers of that being. Rather than naming the general tendency toward whatever is suitable for a creature, "sensitive appetite" picks out the specific inclination toward those things that are apprehended as desirable by the creature that possesses sensation.

The simplest case is the inclination toward what is sensed to be pleasant. If a thing is not sensed to be pleasant in itself, but nonetheless estimated as useful for obtaining what is pleasant, then the sensitive appetite may tend toward that thing as well. This dual direction of the sensitive appetite toward what is pleasant and what is useful constitutes (or so I will argue later) the basis of Aquinas' division of the sensitive appetite into a "concupiscible" and an "irascible" power (§2.4).

The first move in Aquinas' preliminary description of the sensitive appetite is to set it off from the natural appetite. The second, and more complicated, move is to distinguish it from the rational appetite, which Aquinas will also call the "intellectual appetite" and (more frequently) "will" (*voluntas*).

1.3 SENSITIVE VS. RATIONAL APPETITE

What is the distinction between the sensitive and the rational appetite? A simple formulation of the distinction would run as follows: the sensitive appetite tends toward concrete singulars that are apprehended by the senses, whereas the rational appetite tends toward universal goods that are perceived by the intellect. Through its acts of cognition, the intellect does not merely know particulars, but also universal concepts by abstraction from concrete things apprehended by sensation. In its essentials, this formulation of the distinction between rational and sensitive appetite is adequate. Yet it gives rise to misunderstandings and objections. To attain an accurate understanding of the difference between sensitive and rational appetite, the difference between the proper objects of each must be considered in some detail.

Anthony Kenny wonders whether Aquinas' apparent confinement of the sensitive appetite to concrete singular objects bears scrutiny. He suggests the following counter-example:

If we express a want in language – say, by giving an order to a waiter – then what eventually satisfies the want will be an individual thing: the particular medium rare steak which he brings. But the initial want was not a want *for that particular steak*. (1993, p. 62; emphasis in original)

Aquinas seems to hold that only particulars (this particular steak) can be the object of the sensitive appetite. Against this, Kenny claims that what moves the sensitive appetite is often not the act of perceiving or imagining a particular member of a class ("This piece of steak looks good"), but simply thinking of the class itself ("Steak would be good").

But does Aquinas actually reduce the object of the sensitive appetite to particulars in the way that Kenny imagines? Kenny appears to have overlooked an important passage from the *QDV*. The sensitive appetite, Aquinas writes,

tends to the appetible thing itself, just as that which is the reason of its being appetible (*ratio appetibilitatis*) is found within it. For it does not tend to the *ratio appetibilitatis* itself, since the lower appetite does not desire goodness or utility or pleasure itself, but this useful thing or this pleasurable thing. (*QDV* 25.1.co)

By itself, this quotation would seem to confirm Kenny's view that for Aquinas, the sensitive appetite tends only to discrete particulars ("this sirloin"). But Aquinas adds:

Since the sensitive appetite tends not only to this thing or only to that thing, but to every thing which is useful or pleasurable to it, it is therefore above natural appetite. On account of this it needs an apprehension by which it may distinguish the pleasurable from what is not pleasurable. (*QDV* 25.1.co; emphasis mine)

It turns out that sense appetite tends toward *anything* that is pleasant or useful. Kenny implies that Aquinas' citation of the *Rhetoric*'s assertion, "we hate the whole class of brigands" (2.4, 1382a6), intends to contrast the universal objects of the rational appetite with the particular objects of the sensitive appetite (2004, p. 62). But Aquinas cites the same passage to establish that "the sensitive powers, both of apprehension and of appetite, can tend to something universally" (29.6.co). Read together, *QDV* 25 and the 1a2ae suggest that the object of the sensitive appetite is both universal and particular, though not in the same respects.

To clarify the issue, we may first identify the respect in which it is impossible for the object of the sensitive appetite to be universal. Aquinas writes: "There are two ways of speaking of the universal: first, according as it is under the intention of universality; secondly, as considered in the nature to which the intention is attributed" (29.6.co). (I will explain the notion of "intention," important for Aquinas' account of the activation of passion, in more detail at §3.3 and §3.4.) In the first sense, the object of the sensitive appetite cannot be universal, because the sensitive apprehension cannot perceive universal intentions. The sensitive appetite is not moved by reflection on the logical concept of a steak. For the sensitive appetite to be moved, there must be some phantasm of a steak. Yet this phantasm *is* a universal in the second way of speaking that Aquinas mentions. It need not be identified with any particular piece of steak.

Rather, it will contain within itself the features common to multiple steaks which are pleasing to the appetite.[7] In this way, Aquinas acknowledges that the sensitive appetite can tend not simply to this or that steak, but to any piece of steak that has the relevant qualities. Kenny wants to contrast Aristotle's view that "we hate the whole class of brigands" (where hatred appropriately has a universal object) with Aquinas' view, which (he thinks) would arbitrarily confine a passion like hatred to particular brigands. But is this really Aquinas' view? In the Treatise he writes:

Hatred in the sensitive part can regard something universally, because this thing, by reason of its common nature, and not merely as an individual, is hostile to the animal – for instance, as a wolf in regard to a sheep. Hence a sheep hates the wolf generally. (29.6.co)

Thomas's view that "the sensitive appetite is an appetite for the particular good, while the will is an appetite for the universal good" (1.64.2. co), cannot be pitted against the ability of the sensitive appetite to tend to something universally, if universality is considered not "under the intention of universality," but rather "in the nature to which the intention is attributed" (29.6.co).

This suffices to show that (*pace* Kenny) Aquinas acknowledges the respect in which the sensitive appetite's object is universal. But why does Aquinas also insist that the object of sensitive appetite is "particular"? Is he not wanting to have his steak and eat it too? It seems that on the reading of Aquinas that I am recommending, the sensitive appetite is not drawn primarily toward particulars (e.g. this piece of candy), but primarily toward universals (e.g. "the sweet") and only derivatively toward particular things as instances of universals (e.g. this piece of candy *qua* sweet thing). If "the sweet" and "the pleasant" are *per se* objects of the sensitive appetite, and this piece of candy its object only *per accidens*, why does Aquinas insist that the proper object of sensitive appetite is something particular? In the 1a *pars*, Aquinas suggests that non-rational animals "are inclined to the good, with some knowledge. It is not that they cognize the very aspect of good (*ipsam rationem boni*). Rather, they cognize some particular good (*aliquod bonum particulare*), just as the sense does, which knows the sweet, the white, and anything else of this sort. The inclination following upon this cognition is called the sensitive appetite" (1.59.1.co).

---

[7] This corresponds to what Collingwood (1938) terms "generalizing representation." As Collingwood observes, "the patron who buys a picture of a fox-hunt or a covey of partridges does not buy it because it represents that fox-hunt or that covey and not another; he buys it because it represents a thing of that kind" (pp. 45–6).

Non-rational animals do not cognize the very aspect of good, but only some "particular good." Here *bonum particulare* denotes not a "bare particular" (this piece of candy), but the pleasant or useful, which Aquinas construes as "some particular goods" in relation to the common *ratio* of goodness. By comparison to the good as such, the "good *qua* pleasant" or "good *qua* useful" stand as particular goods. This reading, I think, not only is faithful to Aquinas' texts, but also suffices to account for how the sensitive appetite tends toward particular good, which nonetheless has an aspect of universality. Yet I do not want to imply that when Aquinas considers "pleasure" or "utility" as examples of *aliquod bonum particulare*, he thinks of them as instances of a single substance called "goodness." Rather, his view is that "good" is predicated of them analogically (§1.1). Only the *bonum honestum* is good *simpliciter*, because it denotes the end that is goodness itself, or else some action that is suitable for attaining that end.

The sensitive appetite cannot directly desire the *bonum honestum*. It is confined to wanting things that are either pleasant or useful. In this sense, it is limited to particular goods. Appetite for goods that are either pleasant or useful does not, according to Aquinas, require the possession of general concepts of pleasure and utility. On the contrary, non-rational animals lack these concepts altogether. They do not know "what pleasure is." But their appetites conform to a pattern; they are drawn *only* to things perceived as pleasant or useful. Because they lack intellect, they are incapable of desiring anything as good in abstraction from pleasure or utility. An irrational animal can desire anything apprehended as pleasant or useful, but it cannot ask itself, "Is it good to want pleasant things?" Only a rational animal can abstract pleasure and utility as universals, and reflect upon their relation to the good as such. It is the human privilege to desire "immaterial goods that the sense does not apprehend, like knowledge, virtue, and other things of this sort" (1.80.2 ad 2m).

The primary object of the sensitive appetite is the pleasant. This accords with Thomas's view that "good" is more properly predicated of the pleasant than the useful. Yet Aquinas does not engage in any crude reduction of the sensitive appetite's object to pleasure and the avoidance of pain. The sensitive appetite also tends to what is useful, and the avoidance of danger. His examples are typically Aristotelian – the sheep flees the wolf because it perceives it to be harmful. Perhaps thinking of *Republic* 436a, Kenny notices that the appetites for sensible goods like food, drink, and sex are "paradigm exercises of the animal appetite" (2004, p. 63). He adds:

But Aquinas also sees the flight of the sheep from the wolf, and the charge of the enraged bull, as manifestations of appetite. There are negative as well as positive appetitions. Indeed, Aquinas divides the sensory appetite into two sub-faculties: one which is the locus of affective drives, and another which is the locus of aggressive drives. It would be unprofitable to follow in detail his justification for this anatomizing: it consists largely of forced assimilation of diverse classifications made by previous philosophers and theologians. (p. 63)

Here Kenny's account is muddled. Though positive appetitions for apprehended goods are primary, as I will argue in the next section (§1.4), there are indeed negative appetitions as well. A "negative" appetition is a tendency *away* from something perceived as evil. But this distinction between "positive" and "negative" appetitions has nothing to do with the distinction between what Kenny calls the "sub-faculties" of the sensitive appetite, viz. the concupiscible and the irascible (§2.4). To see that Kenny has confused the point, consider that for Aquinas hatred is both an "affective drive" (i.e. a concupiscible passion) and a "negative appetition" (a repugnance against perceived evil). Likewise, hope is both an "aggressive drive" (i.e. an irascible passion) and a "positive appetition" (an inclination toward perceived good).

To summarize: the sensitive appetite is the inclination in beings possessing sensation (i.e. animals with bodies) toward particular goods perceived as pleasant or useful. So far, in accordance with Aquinas' own emphasis, I have stressed the tendency toward good. But is the sensitive appetite restricted toward what an animal apprehends as good? Are there appetites that tend away from evil, without necessarily tending toward good? Can there be an appetite to evil, or an appetite directed away from the good? To understand Aquinas' thinking about these questions, we must grasp his appropriation of an idea that he derives from Augustine and Dionysius, namely the idea that good is radically prior to evil.

1.4 THE PRIORITY OF GOOD TO EVIL

Appetite is a kind of motion toward good. Cannot appetite equally be a motion toward evil? Thomas addresses this question early in the 1a *pars*. "Since the *ratio* of good is the *ratio* of appetibility, and since evil is opposed to good, it is impossible that any evil, as such, should be desired (*appetatur*), whether by the natural, the animal, or the intellectual appetite, i.e. the will" (1.19.9.co). But how to explain the apparent inclination to what is evil? Thomas continues: "Nevertheless evil may be desired *per accidens*, so far as it follows some good; and this appears in each appetite" (1.19.9.co). A natural agent with only a natural appetite (§1.2) never intends its own corruption, but the preservation or generation of something, which may imply the corruption of something else. The same holds for agents with sensitive appetite. "When a lion kills a deer, he intends food, to which the killing of the animal is joined as an accompaniment" (1.19.9.co). The lion is drawn only to what is useful or pleasing to it.[8] This is also true, Thomas holds, of the rational appetite, even when it seems to intend evil for its own sake. "Similarly, the fornicator intends pleasure, to which the deformity of sin is joined as an accompaniment" (1.19.9.co). The basic structure of *appetitus* ensures the impossibility of seeking evil *as* evil. "Never therefore would evil be desired, not even *per accidens*, unless the good to which the evil is joined as an accompaniment were desired more than some good which lacks that evil" (1.19.9.co; see also 1.63.4 ad 1m).

As we have seen, *appetitus* names primarily the inclination toward good. Yet this does not exhaust the notion. Because appetite is a tendency toward what is perceived as good, it correlatively implies a motion away from evil. Can these two forms of appetite exist on an equal footing? Aquinas denies that they can. Inclination toward a perceived good is the cause of repugnance from evil, but the converse is not true. Repulsion from evil occurs solely as a reflex of the more basic attraction toward some good, of which the shunned evil is the privation. Thus Aquinas writes that evil is the object of the appetite only secondarily and indirectly, and that "the acts of the will and appetite that regard good must naturally be prior to those that regard evil, as joy is prior to sorrow and love is prior to hate. For what exists *per se* is always prior to that which exists *per aliud*" (1.20.1.co). Our notion of the sensitive appetite must therefore be enlarged to include *both* its inclination toward the apprehended good and its tendency away from the perceived evil. Yet these can never hold the same rank, since the latter exists only by the power of the former. Thus William Wallace is correct to observe that for Aquinas, "since avoiding evil is itself a good, one may define the appetite as ordered simply to the good, and this either directly or indirectly, the latter by avoiding its opposed evil" (1997, p. 174).

Appetitus names a primary tendency toward good, and a derivative inclination away from evil. Is there any such thing as motion away from good, or toward evil? Peter King (1998, p. 116) writes:

---

[8] In his own fashion, Nietzsche (1967) affirms the priority of good. As he imagines birds of prey to observe: "We don't dislike them at all, these good little lambs; we even love them: nothing is more tasty than a tender lamb" (p. 45).

It is one of Aquinas's fundamental principles that all of creation tends towards the good. In the case of creatures that have at least sensitive abilities, he takes this principle to have the consequence that all action is directed to the (apparent) good. Since the passions are part of the affective structure of living creatures, they tend toward something only to the extent that it is seen as a good. Hence there cannot be any passion that tends towards (apparent) evil.

King accurately captures the sense in which Aquinas' doctrine of the passions is embedded in the larger metaphysics of creation. But it is not strictly true for Aquinas that "there cannot be any passion that tends towards (apparent) evil," or away from good. Daring tends toward evil, according to Aquinas, although for the sake of overcoming it. Likewise, despair is the passion that withdraws from what appears to be good. (I discuss these apparent anomalies in more detail at §2.5, §9.1, §11.1, and §11.2.)

The superiority of good to evil grounds the most basic hierarchy among the particular acts of the sensitive appetite. Thomas builds this hierarchy into the very structure of his exposition of the particular concupiscible passions. Love (Questions 26–8) is prior to hatred (Question 29); desire (Question 30) is prior to aversion (there is no question on aversion); pleasure (Questions 31–4) is prior to pain and sorrow (Questions 35–9). Because the tendency of the sensitive appetite is toward the apprehended good, love appears first in the sequencing of the passions. Why this priority of love? Aquinas writes:

For nobody desires anything except as a loved good (*bonum amatum*); nor does anyone rejoice except in the loved good; nor does hate concern anything except what is contrary to the loved good. Similarly, it is manifest that sorrow, and other things like it, are referred (*referri*) to love as to their first principle. Whence in whomever there is will and appetite, there must be love. For if the first is removed, all the rest is also removed. (1.20.1.co)

What leads Thomas to affirm the radical priority of love is not sentimentality, but basic ontology. Love's priority not only grounds the hierarchy within the concupiscible passions, but also informs the priority of the concupiscible passions, which in some way concern good as such, to the irascible passions, which are directed toward good as specified under the condition of the "arduous" or "difficult." What gives Aquinas the confidence to order the passions in this manner is his metaphysical conviction (held in common with Augustine and Dionysius) that good is radically prior to evil, and that evil is not intelligible except as a privation of good. I will attend in more detail to the specific work done by the priority of good in Aquinas' thinking about relations of the passions to one another (§3.5). For now, it suffices to note the importance of the priority of the good in his initial account of sensitive appetite.

I have given an account of what Aquinas means by "sensitive appetite." Such an account is necessary, in order to grasp the fundamental claim that whatever else the passions may be, they are acts of the sensitive appetite. But what does Aquinas mean by "acts of the sensitive appetite"? It is time to turn to Aquinas' strategy for defining the passions.

CHAPTER 2

The definition of passion

*Having located the passions in the sensitive appetite, Aquinas may be
expected to offer a general definition of passion. Aquinas seems to
nourish this expectation. His actual procedure is somewhat different
and more interesting. Rather than provide a general definition at the
outset, Aquinas takes the reader through a series of considerations that
throw light on the matter (§2.1). But the illumination seems quickly to
turn into darkness. First, why does Thomas restrict passions to the
sensitive appetite? Are there not experiences that involve no sensory
component, yet count as passions (§2.2)? Second, Thomas's apparent
endorsement of the claim that passions are "motions" has struck many
readers as not only antiquated and confusing, but also inconsistent with
what he says about other passions, especially love and pleasure. Why does
Thomas use the language of motion to describe the passions? If the
passions are invariably accompanied by physiological effects that are
bodily motions, is it the case that Thomas equates the passions with
somatic events (§2.3)? Aquinas does not stop with the claim that every
passion is a motion of the sensitive appetite. He finds it important to
divide the passions into "irascible passions" and "concupiscible passions."
Is this simply an instance of Aquinas's deferring to a long tradition? Does
he recognize any intrinsically compelling reason to divide the sensitive
appetite into an irascible power and a concupiscible power? In the
1a pars, Aquinas grounds the irascible/concupiscible distinction in the
more basic difference between the useful good and the pleasant good
(§2.4). He provides an elaborate application of the distinction in
Question 23 of the 1a2ae. I argue that the fruitfulness of Question 23's
application amounts to a second justification of the distinction (§2.5).*

2.1 DEFINING "PASSION"

To say that Thomas refuses to provide a complete definition of "passion"
may seem perverse. In the first Question of the Treatise (Question 22),
Aquinas establishes that passions are in the soul (Article 1), in the soul's
appetitive rather than apprehensive part (Article 2), and in the sensitive

29

rather than the rational appetite (Article 3). The Question appears to culminate in the definition of the passion given by John Damascene. In the argument *sed contra* of Article 3, Thomas quotes Damascene, as translated by Burgundio of Pisa:

A passion is a motion of the power of the sensitive appetite regarding the imagination of good or evil. To say this differently: a passion is a motion of the irrational soul occurring through a suspicion of good or evil. (22.3.sc; cf. Damascene 1857–66, cols. 940–2)

Both the importance and the incompleteness of Damascene's definition should be observed. The importance is evident. Aquinas might have quoted an Aristotelian definition of *passio*, but he chooses not to. The movement of Question 22 culminates in Damascene rather than Aristotle. In the Prologue of the 1a2ae, Damascene's authority testifies to the role of "free choice and power through oneself" in the rational creature's motion toward the end. It is fitting that the same *auctoritas* be used to illuminate the sense in which human beings not only direct themselves, but also are directed, toward the end. (Compare 1.1 of the 1a *pars* – a person must "order" [*ordinare*] her intentions and actions to the end, even as she finds that she is "ordered" [*ordinatur*] toward an end which surpasses human reason.) Yet the definition is incomplete. As Ramírez comments: "For any form which is determined in matter, its definition is insufficient unless matter is included within its definition" (1973, p. 33). A complete definition of passion would include both its formal and its material element – that is, both the soul's appetitive motion and the associated change in the body.

Why does Aquinas offer a truncated definition of passion when he might have offered a complete one?[1] It is difficult to believe that Thomas somehow "forgot" to include the bodily change in the definition. In fact, he explicitly argues at 22.1 that passion, in the most proper sense of the term, essentially involves a somatic component. A more plausible answer to the question is that Aquinas judges it useless, and possibly harmful, to hand the reader a definition at the outset, however accurate it might be. Certainly Aquinas might have chosen to save his readers some work and offer something like the definition proposed by Ramírez:

---

[1] Murphy (1999) notices Aquinas' reluctance to offer a definition. She introduces a quotation from *QDV* 26.2 with these words: "Here's as close as Aquinas comes to a definition" (p. 172).

Passion ought to be defined thus: "A motion of the sensitive appetite following the sensitive apprehension of sensitive good or evil with a corresponding bodily or organic transmutation (alteration)." (1973, p. 33)

But Aquinas, like Wittgenstein, does not desire that his writing should spare his readers the trouble of thinking. Rather than provide a complete definition of passion at the beginning, Aquinas employs a more subtle strategy. He desires that the reader should sift through the proposals of a range of *auctoritates* – Aristotle, Cicero, Damascene, Nemesius, and Augustine among them – so that she might arrive at a conception that includes elements of the integral tradition. This means: *not* giving a formula that would enable her to cast the tradition aside, like a ladder that can be discarded when it is no longer useful (see Wittgenstein 1922, 6.54). Paul Gondreau claims that the *sed contra* of 22.3 and other texts "expose the error" (2002, p. 204) of a commentator (G. Blanco) who claims that Thomas never provides "a proper definition of passion" (Blanco 1948, p. 133). I think this is wrong. Blanco is right to notice that Thomas does not offer a "proper definition," for two reasons. First, Aquinas does not directly commend the definition himself. The function of the *sed contra* is to provide a counter-appearance to the set of appearances that constitute the "objections." It is no substitute for Thomas's own determination (the *raison d'être* of the response). Second, Damascene's formula does fall short of a "proper definition," as Ramírez holds, since it fails to include the fact that passion essentially contains a *transmutatio corporalis*. On my reading, however, the lack of a complete definition is not an embarrassment against which Aquinas requires defense. Rather, it accords perfectly with his usual manner of proceeding dialectically.

Let us pick up the dialectic at its beginning, the first Article of Question 22. Here Aquinas asks an apparently obvious question: Are passions in the soul? The answer seems to be implied by the very phrase *passiones animae*, "passions of the soul." Closer inspection, however, reveals that the verbal association of passion with the soul conceals a host of difficulties. *Pati*, "to be acted upon," is proper to matter, as the first objector claims (22.1 arg. 1). If passions are motions, they cannot be in the soul, since "the soul is not moved," as the second objector argues (22.1 arg. 2). The third objector argues that passion is connected with what is corruptible, but "the soul is incorruptible" (22.1 arg. 3). The argument *sed contra* cites a passage from Romans 7, where Paul speaks of "passions of sins." If sins are properly said of the soul, it seems that passions must also bear some relation to the soul (22.1.sc). The dialectic of Article 1 heightens the question: Is it proper to speak of "passions of the soul"?

In the response, Aquinas begins by noticing what might be considered an easy way out. *Pati*, "to be acted upon," may in the widest sense be said of anything that can receive (*recipere*) the act of another. In this sense, passions evidently belong to the soul, because its act of understanding (*intelligere*) involves reception. But Aquinas immediately distinguishes between this extended use of *pati* and its proper sense. When *pati* is said properly, the reception of one thing is always accompanied by the "casting-off" (*abjectio*) of another (22.1.co). Can an act of this sort be attributed to the soul? Aquinas answers: not unequivocally. Any act whereby an animal receives one thing by casting off its contrary – what Thomas calls *passio cum abjectione* – necessarily includes a bodily change (*transmutatio corporalis*). Thus Aquinas draws the conclusion: "*passio*, said properly, does not relate to the soul except *per accidens*, inasmuch as it is the composite that is acted upon" (22.1.co). The objectors are substantially correct. If we continue to speak of the *passiones animae*, we must remind ourselves that their actual subject is not the soul, but the composite.

To say this differently: the passions are in the sensitive appetite, but the sensitive appetite itself belongs to the form/matter composite, since it requires a bodily organ for its operation. With the unique exceptions of intellect and will, every power of the human soul requires a bodily organ for its operation. Aquinas has already argued in the 1a *pars* that the sensitive soul has no *per se* operation of its own. Since the acts of the sensitive appetite necessarily involve a bodily organ, passions cannot be essentially attributed to the soul (unlike thoughts or volitions). And yet because they are formally shaped by the soul's apprehension, they are not simply acts of the body. Hence Thomas concludes that their subject can only be the composite.

Passio cum abjectione – passion accompanied by a casting-off or loss of something – corresponds to the proper sense of "being acted upon" (*pati*). Within this sense, Aquinas distinguishes two modes of being acted upon. A person may exchange something worse for something better, as when a person casts off illness and gains health. Conversely, a person may lose his health and become sick, thereby exchanging something better for something worse. Thomas claims that *pati* is "most properly" said in the latter case. If the bodily change is for the worse, then the act "most properly has the character (*ratio*) of passion" (22.1.co). Why does Aquinas connect *passio*, in the strictest sense, with a change for the worse? It would be easy to explain this by attributing to Aquinas a rationalist animus against the passions. In fact, this move would only explain away what requires attention.

To understand what Aquinas means, one should consider the possibility that he wants to remain close to ordinary speech and experience. An example may be helpful. A man on horseback who encounters a sudden gust of wind is acted upon. The gust may speed him more quickly to his destination, if it comes *a tergo*, or else it may knock him to the ground. While he is "acted upon" in either scenario, he is "most properly" acted upon in the latter case, when he is violently knocked off course. Experience confirms this. When a person is affected by an outside force, but in a way that coincides with what he antecedently desired, his disposition is far brighter than when he is acted upon in a manner that he experiences as violent. In the latter case, he feels more at the mercy of outside forces, that is, more acted upon. Victorian English speaks of being "buffeted about" by forces beyond one's control. More recent idioms suggest that when a person is acted upon against her will, she is being "messed with" or "jerked around."[2] All this confirms Thomas's fidelity to experience in his association of "being acted upon in the most proper sense" with passions that divert a person from her natural end. Thus Aquinas declares that "*pati* is said when something is dragged (*trahitur*) toward an agent; and when something recedes from what is suitable to it, it seems especially that it is dragged (*trahi*) toward another" (22.1.co).[3]

If Aquinas is correct to distinguish two senses of *pati* within its proper meaning, and to identify one of these as more proper than the other, one might expect that the most proper sense would control the discussion that follows. But does this happen? Eileen Sweeney observes:

For Aquinas begins pessimistically, taking passion in its most proper sense as the *loss* of what is natural and the receiving of what is not; hence sorrow is more a passion than joy. He then works through the next 24 questions to construct an account which emphasizes just the opposite, converting the reader to a vision of

---

[2] "Buffeted," "messed with," "jerked around" – these are passive participles. Gordon (1986) observes that "the great majority of adjectives designating emotions are derived from participles: for example, *amused, annoyed, astonished, delighted, depressed, frightened, horrified, irritated, miffed, overjoyed, pleased, terrified, surprised, troubled, upset,* and *vexed*" (pp. 373–4). He suggests that the "grammatical passivity of emotion descriptions," far from being accidental, is an important clue to the essentially passive character of emotions.

[3] White (2002) observes that *trahi* (in this context) suggests the violence implied by "pulling" or "yanking" or "jerking" (p. 103).

the passions as forces for good, moving away from seeing them as a detriment or something to be merely tolerated or controlled. (1999, p. 220)[4]

Later I will consider this conclusion in more detail (§4.4). At the very least, Sweeney is right to suggest that Aquinas' identification of the most proper sense of "being acted upon" bears no straightforward relation to what he considers most important about the passions.

Article 1's link between "being acted upon" and "being dragged toward something alien" determines the second Article of Question 22. Is passion more in the appetitive or the apprehensive part of the soul? Because "the name of passion implies that the patient is drawn (*trahatur*) toward that which is of the agent" (22.1.co), it follows that the *ratio passionis* is found more in the appetitive part than in the apprehensive part." Notice, however, that Aquinas does not sever the connection between passion and apprehension. Both apprehension and appetition are instances of "being drawn to another." The "frontier" status of passion persists; it is *more* found in appetition than apprehension. The difference is that the apprehensive power is drawn to its object, but mediately. It cannot operate except *secundum intentionem*. Appetite, however, is drawn essentially to things themselves. Aquinas cites the Aristotelian maxim that "good and evil, which are the objects of the appetitive power, are in things themselves" (22.2.co; cf. Aristotle, *Metaphysics* 6.4, 1027b25). Not mediated by "intentions," the appetitive power's contact with its objects is more palpable than apprehension's. Desire places us in a more intimate relationship to the good than perception. Discussing the effects of love, Aquinas holds that "love is more unitive than cognition" (28.1 ad 3m). More forcefully, he declares in the same Question that

the lover is not content with a superficial apprehension of the beloved, but strives to investigate from the inside all particular things that belong to the beloved, so as to penetrate to his inmost being. (28.2.co)

This partly explains why Aquinas devotes so many of the Questions in the 1a2ae to the appetitive power. The 1a2ae does not simply want to describe the rational creature's detached apprehension of the end. Its aim is to speak of creaturely motion toward the good (§4.2). But in light of the dependence of appetition upon apprehension – a person cannot desire

---

[4] Not everyone has seen that Thomas's deployment of *pati* proceeds according to this order, or any order at all. Thus James (1997): "In the *Summa* no attempt is made to reconcile these senses; Aquinas simply registers the differences between them and appeals sometimes to one, sometimes to the other" (p. 51).

a good unless he apprehends it as something desirable – the 1a2ae begins with a consideration of the *finis* before discussing motion toward the end. In the particular case of the passions, Thomas preserves this general dynamic by assigning passions to the appetitive part of the soul, but without breaking their connection to the apprehensive power. Thus the passions are "more" (*magis*) in the appetitive than in the apprehensive part of the soul (22.2.co).

While irrational animals have a natural and a sensitive appetite, according to Aquinas, humans have in addition a rational appetite, an inclination toward goods perceived by intellect and subject to rational deliberation. Why does Aquinas, in the final Article of Question 22 and elsewhere, associate the passions exclusively with the sensitive appetite? On what ground does he reject the apparently broader view that passions belong to appetite as such?

2.2 PASSIONS AND PSEUDOPASSIONS

In an important article, Peter King suggests a distinction between passions in the proper sense (acts of the sensitive appetite) and "analogues to the passions pertaining to the purely intellective part of the soul – call them 'pseudopassions'" (1998, p. 105). God and the angels may have pseudopassions, but they cannot have passions proper, since they are beings that lack bodies.[5] If the passions necessarily involve a bodily change, as Aquinas holds, they cannot be located in the intellectual appetite, since the will's proper act requires no bodily change. Pasnau correctly observes that "only beings with sensation (and therefore sensitive appetite) can have passions in the strict sense" (2002, p. 241).

In proposing the distinction between passions and pseudopassions, King is not at odds with Aquinas' own usage. Thomas consistently reserves *passiones* for acts of the sensitive appetite. He uses *affectiones* (and, less frequently, *affectus*) for acts that may or may not belong to the sensitive appetite.[6] Ramírez proposes a contrast between later

---

[5] Can God have emotions? Everything depends, of course, on what is meant by "emotion." Though God cannot have passions in the strict sense of the term (since God has no sensitive appetite), Aquinas does not hesitate to attribute at least some affections to God. (Here he differs from Anselm, who at *Proslogion* 8 argues that while God is necessarily compassionate from our point of view, no experience of emotion can actually be attributed to God.) The best discussion of this point in Aquinas remains Westberg 1996. Also helpful are Floyd 1998 and Weinandy 2000.

[6] There is some correspondence between Aquinas' use of *affectiones* and "emotions" in contemporary parlance. Leget (2003) observes that "the common sense account of 'emotion' is closest to Aquinas's

scholastics, who distinguish *passio*, *affectio*, and *emotio*, and Aquinas and his predecessors, for whom these three terms allegedly mean the same. "Patet – inquit Thomas – quod passiones animae sunt idem quod affectiones" (1973, p. 22).[7] This proposal does not bear scrutiny. The "inquit Thomas" is interpolated by Ramírez himself between Aquinas' own words in the *sed contra* of 22.2. Typically in the arguments *sed contra*, Thomas speaks dialectically. He does not himself endorse the view that "the passions of the soul are the same as affections." The "evidence" cited by Ramírez requires that we simultaneously misconstrue the function of the *sed contra* in the disputed question and ignore texts where Aquinas explicitly argues that a range of volitions belonging to God, angels and humans are affections, but not passions.[8]

From a different angle, Roberts has taken Aquinas to task for assigning the emotions to the sensitive rather than the rational appetite (1992, p. 292).[9] Does Thomas do this in any objectionable sense? Were he to argue that all emotional phenomena are acts of the sensitive appetite, Roberts's critique would hit its target. But it is clear that while Aquinas restricts passions, in the proper sense of the term, to acts of the sensitive appetite, he neither overlooks nor denies affections that belong to the rational appetite (pseudopassions). He simply does not label them as *passiones*. Aquinas says explicitly:

Love, joy and the like, when attributed to God, or the angels, or to humans according to intellectual appetite, signify simple acts of the will with like effects but without passion. Hence Augustine says: "The holy angels feel no anger while they punish . . . no fellow-feeling with misery while they relieve the unhappy; and

---

concept of *affectus* in the broad sense – comprising the movements in the intellective and sensitive part of the appetitive faculties" (p. 574). Faulting Aquinas for using "Aristotelian faculty psychology," Roberts (1992) asks: "Why not conclude, instead, that emotions don't (all?) belong to the sensory appetite?" (p. 291). With appropriate qualifications, this conclusion would echo rather than oppose Aquinas.

[7] James (1997) exhibits the same failure to differentiate between the speech of the *sed contra* and Thomas's own *determinatio* ("as he remarks in a comment on Augustine's discussion of the translations of *pathe*, *passiones* are identical with *affectiones* or affections," p. 48). In view of these considerations, I concur with Gondreau's criticism of translations of *passio* as "affection of the soul" (2002, p. 31).

[8] See e.g. 1.20.1 ad 1m; 1.21.3.co; 1.57.4.co; 1.59.4 ad 2m; 1.64.3.co; 1.82.5 ad 1m; 1.113.7 ad 1m.

[9] Regarding the presence of such affections as anger and pity in beings without bodies, such as God and the angels, Roberts (1992) alleges that Aquinas' "response to these examples is to deny that they are emotions" (p. 295). That is the one thing Aquinas does not do. He clearly holds that while they are not *passiones*, they are *affectus*. Roberts's inattention to the *passio/affectio* distinction in Thomas vitiates his entire discussion, to the extent that it claims to understand Aquinas. The decision to speak indifferently of "emotions" in Aquinas is a particularly serious error. Solomon (1999) rightly observes that "'emotions' is something of a grab-bag term" (p. 132).

yet ordinary speech is accustomed to ascribe to them also these passions by name, because, although they have none of our weakness, their acts bear a certain resemblance to ours." (22.3 ad 3m)

Roberts reads this passage on love and joy as an attempt of Aquinas "to deny that they are emotions" (1992, p. 295). This is a simple mistake, since Aquinas thinks that while they are not *passiones*, they are *affectiones*. Roberts might concede this point, yet continue to ask what justifies the location of the passions in the sensitive appetite, since the object of a passion may include elements that are not perceivable by the senses. I will respond to this line of argument more fully in later chapters (§3.4, §6.4, §11.4). For now, it suffices to notice that Roberts seems to have grabbed the stick at the wrong end. Aquinas does not think that we first know what passions are, and then proceed to determine whether they are located in the sensitive or the rational appetite. On the contrary, the passions *just are* the acts of the sensitive appetite.[10] If we experience other acts that resemble the formal element of the passions, but lack any corresponding somatic element, we may take due account of these acts. (King goes so far as to suggest that the pseudopassions "play a major role in Aquinas's theology and merit investigation in their own right" [1998, p. 105n7].) But doing so generates no reason to disconnect the passions, understood strictly, from the sensitive appetite.

Roberts might reply by questioning the distinction that Aquinas makes between sensitive and rational appetite in human beings (§1.3). At one point, he suggests that "if the will and the sensory appetite were as distinct as Aquinas wishes to make them" (1992, p. 295), then it would be true that non-sensory apprehensions would never generate bodily changes (as they plainly do). But this is to foist on to Thomas a view that he does not hold. Aquinas explicitly acknowledges the large role played by rational apprehension in the activation of the sensitive appetite, as I will show in some detail (§3.4). (Roberts fails to see this clearly, perhaps because he has misconstrued Aquinas' notion of sensitive appetite, as Claudia Murphy has suggested [Murphy 1999, p. 169].)[11] Without a doubt, the issue is complex. There are good reasons for holding that the passions, strictly

---

[10] Though I derive it independently from him, both my position and my formulation are quite similar to Pasnau's (2002): "The passions just are the activities of sensory appetite" (p. 243). Pasnau cites 35.1.co: "every movement of sensory appetite is called a passion."

[11] Expounding Aquinas, Uffenheimer-Lippens (2003) comments insightfully: "The passions of the soul are never to be considered as mere instincts in man. They do not belong to an 'irrational soul' that stands over and against a rational soul. Rather, what defines the passions is that they contain in themselves the tension between the rational and nonrational" (p. 545).

speaking, necessarily involve a sensitive component at the level of both apprehension and appetition. In non-rational animals, there is no "rational" component, although Aquinas' willingness to attribute to them an "estimative power" that goes beyond sense-perception (§3.3) suggests that he is not blind to the complexities that attend the animal case. For human beings, however, the interaction between the rational and sensitive apprehensive powers plays a decisive role in the activation of passion. This interaction will be examined in more detail at §3.4. For the moment, it suffices to note that Aquinas' conception of the sensitive appetite involves no reduction to a set of instinctive drives. As Pinckaers (1990) notes:

We quickly observe that the author, who has defined the passions as motions of the sensitive appetite, nonetheless does not hold strictly to the level of sensibility. Already the problem of the moral quality of the passions situates them in their relation with reason and will, and endows them with a dimension that they do not have among animals, for example. (p. 381)[12]

Aquinas does not reduce the passions to instinctive reactions that are impermeable to rational apprehension. King rightly concludes that for Aquinas "the passions are not, after all, similar to our reactions to hot peppers. They can be affected by reasons and beliefs," while remaining motions of the sensitive appetite (1998, p. 131). To clarify the relations between passions, emotions, affections, and pseudopassions is useful, because it clears one obstacle to understanding how Aquinas thinks about the passions. I now turn to another, quite different obstacle.

2.3 PASSIONS AS MOTIONS

According to the partial definition that Aquinas takes from Damascene, the passions are "motions" of the sensitive appetite. In precisely what sense are the passions "motions"? Eric D'Arcy suggests that "for the philosopher" no matter in Aquinas' treatment of the passions "is of greater interest than the role assigned to physical movement as a model of emotional experience" (2006, p. xxvi). Without wanting to pronounce on what is "philosophically interesting" – all such pronouncements questionably presuppose a particular conception of philosophy and its relation to what is allegedly non-philosophical – it is true that Aquinas' use of

---

[12] A shortened English version of Pinckaers's original essay appears in *The Pinckaers Reader* (2005) as "Reappropriating Aquinas's Account of the Passions." Unfortunately, the translation shifts unpredictably from "emotions" to "passions" (in contrast to Pinckaers's own consistent use of *passions*), and thus invites the kind of confusion found in Roberts 1992.

motus raises interesting questions. Contending that Thomas uses motion "strictly as a model," D'Arcy makes the further assertion that "it is physical movement, involving local motion in the ordinary sense, that St Thomas plainly has in mind" (pp. xxvii–xxviii). But is this true? Early in the 1a *pars*, Aquinas defines appetite as "a kind of motion (*quidam motus*) toward a thing" (1.5.4.co). The qualifying *quidam* is important; it suggests that Thomas has something more subtle in mind than the crudely literalizing interpretation urged by D'Arcy. This is not a hapax legomenon; in the Treatise, Aquinas declares that "passion is a kind of motion" (*passio quidam motus est*) (23.2.co).

D'Arcy is not the only commentator who would impose a univocal sense of motion upon Aquinas. Alleging that Thomas sometimes describes desire "as a motion toward a pleasurable object and sometimes as a motion of the appetite toward a pleasurable object," Simo Knuuttila indicts him for "terminological vacillation" and infers "a sign of some problems in Aquinas's approach" (2002, p. 74). Once again, we can look to relevant passages that occur early in the *ST*, so frequently overlooked by commentators. Near the beginning of the Question on divine simplicity, Aquinas gives this response to an objector:

We draw near to God not by bodily steps, since he is everywhere, but by affections of the mind, and recede from him in the same way. And thus approach and withdrawal designate a spiritual affection under the likeness of local motion. (1.3.1 ad 5m)

One may wonder: does not this passage confirm the view of D'Arcy and Knuuttila? Is not Aquinas implying that while "spiritual affections" (the pseudopassions) are likenesses of local motions, the passions just are instances of local motion? But this view cannot be reconciled with the texts. In the 1a2ae, Aquinas speaks of "a kind of motion (*motus quidam*) of the irrational appetite," that is, a passion (24.2.co). Both the passions and the pseudopassions lend themselves to description "under the likeness of local motion." Neither is to be identified with particular instances of local motion.

Noticing that the passions are not local motions, Susan James remarks that "it looks as though we need a conception of motion which is not explicated in terms of place" (1997, p. 63). James seems unaware that in the *Physics* Aristotle both gives a general definition of motion ("the actualization of what exists potentially, insofar as it exists potentially" (*Physics* 3.1, 202a11) and proceeds to identify three distinct types of motion – motion in respect of quality (alteration), motion in respect of quantity (increase or decrease), and motion in respect of place (locomotion).[13] Which kind of motion is a passion? The answer seems clear enough: a passion is an alteration that involves a change either from one contrary to another (e.g. from pleasure to sorrow), or from a privation to a quality (e.g. from being calm to being angry).[14] Murphy wants to qualify this, on the ground that the "psychological constituent" of the passion is "in the soul" and therefore "not a genuine alteration (the soul is not being capable of being altered)" (1999, p. 167). Aquinas would not grant this qualification. Though he locates formal and material elements within any passion, he does not assign the formal element exclusively to the soul. Rather, passions are predicated neither of the body nor of the soul, but of the body/soul composite (22.1 ad 3; see §2.1). Since the body/soul composite can undergo alteration, in the technical sense of the term, it is reasonable to conclude that when Aquinas speaks of passions as "motions" of the sensitive appetite, he is rigorously speaking of motion *qua* alteration, and not (as Murphy thinks) of a quasi-alteration.[15]

When Aquinas describes passions as motions, he is not merely speaking metaphorically. Yet the literal sense of *motus*, when applied to the passions, does not correspond to local motion. D'Arcy is mistaken when he asserts that "it is physical movement, involving local motion in the ordinary sense, that St Thomas plainly has in mind" (2006, pp. xxvii–xxviii). On the contrary, "motion" takes the meaning of "alteration" in Aristotle's sense. Nonetheless, it may be necessary to say that the correct identification of motion as alteration does not exhaust the significance of Aquinas' usage of "motion." In particular, the metaphorical designation of "a spiritual affection under the likeness of local motion" (1.3.1 ad 5m) suggests that the passions are involved in "motion toward the end" (§4.2).

---

[13] See e.g. *Physics* 3.1, 201a10–11; 5.1, 225b8; 5.2, 225a23–36. For Aristotle's identification of both actions and passions with motions, see *Physics* 3.3, 202a25. That alteration cannot be collapsed into local motion, Aristotle makes quite clear: "alteration is different generically from local motion" (*Physics* 5.4, 227b6).

[14] For Aristotle, the latter event is a change, but not strictly a motion: "a process simply to a contrary, e.g. that denoted by the expression 'becoming white,' where no starting-point is specified, is a change but not a motion" (*Physics* 5.5, 229b10–12). As far as I can tell, Aquinas does not lay any emphasis on this particular distinction.

[15] Additional support for this interpretation may be had by comparing the Treatise's opening description of passion with Aquinas' exposition of Aristotle's use of *passio* in the *Metaphysics*. Expounding *Metaphysics* 5.21, 1022b15–22, Aquinas observes that Aristotle distinguishes four senses of *passio*: (1) quality or alteration; (2) acts brought about by a quality or alteration; (3) specifically bad alterations; (4) specifically bad alterations of great magnitude (*InMet* 5.20.8–11; cf. Thomas Aquinas 1961, pp. 401–2). For Aquinas *passio* evidently belongs within (1). The only question is: which kind of alteration? What 22.1 identifies as "propriissimus modus passionis" corresponds with (3) above. But Aquinas also uses the term freely in the other senses, especially (2).

To see this more clearly, it is helpful to look at the framework in which Aquinas situates the "concupiscible passions."

In the motions of the appetitive part of the soul, good has an attractive force as it were, and evil a repulsive force. Therefore, good first causes in the appetitive power a certain inclination or aptitude, or connaturality toward the good, which belongs to the passion of love, to which corresponds the contrary of hatred from the side of evil. Second, if the good is not yet possessed, it gives the appetite motion toward pursuing the loved good, and this belongs to the passion of desire or concupiscence, and the opposite from the side of evil is aversion or abomination. Third, when the good is attained, it gives the appetite a certain rest in the very good attained, and this belongs to pleasure or joy, to which is opposed from the side of evil pain or sorrow. (23.4.co)

As Sweeney observes, this three-stage narrative sequence is "not unlike that of a quest-romance" (1999, p. 216). Beginning from the first inclinations, the rational creature undergoes motion in accordance with those inclinations, aspiring to reach a destination that brings this motion to rest. It is difficult to imagine a conception of the passions more appropriate to *homo viator*. Aquinas privileges the category of "motion" not because he intends a crude physicalism, but because he wants the likeness of motion to evoke the pattern of human life itself, conceived as a return to the end. Nonetheless, one may still wonder: Is not Thomas unfaithful to his own conception? Even analogically, the category of motion appears to apply only to the passions in the middle of the sequence: desire and aversion. Thus Knuuttila: "One obvious problem of the movement terminology is that of the stages of natural processes (inclination, movement, rest) the first precedes a temporal process and the third follows it. Only the middle part seems to be a movement" (2004, p. 249).

Is Aquinas aware of this "obvious problem of the movement terminology"? At 26.2 he asks "whether love is a passion." Here is the third objection:

Love does not imply the motion of the appetite; for this is desire (*desiderium*), of which motion love is the origin (*principium*). Therefore love is not a passion. (26.2 arg. 3)

The problem is to describe love both as a "principle of motion" and, in some sense, itself a motion. If love is in no sense a motion, but only a principle of motion, then one of two things would follow: either love is not a passion, or the passions cannot be understood, even analogically, under the likeness of motion. Aquinas' strategy is to argue that while love is certainly not a motion in the same respect as desire, it is nevertheless a motion.

	Aptitudo	*Motus*	*Quietatio*
Accessus ad bonum	Love (*amor*)	Concupiscence or desire (*concupiscentia vel desiderium*)	Pleasure or joy (*delectatio vel gaudium*)
Recessus ab malo	Hate (*odio*)	Aversion or abomination (*fuga vel abominatio*)	Pain or sorrow (*dolor vel tristitia*)

Figure 2.1. The narrative structure of the concupiscible passions

Although love does not name the motion of the appetite (*motus appetitus*) that tends toward the appetible thing, it does name the *motus appetitus* whereby the appetite is changed by means of the appetible thing, so that the appetible thing might be pleasing to the appetite. (26.2 ad 3m)

Though not every change is a motion (see e.g. Aristotle, *Physics* 229a30), love qualifies as a motion because it is a genuine alteration, an *immutatio* of the appetite. Moreover, it is not just any alteration, but the *prima immutatio* that makes possible all subsequent motion toward the good (26.2.co). Thus Aquinas confidently describes it as a motion, finding it not only possible, but actually necessary, to say that love is both "a principle of motion" and a motion itself.

Stronger support for Knuuttila's claim that the "movement terminology" is problematic may be gleaned from the discussion of pleasure. As can be seen from figure 2.1, Aquinas appears to identify pleasure with rest – that is, with the exact opposite of motion. More formidably than Knuuttila, Costantino Marmo argues that Aquinas is grossly inconsistent on this point, and that this inconsistency was noticed shortly after Aquinas' death by Giles of Rome, who "implicitly accuses Thomas of incoherence" (1991, p. 299). What Giles leaves implicit, Marmo is happy to make explicit: "It is not, in fact, admissible to define *delectatio* as motion (according to its genus), while also defining it as rest, without falling into contradiction" (p. 299). Though "rest" might be the end of external operation, he argues, pleasure itself must be rigorously conceived as motion, that is, as the final stage of a dynamic process rather than as a state of rest. Abandoning explicative models that are "substantially extraneous to the concept of passion," Giles proposes (on Marmo's reading) "a coherently 'structuralist' model organized according to binary oppositions which manages to avoid the inelegance of recourse to 'processuality' in the justification of a system" (p. 298). Giles's account seems to preserve many of Aquinas' particular psychological observations, while placing them on a more secure theoretical foundation. If Giles's own scheme seems heavily derivative, that only increases its power as an internal critique. Far from being a modern analyst whose criticisms are predicated on shallow reading, Giles comes across as a close successor of Aquinas who (concludes Marmo) "attempts to use Thomas against Thomas himself" (p. 314).

I want to argue that Marmo is too quick to conclude that Giles makes a genuine improvement on Aquinas. Thomas himself is aware of the tension between (1) the claim that pleasure is motion – as it must be, if it is to qualify as a passion – and (2) the claim that pleasure is rest – as it must be, if it is to be the *telos* of the other passions. Aquinas signals his awareness of the tension when he has an objector make the following argument:

Being acted upon (*pati*) is being moved (*moveri*), as is said in chapter 3 of the *Physics*. But pleasure does not consist in being moved, but in having been moved, for pleasure is caused by the good already attained. Therefore pleasure is not a passion. (31.1 arg. 2)

In replying to this objection, Aquinas distinguishes between two senses of *motus*. In one sense, motion is "according to intention of the end, which belongs to appetite." In another sense, motion is "according to execution, which belongs to the exterior operation" (31.1 ad 2m). When a person obtains a desired good, does motion come to an end? The answer depends upon which of the two senses of motion is being entertained. In the second sense, motion is simply replaced by rest. Once the desired good is obtained, execution ceases until it is replaced by a new intention. In that sense, pleasure is equivalent to rest, not motion. But what about motion in the first sense? When a person is experiencing pleasure, is it right to say that the condition of her appetite shifts from motion to rest? Aquinas says directly: "in the person who has already obtained the end in which she takes pleasure, the motion of the appetitive part does not come to a stop" (*non cessat*). In this sense, pleasure is a motion. Is pleasure a motion in the same sense as desire is a motion? Or does it qualify as a motion in another sense? Aquinas answers:

For though pleasure is a certain rest (*quies quaedam*) of the appetite, if we consider the presence of the pleasurable good which satisfies the appetite, nevertheless there remains the change (*immutatio*) of the appetite by the appetible object, by reason of which pleasure is a certain motion (*motus quidam*). (31.1 ad 2m)

The "*quidam*" and "*quaedam*" are not trivial. Pleasure is rest in at least two senses: it marks the cessation of exterior motion, and it quiets the desire. But since it involves a genuine *immutatio* of the appetite, it is a motion in the same sense that love is. Throughout the Treatise, Aquinas uses "rest" and "motion" as labile terms whose exact meaning may shift from one context to another.[16]

When Thomas describes the passions as "certain motions of the appetite," he does not intend to identify them with bodily motions. But he does hold that every appetitive motion which is properly called a passion is accompanied by a bodily motion. This has not been obvious to all commentators, nor is it obvious in itself. Some interpreters have wanted to argue that the passions *just are* physiological events, that is, bodily motions. Pasnau makes the strongest argument for this view. While acknowledging that "there is room for disagreement over whether Aquinas is in any sense proposing a materialist theory of the passions," he concludes that we should "decide to identify the theory as a version of materialism" (2002, p. 243). Without pretending to settle the matter, I would cite a relevant passage from the 1a *pars*:

> The act of the sensitive appetite is always accompanied (*concomiatur*) by some change of the body (*aliqua transmutatio corporis*), and especially about the heart, which is the first principle of motion in animals. Therefore acts of the sensitive appetite, inasmuch as they have a conjoined bodily change (*inquantum habent transmutationem corporalem annexam*) are called passions, but not acts of the will. (1.20.1 ad 1m)

Were it the case that the appetitive motion *just is* the somatic event, it would be difficult to see why Thomas uses the language of "accompaniment" or "conjunction," rather than identity, to describe their relation. The act of the sensitive appetite, though an appetitive motion that is accompanied by a physical change, is not itself a bodily motion. As I will show (§5.5) in examining what Aquinas means by describing "union" as an effect of love, Thomas typically refrains from speaking of two things that are "conjoined" or "united" as identical. On the contrary, he characteristically insists that the two things, while united, remain distinct. Pasnau

---

[16] One exception to the general insensitivity on this issue that obtains among commentators is King 1998. While "the theory of motion he relies on may be quaint," the point of his comparisons of the passions to forms of motion "should be evident" (p. 119). D'Arcy's imposition of a literalizing reading on Aquinas does not arise from a close reading of his texts. It is evidently generated by his desire to draw a strong contrast between his self-predicated quasi-Wittgensteinian openness and "the use of a model [that] seems to have created a kind of *a priori* framework into which a writer has been led to squeeze his concepts, rather than seeking to make explicit the logical structure already present in the language which expresses them" (1967, p. xxix).

might argue that even if the appetitive act is distinguishable from the somatic event, it does not follow that both are not, or cannot be, material entities. While I am not sure how to show that this position is impossible, I see no evidence that Aquinas actually holds it. Ultimate adjudication of the issue would depend partly on how liberal one decides to be as to what counts as a "version of materialism," and partly on how one evaluates the claim that "Aquinas does not ascribe to a metaphysical dualism of matter and form, potentiality and actuality. His is a reductive hylomorphism" (2002, p. 44).

Materialist or not, Aquinas clearly holds that the appetitive act stands to the somatic event as form to matter.[17] Does this imply that the appetitive motion "causes" the somatic event? It might seem so. Consider, for example, how the experience of fear characteristically produces the physiological symptoms that Aquinas identifies: trembling, quivering of the lower lip and jaw, arms and hands shaking, knees knocking (see 44.4 ad 2m). Nonetheless, Aquinas does not regard appetitive motions simply as efficient causes that produce separate physiological events. Anthony Kenny's observation is apposite:

The medievals did not regard the philosophy of the emotions as a search for causal mechanisms. For Aquinas, the relation between an emotion and its bodily manifestations was not one of efficient causality. The increase in one's blood pressure when one is angry is, according to him, neither a cause nor an effect of one's anger; it is its *materia*. (1963, p. 16)[18]

Kenny's point is a useful corrective to any crude assertion that events in the soul produce bodily motions, as the motion of a billiard cue produces the (quite separate) motion of a billiard ball. The relation between the appetitive motion and the corresponding bodily event will be more intimate than that – as it must be, if Aquinas' comparison to the form/matter relation is to make any sense. Yet Kenny slightly overstates his point, since Aquinas often treats the somatic events associated with any particular passion within a Question on its "effects." Perhaps a more adequate formulation would run as follows: For Aquinas, events within the soul produce distinct bodily events. But the distinction is not a separation. Because the body and soul are fundamentally integrated, there

---

[17] See particularly 28.5.co; 37.1 ad 3m; 44.1.co; 45.3.co; 48.3 ad 1m. Also pertinent is 1.20.1 ad 2m.

[18] Uffenheimer-Lippens (2003) makes a similar observation: "body and soul are not related as cause and effect – as they were for Descartes. Rather, they are the material and formal aspects of one and the same event/movement" (p. 536).

will always be an ordered connection between them.[19] The connection is one of formal rather than efficient causality. Aquinas writes:

Just as the formal aspect (*formale*) is the very motion of the appetitive power (*ipse motus appetitivae potentiae*), so is the bodily change (*transmutatio corporalis*) the material aspect (*materiale*), of which one is proportioned to the other (*quorum unum alteri proportinatur*). (44.1.co)

To describe the connection between the soul-event and the body-event as a proportion is to imply a resemblance between the two. "According to the likeness and character (*similitudo et ratio*) of the appetitive motion, the bodily change follows" (44.1.co). What happens "from the side of the body" (*ex parte corporis*) imitates what occurs "from the side of the soul" (*ex parte animae*), that is, the alteration of the sensitive appetite. Knuuttila wonders whether Aquinas indulges in an illegitimate transition from the bodily to the spiritual. "All emotions involve internal physical movements," he claims, "but Aquinas did not refer to them in explaining why emotions are movements" (2004, p. 251).[20] From Aquinas' perspective, this appears as a pseudo-problem. In describing the passions as motions, Thomas assumes that the reader is familiar with the *Physics* and *Metaphysics*, and therefore knows that "motion" takes three distinct (but analogically related) senses.[21] He also assumes that the reader will know that "alteration" names a genus with various species. On that basis, he describes the three concupiscible passions (love, desire, pleasure) as motions toward the good, without holding that "motion" is predicated univocally of each passion.

2.4 THE IRASCIBLE/CONCUPISCIBLE DISTINCTION IN THE IA 'PARS'

When Aquinas divides the sensitive appetite into an irascible power and a concupiscible power, he inherits a long tradition. Peter King notices that

---

[19] Aquinas does not simply note the accompaniment of appetitive motions by somatic reactions as an interesting fact. More profoundly, he views the interplay between the formal and material as beneficial for flourishing. Terruwe and Baars (1972) observe: "In the case of the pleasure appetite this somatic arousal serves the purpose of optimal involvement; in that of the utility appetite, optimal intensity of action" (p. 41).

[20] Gondreau (2002) is helpful: "By defining passion as a 'movement' of the sensitive appetite, or by affirming that affectivity is characterized by a movement 'towards things,' Thomas of course does not have 'local motion' in mind, i.e., physical displacement in time and place, as may *prima facie* be understood by the modern reader" (p. 209).

[21] See Aristotle, *Physics* 5.2, 226a25, and Aquinas, *InPh* 5.4.2–6.

Medina "flaunts his renaissance erudition" by drawing arguments for the irascible/concupiscible distinction not only from Aristotle, but also from Hippocrates and Plato (2002, p. 233).[22] Eric D'Arcy traces the distinction back to Aristotle, pointing to William of Moerbeke's translation of *thumike* by *irascibilis* and *epithumetike* by *concupiscibilis* (2006, p. xxvi). The basic idea may be stated concisely. Whereas the concupiscible simply seeks pleasure and shuns pain, the irascible inclines the sensitive appetite to resistance and defense, even when this seems to involve what is unpleasant or entails pain. Because the soul can be simultaneously attracted and repelled by what is "arduous" or "difficult," there must be distinct powers to account for both the attraction and the repulsion. Hence the concupiscible is repulsed by the arduous, whereas the irascible is (under certain conditions) drawn toward it.

Though Aquinas uses terminology that has Aristotelian origins (though mediated by Damascene and Nemesius), something like the irascible/ concupiscible distinction goes back to Plato. In the *Republic*, Socrates invents a version of the "powers of the soul" doctrine (see 477c–d), which will receive more technical formulation in *De Anima*. Socrates identifies one appetitive power of the soul with its lowest part, naming it *epithumia*. *Epithumia* is the principle of desire for bodily goods, especially those associated with food and sex (see *Republic* 436a). In medieval Latin, *epithumia* will become *concupiscentia*. Socrates proceeds to distinguish another appetitive part, the desires of which may (or may not) stand in opposition to *epithumia*. This is *thumos*, the "spirited" part of the soul. In medieval Latin, *thumos* will become *ira*. Kenny acknowledges the distinction's history, but finds that Aquinas' use of the distinction "consists largely of forced assimilation of diverse classifications made by previous philosophers and theologians" (1993, p. 63). Against this uncharitable reading, it seems more plausible to hold that Aquinas refines and clarifies a division that goes back to Plato, if not (as Medina suggests) Homer and Hippocrates.

Aquinas holds (§1.1) that appetite seeks the good under the "formal aspects" (*rationes*) of the befitting good (*bonum honestum*), the pleasant (*delectabile*), and the useful (*utile*). The threefold division of good corresponds neatly to the single formal object of rational appetite and the two formally distinct objects of sensitive appetite (§1.3). The will formally tends

---

[22] Others have also noted Medina's erudition in this connection, e.g. Ramírez (1973): "Medina inquires at length into the origin and etymology of the word 'love' in Hebrew, Greek, and Latin" (p. 86).

toward the *bonum honestum*, even if what is willed is materially unsuited to human flourishing. Within the rational appetite, Aquinas argues, the useful/pleasant distinction does *not* generate a difference of irascible and concupiscible powers (1.82.5). Whether the intellect apprehends something as pleasant (or painful), or as useful (or dangerous), makes no difference for volitions. The will chooses pleasant and useful things in the same way, "according to the common notion of goodness," that is, the *bonum honestum* (1.59.4.co). In relation to sensitive appetite, things are different. Sensitive appetite is inclined in one way toward something apprehended as pleasant, and in quite another way toward something estimated as useful (§1.2). Therefore, it must be subdivided into two powers, unlike the rational appetite (which admits of no subdivision).

Aquinas does not spring the irascible/concupiscible distinction upon the unsuspecting reader toward the end of the 1a *pars*. On the contrary, the ground is prepared quite early, beginning with Question 5 on the nature of goodness in general. The foundational significance of the pleasant/useful distinction for the concupiscible/irascible division usually escapes those who are quick to dismiss the latter. According to James, Aquinas

claims, rather confusingly, that these powers [the concupiscible and irascible] are distinguished by their objects. In fact, however, they are differentiated not by the kind of objects that they are appetites for or aversions to, but rather by the relation that an agent has to an object as easy or hard to obtain. (1997, p. 56)

This reflects a basic misunderstanding of what Thomas means by a formal object of appetite. Since the formal object of a passion (see §3.1) is partly constituted by the manner in which an agent apprehends some material object, it is difficult to know why James attributes confusion to Aquinas.

To attain a better grasp of the irascible/concupiscible distinction, I would like to consider in more detail its grounding in the difference between the *utile* and the *delectabile*. If these are formally different kinds of good, and if the sensitive appetite responds to each kind of good in distinct ways, there is – at least *prima facie* – a division of powers in the sensitive appetite. But what prevents the useful's reduction to the pleasant? Attending to the surface of human experience (all too often neglected by philosophers), Aquinas writes:

Sometimes the soul sets itself against painful things (*tristia*), contrary to the inclination of the concupiscible, so that according to the inclination of the irascible appetite, it may fight obstacles. (1.81.2.co)

Fighting obstacles is unpleasant work. Often it conflicts directly with what is pleasurable, *secundum inclinationem concupiscibilis.* Yet we may be drawn to put up a fight, in spite of the fact that offering no resistance would be more pleasant (at least in the short run). To corroborate this, Aquinas makes an observation about the two passions (*ira* and *concupiscentia*) after which the irascible and concupiscible are named.

The passions of the irascible seem to go against the passions of the concupiscible, since when concupiscence is inflamed (*accensa*), it diminishes anger, and when anger is inflamed, it diminishes concupiscence in many cases. (1.81.2.co)

As experience and observation attest, a person who is genuinely angry cares little about satisfying her appetites for food, drink, or sex. Her first concern is vengeance; she brushes aside her inclinations toward pleasure. And yet what she ultimately desires is the pleasure, sweeter than honey, that vengeance promises to deliver. Aquinas explains:

The irascible is, as it were, the champion and defender of the concupiscible, when it rises up against what hinders the acquisition of the suitable things which the concupiscible desires, or when it sets itself against the harmful things which the concupiscible flees. (1.81.2.co)

The concupiscible power seeks pleasure here and now. The irascible power inclines the sensitive appetite to resistance and defense, even when this appears difficult and unpleasant. Because the soul can be simultaneously attracted and repelled by what is "arduous" or "difficult," there must be distinct powers to account for both the attraction and the repulsion.

Impressed by the connections between the concupiscible power and pleasure, and the irascible power and utility, the Thomist psychiatrists Anna Terruwe and Conrad Baars rename the two powers the "pleasure appetite" and the "utility appetite" (1972, pp. 32–7). While I do not want to rename the powers in this manner, I think the basic intuition is correct, since Aquinas grounds the irascible/concupiscible distinction in the difference between the useful good and the pleasant good. According to Aquinas, the irascible seeks the difficult or arduous good, and avoids the difficult or arduous evil,

not because it is suitable according to the pleasure of the senses, but according as it is useful to the animal for its own defense. (1.81.2 ad 2)

This is important textual evidence for the claim that Aquinas grounds the irascible/concupiscible distinction in the difference between the *utile* and *delectabile*. But why should we believe what Aquinas has claimed? Apparent counter-examples may spring to mind. Suppose I want a hammer, as something useful. Is this the irascible power at work? It seems not. This is not, however, a genuine counter-example. Aquinas' argument is not that *any* desire for what is useful is an act of the irascible power. If I judge that a hammer would be useful to drive a nail, and elect to use a hammer, I have performed an act of the rational appetite. Aquinas' argument may be laid out as follows. For any act that is proper to the sensitive appetite, the object of that act is desired as either pleasant or useful. For any object desired as pleasant (or shunned as painful) by the sensitive appetite, the corresponding passion belongs to the concupiscible. For any object that the sensitive appetite desires not as pleasant, but as useful for obtaining something that is pleasant (or avoids as dangerous because it will lead to what is painful), the corresponding passion belongs to the irascible.

The irreducible distinction between the pleasant (painful) and the useful (dangerous) accounts for Aquinas' differentiation of the sensitive appetite into a concupiscible and an irascible component. As long as the distinction between responding to a thing as pleasant and responding to it as useful remains intact, the justification for the irascible/concupiscible distinction appears secure. One might try to collapse the latter distinction from another angle. Since all the acts that Aquinas attributes to the irascible are ultimately reducible to the maximization of pleasure, one might argue, it follows that they should be assigned to the concupiscible power. For Aquinas, this argument fails, because it merely restates the ordering of the useful toward the pleasant, without negating the essential incommensurability between them. (By "incommensurability," I refer simply to the impossibility of collapsing our perception of something as useful into our perception of something as pleasant. For example, no matter how convinced I am that taking a particular distasteful medicine is useful and will assist in producing a future state of affairs that contains much pleasure, I am unable to construe the actual ingestion of that medicine as anything but unpleasant.[23]) Thus Aquinas concludes:

---

[23] What inspires my appeal to "incommensurability" in the present context is Pasnau's detection of "two incommensurable sides to sensory appetite, one aimed at pleasure and the other at combat" (2002, p. 240). To say that the pleasant and the useful are incommensurable is compatible with the possibility that there are also "incommensurable goods *within* each of the three regions of the good," as Vogler (2002) points out (p. 62). Moreover, the claim that pleasure and utility are, in a certain sense, incommensurable need not entail the denial of Vogler's observation that it is possible "to make appropriate trade-offs between doing what's useful, doing what's pleasant, and doing what's fitting" (p. 63). For Aquinas, the capacity to make such trade-offs is restricted to the possessor of rational appetite, which alone can make the comparisons required for a "trade-off."

All the passions of the irascible have their *incipit* from the concupiscible passions and are terminated in them, just as anger is born from experienced sorrow and, achieving vindication, terminates in gladness. For this reason as well, fights between animals are about things concupiscible, viz. food and sex, as is said in *de Animalibus* 1.9. (1.81.2.co; see also Aristotle, *History of Animals* 8.1, 589a5)

The object of the sensitive appetite is the suitable good, as it appears under the primary aspects of the pleasant or the useful. (The painful and the dangerous are secondary aspects, since minimizing pain is an indirect way of maximizing pleasure, and avoiding danger is an indirect way of maximizing utility. Both are cases of the general priority of good to evil [§1.4].) Kenny is puzzled by the apparent absence of a single criterion by which something may be estimated as an object of sensitive appetite. One might propose, he suggests, that "sensory wants are wants for sense-gratification" (1993, p. 63). But "the use of this criterion will rule out many things which Aquinas sees as manifestations of animal appetite, such as the flight of the lamb and the charge of the bull" (p. 64). This does not qualify as a serious objection. Precisely because the object of the sensitive appetite can be either the pleasant (painful) or the useful (dangerous), Kenny's demand for a "single criterion" is idle.

According to Aquinas, the sensitive appetite necessarily subdivides into two distinct powers. In an extraordinarily illuminating work of scholarship, Peter King has examined the ways in which Aquinas' subdivision of the sensitive appetite was challenged, beginning with Scotus and culminating in Suárez. (In the light of Suárez's formidable attack, as King shows, Descartes's famous dismissal of the concupiscible/irascible distinction appears as something of an epiphenomenon [2002, p. 251].)[24] After examining various attempts to establish a "real distinction" between the irascible and concupiscible powers, Suárez concludes that the names *irascibilis* and *concupiscibilis* "do not signify two appetites (*duos appetitus*) but one and the same conceived in different ways."[25] It would appear that Suárez directly confronts Aquinas' own teaching on the matter. That

---

[24] As King (2002) notes, Descartes dismisses the distinction in §68 of *Les passions de l'âme* (1649). King concludes that in affirming the (at most) merely conceptual (and thus entirely non-binding) status of the irascible/concupiscible distinction, Descartes is "the inheritor of Suárez, and stands indebted to the complex development played out within the Thomist tradition – not the radical innovator he is sometimes portrayed as" (p. 251).

[25] Suárez, *Tractatus quinque ad Primam Secundae*, IV, disp. 1, §3.2, 458b, quoted in King 2002, p. 239, and Suárez's Latin text at p. 254n21.

Aquinas teaches the existence of "two appetites," the irascible appetite and the concupiscible appetite, seems clear enough. Thus Pasnau:

Because the will takes reasons for its inputs, the will's operation is different in kind from the operation of the sensory appetites. (2002, p. 241)[26]

Notice that Pasnau speaks of two plural "sensory appetites." Similarly, Ramírez persistently speaks of the "*appetitus concupiscibilis*" as distinct from the "*appetitus irascibilis*."[27] More recently, Gondreau expounds what he regards as Aquinas' authentic teaching by suggesting that "the one sensitive appetite is composed of two faculties, the concupiscible appetite and the irascible appetite" (2002, p. 214; see also p. 202). Commentators who otherwise disagree sharply with one another seem to concur that Aquinas holds for "two appetites."

I do not think that close attention to Aquinas' texts supports this consensus. It may be true that Aquinas would support a "real distinction" between the irascible and the concupiscible. Unless the distinction between the pleasant and the useful is merely conceptual, it is reasonable to affirm that the irascible/concupiscible distinction is "real" (in some sense). Yet this affirmation does nothing to establish, or even suggest, that Aquinas would consent to the division of the sensitive appetite into two separate appetites. It is no accident that the phrases *appetitus concupiscibilis* and *appetitus irascibilis* do not appear once in the *ST*'s treatment of the passions, or (as far as I can tell) in the *QDV*, the *QDM*, or any of the Aristotelian commentaries. Aquinas thinks that the sensitive appetite, while dividing into two powers, is fundamentally one. This explains why, though he occasionally uses the phrases "irascible power" and "concupiscible power," his far more frequent practice is simply to speak of the "irascible" and the "concupiscible." Forgetting that the irascible and the concupiscible are powers of the same appetite, Ramírez and Gondreau reify them into two separate appetites. In this respect (if no other), they do not reproduce Aquinas' teaching, but Suárez's representation of Aquinas' teaching. Though Pasnau errs on this point less frequently, he seems to think that Aquinas disregards Aristotle's remark (at *De anima* 3.9, 432b4–5) that "it is absurd to split it up" (2002, pp. 237–8). But the rigorous avoidance of the phrases "*appetitus concupiscibilis*" and "*appetitus*

---

[26] Elsewhere in the same text, Pasnau (2002) more accurately speaks of a "concupiscible and irascible component" within the sensitive appetite (p. 202). What must be recognized is the difference between speaking of two distinct capacities of the same unified appetite, and speaking of two separate appetites (implying "disunity" within the sensitive appetite).

[27] See Ramírez 1973, pp. 45, 46, 57, 59, 67, 69, 90, 91, 361, 372, 373.

irascibilis" suggests that Aquinas heeds the Aristotelian warning. While he argues for a subdivision of sensitive appetite, grounded in the irreducible distinction between the useful and the pleasant, he does not want to split it up into two separate things.

<h2 style="text-align:center">2.5 THE IRASCIBLE/CONCUPISCIBLE DISTINCTION
IN THE 1A2AE</h2>

I have sought to follow Aquinas' argument for the irascible/concupiscible distinction.[28] However persuasive the argument, the distinction is not without difficulties. Suárez makes other objections that would require different responses (see King 2002, pp. 238–44). In *QDV* 25.2, Aquinas himself notes nine objections that might be made to the distinction. In what follows, I want to argue that Aquinas' most extended justification of the distinction is to be found within the Treatise at Question 23.

At 23.1, Aquinas asks whether the passions that are in the irascible power are diverse from those that are in the concupiscible. The response: the irascible differs from the concupiscible according to a difference of formal object. The generic object of the concupiscible power (*obiectum potentiae concupiscibilis*) is "sensible good or evil taken simply, which is the pleasurable or the painful" (23.1.co). The object of the irascible power is something different. Why? As in 1.81.2, Thomas appeals to an experience that justifies the distinction of objects (and thereby powers):

> Necessarily the soul sometimes suffers (*patiatur*) a difficulty or a fight in attaining a pleasant good or fleeing a painful evil, inasmuch as this is in a certain way elevated above the easy power of an animal. Whence this very good or evil, according as it has the character of the arduous or the difficult, is the object of the irascible. (23.1.co)

Some things we desire are easy to get, and other things are hard to obtain. But why should the opposition of *facile* and *difficile* justify a distinction of powers? Why does it generate passions that are different in kind? The arguments given by Aquinas seem to establish only that some passions concern what is easy, and others what is difficult. They do

---

[28] King (2002) notices how striking it is that Aquinas would even make an argument for the division of the sensitive appetite into two powers: "Perhaps the most remarkable thing about these arguments [for the irascible/concupiscible distinction] is that Aquinas gives them at all. Imagine the analogous case for metaphysics: after dividing the genus *animal* by the differentia *rational*, further arguments are given to establish that rational animals really are not the same as irrational ones!" (p. 111).

Concupiscible passions	Love/hate	Desire/aversion	Pleasure/pain
Irascible passions	Hope/despair	Hope/fear	Fear/daring

Figure 2.2. The passions as ordered pairs (*coniugationes*)

not seem to motivate the stronger claim that two separate powers are required. I want to argue, however, that Aquinas is aware of this. He does not intend either the distinction's initial presentation in the 1a *pars* or at 23.1 as a demonstration of the necessity of the concupiscible/irascible division. King suggests, persuasively, that the "taxonomic structure" that proceeds according to the irascible/concupiscible distinction "has no independent explanatory value; its worth is cashed out in its fidelity to the phenomena it seeks to explain and the utility of its classification scheme" (1998, p. 112). The aim of 23.1 is simply to lay the ground of the distinction's possibility. Only in the remainder of the Question does Aquinas endeavor to exhibit the appropriateness, if not the strict necessity, of the division. When the division is made, he will show, multiple relations among the passions naturally fall into place that would otherwise be difficult to explain or even acknowledge.

The first of these relations is designated by *contrarietas*, the key term of Article 2. A "contrariety" is a principle whereby two things are mutually opposed. With the exception of anger, each of the passions has at least one contrary. We may summarily depict these by listing the passions in ordered pairs, as in figure 2.2.

An asymmetry between the concupiscible and irascible appears at once. Each of the concupiscible passions has one, and only one, contrary. Two of the irascible passions – hope and fear – have two contraries, and anger has no contrary. How do we explain this? Thomas appeals to the different character of the *contrarietas* in each power. The concupiscible presents the simpler case. The members of all three of its ordered pairs are opposed according to the same principle. This is what Aquinas calls "contrariety of objects." The object of love (desire, pleasure) is good; the object of hate (aversion, pain) is evil. Since good as such is inherently attractive – "nothing shuns good, insofar as it is good, but all things desire it" (23.2.co) – it can only be a terminus *ad quem*. Thus each of the basic concupiscible passions – love, desire, and pleasure – is an inclination toward good. The inverse is true of evil. Since it is repulsive by its nature – "likewise nothing desires evil, insofar as it is evil, but all things flee from it" (23.2.co) – it can only be a terminus *a quo*. Thus hate, aversion, and pain are repulsions from evil. Within the realm of "sensible good and evil considered absolutely," there can be no repulsion from good or attraction from evil. Because things appear thus from the vantage point of the concupiscible, the principle behind each of the ordered pairs is the same. There is but one *contrarietas*, the opposition of good and evil.

If one looks at the ordered pairs of passions within the irascible, things are more complicated. Hope and fear are related by the "contrariety of objects," since hope is motion toward the (difficult) good, and fear is flight from the (difficult) evil. But hope and fear are the *only* ordered pair within the irascible to be governed by this contrariety. Hope and despair cannot be explained by the *contrarietas obiectorum*, since they have the same object, namely the difficult or arduous good. Yet, since they are genuine contraries, there must be some other principle of opposition. This is what Thomas describes as the contrariety "according to approach (*accessus*) or withdrawal (*recessus*) from the same terminus" (23.2.co). Thus hope and despair are contraries in that hope is an *accessus* toward the "difficult good," and despair a *recessus* from the same. How do we reconcile the latter – that is, a withdrawal from the good – with the principle that *nihil refugit bonum, in quantum bonum, sed omnia appetunt ipsum*? We must attend to the aspect that distinguishes the irascible's object, the *ratio ardui vel difficilis*. Despair is a withdrawal from the good not because it is good, but because its attainment is perceived as too difficult. The hallmark of despair is that its possessor continues to regard the desired object as good, although she has abandoned any hope of attaining it. The contrariety that relates hope and despair, then, is not the "contrariety of objects" (since both have the same object), but the contrariety of approach or withdrawal from the same object or term.

This same *contrarietas* also relates fear and daring. While fear and daring both regard an impending evil, fear is a *recessus* from the evil, and daring is an *accessus* toward it. Daring appears as the inverse of despair; it proposes the possibility of motion toward a perceived evil. How to reconcile such motion with the principle *nihil appetit malum, in quantum huiusmodi, sed omnia fugiunt ipsum*? Once again, the *ratio ardui vel difficilis* is decisive. Daring moves toward a thing not because it is evil, but because it stands as a difficult obstacle that must be removed for the sake of attaining the good.

Aquinas has shown that the two principles of relation among the irascible passions (contrariety of object, contrariety of approach and withdrawal) cannot be reduced to the single principle that relates the opposed concupiscible passions (contrariety of object). This provides decisive confirmation of the irascible/concupiscible distinction. If the *contrarietas* governing each ordered pair of irascible passions were in every case identical to that of the concupiscible passions, the division would appear arbitrary. But in the light of the "twofold contrariety" (*duplex contrarietas*) that governs the irascible, the distinction's point begins to emerge. Article 2's difference of *contrarietas* secures the division that was proposed in Article 1 according to difference of object.

Article 3 highlights a third difference of the irascible from the concupiscible. Only the irascible contains a passion with no contrary. In its response, Aquinas asserts that the passion of anger "is singular in that it cannot have a contrary, either according to *accessus* and *recessus*, or according to the contrariety of good and evil" (23.3.co). Why does the first *contrarietas* play no role? Thomas explains: insofar as anger is aroused by a present evil, it assumes the form of an approach toward that evil, a tendency to attack it. The opposed withdrawal, the motion away from that evil, would simply be sorrow (*tristitia*). Why does the other contrariety, the contrariety of objects, fail to generate a passion contrary to anger? Aquinas answers that anger ends either in sorrow (produced by failure to achieve vindication), or in joy (produced by success in vindication). *Tristitia* and *gaudium* are mutual contraries, but neither is the contrary of anger. To the suggestion that calm would qualify as the contrary of anger, Thomas replies that it is, but only negatively or privatively. Neither contrariety furnishes a passion contrary to anger. Aquinas does not aim in Article 3 to provide a full explanation of anger. Indeed, he does not even provide a basic explanation. The elucidation of anger must wait until Questions 46–8. The point of Article 3 is to provide additional confirmation that the sensitive appetite is appropriately divided into the irascible and concupiscible. It does so by pointing to yet another characteristic that the irascible power has, but the concupiscible power lacks, namely the presence of a passion that has no contrary.

The final Article of Question 23 completes the extended justification of the irascible/concupiscible distinction. In Article 4's response, Aquinas shows that the irascible passions are framed within the concupiscible. The irascible passions cannot arise at the first stage, since they presuppose an initial tendency toward some good or away from some evil. They appear in the middle stage, when there is a difficult good (or evil) on the horizon but not yet present (otherwise there would be no difficulty). Thus "in respect of good not yet attained there is hope and despair; in respect of evil not yet encountered there is fear and daring" (23.4.co). With respect to the final stage, no irascible passion corresponds to the attained good, because once it has been attained, "it does not have the character of the arduous." With respect to present evil, anger may arise. But like the other irascible passions, anger cannot be ultimate. It necessarily terminates in either joy or sorrow.

To summarize: Question 23 justifies and applies the irascible/concupiscible distinction in four stages. First, Aquinas appeals to a generic difference of object (Article 1). Second, he argues that while only one contrariety suffices to explain each ordered pair of passions within the concupiscible, two contrarieties are required to account for the ordered pairs of passions within the irascible (Article 2). Third, he argues that only the irascible power contains a passion with no contrary (Article 3). Fourth, he appeals to the non-ultimacy of the irascible passions (Article 4). Before accepting Descartes's dismissal of the irascible/concupiscible distinction, careful consideration ought to be given to Aquinas' presentation of the distinction in both the 1a *pars* and the 1a2ae.

CHAPTER 3

The activation of passion

Because the passions are "passive potencies" in Aristotle's sense, they remain inert unless they are activated by an agent outside themselves. What activates the passions? Since appetite follows apprehension, certain types of sensation, imagination, and perception will reliably activate certain passions. Here what matters is not the particular object of perception, but the "form" or "aspect" under which that object is perceived. This is the "formal object" of the passion. While the formal object activates the passion, it must be distinguished from the "material" or "dispositive" cause of the passion (§3.1). The apprehension of a singular concrete object by sensation or imagination plays a crucial role in the activation of the sensitive appetite (§3.2). But is sensitive apprehension the only act relevant for understanding the activation of passion? In rational animals, the sensitive soul is influenced to no small degree by the intellect. Careful attention must be paid not only to sensation and imagination, but also to the "estimative power" and "memorative power" in non-rational animals (§3.3), which in human beings assumes the form of the "cogitative power," also known as the "particular reason" (§3.4). What else would activate the passions? Because the passions are intrinsically related to one another, Aquinas holds that some passions reliably cause other passions, in a set of predictable sequences (§3.5).

3.1 FORMAL OBJECTS OF THE PASSIONS

A passion is an act of the sensitive appetite. Such acts are properly "passive" because they require something outside themselves to activate them. Robert Gordon contrasts "changes of state" that do not require the intervention of an outside agent or catalyst (e.g. freezing, rotting, congealing, solidifying) with other changes of state that will happen only if such intervention occurs. Gordon observes:

A food is salted or pickled, on the other hand, only if has been salted or pickled, typically by a person using the appropriate substance (salt, a pickling solution, etc.): it doesn't just "salt" or "pickle." Likewise, a person is *intoxicated* only if something (an intoxic*ant*) is, or at least has been, intoxicating him. One does not simply "intoxicate." *Intoxicated* is an adjective that characterizes a state as resulting from an *operation* performed by some "agent". (1986, p. 375)

For Aquinas, the motions of the sensitive appetite are passive in precisely this sense. In any particular case, no passion will be triggered in the absence of the appropriate "agent" or "activator." Just what kind of thing is the activator of a passion? Aquinas writes:

passions differ in accordance with their activators (*activa*), which, in the case of the passions of the soul, are their objects (*obiecta*). (23.4.co)[1]

We seem to have a clear first answer to the question. The activators of a passion coincide with its objects. Activators of the passion of concupiscence, for example, may be nothing other than its objects: a warm bath, a cold dessert, a cup of hot coffee. Each item on this list counts as a "material object" of the passion, a concrete thing numerically different from other concrete things on the list. Any material object would thus be related to the passion as its activator. But what do concrete objects have in common that makes them activators of passion? In virtue of what "form" are they able to serve as activators?

To answer these questions is to specify the "formal object" of the passion. Peter King notices that Aquinas often tends to speak only of the "object," rather than the "formal object" (1998, p. 107); the text quoted above from 23.4 is one example of this tendency. But Aquinas does make clear that when distinguishing the passions, the main quarry is the formal difference. The general object of appetite is the good (§1.1). Any passion, therefore, will formally be a motion either toward the apprehended good, or away from a perceived evil which occurs only on account of the appetite's inclination toward the contrary good (§1.5). But to say that the object of appetite is good does nothing to differentiate the particular passions. If, as Sweeney observes, "all passion is in some way reducible to the tendency of things to seek what is suitable to their nature, all are movements which presuppose a likeness or aptness to that toward which they tend" (1999, pp. 220–1), then how are particular passions to be distinguished from one another?

Aquinas addresses this question with special clarity in his treatment of concupiscence. In Article 2 of Question 30, the objectors wonder why

---

[1] Similar passages occur at 30.2.co; 31.8 ad 3m; 35.4.co; 36.4 ad 3m; 40.1.co; 40.2.co.

"concupiscence" should name a specific passion, rather than any act of appetite that tends to whatever is perceived or imagined as pleasurable. Aquinas answers: if concupiscence is a specific passion, its object cannot simply be the "good," or even the "pleasurable good according to the senses" (*bonum delectabile secundum sensum*). As a particular passion, *concupiscentia* must have a correspondingly particular object. If this particularity is sought at the level of concrete singular objects, there will be as many concupiscences as there are material objects. This particularity generates what Thomas calls a "material difference of the passions," which occurs whenever there is difference in the object "according to the nature of the thing" (*secundum rei naturam*) (30.2.co). But Aquinas is not concerned with material differences. Rather than dwell on concrete singular objects, he looks for "formal differences." He finds these differences in a "diversity which is according to the activating power" (that is, the power of apprehension) and which "makes a formal difference among the passions, according to which passions differ in kind" (30.2.co). Because it is possible to apprehend sensible goods under distinct *rationes* – "aspects" or "descriptions" – there are formal differences among sensible objects.[2]

What generates formal differences within the common field of the "pleasurable good according to the senses"? The most decisive factor is the capacity to apprehend a pleasurable good either as present or absent. When an appealing object is apprehended as present, the result is pleasure. When the same object is apprehended as absent, the result is concupiscence or desire. What if the object is simply apprehended as pleasant, abstracting from whether it is presently possessed or not? In that case, the passion is love. Aquinas writes:

There are certain acts of the will and appetite that regard good under some special condition, as joy and pleasure regard good present and possessed, whereas desire and hope regard good not yet attained. But love regards the good in general, whether it is possessed or not possessed. Whence love is naturally the first act of will and appetite. On account of this, all other motions of the appetite presuppose love as their first root. (1.20.1.co)[3]

---

[2] The argument that only a plurality of formal *rationes* (as opposed to material differences) can bring about formal differences in another order (e.g. the *scientiae*) occurs *very* early in the *ST* (see 1.1.3.co).

[3] Meyer (1994) seems to have overlooked this passage when he suggests that for Aquinas joy and sorrow correspond to the past, love and hate correspond to the present, and desire and aversion correspond to the future (pp. 365–6). (Elsewhere Meyer [1991, pp. 119–20] implausibly attributes the view to Étienne Gilson.) In light of this basic exegetical failure, it is amusing to hear Meyer address "la confusion de Thomas" (p. 372).

Table 3.1 *The concupiscible passions according to their formal objects*

	Thing perceived as bonum	*Thing perceived as* malum
Present	Pleasure	Pain or sorrow
Absent	Concupiscence	Aversion
Abstracting from presence or absence	Love	Hatred

Table 3.1 individuates the passions according to their "formal objects."

Like the concupiscible passions, the irascible passions are also individuated according to a formal difference in their objects. Hope, despair, fear, daring, and anger each have distinct formal objects. Specifying these formal objects is a relatively complex affair.[4] The irascible passions are not tendencies toward the good considered as pleasant, but rather appetites for something considered as arduous or difficult, but worth pursuing for the sake of attaining the pleasant good or avoiding the painful evil (§2.4). In other words, the formal object of the irascible passions is the useful rather than the pleasant. But to identify the object of the irascible passions as the "difficult or arduous good" is not to say what distinguishes the irascible passions from one another. Aquinas must locate formal differences *within* the field of the difficult or arduous good.

How Aquinas performs this feat may be seen in Question 40's identification of the formal object of hope. As an irascible passion, hope concerns the arduous good. Goodness and difficulty constitute two of the "four conditions" that anything must satisfy in order to be hope's formal object. What are the other two conditions? The object of hope necessarily exists in the future; we do not hope for what we presently have. In this respect, hope is akin to desire; the difference between hope and desire lies in the first condition. While only arduous goods are the object of hope, the object of desire may be either easy or difficult to obtain. Finally, the

---

[4] As King (1998) notices, for any full treatment of the passions, "the formal object of each passion needs to be spelled out in precise detail" (p. 120n37). King performatively demonstrates the need for extreme care in this matter when he writes that "anger has for its object a difficult evil already present which it strives to attack and overcome (revenge)" (p. 118). This is only half the story for Aquinas. Anger's object includes not only the overcoming of the difficult evil, but also – and perhaps especially – the perception of such overcoming as essentially pleasant (see §12.1).

Table 3.2 *The irascible passions (except for anger) according to their formal objects*

	Thing perceived as bonum	*Thing perceived as* malum
Approach	Hope	Daring
Withdrawal	Despair	Fear

object of hope must not only be good, difficult, and future. It must also be possible to obtain. If these conditions are met, the appetite will move toward the difficult possible future good. This "approach" of the appetite is hope. If the same object is apprehended as not simply difficult, but impossible, the motion of the appetite will be "withdrawal" (see table 3.2).

Anger is conspicuously absent from the table. The reason is that Aquinas holds that anger has a complex formal object, containing one element perceived as good (vindication) and another element perceived as evil (offense or slight against oneself). (Anger's formal object will receive careful consideration at §12.1; see also figure 3.5 later in this chapter.)

Considering the formal differences within the fields of the pleasant good and the arduous good, according to Aquinas, yields eleven primary passions. Question 23 summarizes:

In the concupiscible are three ordered pairs of passions, viz. love and hate (*amor et odium*), desire and aversion (*desiderium et fuga*), joy and sorrow (*gaudium et tristitia*). Similarly in the irascible are three groups, viz. hope and despair (*spes et desperatio*), fear and daring (*timor et audacia*), and anger (*ira*), to which no passion is opposed. Therefore all the passions differing in species are eleven in number, six in the concupiscible, and five in the irascible, under which all the passions of the soul are contained. (23.4.co)

Aquinas gives the appearance of having created an exhaustive catalog of the passions. There is something true about this appearance. The eleven passions are privileged. They are the passions that Aquinas will subject to deeper analysis in Questions 26–48. But the list is hardly exhaustive. Thomas knows that other passions exist. Question 31 on sorrow explicitly notes pity, envy, anxiety, and torpor. Question 41 on fear mentions sloth, blushing, shame, wonder, torpor, and agony. But, according to Aquinas, each of these passions can be rightly described as subspecies of one of the basic eleven passions. While the list of eleven is not exhaustive, it is subsumptive.[5] Other passions (passions in the strict sense, not the pseudopassions) will appear as subspecies of one or another of the eleven primary passions.

This judgment must be nuanced in one respect. The summarizing conclusion of Question 23 suggests that each of the eleven passions comfortably bears a single name. But earlier in the same Question, Aquinas says that four of the concupiscible passions have more than one proper name: "concupiscence or desire," "pleasure or joy," "pain or sorrow," "aversion or abomination." Why the multiplicity of names? Are they merely synonyms? It might seem that the first term of each couplet names the passion, and the second the corresponding pseudopassion. While this suggestion might be plausible for "concupiscence or desire" and "pleasure or joy," it does not hold for "pain or sorrow." Sorrow is an act of the sensitive appetite; it is a genuine passion, not a pseudopassion. In the absence of sound generalizations, the relations between each term will have to be closely examined in the chapter devoted to the particular passion.[6]

To know what a passion is, in no small part, to know its formal object, "the most general characterization which anything that counts as the object of the potency can fall under," in King's formulation (1998, p. 108). Some might deny this, on the ground that while some passions have objects, there are also "objectless" emotions, such as "dread."[7] From

---

[5] This does not mean that the eleven are well understood as "elements." Aquinas does not think that other passions are formally constituted by their combination. That several passions can work together to generate other passions, as love and desire combine to generate hope, is true. But this concerns causality rather than formal constitution. King (1998) observes that whereas Descartes's primitive passions (wonder, love, hate, desire, joy, and sadness) are like chemical elements whose combination produces psychological experience, "Aquinas's model is biological rather than chemical. He takes the passions to be essentially different from one another, so that they are related causally rather than by mixture" (pp. 112–13). Gondreau (2002) emphasizes that Thomas's list of eleven passions is unique, adding that Aquinas "supplies his doctrine with enough latitude to respond to the criticism that his index of eleven passions fails to account for all the emotional reactions that characterize human behavior, as he explicitly admits that the eleven principal passions do not include all the specific passions that a human being may undergo" (p. 217).

[6] Attending to the diversity of emotional phenomena, Gordon (1986) confesses it "useless to generalize about 'the emotions'" (p. 385). I do not think that Aquinas would go quite so far. We can and do generalize about the passions and emotions; Questions 22–5 are about the passions "in general." Yet Gordon has an important point about the limits of generalization. In his own way, Aquinas acknowledges this point by placing the emphasis of the Treatise squarely on the particular passions. He knows that generalizations, however helpful for the purpose of orientation, are no substitute for detailed analysis of particular phenomena.

[7] Kenny (1963) notes "the problem of objectless emotions, such as *Angst*, which exercised Freud and Wittgenstein" (p. 17). Deigh (1994) also notes the problem, only to suggest that "charity and just good sense advise us to let the problem of objectless emotions pass" (pp. 826–7).

Aquinas' perspective, the very idea of "objectless" passions rests on a fundamental confusion. Since appetition follows apprehension (§1.1), any passion is necessarily caused by some act of sensation, imagination, perception, or cognition, and thus has a formal object. Why the temptation to suppose the existence of objectless emotions? Acknowledging many of the phenomena observed by Freud, while arguing that Aquinas offers resources for a more adequate explanation of the facts, Terruwe and Baars (1972) make the following claim:

> We experience anxiety because we *are, know,* or *believe* ourselves unable to avoid the threatening evil. For example, we *are* unable to come to grips with the object of our fear when we suffer from repressive neurosis. This is so because the object of fear has been repressed and, though still present in the subconscious, is no longer known as clearly as before, if at all. On the other hand, we may experience anxiety, and without necessarily being neurotic, in the presence of a danger *known* to us. (p. 12)

If Terruwe and Baars are correct, what characterizes neurotic anxiety is not the absence of a feared object, but precisely the conjunction of its presence with its psychological repression. While the particular object causing the fear is not present to consciousness, it is hardly ineffective or non-existent.

Were we unable to specify the formal objects of the passions, we would not understand how the passions differ from, and are related to, one another. At best, we would know only that some of the passions incline a person toward a perceived good, and others away from a perceived evil. We would not know (for example) how desire differs from hope, or how despair differs from fear. Despite its central importance, the notion of formal object does not exhaust the question of what activates a passion. This is true for several reasons. For one thing, as I have already suggested, when we want to know about a passion's activator, we may be asking a question about the relevant material object. If I ask another person, "What set off that attack of concupiscence?" I may not want a general description that corresponds to concupiscence's formal object. I may be looking for the material specification of the formal object – a concrete singular designated by a proper name.

The clearest indication that Aquinas recognizes a strong distinction between the object of a passion (whether formal or material) and its "cause" is found in the consideration of fear, which devotes one Question to the *obiectum* of fear and a separate Question to its cause (see §10.3). What disposes us to perceive some particular face (the material object) as an instance of the terrible evil (the formal object), and thereby as an activator of fear, may be some feature of our condition, a dispositive cause "from the side of the subject" (*ex parte subiecti*) similar to what Gordon calls the "cognitive and attitudinal 'components'" that are the "sustaining causes" of a passion (1986, p. 381). Alternatively, the "cause" may be a feature of the thing itself, a dispositive cause "from the side of the object" (*ex parte obiecti*). Or it may be something that seems to transgress the subject/object distinction, corresponding roughly to what Gordon terms a "side condition" without which the passion will not occur (1986, p. 383). Similarly, when Aquinas gives an account of the "cause of love" (see §5.4), he does not simply reiterate that the formal object of love is an object apprehended as good. Rather, he isolates and describes the forces ("knowledge" and "likeness") that typically dispose a person to see things under the aspect of good. The same holds for the account of the "cause of pleasure." In the treatment of pleasure in itself (Question 31), Aquinas focuses on the formal object. But in the separate question on the cause of pleasure (Question 32), he provides an analysis of the "activity" that disposes a person to apprehend an object as pleasant.

It is vital to keep these distinctions in mind. When a person asks about the "cause" of a passion, she may be asking about either the formal object, the material thing perceived under a certain formality, or the factors (whether in the perceiver or the thing perceived) that lead a person to construe the concrete thing in a manner that activates the passion. She may even be asking about all these things simultaneously. Alternatively, her question may concern the multiple "inputs" possessed by animals which, under the right circumstances, reliably activate the full range of passions. The most basic of these inputs are sensation and imagination.

3.2 SENSATION AND IMAGINATION

At 1.78.4, Aquinas distinguishes four apprehensive powers of the sensitive soul. In their most basic forms, the following powers are common to all animals:

1. Sensation, including both the proper senses and the common sense
2. The imagination
3. The estimative power
4. The memorative power

Each power is capable of activating the sensitive appetite. Aquinas states this directly:

The sensitive appetite is moved not only by the estimative power in other animals, and in man by the cogitative power which the universal reason guides, but also by the imagination and sense. (1.81.3 ad 2m)

With Aristotle, Aquinas holds that "in whatever there is sense, there is also appetite, as said in *De anima* 2.3" (78.1 ad 2m). That motion of the sensitive appetite would follow directly upon sensation seems evident. If I put my hand on a stove, I feel pain at once. Greek and Latin capture the closeness of the connection between sense perception and appetitive motion; *aisthesis* and *sensus* signify both "sensitive apprehension" and "feeling."

The matter is complicated slightly by Aquinas's reworking of the Aristotelian "common sense." The "proper senses," as distinguished from the "common sense," are those through which an animal perceives (1) "proper sensibles," that is, qualities that "make an impression on the sense primarily and *per se*" (e.g. color, sound, smell, sweet, bitter, hard, soft) and (2) "common sensibles" (e.g. size, number, shape, motion, rest). Though one might suppose that the common sense would perceive the common sensibles, Aquinas thinks that the proper senses suffice for this function.[8] Sight perceives shape; touch perceives that there are three jelly beans on a table. Both kinds of sensibles, proper and common, belong to the "*per se* objects of the senses." So why is the common sense necessary? It is required, Aquinas answers, to account for the capacity of an animal not only to apprehend *per se* sense objects, but also to perceive that such qualities exist in a single thing. An animal does not simply apprehend black and white patches, as well as a spherical shape. It perceives that the white and black patches are united in a single thing, this soccer ball. (What the non-rational animal *cannot* do is to judge that the single thing it perceives is an instance of the kind "soccer ball.")

The main function of the common sense is to perceive the union of *per se* sensible qualities in a single thing. How do the proper senses and the common senses interact in moving the sensitive appetite? At one level, no interaction is necessary. When a horse with a parched throat takes a drink, receiving the form of wetness on its dry throat, it feels

---

[8] Here Pasnau (2002) is quite helpful. Common sense "does not receive any special sense object of its own; it does not, in particular, have common sensibles as its special object" (p. 191). As Pasnau notes, Aquinas makes this claim directly in his commentary on *De anima* 2.13: "It is impossible for the common sense to have a proper object that is not the object of a proper sense" (*InDA* 2.13.8; cf. Thomas Aquinas 1999, p. 206).

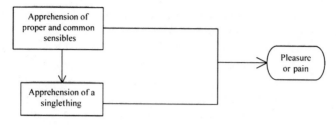

Figure 3.1. Appetition follows sense apprehension

pleasure, regardless of whether it perceives the wetness and the color of the liquid to belong to the same thing. This does not prevent, however, the possibility of other instances in which the act of the common sense plays a decisive role in moving the sensitive appetite. If I perceive a certain combination of qualities as united in the same painting, I may be affected by the painting as a whole in a way quite different from how I would be affected if I were only to perceive the proper sensibles of texture, color, shape, etc., without recognizing them as belonging to a unified object (see figure 3.1).

This model fits the cases in which animals experience pleasure or pain upon the perception of something in their immediate environment. Are animals capable of feeling pleasure or pain even when nothing is directly present to be sensed? Aquinas writes:

> It is required for the life of a complete animal that it should not only apprehend a thing in its presence, but also in its absence from sensation. Otherwise, since animal motion and action follow apprehension, an animal would not be moved to seek something absent. Most of all we observe the contrary of this in perfect animals, which are moved by a processive motion, for they are moved toward something apprehended and absent. Therefore an animal through the sensitive soul must not only receive the species of sensible things, when it is actually changed by them, but also retain and preserve them. (1.78.4.co)

Images of both *per se* sense objects and the things in which they inhere (the *per accidens* objects of the senses) may be possessed, even when they are not directly present to sensation. The capacity of not only receiving forms, but also retaining them, is what Aquinas calls "imagination," following Moerbeke's rendition of *phantasia* by *imaginatio*.

Frequently (but not necessarily) sensation and imagination work together to produce a passion. If I have an immediate sensation of a waterfall that I have seen before, nothing precludes my also having images of that waterfall, stored in my imagination. In any such case, it is probable that movement of my sensitive appetite will result neither from just the sensation I experience in the presence of the waterfall, nor exclusively from the stored images. Rather, appetitive motion will result from the interaction between sensation and imagination. This interaction explains why appetitive motion sometimes seems "out of proportion" to the thing sensed. A person (call her Marnie[9]) may perceive something ordinary, such as a red patch, that produces a weak reaction (if any at all) in others. But when Marnie senses the red patch, she also recalls images of violence and blood, stored in the imagination from prior acts of sensation. As a result, when she senses a red patch, she undergoes a strong reaction on the part of her sensitive appetite. While triggered by sensation, what causes the passion can be understood only by attending to the interaction between sensation and imagination. (Sensation is not the only power that can arouse the imagination. Aquinas thinks that the will is also capable of this [§4.4].)

The first passion that imagination will produce is either pleasure or pain. Any image that moves the sensitive appetite is, as such, experienced as either pleasant or painful. But when the image is present and the thing is absent, another passion will be experienced. If the image is experienced as pleasant, then the combination of the image's presence and the thing's absence will produce desire. Should the image be painful, the thing's absence and the image's presence will yield aversion. If Steve is a carnivore who likes steak (and has not just gorged himself on sirloin), then recalling an image of steak will produce pleasure. (If Stephanie is a vegetarian who has a repugnance toward eating flesh, the same image may lead to pain.) But the recognition that the steak presently exists only in the imagination will produce the distinct (and possibly painful) passion of desire (§3.1). (For Stephanie, the result will be aversion.) To take account of the possibility of interaction between sensation and imagination, the diagram may be revised as in figure 3.2.

Is this a radical modification of the model? It appears not. In both cases, what moves the sensitive appetite are sensible forms that are somehow present to the apprehension. The only difference is that the object from which the sensible forms derive need not be present *secundum rem* in order to move the sensitive appetite. It may be present in imagination. Sensation and imagination bring the same type of sensible qualities before the apprehension, and thereby move the sensitive appetite in

---

[9] Admirers of the films of Alfred Hitchcock will understand the reason for this apparently strange choice of name.

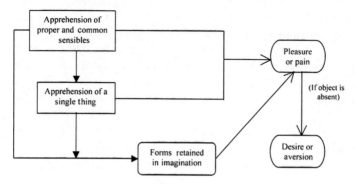

Figure 3.2. Appetition follows sensation and imagination

essentially the same way. There may, of course, be differences of intensity. Imagining one's finger burning on a hot stove does not cause the pain that results from actually placing one's finger on the stove. Provided that the finger is not actually on the stove, the (perhaps negligible) pain produced by imagining the finger on the stove will yield to aversion. Yet it is not invariably the case that passions activated by the imagination are "weaker" than those produced by immediate sensation. At times the act of imagining sensible qualities can move the sensitive appetite more powerfully than the presence of the "real thing." The pleasures of anticipation may outstrip the pleasures of consummation.

3.3 THE ESTIMATIVE AND MEMORATIVE POWERS

Because the sensitive appetite is a "passive power," it is not moved by itself. It requires something else to activate it. In the first instance, what moves the sensitive appetite is sensation or imagination of the appetible object. But Aquinas does not leave the matter at this point. What rational animals actually perceive as appetible is always influenced by intellect. It is precisely because the sensitive appetite can obey reason that it can be harnessed to play an important role in the rational creature's motion toward the good (see §4.2).

Before directly considering the mode in which the intellect acts upon the sensitive appetite for human beings, through the mediation of particular reason, it is necessary to understand how Aquinas thinks that even non-rational animals have passions that are activated by something other than sensation or imagination of the pleasant or painful. I have anticipated this in accounting for the distinction of the irascible power from the concupiscible power in terms of the difference of the useful from the pleasant (§2.4). Now I want to show precisely how Aquinas thinks sensitive appetite in non-rational animals is activated by estimations of what is useful or dangerous, estimations that are not collapsible into sensations or images of what is pleasant or painful. To show this, it is helpful to look more closely at what Aquinas says about the "estimative power" in non-rational animals, which in human beings becomes the "particular reason" or the "cogitative power" (§3.4).

From what does the need arise to posit an estimative power? Thomas explains:

If an animal were moved only on account of what is pleasant and painful according to the sense, it would not be necessary to suppose in an animal anything besides the apprehension of the forms that the senses perceive, and in which the animal takes pleasure, or else bristles from. (1.78.4.co)

Why does Aquinas think that an animal can be moved by something other than what is *delectabile et contristabile secundum sensum*? What makes a purely hedonistic account inadequate? He answers: "The sheep runs away when it sees a wolf, not on account of its unbecoming color or shape, but as though it were a natural enemy. And similarly a bird gathers straws, not because doing so pleases the senses, but because it is useful (*utilis*) for building its nest" (1.78.4.co). At least on occasion, non-rational animals respond to their environment in a manner that goes beyond the perceptual content of what they sense or imagine. "It is necessary to an animal that it seek or avoid some things," Thomas says, "not only because they are suitable or not suitable for sensing, but also on account of other benefits and uses, or else harms" (1.78.4.co). If these other uses and disadvantages are not perceived by sense, they must be apprehended by some other power. This is what Thomas calls the "estimative power" (*vis estimativa*). The object of the estimative power is not proper or common sensibles (or images thereof), but rather "intentions which the exterior sense does not perceive" (1.78.4.co). Because to receive these *intentiones* is not the same as to retain them, a fourth power that preserves the intentions in memory must be supposed. What the imagination is to sensation, the memorative power is to the estimative power.

What precisely are the *intentiones* perceived by the estimative power in non-rational animals? Aquinas does not describe them in detail. The text quoted above suggests that they are non-empirical valuations of a perceived thing as either useful or dangerous. They are not perceived by the senses, but "only by some natural instinct" (1.78.4.co). In distinguishing intentions from sensible forms in this manner, Aquinas draws from the first book of Avicenna's *Liber de anima*.[10] When a sheep apprehends a wolf's "shape, condition and color," according to Avicenna, it is perceiving "forms." But when it perceives that the wolf is dangerous, it performs a distinct act.

An intention is that which the soul apprehends of the sensible, even though the external sense has not previously apprehended it – for example, when a sheep apprehends the intention that it has of the wolf: that it ought to fear it and flee from it – even though its senses do not in any way apprehend this. (Avicenna 1972, p. 86, quoted in Pasnau 2002, p. 269)

Aquinas makes Avicenna's distinction his own.[11] Neither Aquinas nor Avicenna implies that the estimative power is a free agent, operating independently of sense and imagination. On the contrary, the animal must first sense or imagine something before its estimative power can be activated. By its proper and common senses, the sheep apprehends the wolf – or, more precisely, the conjunction of sensible forms that it recognizes as existing in a single thing, but not as an instance of the concept "wolf" (§3.2). Through the estimative power, it proceeds to apprehend an intention of the wolf as dangerous. These acts may be difficult to distinguish temporally: the sheep may estimate the wolf as dangerous "as soon as" its sensible qualities are perceived. Yet, Aquinas thinks they are genuinely distinct. Other perceivers, capable of apprehending the same sensible forms in the wolf, do not necessarily estimate the wolf as dangerous. (The relevant set of "other perceivers" ranges from Little Red Riding Hood to other animals not known to fear wolves, though they perceive their sensible qualities no less clearly than sheep.)

When Aquinas assigns animal nature an estimative power, beyond the capacities for sensation and imagination, he reiterates the essential incommensurability between the useful/dangerous and pleasant/painful (§2.4). With Avicenna, he agrees that what leads the sheep to perceive the wolf as harmful is not repugnance caused directly by the sharpness of its teeth or

---

[10] Pasnau (2002) offers a clear account of the extent to which Aquinas borrows from Avicenna (pp. 268–9); see also Wolfson (1935). Klubertanz (1952) observes that Avicenna's explanation of "purposive or quasi-intelligent activity of brutes" was "readily adopted by the Latin writers"; he cites Gundissalinus and William of Auvergne (p. 269). But he adds that the "school of Avicenna breaks up into a number of divergent and irreconcilable theories" (p. 270).

[11] Though I arrived at the point independently, my formulation converges with that of Klubertanz (1952). Aquinas "studied Avicenna's arguments and made them his own with some modifications" (p. 270).

the color of its coat. Nonetheless, the sheep avoids the wolf, "whose hostility it has never sensed" (*QDV* 25.2.co).

These considerations illuminate the necessity of the estimative power for Aquinas. Why the memorative power? If intentions were largely discovered, the answer to this question would be evident. One power would be required to make the initial estimations; another would be needed to store the estimations. Something like this seems to hold for the distinction in humans between the cogitative and memorative powers (§3.4). But if non-rational animals do not discover intentions, but simply hold them within the natural estimative power, why posit a separate capacity for their retention? In this respect, the sheep example may be misleading.[12] Aquinas does not exclude the possibility that, beyond possessing innate reactions to things, non-rational animals are also capable of discovering that some things are useful or dangerous, and retaining those estimations in memory. Not all animals are likely to excel at such discovery. A mouse lucky enough to survive three or four failed mousetraps, each of which uses cheese as bait, may still never be able to estimate that cheese is dangerous. But other, more intelligent animals are capable of associating particular complexes of sensible qualities with the estimation of "danger." (If beaten often enough by the same person, Fido will learn to run away whenever he smells him, despite his natural tendency to be faithful to his master.)

Aquinas himself suggests a slightly different justification for the memorative power. Though he would agree with Nietzsche that non-human animals excel in forgetting, he also credits animals with the power to store intentions in memory. This happens particularly when the animal estimates something as useful or dangerous: "the principle for remembering is formed in animals from an intention of this kind – for instance, that a thing is harmful or agreeable" (1.78.4.co). Thus, Aquinas concludes, non-rational animals behave in accordance with some distinction between immediately present sensible qualities and intentions of things, including

[12] I work on the assumption that extended analysis of the sheep/wolf example is useful for grasping what Aquinas thinks. But the following remark of Kenny (2004) ought not to be neglected: "Aquinas, in common with other great mediaeval scholastics, is very sparing with illustrative examples, and when he does offer them they are often second-hand or worn out. Commentators, therefore, in order to render the text intelligible to a modern reader, have to provide their own examples, and the choice of examples involves a substantial degree of interpretation" (pp. 457–8). Kenny thus provides an apologia for my own habit, in this chapter and others, of generating examples of a sort that Aquinas may or may not provide. Solomon (1999) rightly notes the oddness of books on the emotions that use virtually no such examples from literature, "real life," or the author's first-person experience (p. 131).

"the very character of being in the past" (1.78.4.co). Such animals cannot, of course, consciously grasp this distinction, any more than they can reflect theoretically on the difference between the useful and the pleasant.[13] But that provides no reason for denying that animals in fact behave according to such distinctions.

While distinct from sensation and imagination, the estimative and memorative powers cannot be moved without a prior act of sensation or imagination. It does not follow that sensation and imagination automatically or necessarily activate the estimative power. On the contrary, many particular acts of sensation and imagination conform to the model illustrated in figure 3.3 (see §3.2). Often an animal will simply sense a thing and react to it as pleasant or painful, with no activation of the estimative power. Conversely, the estimative power seems to function when (in special cases) a thing is perceived as useful or dangerous, *without* there being any prior perception of that thing's qualities as pleasant or painful. In light of this, it seems reasonable to depict the estimative power's apprehension of intentions and the impact of those intentions upon the sensitive appetite without supposing any essential relation to pleasure or pain.

As the diagram shows, the irascible passions (hope, despair, fear, daring, anger) are generated from acts of the estimative and memorative powers. Because the estimative power may be activated without an initial sensation of something as pleasant or painful, pleasure and pain do not appear. But what becomes of Aquinas' insistence that the irascible power begins from and terminates in the concupiscible passions (§2.4)? The origin of the irascible passions in the concupiscible means only that they presuppose some basic inclination toward what is suitable for the animal. The sheep will not perceive the wolf as a repugnant evil to be fled, unless it has a prior connatural inclination toward its own preservation (a form of love). Nonetheless, the diagram is not misleading in this respect; while love is a "universal cause" of the other passions, it remains that no separate motion of the concupiscible is required to activate the estimative power. A more potentially misleading feature of the diagram is its implicit suggestion that the estimative power is sufficient to motivate action. Aquinas occasionally speaks as if this were the case. The sheep (1) perceives a wolf by sensation, (2) apprehends the wolf as dangerous by the irascible power, (3) experiences the passion of fear, and (4) flees as fast

---

[13] Klubertanz (1952) observes: "the estimative does not know what usefulness and the like are, but it does determinately and accurately apprehend a particular concrete useful thing" (p. 236).

The activation of passion

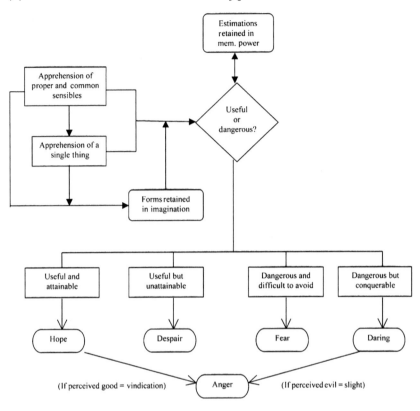

Figure 3.3. The estimative power, activated by sensation and imagination

as its sheep-legs will carry it. On this picture, action immediately follows the motion of the irascible.

But how can this be the case, if the irascible passions terminate in the concupiscible passions? One might try to describe Aquinas' view as follows. Inspired by fear, Little Red Riding Rood flees the wolf. Either she escapes successfully, and experiences relief (a form of pleasure), or she fails to escape and feels the sharp bite of the wolf's incisors (a form of pain). In this sense, the fear that she experiences will ultimately terminate in pleasure or pain. However plausible in itself, this is not Aquinas' view. Thomas states that, at least in the case of non-rational animals, action does not ensue until the act of sensitive appetite culminates in pleasure or pain. The text in which Aquinas advocates this view most clearly is probably the *De anima* commentary.

Therefore it is clear that the motion of a sensible thing in a sense proceeds, as it were, by three steps. First, the sense apprehends the sensible thing itself as either suitable or harmful (*ut conveniens vel nocivum*). Second, from this follows pleasure and pain (*ex hoc sequitur delectatio et tristitia*). And third, follows desire or flight (*sequitur desiderium vel fuga*). (*InDA* 3.12.5)

The above story about Little Red Riding Hood is not false, but it is incomplete. The experience of fear is itself apprehended as unsuitable, and therefore painful. Little Red Riding Hood runs away not simply because she is afraid, but because she is both afraid and pained by her fear. This explains how Aquinas can simultaneously reject simplistic models according to which animals are solely motivated by sensed pleasures or pains, and agree with Aristotle's claim that avoidance and pursuit in animals are generally traceable to an experience of pleasure or pain (see *De anima* 3.7, 431b8–9). Insofar as Little Red Riding Hood shares the characteristics of non-rational animals, fear will be followed by pain, and her action takes the form of flight. (This is true unless her apprehension of the wolf changes from "an evil difficult to avoid" to "an evil absolutely impossible to avoid," in which fear will succumb to despair, and flight will cease.) What is likely to hold for Little Red Riding Hood is invariably true of the sheep, for which action necessarily follows the last motion of sensitive appetite. In the case of non-rational animals generally, there is no possibility of a hiatus between the motion of sensitive appetite and action. But for Little Red Riding Hood and other beings with rational appetites, such a hiatus is always possible. Aquinas writes:

To the will also is the sensitive appetite subject in execution, which is accomplished by the moving power. For in other animals motion follows at once from the concupiscible and irascible, as the sheep, fearing the wolf, flees at once, because there is no higher appetite which would oppose flight. But man is not moved at once, according to the irascible and concupiscible. Rather, he awaits the command of the will, which is the higher appetite. (1.81.3.co)

Humans can be moved in one direction by the motion of sensitive appetite, and yet refrain from actions that would follow this motion. No matter how afraid, and therefore inclined to run away, Little Red Riding Hood can stand her ground, because her rational appetite can oppose her sensitive appetite. It does not follow, of course, that in any particular case, the rational appetite should oppose the sensitive appetite. In non-rational animals, the natural estimative power is remarkably accurate; its quasi-judgments about what is useful or dangerous are not typically erroneous.[14] Something analogous may hold for human beings. Because the passions are part of basic human nature, one of their natural functions is to promote self-preservation, the good of natural appetite (§1.2). At the other extreme, the passions may provide a kind of "affective knowledge" (to use Victor White's term) about the highest things, knowledge that is difficult to acquire by the intellect without passion (§4.3). Yet the contrary is also possible, and probably more familiar to us. What exists naturally in animals is deformed in human beings by both fallen nature and bad acquired habits. If the passions are to perform their highest function of assisting the rational creature's motion *ad finem* (§4.2), the possessor of those passions must know how they are moved by sensation and imagination. She must also discern how they might be activated and shaped over time by reason and will. Thus the necessity arises of examining Aquinas' thinking about the counterpart of the natural estimative power in human beings.

3.4 THE ROLE OF THE PARTICULAR REASON

Strictly speaking, human beings do not have an estimative power. But they have something like it. Comparing the capacity of human beings to perceive estimations of the useful and dangerous with that of non-rational animals, Aquinas writes:[15]

Other animals perceive these intentions only by some natural instinct, but man perceives them by means of a kind of collation (*per quamdam collationem*). Therefore what in other animals is called the natural estimative power in man is called the cogitative power (*cogitativa*), which by a kind of collation (*per collationem quamdam*) discovers these intentions. Whence it is also called the particular reason (*ratio particularis*) to which medical men assign a determinate organ, namely, the middle part of the head; for it is collative of individual intentions (*collativa intentionum individualium*), just as intellective reason is

---

[14] There may be instances of failure, but these are necessarily the exception. Perhaps a sheep can be deceived by a wolf dressed in sheep's clothing. But even here, the fault would lie not in the estimative power, but in a prior deception of sense.

[15] It is important not to miss the order of Aquinas' procedure, which is to understand what is more complex (the particular reason/cogitative power in rational animals) on the basis of what is simpler (the estimative power). Aquinas' use of the term *vis cogitativa* apparently derives from Averroes' assignment of a *virtus cogitativa* to the soul. Klubertanz (1952) makes this point (p. 275) and goes on to protest (too much, I think) that Averroes' use of *virtus cogitativa* is only an "occasional cause" of Aquinas' *vis cogitativa*, since "there is no discernible historical ancestry" (p. 279).

collective of universal intentions (*ratio intellectiva est collectiva intentionum universalium*). (1.78.4.co)[16]

The task of universal reason is to abstract universals from concrete objects perceived by the senses. It does this, Aquinas says, "by composing and dividing" (85.5.co). Particular reason does something analogous, but at a lower level. Through a process of "collation," a rudimentary form of composing and dividing, it discovers not universal concepts, but "individual intentions." Because they are perceived by a power assigned to a bodily organ, these intentions cannot be genuinely universal. (Only a power whose act is not the act of a bodily organ, according to Aquinas, is capable of apprehending immaterial species [1.12.4.co; 1.78.1.co; 1.79.6.co].[17]) Yet the intentions perceived by the cogitative power are

---

[16] Here I quote from the edition of the *ST* presented to Cardinal Pecci (Thomas Aquinas 1887–9). The text reproduced by other editions, including the Leonine (Thomas Aquinas 1882–) and the electronic edition of Alarcón (Thomas Aquinas 2006e), reads: "est enim collativa intentionum individualium, sicut ratio intellectiva intentionum universalium."

[17] The claim is controversial and worth taking seriously. As Pegis (1955) shows, it is the main issue that separates Aquinas' interpretation of Aristotle from that of Averroes. Most who are generally sympathetic with Aquinas' philosophical psychology have wanted to defend this claim, or at least argue that objections to it fail. One recent exception is Stump (2003), who suggests that Aquinas "turns out to have been wrong in his view that the intellect uses no bodily organ" (p. 264). Observing that this stands as an exception to Stump's general tendency to defend what she takes to be Thomas's view, Kenny (2004) comments: "Ironically, on this issue, I believe Aquinas is right and Stump is wrong" (p. 462). To say that the proper *act* of the intellect is not the act of a bodily organ is not to deny that the intellect may make some kind of "use" of sensitive powers, whose acts are the acts of a bodily organ. For Aquinas, as a general rule, the higher can always "use" the lower, without ontologically *depending upon* the lower. Pegis (1955) sets up the problem in an interesting manner. Against Averroes, Aquinas holds that the human soul can be the immaterial form of matter without itself being "immersed" in matter, because he regards the alternative as entailing the unacceptable consequence that either the intellect by which the soul knows is material and therefore corruptible (Alexander of Aphrodisias' interpretation of Aristotle), or that the intellect is not a part of the soul, but exists separately from it (Averroes' interpretation). If the human soul informs matter without being immersed in it, then it is capable of including as parts both an immaterial intellectual power that does not require a bodily organ for its act, and sensitive powers that do require bodily organs for their acts. The interesting question then becomes not "Does the intellect require a bodily organ for its act?" (it does not), but rather "Why does the human soul need any powers other than the intellect, i.e. sensible powers?" Pegis's suggestion: for Aquinas "the human intellect is not fully an intellect *without the sensible powers*" (p. 169). Knowledge of abstract concepts is incomplete; the type of knowledge we desire – abstract knowledge together with individuals – requires that the power of intellect be completed by the senses. "To know not only *man* but also *John Smith*, indeed to know *man as John Smith* and *John Smith himself as a man*, the human intellect must work with the senses, so that the co-operative whole of intellect and the senses knows the individual John Smith adequately" (p. 171). While these considerations drawn from Pegis hardly settle the issue, I think they suggest a profitable line of approach.

not sensible forms. They resemble abstract concepts known by intellect in that they are not directly perceivable by sensation or imagination.[18]

How does the cognitive power arrive at these intentions by means of "collation"? Aquinas gives us little to go on.[19] The example of Marnie's associating red patches with blood and violence might be an example of the particular reason at work. By associating instances of the color red with violence, the particular reason derives the quasi-universal judgment that "all red objects of a certain type are dangerous." I say "quasi-universal," because the particular reason has no access to either the concept "red" or "dangerous." Yet it accurately locates what is common to instances of a certain shade of red, and connects these instances with the estimation that "this signals danger." Attaching the estimation "useful" or "dangerous" to a set of objects sharing particular features seems to be the job of the cogitative power. Earlier (§3.2), I argued that sensation of a certain kind of object (e.g. a red patch) has the power to recall images that are stored in imagination. The particular reason, according to Aquinas, is the power that enables a person to attach a set of particular sensible qualities to images stored in the imagination that are directly connected with experiences of pain. Through making this connection between sensible forms and painful images, it estimates the sensed forms as "dangerous," despite the fact that nothing about these forms directly produces pain. In this way, its function is precisely analogous to the estimative power's capacity to apprehend some sensed objects as dangerous, although nothing about the sensible forms themselves is painful.

The particular reason is the capacity to arrive at estimations of utility or danger by associating sensible forms, neutral in themselves, with stored images that are charged with pleasure or pain. As such, it presupposes the imagination. Another example may be helpful. Consider several items that a two-year-old child (call her Louisa) can sense.

---

[18] Most commentators, rather than emphasizing the "collation of individual intentions" (as I am doing), stress another feature of the particular reason that Aquinas identifies at 1.81.3.co, namely, its capacity to particularize what is known abstractly by universal reason. An exception to the rule is King (1998), who correctly notes that 1.78.4's description of the particular reason as the faculty of collating individual intentions "seems unlike any inferential ability" (p. 129n52).

[19] One might wonder how the cogitative power, which Aquinas locates as a part of the brain, can perform some of the tasks of reason. Pasnau (2002) raises this issue, wondering whether the ascription of reasoning ability to the cogitative power is in tension with the claim that the intellect is incorporeal. Pasnau's own account of Aquinas on this point seems persuasive: "In fact Aquinas sees less to explain than one might suppose, because he does not believe that reasoning requires immateriality. What requires immateriality . . . is the capacity to form universal concepts. This is precisely what the cogitative power cannot do. It 'compares individual conceptions just as intellective reason compares universal conceptions'" (p. 254).

A burner on an electric stove
A flame from a lighter
A set of burning coals in a grill

If Louisa touches all three of these items, she receives their forms by sensation and stores the phantasms (charged with pain) in her imagination. Suppose Louisa next sees:

A fire burning in a fireplace

When she sees the fire, will she touch it? The answer to this question depends upon whether her cogitative power has begun to function. If it has not, she will probably touch the fire, since she is naturally attracted to bright and warm objects. But what happens if she has learned to perceive the fire not simply as bright and warm, but as having something in common with the images of painful objects? At some point Louisa will learn to make this "collation." Once she groups the fire with the images that she associates with pain, she will not be attracted to it. Rather, the particular reason will tell her that the fire burning in the fireplace is dangerous, despite the fact that she has no direct acquaintance with the capacity of that particular fire to cause pain. Having made this estimation, she will store it in the memorative power. On this basis, she will estimate other objects with like sensible features as dangerous.

This example preserves what the particular reason has in common with the estimative power. Yet it also illuminates the difference. Unlike the sheep who avoids the wolf by instinct, Louisa has no instinct that leads her to avoid touching the fire. On the contrary, she learns this by collation of the sensible forms attached to the fire with other sensible images that have previously caused her pain. Through this process of discovery by the particular reason, Louisa has learned to protect herself from some significant dangers, well before her universal reason has developed in any significant way. (Indeed, she may still call all men "father" and all women "mother," as Aristotle suggests at the beginning of the *Physics* [184b13–15].)

How does a person discover certain things to be useful or dangerous without experiencing directly their sensible qualities which arouse pain or pleasure? Thomas's teaching on the particular reason is designed to answer this question. It explains how a thing can look appealing, and yet be perceived as dangerous and to be avoided. Because it is natural (like the natural estimative power in non-rational animals), the particular reason is designed for the reliable preservation of the organism. Yet, in a way that is impossible for the estimative power, it is vulnerable to error and distortion. Since its *intentiones* are largely given by instinct, non-rational animals discover very little by the estimative power. The sheep does not learn from prior experience that the wolf is dangerous; it already "knows" this. By contrast, much of particular reason's work consists in the actual discovery of intentions. Certainly humans are able to make some estimations innately, as can a baby searching for the mother's breast.[20] Generally speaking, however, humans do not know by instinct what is useful or dangerous for them; they must learn this from experience.

Aquinas' account of particular reason, despite its relative lack of detail, offers a powerful way of accounting for persons who systematically make erroneous or dysfunctional judgments about what is useful or dangerous for them.[21] Why are the estimations of particular reason, especially those made early in life, so difficult to overcome, notwithstanding that universal reason may have learned to make the opposite judgment?[22] Aquinas explains that the estimations stored in the memorative power are literally ingrained in a person's soul. To say this is not merely metaphorical. Because the estimations of the interior sensitive powers require a bodily organ, they are literally "immuted" or imprinted on the soul. Modern readers are entitled to smile at Aquinas' location of the cogitative power "in the middle part of the head." But the vital point is that a person will approach maturity with a system of neurological correspondences between sensible patterns and estimations of usefulness and danger. Since these correspondences have become a part of her material being, they are extremely difficult to alter.

---

[20] I take the example from Terruwe and Baars (1972), p. 28. Terruwe and Baars also suggest the "young man and girl in whom the sexual urge awakens" as an example of the human analogue of the natural estimative power. This strikes me as questionable, since it seems easy to account for this primarily in terms of the concupiscible. Perhaps a better instance of an instinctual estimation of something as useful or dangerous, independent of sensations of pleasure and pain, is the innate reaction we have to snakes and spiders. (Robert Pasnau suggested this example to me.) I agree with Klubertanz (1952) that while "there are a very few primitive reactions which are innately determined," it is nonetheless true that "for the most part, man has to learn what is good for him concretely by instruction and experience" (p. 239; see also p. 279).

[21] Writing from a clinical perspective, Terruwe and Baars (1972) clearly notice the importance of the particular reason: "This conception of particular reason has a profound bearing on the subject of our discussion because certain of the disorders of emotional life can be traced to this faculty. The transition from instinct to particular reason, or the penetration of the purely sensory estimative power by reason, constitutes one of the most important developmental processes of the human mind" (p. 29).

[22] Klubertanz (1952) notices the difficulty: "Properly to understand the operation of the estimative, we would have to remember why and how, as little children, our sense appetites were aroused" (p. 237).

Despite this difficulty, Aquinas does not conclude that the estimations stored in the memorative power are impossible to change. He acknowledges that the particular reason may be gradually reshaped by reason and will. In Question 81 of the 1a *pars*, he writes:

> In the place of estimative power in man, as we have said above (1.78.4), is the *vis cogitativa*, which is called by certain people the *ratio particularis*, because it is collative of individual intentions. Whence by nature the sensitive appetite is moved in man by the particular reason. But the particular reason itself is naturally moved and guided in man according to the universal reason: whence in syllogistic matters singular conclusions are drawn from universal propositions. Therefore it is clear that universal reason commands the sensitive appetite, which is distinguished into the concupiscible and irascible; and this appetite obeys it. But since to draw singular conclusions from universal principles is not the work of simple intellect (*simplex intellectus*), but of reason, it follows that the irascible and concupiscible are said to obey the reason more than the intellect. Anyone can put this to the test in himself, for by applying certain universal considerations, anger, fear or the like may be modified or excited. (1.81.3.co)

When Dorothy sees a man who reminds her of her abusive uncle, her first reaction is fear. But after therapy, she may have learned to apply what she knows by universal reason ("not all men are like my uncle") to particular cases, and thereby replace the estimations stored in her memorative power with new estimations that are more adequate to reality. If she has good evidence that someone genuinely loves and cares about her, she will be in a position to take the first step toward replacing fear with intimacy. (The road may be a long one, depending on the severity of the case.) This is the best-case scenario. Aquinas is not blithely optimistic that universal reason will always work to correct distorted estimations of particular reason. On the contrary, universal reason may only make things more dysfunctional. Without appropriate guidance, Dorothy may go from estimating certain men as dangerous to the universal judgment that "all men are threatening," and proceed to adopt this stance as a conviction. Without virtue (both infused and acquired), universal reason stands a poor chance of being able to revise and reshape the historically established judgments of particular reason. Instead, it will merely perform induction on the estimations already stored in the memorative power.

If Dorothy (or anyone else in a structurally parallel situation) is to avoid this bleak scenario, at least two things are necessary. First, her universal reason must possess knowledge (or at least true opinion) that is adequate to reality, in a way that contradicts everything her particular reason has told her. (This in itself cannot be taken for granted.) Second,

Dorothy must somehow acquire the *habit* of applying this knowledge to particular situations, until the estimations she learned to make early in life are replaced with better estimations. The mere knowledge that "dangerous" or "threatening" is not essentially predicated of "man" is not enough. She requires, additionally, a series of judgments and actions that reshape her particular reason and memorative power. Cultivating the particular reason so that it conforms to the judgment of rightly directed universal reason is the key to perfecting the passions.[23]

3.5 PASSIONS AS CAUSES OF OTHER PASSIONS

Question 25 of the Treatise considers the "order of the passions to one another." As so often for Aquinas, there is more than one possible order. Thomas distinguishes between the "order of sequence" (*ordo consecutionis*), which he also calls the "order of generation" (25.3.co), and the "order of intention" (*ordo intentionis*). In the order of intention, the first passion that causes the others is pleasure. The intention of pleasure generates the passion of love. Love is not only a *connaturalitas* toward some good. Aquinas also calls it a *complacentia*, in order to indicate its close relation to the pleasure that is prior to love in the order of intention. In the order of sequence, the relation is the opposite. Pleasure is the last thing attained; love is the inclination that must be present prior to both desire and achieved pleasure. "Since rest is the end of motion, it is the first in the order of intention, but last in the order of execution" (25.1.co). Throughout the Treatise, Aquinas places the emphasis strongly on the order of execution.

In the order of execution, at least some concupiscible passions must precede the irascible passions, because "the passions of the irascible add something over and above (*supra*) the passions of the concupiscible, just as the object of the irascible adds arduousness or difficulty over and above the object of the concupiscible" (25.1.co). From this Thomas shows that desire and aversion necessarily precede hope and fear. "Over and above desire, hope adds a certain effort (*conatus*) and a certain elevation of the soul toward pursuing the arduous good. In like manner, over and above aversion or abomination, fear adds a certain depression of the soul on

---

[23] What holds for the intellect and the will also turns out to apply to the interior senses that move the sensitive appetite. It is true that Aquinas gives little detail regarding the specific operation of particular reason. But that Aquinas considers particular reason to play a decisive role in activating the sensitive appetite in cases where more than sensation and imagination are involved is clear. Thus one may question the view that Aquinas' "resolute division of the faculties diverts him from vigorously using the concept of the particular reason" (Roberts 1992, p. 297).

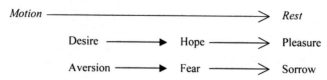

Figure 3.4. Passions in the order of generation: a simple scheme

account of the evil's difficulty" (25.1.co). After hope comes joy, since hope causes joy, either by way of immediate anticipation or eventual attainment. Likewise, sorrow comes after fear, since "when one meets the evil that was feared, sorrow is caused (*causatur tristitia*)" (25.1.co). We thus have the simple scheme represented in figure 3.4.

This scheme must be complicated at once. In Question 22, Aquinas holds that what makes sorrow a passion in the strictest sense is its radical unsuitability for human beings who seek what completes them by nature. The soul does not naturally reconcile itself to sorrow. Its irascible side rises to the occasion. Thus *ira* follows sorrow, "since from a preceding sorrow someone rises up to set things right (*aliquis insurgit in vindictam*), and this belongs to the motion of anger" (25.1.co). When vindication is achieved, joy ensues. "Because to pay back an evil is apprehended as a good, when the angry person has acquired vindication, he rejoices (*gaudet*)" (25.1.co). The model can be modified as in figure 3.5. Aquinas can now say that "the irascible passions both have their origin (*principium*) from the concupiscible passions, and are brought to a conclusion (*terminatur*) in the concupiscible passions" (25.1.co).[24]

Article 1 provides an abbreviated model of the passions' order to one another. It omits love, hate, despair, and daring. Why the lacunae? Articles 2 and 3 exist to fill them in. Article 2 asks whether love is the first of the concupiscible passions. It is, Aquinas says, citing Augustinian authority in the *sed contra*. If desire is appetitive motion toward the good, love is the principle of any such motion. Love is the principle not only of desire, but of all the passions. Every passion is caused by love, Augustine says, since (Aquinas quotes from *De civitate Dei* 14) "love wanting to have what is loved is desire (*cupiditas*), but having it, and enjoying it, is gladness (*laetitia*)" (25.2.sc). This is precisely the structure of the concupiscible passions that Thomas makes his own.

---

[24] Figure 3.5 should not mislead anyone into supposing Aquinas to hold that anger *necessarily* comes between hope and joy. On the contrary, I do not (at least not yet) want to exclude the possibility of going straight from hope to joy.

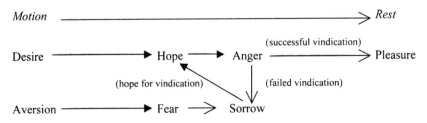

Figure 3.5. Passions in the order of generation: adding sorrow and anger

Why did Aquinas not include love at the beginning of the Question? The presentation of the concupiscible motions without their head, shorn of their *principium*, prepares the delayed entrance of *amor*, and thereby emphasizes its status as the origin of every passion. The transition from Article 1 to Article 2 is a motion from effect to cause. As Aquinas says in the *ad primum*, we often name a thing from what is most familiar or strongly felt. Thus the concupiscible power is named from *concupiscentia*, since we feel that passion most. But the cause of the concupiscible power is love.

The priority of love among the passions is an instance of the basic priority of good to evil (§1.4). Thomas's *auctoritas* for both priorities is Augustine. "Now good is naturally prior to evil, since evil is *privatio boni*, whence all the passions whose object is good are naturally prior to the passions whose object is evil" (25.2.co). We repel evils only in the name of some good to which the evil is opposed. Only good, according to Aquinas, has the "character of an end" (25.2.co). Since the end is first in intention but last in execution, the passions may be ordered either "according to intention (*secundum intentionem*)" or "according to sequence (*secundum consecutionem*)" (25.2.co). The order that Aquinas privileges, here and throughout the Questions on the passions as a whole, is order of generation. Thus love is first, since love is what "first comes to be in that which tends to an end." Love is thus an "aptitude or proportion toward some end" (25.2.co). As the proportion *ad bonum*, love is nothing other than the "complacency in good" (*complacentia boni*). From the aptitude springs motion: "motion toward the good is desire or concupiscence." Motion is ordered to rest: "rest in the good is joy or pleasure" (25.2.co). As if to emphasize the priority of good, Aquinas does not even bother to mention the opposed passions of hate, aversion, and sorrow. (He will make good the omission in the next Article.)

Love, desire, pleasure – the concupiscible passions follow this sequence in the *ordo generationis*. Aquinas closes Article 2's response with a brief acknowledgment that they can also be disposed "according to the order of intention." This order inverts the order of generation, because "intended pleasure causes desire and love. For pleasure is the enjoyment of the good, which in a certain way is the end, just as the good itself is, as was stated above" (25.2.co).[25]

What is the sequencing that occurs within the irascible passions? Etymology would suggest that *ira* is first among the irascible passions. The opposite is nearer the truth; anger is last of the irascible passions. As with the concupiscible, the irascible is named from its most familiar or deeply felt effect, rather than according to its origin or essence. Article 1's abbreviated model of the order of the passions captured the priority of hope among the irascible passions, while omitting daring and despair. Aquinas now fills the gap in Article 3. Using the radical priority of good to evil to establish that hope precedes despair, fear precedes daring, and that hope and despair precede fear and daring, he writes:

That hope and despair are naturally prior to fear and daring is manifest from this – that as the appetite for good is the reason whereby one shuns evil, so hope and despair are the *ratio* of fear and daring. For daring arises from (*consequitur*) the hope of victory, and fear arises from despair of overcoming. Now anger arises from daring, "for no one is angry while seeking vindication, unless he dare to vindicate himself," as Avicenna says in the sixth book *De naturalibus*. Thus it is clear that hope is first among all the irascible passions. (25.3.co)

Aquinas continues:

If we wish to know the order of all the passions according to the way of generation – first occur love and hatred. Second, desire and aversion. Third, hope and despair. Fourth, fear and daring. Fifth, anger. Sixth and last, joy and sorrow, which follow from all the passions, as stated in the *Ethics* (2.5): yet so that love is prior to hatred, desire is prior to aversion, hope is prior to despair, fear is prior to daring, and joy is prior to sorrow, as can be gathered from the preceding statements. (25.3.co)

If we combine this model with Article 1's suggestion that sorrow belongs between the irascible passions of fear and anger, we may draw (in sand) one last diagram, figure 3.6.

---

[25] The identification of *delectatio*, *fruitio*, and (*quodammodo*) *finis* implicitly refers the reader back to Question 11 on *fruitio*, and points ahead toward 34.3, where Aquinas will link a certain pleasure with attainment of the highest good.

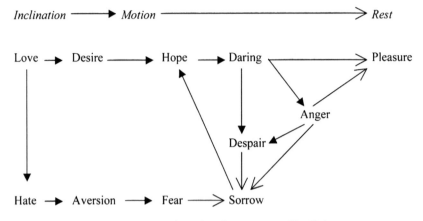

Figure 3.6. Passions in the order of generation: a "final" diagram

Articles 1–3 complete the ordering of the passions in relation to one another. Question 25 ends by raising a question. How might this complex ordering be reconciled with the ancient tradition that designates joy, sorrow, hope, and fear as the "principal passions" (*principales passiones*)? Why regard these four as the principal passions? It seems easy enough to understand the sense in which joy and sorrow are "principal"; they complete the motion of every other passion. But what makes hope and fear principal? In what sense do they complete the motions of the passions that precede them in the order of generation? One way to approach this question is to examine the tradition upon which Aquinas draws. Cicero locates four relations between object (good and evil) and temporal status (future and present). Hope seeks the future good; fear avoids the future evil; joy delights in the present good; sorrow recoils from the present evil (*Tusculan Disputations* 4.6.11–12). Aquinas makes a slightly different argument. Hope and fear are "principal," not because they are the first appetitive motions (they are not). Rather, they complete the particular motions that begin in love or hate and proceed to desire or aversion. If hope and fear do not lead directly to joy or sorrow, they generate new *per accidens* motions, either toward an evil for the sake of conquering it (daring), or away from good because its attainment is perceived as too difficult (despair).[26] Anger, likewise, cannot be a principal passion, since it is a "certain effect of daring" (25.4 ad 2m).

[26] In a diagram, Brennan (1941) identifies courage (i.e. daring) as "affective retreat from the vincible" (p. 158). The explanation for this (serious) error may lie in the difficulty of seeing how any passion whose formal object is an evil can involve anything other than repugnance or "affective retreat."

How well does Aquinas' complex ordering of the passions *ad invicem* mesh with the simpler scheme of Cicero and Boethius? Thomas strives to suggest an appearance of harmony. Does he succeed? There may be something forced about the argument.[27] Superficially, hope and fear resemble joy and sorrow in that they are "completive" (*completivae*) of the appetite's motion. But *completiva* is equivocal; hope and fear do not terminate the appetite's motion in the same sense as joy and sorrow do (as can be seen from figure 3.6). They are relative termini. Far from bringing the appetite to rest, they generate other passions.

If the schemes are not quite as harmonious as the textual surface would suggest, Aquinas is nonetheless right to acknowledge profound continuity between the tradition and his own thinking. The distinction of passions according to good/evil and present/future found in the *Tusculan Disputations* appears foundational for Aquinas' own thinking. Thomas's use of Cicero is likely mediated by Augustine at every point, although he seems to have read parts (at least) of the *Tusculan Disputations* on his own. What seems clear is that Aquinas' ordering of the passions owes remarkably little to Aristotle. The continual insistence that passions tending toward good are naturally prior to those which shun evil derives from Augustine and Dionysius, not Aristotle. While the notion of sensitive appetite is Aristotelian, its explicit division into concupiscible and irascible is only questionably so.[28] Aristotle does claim in *Ethics* 2.5 that the passions terminate in joy and sorrow. But he never arranges them sequentially, let alone in the particular *ordo generationis* that Thomas provides. Inspection of the arguments *sed contra* in Question 25 confirms the point. The first and third Articles cite no *auctoritas*; the second quotes Augustine on the power of love to generate desire and culminate in joy. Aristotle's authority plays only a small role in securing the architectonic principles that inform Thomas's ordering of the passions.

---

[27] The judgment found in James (1997) that Aquinas considers the Ciceronian view "in order to reject it" (p. 59) is too blunt. In both the *ST* and the *QDV* (see 26.5), Aquinas attempts to preserve the truth contained in the designation of hope, fear, joy, and sorrow as the four principal passions. Nonetheless, I agree that the designation plays a small role in Aquinas' overall own approach; Roberts (2003) seems to accord it more importance than it actually has for Thomas (p. 186).

[28] Gondreau (2002) finds that the "immediate source" of the distinction is Nemesius and Damascene (pp. 201–2). As he observes, the distinction is also present explicitly in the anonymous author of the late twelfth-century *De spiritu et anima*, John of La Rochelle (fl. 1233–9), and Vincent of Beauvais (fl. 1250). Lagerlund and Yrjönsuuri (2002) suggest that John's influence is so strong as to justify the claim that Thomas's entire discussion of the emotions is "hardly original" (p. 15).

CHAPTER 4

The morality of the passions

In Question 24, Aquinas examines the passions in relation to good and evil. Against both the Stoics and the Epicureans, and taking Augustine as his model, Aquinas elaborates and defends the view that, when governed by reason, the passions can make an important contribution to the moral goodness of actions (§4.1). Thomas does not, however, restrict the potential moral goodness of the passions to discrete human actions. He assigns the passions a surprisingly large role in the overall return of the rational creature toward the ultimate end. This assignment goes some way toward explaining why Aquinas would devote such a large portion of the 1a2ae to the passions (§4.2). If the passions are potent sources of energy for the journey of the human person (and not simply the mind) toward God, do they have any cognitive value? Some have doubted that they do, at least for Thomas. I argue that, to the contrary, Aquinas considers the passions to play an important role in elevating the power of human cognition (§4.3). In light of the close relation of the passions to moral action and human cognition, it would seem that we are responsible for our passions. Yet it is difficult to see how we can be directly responsible for the passions, since (as Aquinas has argued, contrary to the Stoics) they are neither judgments nor acts of will. Nonetheless, Aquinas argues that we are ultimately responsible for our passions, even if it is beyond our power to control the occurrence of a passion in any particular case (§4.4).

4.1 PASSIONS AS CONTRIBUTORS TO THE MORAL GOODNESS OF ACTIONS

In Questions 23 and 24 of the 1a2ae, Aquinas describes the passions with all the clarity (and perhaps clinicality) of the detached taxonomist. By anatomizing the primary passions by reference to the sensible good, he has suspended the ancient question of the morality of the passions, or what Jordan (1986) calls the "teleological problem about incorporating the passions into the rational, that is, into morality" (p. 88). Aquinas takes up this problem in Question 24 of the 1a2ae. His procedure is, first, to consider two views, both of which are conceptually simple and perennially attractive. One holds that passions are morally neutral, the other that they are evil (Articles 1 and 2). Second, Aquinas outlines a more nuanced conception of the manner in which the passions are related to moral good and evil (Article 3), but not without an important qualification (Article 4).

Can moral good and evil be found in the passions? Addressing this question in Article 1, Aquinas suggests that considered "in themselves" (*secundum se*), purely as acts in common with other animals, the passions are morally neutral. This appears when one looks at the passions simply as "certain motions of the irrational appetite" (24.1.co). But, for human beings, another standpoint is available. The passions in rational creatures may be considered – and must be considered – as "lying under the command of reason and will" (*subiacent imperio rationis et voluntatis*) (24.1.co). While the passions are susceptible to a form of naturalistic description that prescinds from what is distinctively human, truncating the description at this point would be an act of false abstraction. The authority *sed contra* for every Article of Question 24, not coincidentally, is Augustine's *De civitate Dei*. Regarding human passions, Augustine says: "They are evil if our love is evil; good if our love is good" (24.1.sc).[1] Placed under the command of reason and will, the passions cannot be morally neutral.

Article 2 asks whether the passions are "morally evil." In the response, Aquinas recalls the debates between the Stoics and the Peripatetics: "the Stoics said that all passions are evil; the Peripatetics, however, said that moderate passions are good" (24.2.co). While Aquinas directly rejects the position he attributes to the Stoics, he wants to honor the school's deeper intention. The Stoic rejection of passions as evil is less scandalous than it may seem, since the Stoics define the passions as *perturbationes animae*, disturbances of the soul that lack reason. Aquinas is happy to agree that progressing beyond the limits of reason is evil. But what leads the Stoics to regard all passions as *perturbationes* that are contrary to reason? A basic error: "The Stoics did not discern between sense and intellect, and consequently neither between the intellectual and sensitive appetite" (24.2.co). Because the Stoics are unable to distinguish passions

---

[1] As Mauro (1974) observes, although many of the conclusions that Aquinas reaches about the morality of the passions are similar to those of Augustine, one important difference is that the latter "does not consider the passions as motions proper to a particular faculty – the sensitive appetite – but rather as 'external' manifestations of the interior motions of the will" (pp. 13–14).

from motions of the will, they are forced to regard the passions as irrational volitions.

In one sense, Article 2's critique of the Stoics is tame. Thomas respects (and shares) the school's ultimate intention to offer an anthropology that enables men and women to lead more human lives by following reason. Jordan suggests that Thomas "abbreviates and softens Augustine's attack" (1986, p. 92).[2] Set next to the longer polemic found in chapters 9 and 14 of *De civitate Dei*, Thomas's critique appears gentle. But it is arguably more penetrating. The basic error of failing to distinguish the rational appetite from the sensitive appetite leads to a distorted view of the passions. How could it not, if passions are defined as "diseases of the soul"?[3] Far more adequate – though it too stands in need of correction and subordination – is the Aristotelian psychology. More attuned to human experience, the Peripatetics leave the goodness of any particular motion of the sensitive appetite as an open question. They "esteem the passions good, when they are moderated by reason, and evil when they go beyond the moderation of reason" (24.2.co). This connects Aristotle with the Augustinian *sed contra* of the preceding Article. When our love is good, our passions are naturally moderated by reason; when our love is evil, our passions revolt against reason. Aquinas uses both the Aristotelian and Augustinian vocabularies to show that human passions always bear a relation to moral good and evil. No contest arises between the rule of reason and love of the good, since "the good of man is founded on reason as its root" (24.3.co). Unlike so many moderns, Aquinas displays no tendency to exalt reason by denigrating the passions, or to exalt the passions by condemning the rule of reason.

The first half of Question 24 eliminates the two simplest options: the passions as morally neutral, the passions as morally evil. In Article 3, Aquinas begins to articulate his own position, asking whether a passion can augment or diminish the moral quality of an act, its "goodness" or "badness." The meaning of this question must be understood precisely. Aquinas is not asking whether a passion will make a person more or less

---

[2] Jordan (1986) adds that "the moderation may not be an incidental part of his project of clarification" (p. 92). One may juxtapose this with Gondreau's characterization of "Aquinas's incessant drive to stamp out the effects of Stoicism" (2002, p. 285).

[3] Cicero himself recognizes the oddity of rendering *pathe* by *morbi*, and chooses *perturbationes* on the ground that *morbi* would not accord with customary Latin usage. Yet despite the terminological choice, he does not seem to question the basic idea that passions are diseases of the soul. Cf. Cicero, *Tusculan Disputations* 3.4.7–9 and 3.5.10.

motivated to perform a morally good act, the *bonitas* of which is independent of the motivational force of the passion. His question is: Can a passion enter into the moral quality of an act, making that act better or worse than it would be without the passion? Aquinas approaches the question by finding common ground with the Stoics. Not all passions are evil, but the motions of sensitive appetite which are disordered subtract from an act's goodness. A work of charity performed "from *only* the passion of pity" may be good (24.3 ad 1m). But it is not as good, Thomas says, as a similar work of charity performed "from the judgment of reason." Aquinas seems almost Kantian in his insistence that only acts approved by reason deserve full moral credit. With Kant, he would agree that the passions cannot be allowed to direct moral action. The sovereignty of reason must remain inviolate. But what if the act is performed *ex iudicio rationis*, yet accompanied by a passion? At this point the parallel to Kant breaks down. For Kant, a passion can have no bearing on an act's intrinsic goodness. Only the presence or absence of the rational perception of duty is morally relevant.[4] Aquinas argues just the opposite. If an act done out of rational judgment is accompanied by a passion that obeys reason, the presence of that passion will increase the moral goodness of that act. Aquinas identifies two ways in which this may occur:

First, by overflow (*per modum redundantiae*), since when the higher part of the soul is intensely moved toward something, its motion follows in the lower part. And thus the passion that consequently exists in the sensitive appetite is a sign of the intensity of the will, and thus points to greater moral goodness. In another way this occurs by choice (*per modum electionis*), as when a man chooses from the judgment of reason to be affected by some passion, so that he may work more promptly by means of the co-working of the sensitive appetite. And thus a passion of the soul adds to the goodness of an action. (24.3 ad 1m)

Within these two modes, Jordan locates the discovery of a "morally positive mutual causality" (1986, p. 92). He extrapolates: "The more intense an act of will, the more it causes an accompanying passion. Alternately, one might cultivate an emotion precisely in order to make an act of will easier and more intense" (p. 92). The work is to govern and cultivate the passions, not to eliminate them.

---

[4] Contrasting Kant's handling of the reason/passion relation with that of Aquinas, Galeazzi (2004) provocatively suggests that for Kant human existence is "split into two independent lives, of which one, having been abandoned to animality, remains irremediable and impenetrable, and not enlightened – notwithstanding the Enlightenment intentions of Kant – by reason and the ethical order" (p. 550).

When governed by reason, passions increase the goodness of individual human acts. One might endorse this position, while supposing that cultivation of the passions remains optional for human life as a whole. Has not Aquinas himself just argued that actions performed "from the judgment of reason" are good, even when done "without passion"? He has. But Aquinas' approach to ethics does not primarily concern the evaluation of discrete acts. His main intention in the Ia2ae is to promote the total flourishing of the human person. We differ from God and the angels, he says, precisely in that our good proceeds "according to the right ordering of the passions or bodily acts" (24.3 ad 2m). To suppose that humans can attain their full good without attending to the totality of their acts, including those shared with other animals, is to commit the mortal sin of angelism.[5]

In the response of Article 3, Aquinas begins by proclaiming the most evident consequence of rejecting the Stoic construal of passions as disturbances or illnesses. "If we name as passions all the motions of the sensitive appetite, then it belongs to the perfection of human good that the passions be moderated by reason" (24.3.co). Exalting the good at the expense of the passions does not create the sole condition under which human acts deserve full moral credit. It guarantees, rather, a person's failure to achieve her complete good. It ensures that she is stuck in a perpetual battle between her reason and her passions. How vital is this point? If Thomas – lover of laconic understatement, hater of *frequens repetitio* – made the point only once, it would retain its full value. But Aquinas – in the response of Article 3 – uses the phrase *perfectio boni moralis* (or some close variant thereof) *five* times. In case this is insufficiently forceful, Thomas follows the final iteration with a quotation from Scripture:

> Just as it is better that man should both will good and do it in his exterior act, so also does it belong to the perfection of moral good, that man should be moved toward the good not only according to will, but also according to sensitive appetite, following what is said in Psalm 83:3: "My heart and my flesh have rejoiced in the living God": where we are to take "heart" (*cor*) for the intellectual appetite, and "flesh" (*carnis*) for the sensitive appetite. (24.3.co)

It would be difficult to imagine a more positive, yet balanced, appraisal of the place of the passions in the attainment of the complete human good.[6]

---

[5] On "angelism-bestialism," see Percy (1971), p. 27 and *passim* (especially p. 254).

[6] Pègues (1912) correctly notices the "boldness" of this teaching, which, as he observes, "will have the most radiant applications in the mystery of the Incarnation itself, when the human nature of the Savior is concerned" (p. 60).

Perhaps in the service of balance, Aquinas concludes Question 24 with a coda reminding the reader that not every passion can play a role in human perfection. What makes this point initially difficult to see is that nothing within the "natural" consideration of passions can exclude them from the moral teleology. But when the passions are viewed in their moral genus, things appear differently. In the response of Article 4, Thomas says that "moral good and evil can belong to the species of a passion" (24.4.co). The response furnishes two examples of passions that are simply evil. Shame (*verecundia*) is evil by its nature, since it is "wicked fear." The example seems puzzling, not least because the *sed contra* of this very Article identifies *verecundia* as a praiseworthy passion. Why does Aquinas appear to contradict himself so blatantly? Possibly he simply failed to pay attention (*etiam Thomas dormit*). Alternatively, Aquinas may wish to remind us that if specifically identical passions sometimes bear different names, it is no less the case that passions differing in species may bear the same name. However this may be, the second example is both simpler and attested by Aristotle (a passage in *Ethics* 2.6 seems to be its direct antecedent).[7] Envy is a passion that is evil in its species. Defined as sorrow for another's good, envy is evil *per se*. It is impossible to suffer envy toward the right person, at the right time, and in the right way.[8]

4.2 PASSIONS AND THE MOTION 'AD FINEM'

Aquinas agrees with Kant that human beings often act from the judgment of reason in a manner that is contrary to their passions:

> For many things we will and work (*volumus et operamur*) without passion and through choice alone, as is clear in those things where reason resists passion. (10.3 ad 3m)

For Kant, the power of the good will shines especially brightly when it acts in accordance with the moral law, contrary to the inclinations. Aquinas would not deny this power. But he would hold that the opposition of the will and the passions is a second-best scenario. When Paul speaks of "the good which I will I do not, but the evil which I will not, that I do" (Romans 7:19), Thomas takes Paul to describe not an inescapable reality,

---

[7] Cf. Aristotle, *Nicomachean Ethics* 2.6, 1107a9–18. In light of this passage, one might have expected Thomas to choose "shamelessness" rather than "shame" as the example of a passion evil *per se*.

[8] This Article qualifies any simple view according to which Aquinas regards the passions as neither good nor evil in themselves.

but a condition from which we seek to be freed. The virtuous person, according to Aquinas, is partly defined by his freedom from this condition: "the sensitive part is wholly subject to his reason" (10.3 ad 2m). A virtuous person's sensitive appetite disposes her to desire the same path that reason would judge to be attractive without the passions. For Aquinas, a primary task in the moral life (perhaps even *the* primary task) is to make the ascent from the condition where the sensitive appetite is an obstacle for the will to overcome, to a better condition where the passions gladly serve reason. This means that reason must govern the passions, without ruling them despotically. Thomas Merton writes:

The control we mean here is not arbitrary and tyrannical control by an interior principle which can be called, variously, a "super-ego" or a pharisaical conscience: it is the harmonious coordination of man's powers in striving for the realization of his deepest spiritual potentialities. It is not so much a control of one part of man by another, but the peaceful integration of all man's powers into one perfect actuality which is his true self, that is to say his spiritual self. (1961, p. 8)[9]

The passions are sources of energy for what Bonaventure calls the "journey of the mind toward God." Would Aquinas speak of the mind's journey toward God? He would not, since he never forgets that the journey belongs to the embodied creature, the soul/body composite. Though the mind may direct the journey, it does not make the journey on its own. It requires the contribution of the passions. In this light we may understand Aquinas' comparison of the relationship between the mind and the sensitive appetite to that of rulers and free subjects. Though subject to their rulers, free subjects

nevertheless have something of their own, by which they can resist the command of the one who rules. And thus the soul is said to dominate the body by a despotic rule, since the members of the body can resist the command of the soul in nothing; but the hand and foot, and any other member that is naturally moved by the motion of the will, is moved at once toward the appetite of the soul. But the intellect or reason is said to rule over the irascible and concupiscible by a politic rule, since the sensitive appetite has something of its own, whence it can resist the command of reason. (1.81.3 ad 2m)

That the sensitive appetite "has something of its own" explains why it can resist the command of reason. But this is not merely a sad fact. It also

---

[9] Merton associates this condition with "the clear inebriation of mysticism" and opposes it to passion. But from Aquinas' standpoint, this opposition cannot be pressed too far, since passions belong to the perfection of the human good.

points to the ability of the sensitive appetite to make a contribution of its own in the return of the rational creature to the ultimate end. If directed by reason, the energy provided by the sensitive appetite can deepen the love by which the rational creature is drawn to her end.

No doubt this seems intolerably general. Just which of the passions are able to play this role? Precisely what do they contribute to the human ascent to the good? These are legitimate questions. The only way to address them is to descend to the particular passions. Parts 2 and 3 of this volume will do this in detail. For now it suffices to notice a key passage in the treatment of love, the first root of all the passions. In Article 3 of Question 26, Aquinas quotes Dionysius in the argument *sed contra*: "Some holy men have held that *amor* means something more divine than *dilectio*" (*Div. Nom.* iv). Thomas agrees:

The reason that some held that, even in the will itself, the name of *amor* is more divine (*divinius*) than the name of *dilectio*, is that *amor* conveys a certain passion, chiefly according as it is in the sensitive appetite; *dilectio*, however, presupposes the judgment of reason. But man is more able to tend toward God through *amor*, drawn passively in a way by God himself, than he can lead himself to God by means of his own reason (*ratio*), which pertains to the character (*ratio*) of *dilectio*, as said above. And on account of this, *amor* is more divine than *dilectio*. (26.3 ad 4m)

Though the love associated with the rational appetite, the pseudopassion (?) named by *dilectio*, is important, it cannot function without the proper passion of love, construed as an act of the sensitive appetite. Love in its most proper sense is sensitive love, because sensitive love is most passive (see §5.2).[10] Allowing oneself to be passively helped by God is the precondition of *dilectio*, of being turned toward God by rational means. The power of God to draw creatures to himself by sensible means exceeds the power of human reason. Thus the passion of love cannot be neglected by the rational creature in her motion toward God. When C. S. Lewis in *The Four Loves* asserts that "the highest does not stand without the lowest" (1960, p. 20), he is expressing an essentially Thomist line of thought.

The teaching that rational love grows, and can only grow, out of sensitive love may be surprising. It disturbs the conventional wisdom that what is most relevant for the rational creature's motion toward the end is

[10] To say that sensitive love is "most passive" implies that rational love, though properly a volition (and therefore active), also has a passive dimension. Ramírez (1973) correctly makes this suggestion. Identifying rational love with *simplex velle*, he writes that *amor rationalis* is the "*prima immutatio passiva*" of the will by the spiritual good apprehended by intellect (p. 97).

the love associated with the rational appetite. Something like this conventional wisdom lies behind the usual lack of attention to the Questions on the passions in the 1a2ae. As Uffenheimer-Lippens observes, the Questions on the passions constitute nearly one quarter of the 1a2ae (2003, p. 530). Why did Aquinas devote so much attention to the passions? Undoubtedly he is convinced, as Pasnau remarks, that they have "tremendous significance" (2002, p. 243). On our reading, the significance lies in the potency to serve as sources of energy that hasten the creature's motion toward the end. Pasnau suggests that the passions are tremendously significant because "they cause irrationality, and irrationality causes us to perform wrong actions" (pp. 243–4).[11] Certainly passions can cause irrationality. But can this be Thomas's primary motive for devoting such a large slice of the 1a2ae to the passions? Many things cause irrationality, yet Aquinas does not devote a cluster of twenty-seven Questions to them. Servais Pinckaers sketches a more adequate account of why Aquinas should accord so much significance to the passions. Noting that the Questions on the passions outnumber those on happiness and human acts, as well as those on the virtues and the gifts, or law and grace, he observes:

This quantitative comparison does not evidently signify that, in the eyes of the Angelic Doctor, the Treatise on the passions is the most important, but it does all the same indicate that it has a particular interest for him. (1990, p. 379)

He proceeds to conclude that

the particular interest of St. Thomas in the passions originates from their contribution to moral action and to the progress of man in his journey toward God (*marche vers Dieu*). (p. 382)

4.3 DO THE PASSIONS HAVE COGNITIVE VALUE?

The passions are valuable because, when rightly directed, they increase the moral goodness of individual actions. Moreover, the proper cultivation of the passions is necessary to supply the psychic energy required for attaining the end. In the *Marriage of Heaven and Hell*, Blake's "voice of the devil" proclaims that "Energy is the only life and is from the Body." Aquinas would agree in part: the passions are located within the appetite

---

[11] Pasnau (2002) proceeds to qualify his position, acknowledging that for Aquinas consequent passions are "admirable" and "valuable," as is "clear especially for the passions of the irascible power, which fight for the things we want" (pp. 262–3). On our reading, the point is no less clear in the case of love and the concupiscible passions generally.

that is common to all embodied creatures. In portraying the passions as a source of bodily energy, Blake does not suggest that the passions have any distinctively cognitive value. For Aquinas, however, the relation to cognition is sufficiently intimate that we may ask: Does the intelligent direction of the passions expand or augment the capacity of the human person for knowing? Do the passions have positive cognitive value?

Martha Nussbaum has argued for a strong contrast between Plato and Aristotle on this question. Plato is the villain, since he (allegedly) thinks that appetite and desire are "potent forces of both distortion and distraction, and that clear and adequate judgments concerning value can be made only by getting the intellect free and clear of their influence altogether" (1990, p. 248; quoted in Pasnau 2002, p. 262). She finds Aristotle to have greater sympathy for the view that passions have cognitive value: "the emotions are themselves modes of vision, or recognition. Their responses are part of what knowing, that is truly recognizing or acknowledging, *consists* in" (p. 79; quoted in Pasnau 2002, p. 262). Setting aside the question of whether these are adequate interpretations of Plato and Aristotle, I want to ask where Aquinas would fall on this spectrum. Pasnau (also responding to Nussbaum) judges that Aquinas "belongs somewhere in the middle" (2002, p. 262). While the antecedent passions that precede judgment "are viewed with Platonic distrust," the consequent passions are "a sign that the mind is fully committed to its choice" and serve to "help one achieve one's aims" (pp. 262–3).

Pasnau's location of Aquinas in the middle is sound, as far as it goes. He persuasively rejects the view that "raw emotion," considered as "passion ungoverned by reason and untrained by discipline" (p. 263), would have any positive value for Aquinas. He may also be correct to ascribe to Aquinas the view that raw emotion does not reliably get things right. Attributing to Pasnau the claim that "Aquinas did not see anything good coming out of passions as immediate reactions, and that he did not provide them with any positive epistemic role," Knuuttila concludes that the claim is too strong (2004, p. 253). I agree that the claim is too strong, but I am unsure that Pasnau actually makes it. Pasnau is careful to restrict the "no positive value" claim to "raw emotion," understood as "passion ungoverned by reason and untrained by discipline" (2002, p. 263). He can easily distinguish raw emotion in this sense from the immediate reactions of the virtuous person. The latter do reliably get things right, even if "raw emotion" does not. Part of what makes the virtuous person genuinely virtuous, as opposed to merely continent, is that her initial emotional reactions do (by and large) get things right.

Or so it seems. The answer to the question "Do the passions add anything to the cognition of the virtuous person?" may not be so obvious. Perhaps the passions merely "second" what the virtuous person already knows without the help of her passions, providing a kind of emotional echo of cognition. Another, complementary possibility is that while the passions provide the virtuous person with motivation to act on what she knows, they make no contribution to the acquisition of her knowledge. I want to argue that neither possibility fully captures what Aquinas actually thinks about the issue. Pasnau might agree; he acknowledges that weighting the passions in the "moral reasoning" of a person with maturity and insight is not incompatible with Aquinas, but adds that "this is not a point that I have found him making" (p. 263). At least one other Thomist philosopher, however, has found him making the point. In a 1943 essay entitled "Thomism and 'Affective Knowledge,'" Victor White declares:

An intellectualist philosophy which is content to ignore or make light of affective experience is not only doomed to impermanence, it must forfeit the claim to be either truly intellectualist or truly philosophical. If intelligence is to be arbiter it is self-condemned if it must confess itself unable to account for the most vital and intimate forms of personal experience. If philosophy is by definition a system of universal applicability, if it is to explain to use the ultimate reasons of all things to the extent that these are discoverable by human powers, it follows that a system which must exclude affective knowledge can make no valid claim to be strictly philosophical. (1943, p. 9)

This declaration does nothing to show that Aquinas actually embraces "affective knowledge." White proceeds to "show by a number of quotations from his writings that St. Thomas was quite alive to the existence of an 'affective,' 'connatural' or 'experimental' knowledge distinct from the purely rational process" (p. 10). White finds ten modes of knowing in Thomas that are not reducible to speculative cognition. This does less, however, than it might seem to support the claim that the passions have cognitive value. Most of White's ten modes refer to intuition, experience, or habits, rather than the passions. Yet one mode does appear to involve a passion: knowledge "*per amorem* (through love)." But even here, one may hesitate. "Love" may denote either a passion, strictly speaking, or a pseudopassion (see §2.2).

Does love, considered strictly as a passion, enter into knowledge in any serious way? The text in the Treatise that speaks most directly to this question is Article 2 of Question 27. Aquinas observes that love for any good requires some apprehension of that good; he accepts Augustine's dictum that "no one can love something that is unknown" (*De Trinitate* 10.1). He proceeds to observe that love outruns knowledge. For example, a person may have minimal knowledge of another (e.g. the mother of a newborn), and yet her love for the other may be far stronger than her knowledge (on any reasonable account, the new mother barely knows the baby). Aquinas makes the point with a rather different example. That a thing can be loved completely, without being perfectly known, is

> most evident in regard to the sciences, which some love on account of some outline knowledge of them: for instance, they know that rhetoric is a science that enables man to persuade others, and this is what they love in rhetoric. (27.2 ad 2m)

What applies to the lover of rhetoric, Aquinas adds, is "likewise to be said regarding the love of God." Though a person cannot know God completely in this life, she can love him completely. In spite of the tendency to attribute a stark intellectualism to Aquinas, it seems that he considers love as a vital prerequisite for knowing. This is true not only of the *scientiae* and other persons, but also of the human end itself. "As a person is, so the end appears to him" (58.5.co). The view expressed by White thus receives textual support. If it is correct to ascribe an "intellectualism" to Aquinas, this cannot be "an intellectualist philosophy which is content to ignore or make light of affective experience" (1943, p. 9).

All this shows that for Aquinas, the passion of love cannot be severed from knowledge, as though knowledge were a thing that could be fully acquired apart from love.[12] Nonetheless, Aquinas would have no reason to accept Nussbaum's claim that "if one *really* accepts or takes in a certain belief, one will experience the emotion" (1990, p. 41; quoted in Pasnau 2002, p. 262). A person's universal reason may "really" judge that the airplane is an extremely safe form of travel, certainly safer than the automobile. Yet the emotion of a person gripped by fear of flying may be at odds with what she knows through universal reason, because her particular reason has built up associations that are contrary to the judgments she is able to make with her intellect (§3.4). For Aquinas, attributing genuine cognitive value to the passions does not require that a passion accompany every act of "real" knowledge. It lies, rather, in the fact that if one does not love a science or a person, the knowledge that one has of that science or person will inevitably be superficial, since one lacks the incentive for the seeking required to deepen one's knowledge.

---

[12] For another version of this argument, see Ricken (1998) on "the cognitive function of love" (pp. 138–40).

4.4 ARE WE RESPONSIBLE FOR OUR PASSIONS?

Though we are responsible for the effects of our passions, and for the actions that are voluntarily performed under the influence of passion, we are not responsible for the passions themselves. This is a common view. Ought this view to be ascribed to Aquinas? It might seem so. Aquinas holds that for non-rational animals, action follows the act of the sensitive appetite. Through the use of the estimative and memorative powers, the sheep "judges" that the wolf is dangerous, and so experiences fear. Once the sheep fears the wolf and is pained by the fear, it flees (§3.3). There is no possibility of a hiatus between the motion of the sheep's sensitive appetite and its exterior action. Rational animals, however, can be moved in one manner by their sensitive appetite, and yet refrain from commanding any action that would be in accord with the passion. So while a person may not be responsible for suffering passion, she is always responsible for her volitions, no matter how strongly she is in the grip of a passion.

It is true that Aquinas holds that violence can never be done to the will, and hence that we are responsible for our volitions. But it does not follow, and Aquinas does not hold, that we are *only* responsible for our willed actions.[13] Some have held that if passions are not actions, but radically distinct from acts of will, then we cannot be responsible for them. The logic is something like this: we are responsible only for what is voluntary; the passions are not voluntary; therefore, we are not responsible for our passions. Against this view, Gordon contends that "it is not a consequence of the passivity of emotions that they are states with respect to which *we* are passive" (1986, p. 372). This point may easily be made in terms of Aquinas' view of the relation between the essence of the soul and its powers (§1.1). Though a part of the soul, the sensitive appetite, is passive, it would be an error to conclude that the whole, the body/soul composite, is passive with respect to the passions. To see that Aquinas does not commit this "fallacy," as Gordon rightly terms it, is to suggest the possibility that we have at least some control over, and hence responsibility for, our passions.

But how are we responsible for our passions? Are there some circumstances under which we are responsible, and others under which we are

---

[13] "Surely what matters is not whether we have voluntary control over experiencing the passions but whether the action that is (at least partially) caused by the passions is voluntary" (King 1998, p. 124n44). The "surely" is out of place here. For Aquinas, *both* our responsibility for actions that are influenced by passions *and* our responsibility for the passions themselves matter a great deal.

not? Though Aquinas does not raise these questions directly, he suggests answers to them. Claudia Murphy argues that Aquinas can accommodate two apparently conflicting intuitions on the matter (1999, pp. 163–5).[14] I would describe the "intuitions" slightly differently, and raise their number to three. They are something like the following:

1. We have indirect but significant control over our passions, and are therefore responsible for them. (I may involuntarily experience fear when I walk into a "haunted house" on Halloween. But no one forces me to walk into the house.)
2. In many particular cases, we have no control over whether we experience a passion. Yet to some degree we are still responsible, because how we experience passions is a part of our character, and we are ultimately responsible for our character. This is true even if a present change of character is impossible. (Aristotle makes a version of this argument, taking it to harmonize with at least one of the commonly accepted opinions.)
3. In some cases (perhaps many), we simply have no control over our passions, and are not responsible for them in any sense. ("I can't help the way I feel.")

Converging with Murphy, I want to argue that Aquinas' perspective is able to capture the truth contained in each of these three intuitions. In Question 24, Aquinas distinguishes two ways that the passions may be related to the "judgment of reason."

In the first way, antecedently. And thus, since they cloud the judgment of reason, on which the good of the moral act depends, they diminish the goodness of the act, for it is more laudable that someone do a work of charity from the judgment of reason, than from only the passion of pity.
In the second way, a passion is related to the judgment of reason consequently. And this happens in two ways. In one way, in the manner of overflow, that is to say, when the superior part of the soul is moved intensely toward something, the lower part follows its motion. And thus passion, when it exists consequently in the sensitive appetite, is a sign of the intention of the will. And thus it points to

---

[14] Murphy (1999) attributes two views to Aquinas: "Passions are directly voluntary, because directly responsive to our reason and will," and "We are indirectly responsible for our passions just in case we could have controlled them if we had tried" (p. 166). Rather than separate these as "two views," it would be more accurate to describe them in Aquinas as two dimensions of a single unified view. Murphy's article itself does an excellent job of showing how the two dimensions hold together in Aquinas' overall perspective. Despite my disagreements with some of her particular judgments, I am deeply indebted to her essay. It stands as the most thorough and perceptive discussion of the topic.

greater moral goodness. In another way, a passion is consequent in the manner of choice, that is to say when a man chooses from the judgment of reason to be affected by some passion, so that he may act more promptly, cooperating with the sensitive appetite. And thus a passion of the soul adds to the goodness of action. (24.3 ad 1m)

I want to begin with the "consequent" passions. How might we be responsible for them? Answering this question seems easy enough. Since these passions follow from an act of reason and will, we are responsible for them to the same degree that we are responsible for the voluntary acts of reason and will on which they depend. The clearest instance of a "consequent passion" is not directly mentioned in the passage quoted above. It occurs when a person decides to use either her imagination (§3.2) or her particular reason (§3.4) to convert an abstract concept (e.g. the health produced by exercise) into a set of concrete images (e.g. the new shape of the body imagined to result from exercise) that produce a passion. In *De veritate*, Aquinas provides a more vivid example:

What is understood universally by the intellect, is formed in a particular manner in the imagination, and thus the lower appetite is moved, as when the intellect of a believer intelligibly grasps future penalties, and then forms phantasms of them, imagining a burning fire and a gnawing worm and other like things, from which follows the passion of fear in the sensitive appetite. (*QDV* 26.13 ad 3m)[15]

Do we often experience this sort of "reason-dependent" passion (to use Murphy's term)? When Aquinas argues that passions obey reason and will, according to Murphy, he does not usually have such cases in mind. This may be correct, but her inference that "most reason-dependent passions are not consciously but unconsciously commanded by the will" is arbitrary. A virtuous person may frequently choose to use her imagination to arouse the sensitive appetite, so that it "adds to the goodness of action" (24.3 ad 1m). The point is not limited to the virtuous. What Murphy calls "the conscious project of forming a certain passion" (1999, p. 185) is not a rare occurrence, but a routine event for a good actress, especially one who has been trained in "method acting" (cf. Stanislavski 1948). She will often and deliberately think of images that reliably lead to the production of various motions of the sensitive appetite, together with the corresponding somatic events (§2.3). That at least some individuals may become accomplished at producing certain passions at will seems

---

[15] Murphy (1999) also cites this example (p. 178). I am indebted to her article for bringing its importance to my attention.

evident. It does not follow, of course, that such a person would be able to produce any passion at will, or even a particular set of passions at any time.

A second type of "reason-dependent" passion corresponds to the first kind of consequent passion described in the passage from 24.3. Such passions occur when the rational appetite wills something so intensely that it produces an "overflow" (*redundantia*) into the sensitive appetite. Since the concern of 24.3 is to identify the ways in which passions can increase the goodness of action, Aquinas emphasizes the advantage of overflow from the higher into the lower appetite. But he says nothing to restrict such overflow to good volitions.[16] Any act of will can be performed so intensely that it produces a corresponding motion within the sensitive appetite. (For example, an employee who hates his boss can work himself up by an act of will, to the point that he experiences a movement of his sensitive appetite.) Thus, in the *De veritate*, Aquinas writes that "insofar as from an apprehension the intellect moves the higher appetite, the lower appetite is moved along with it by a certain overflow or command" (*QDV* 26.3 ad 13m). Just how does the higher appetite "overflow" into the lower? Though Aquinas is acquainted with the phenomenon of overflow by experience and observation, there is no reason to suppose that he knows, or is particularly interested in, the nature of the mechanism by which this occurs. It seems that Aquinas is content to use the metaphor of overflow, without any further explanation.[17]

Are we responsible for the passions that occur by way of "overflow"? If they are dependent on reason and will, it seems that we are responsible for them, since we are responsible for the acts of will that cause them. This remains true even if such passions are "unconsciously commanded," as Murphy puts it. Yet it is difficult to see why Murphy saddles Aquinas with

---

[16] In discussing overflow exclusively within "the positive contribution of the passions to the rational act," Uffenheimer-Lippens (2003) in an otherwise insightful discussion misses this important point (p. 555).

[17] King (1998) suggests that Aquinas generally "describes psychological activity at a high level of abstraction," and does not try to find the underlying neurophysiological mechanisms. He adds that this is "one of the virtues of his account," since "he was, rightly, more concerned with the logic of such interaction than with the nuts and bolts of how it worked" (pp. 131–2). If this is true, the suggestion of Pasnau (2002) that Aquinas "considers the precise mechanisms at work" when discussing the relation of passion to will requires some qualification (p. 253). Klubertanz (1952) makes the point in a different way, suggesting that while Aquinas was "aware of the complex physiological mechanisms so ingeniously constructed by his contemporaries," he rejects Albert's tendency to base the distinction among internal powers of the soul "on physiological and even physical doctrines" because he "knows where the primary consideration lies (in the idea of potency as such)" (p. 227).

the view that "we are somehow *more* responsible for unconsciously commanded than for consciously commanded acts" (1999, p. 185). On the contrary, the image of spontaneous "overflow" suggests that while we are responsible for the act of will, and thus indirectly for the consequent passion, we have no control over whether the passion follows upon the act of will.

The second type of "consequent passion," according to Question 24, occurs when a person may choose "from the judgment of reason to be affected by some passion, so that he may act more promptly, cooperating with the sensitive appetite" (24.3 ad 1m). Murphy comments on this passage as follows:

> What is being described here . . . is not another case of a reasoned judgment *causing* a passion. Choosing to be affected by a passion is not choosing to elicit a passion, but rather choosing that an already occurring passion should have its full effect on oneself, because one endorses or approves of the passion. (1999, p. 183)

Though Aquinas clearly describes this case as an instance of "consequent" passion, it seems to have something important in common with "antecedent" passion, since the passion is "already occurring" prior to an act of reason. (This explains why Murphy's distinction between "reason-dependent" and "reason-independent" passions cuts across the antecedent/consequent distinction.) Are we responsible for such passions? Since "choosing to be affected" by the passion is an act of will, we are at least responsible for the manner in which the passion affects us.[18] But are we responsible for the initial occurrence of the passion? This is a special case of the more general question: How, and under what conditions, are we responsible for antecedent passions?

To address this question, I begin with the simple observation that no passion occurring prior to reason's judgment is directly caused by an act of will. Yet this observation does not settle the question of responsibility, since (as the first intuition described above would suggest) we are responsible for many passions that occur without an act of will's directly causing them. Certain passions may involuntarily follow the ingestion of a specific amount of alcohol. Intoxication itself is a passive state of affairs, occurring only when an operation has been performed by an "agent" (e.g. the ingestion of alcohol under certain conditions). The emotions produced

---

[18] On this point Barad (1991) is illuminating. She suggests that for Aquinas "failing to modify a negative emotional response when one is able to do so is just as morally culpable as voluntarily intensifying it" (p. 404). Both failure to moderate and voluntary intensification would count as instances of "choosing to be affected by a passion."

by intoxication are instances of "reason-independent" passions. But does reason-independence imply our lack of responsibility? It does not, as Gordon argues, because understanding the passive character of being intoxicated and the resultant emotions "rules out none of the following":

that a person may *cause himself to be* intoxicated; that a person may prevent himself from being intoxicated, by preventing the administration of an intoxicant; by taking measures that prevent an intoxicant, once present, from "taking effect"; or perhaps simply by refusing to "assent" to being intoxicated. (1986, pp. 383–4)

When intoxication occurs, Aquinas writes, "the use of reason is fettered or hindered" (33.3.co), and this paves the way for the occurrence of multiple antecedent passions. But I may be held responsible for any passion that is ultimately caused by an act for which I am responsible, even if the passion is an antecedent passion that occurs spontaneously without the use of reason. Why? Aquinas answers: "It could have been prevented by reason if it had been foreseen" (17.7.co). Lack of immediate control over an antecedent passion does not suffice to show that one is not responsible for that passion. We may possess what Murphy (1999) terms "indirect counterfactual control" (pp. 190–1).

Not all antecedent passions are amenable to such control. Every so often, as the third intuition described above would suggest, a person who claims, "I can't help the way I feel," may be telling the truth, rather than simply making an excuse or deceiving herself. In such instances, a person experiences a passion, without foreseeing either that certain acts of sensation and imagination would occur, or that such acts would generate the passions they cause. Thus it follows that we are not responsible for at least some antecedent passions. But a further distinction is necessary. There is a difference between (1) the case where a person could not have foreseen the causal connections between acts of apprehension and appetition, but would have been able to foresee them if she were of better character, and (2) the case where even the virtuous person would not have been able to foresee such connections. In the first case, "indirect counterfactual control" *for that particular person, having the character she does*, is not a real possibility. She may nonetheless be responsible for her character, as Aristotle suggests in accordance with the second intuition listed above.[19] To the extent that she is responsible for her character,

---

[19] Murphy (1999) makes the point: "Sometimes we are responsible for our emotions even when we could not have avoided them" (p. 165).

she is responsible for the passions which accompany that character. This suggests the possibility that the relevant habits and passions may be susceptible to change (unless the character is literally unalterable). As Murphy comments, "We can then, with some effort, form good emotional habits in ourselves and rid ourselves of those we judge to be bad" (1999, p. 193).[20]

In the second case, however, the passions simply occur, without a person's being responsible for them in any sense. Though a man of virtue is not insensitive to feminine beauty (unless he is a boor, but in that case he is hardly a man of virtue), he will experience no arousal at the sight of a beautiful woman. His sensitive appetite is perfectly aligned with his rational appetite. One may object: if the woman is sufficiently beautiful, is it not implausible to suppose that he would have *no* sensitive reaction? Aquinas would grant this objection some validity. Though the virtuous man's sensitive appetite may indeed register something, it will not have been acted upon to any significant extent. The man will have experienced a "propassion" rather than a passion in the proper sense.[21] Aquinas does not think that we are responsible for experiencing propassions.[22] They are an inevitable effect of sensuality, and "sensuality in this life cannot be cured except by a miracle" (*QDV* 25.7.co).

In discussing Aquinas' thinking about our responsibility for our passions, I have acquiesced in the widespread habit – shared by commentators who otherwise differ significantly – of describing the reason/passion relation as one of "control."[23] One interpreter, however, has directly

[20] This judgment requires one important qualification. Aquinas would not simply say that we can reform our emotional life "with some effort." The necessity of grace must be emphasized, lest we confuse Aquinas' view with Pelagianism. "Cognition alone is not enough for the healing of the incontinent; the interior help of grace which alleviates concupiscence is required, as well as the application of the exterior remedy of admonishment and correction, from which a person begins to resist particular concupiscences, so that concupiscence itself is weakened" (2-2.156.3 ad 2m). Pasnau (2002) rightly calls attention to this passage (p. 260).

[21] Aquinas knows the doctrine of the propassions most directly from Augustine, as 59.3.co makes clear. On Augustine's use of the propassions, particularly in his sermons, see Byers 2003. Aquinas also seems to be acquainted with Jerome's use of the term *propassio* (see Gondreau 2002, p. 29). The *ST* glosses Matthew 26:37 in the following manner: "Sorrow is removed from Christ according to complete passion, yet it was initiated in him according to propassion" (3.15.6 ad 1m).

[22] Though even the virtuous person cannot help propassions (even if she can foresee their arrival generally), and is therefore not responsible for them, "she may still be responsible for her attitude to them, and for their continuing and developing. She is not responsible for the first stirrings of adulterous lust, or triumphant pride, or jealousy, and envy. But she may very well be responsible for all of those if they last more than a moment, or if she does nothing to fight them" (Murphy 1999, p. 194).

[23] Some examples: Jordan 1986, pp. 96–7; Pasnau 2002, pp. 257–62; King 1998, p. 126; Murphy 1999, p. 174. Uffenheimer-Lippens (2003) also speaks of control, but adds this crucial qualification: "It is

challenged the adequacy of speaking of Aquinas in these terms. Eileen Sweeney writes:

What Aquinas does not do is express any fundamental distrust of the passions or engage in any heavy-handed appeals to the need for rational control of the passions. (1999, p. 222)

Is this correct? Defending the view that has become entrenched orthodoxy among Aquinas commentators, Simo Knuuttila dismisses Sweeney's proposal as an "exaggerated view" (2004, p. 254). He maintains that because "the sensitive appetite can be obedient to reason, the control of the emotions is an essential element of moral goodness" (p. 254). This is to miss Sweeney's point. It is not that Aquinas denies the subordination of the sensitive appetite to reason (and if by "control" one means only "subordination," then there is no objection). But does the metaphor of "control" adequately capture Aquinas' understanding of the relation between reason and the passions?

There are good reasons to think that it does not. First, and most obviously, Aquinas endorses the Aristotelian distinction between "despotic rule" and "politic rule," and explicitly denies any kinship between the reason/passion relation and despotic rule. The passions are "subject" to reason and "obey" reason, but in the same manner as free citizens obey their rulers (not controllers). Correctly, Pasnau suggests that the ability of the sensitive appetite to "resist" reason "gives the passions a curious in-between status" (2002, p. 257). They are neither rational volitions nor bodily reactions. What Pasnau does not notice is that the analogy to politic rule implies not only negative resistance, but also the potential for positive contribution. As free citizens contribute something of their own to the life of the well-governed *polis*, beyond what is already known or prescribed by the rulers, so the passions are able to contribute "something of their own," as Aquinas says (1.81.3 ad 2m) to the life of the human being.[24] This conclusion does not proceed from any desire to

---

very important, however, to understand what Thomas means by this 'control' of reason. We must stress that Thomas speaks always of the 'mitigation' of the passions and never of their total exclusion. When he does use the verb 'to suppress' in relation to the passions, he refers only to the lack of rational order that must be repelled, not to the passions as such. One must keep in mind that the passions are not by nature *perturbationes animae*" (p. 548).

[24] It is true that in 1.81.2 ad 2m Aquinas uses the phrase "appetitus sensibilis habet aliquid proprium" in the immediate context of the lower appetite's (negative) resistance to reason. But he does not preclude the possibility of a positive contribution, which is implicitly present in the comparison to politic rule. Elsewhere he makes it clear (e.g. 24.3) that passions are able to contribute positively to the moral goodness of an action. Kevin White (2002) makes a pertinent observation: "Although

romanticize the passions; it is strictly contained in the analogy of the reason/passion relation to politic rule (as opposed to despotic rule).

Pasnau asserts that "it is the very materiality of the sensory appetite that explains, most fundamentally, why we cannot entirely control them" (2002, p. 257). But is this Aquinas' view? In asking whether the passions existed in the soul of the first man, Thomas answers that Adam's sensitive appetite was constituted by materiality, and yet "was wholly subject to reason" in the state of innocence (1.95.2.co). This shows that while materiality in the fallen state may be part of the problem, what leads to the revolt of the appetites against reason is not essentially materiality. To locate the *non serviam* in materiality is to hold a crypto-gnostic view from which Aquinas is careful to distance himself.[25]

"What would it mean for the passions to be 'perfectly subjected to the rational soul'?" Pasnau asks. "It can sometimes look as if Aquinas's ideal for human nature is a life entirely free of the passions, a life of reason alone, with the passions held firmly underfoot" (2002, p. 262). This appearance (which Pasnau does not endorse without qualification) derives much of its plausibility from the conflation of "subjection" (the condition of politic rule) with "domination" or "control." Perfect subjection of the passions entails their responsibility to reason and will, in the different ways that I have described. It does not imply, or even remotely suggest, a "life entirely free of the passions." For Aquinas, the passions are a fundamental part of human nature. They are to be cultivated and directed, but not extirpated. Holding this view generates further questions. For example, what is the difference between the appropriate cultivation and the irrational dominance of a passion? How does "moderate sorrow" differ from "immoderate sorrow"? On what basis should righteous anger be distinguished from wrath? For insight into these matters, we may follow Aquinas' own procedure in the Treatise and turn to an examination of the particular passions.

---

sense-appetite's resistance to reason is a result of sin, its partial self-possession is an essential, spirited aspect of human nature as it was in the beginning" (p. 105).

[25] Later in his discussion, Pasnau himself cites a relevant passage from the *Sentences* commentary, where Aquinas holds that when the blessed are resurrected with their bodies, the "human body will be perfectly subjected to the rational soul" (2002, p. 262; the passage is from IV *Sent.* 44.2.1.1c). Materiality as such is not the problem, even if materiality in the fallen state is a contributing factor to the difficulty of rational governance.

PART 2

Particular passions:
the concupiscible passions

CHAPTER 5

Love

The treatment of the passions "in particular," comprising twenty-three Questions, is both more intricate and more extensive than the four Questions on the passions "in general." Why does Aquinas accord such weight to the particular passions (§5.1)? First among the particular passions is love. In its proper sense, the passion of love is "sensitive love." Though rational love is more elevated than sensitive love, Aquinas does not hesitate to point out the superior potency of sensitive love in drawing a person nearer to the divine (§5.2). He proceeds to illuminate the nature of love by examining the distinction between "love of friendship" and "love of concupiscence" (§5.3). What causes love? Ultimately, the good, but in order for the good to cause love, it must be cognized in a way that involves some kind of likeness between subject and object (§5.4). What does love do to a person? What are its effects? Aquinas treats this large question by identifying the primary effect of love as "union," and treating the remaining effects in terms of union (§5.5).

5.I INTRODUCTION TO THE PARTICULAR PASSIONS

Those interested in Aquinas' thinking about moral and anthropological topics in the Ia2ae – the last end, acts of the will, virtues and vices, natural law – have frequently overlooked the Questions on the passions. Even those who notice the passions tend to focus on Questions 22–5 of the Ia2ae, with an occasional glance at *QDV* 25–6, or else concentrate on *QDV* 25–6 with the odd comparison to the Ia2ae. This mode of reading places strong emphasis on the passions "in general." Aquinas' own textual practice is radically different. He devotes four Questions, comprising fifteen Articles, to the passions *in generali*, whereas the passions *in speciali* receive twenty-three Questions comprising 117 Articles. That Aquinas would give eight times the space to the particular passions that he gives to the passions in general is striking. It suggests that in order to understand Thomas as he wishes to be understood, the usual practice of simply focusing on the passions in general must be abandoned.

Careful attention must be given to the twenty-three Questions on the particular passions.

Why does Aquinas find it so important to give such extended consideration to the particular passions? What is gained by knowing the passions in particular? One reason for undertaking a detailed examination of Questions 26–48, the purpose of Part 2 of this book, is precisely to address such questions. A partial answer would build on what Aquinas has said about the particular reason (§3.4). Up to a point, the passions can be reshaped by the proper habituation of the particular reason. But the particular reason does not activate the passions "in general." Its acts correspond to specific instances of this or that particular passion. If I wish to acquire real knowledge of the multiple ways in which I am acted upon, I will gain little simply by thinking about the passions in general. Rather, I must pose specific questions: What do I love? What causes me to experience desire? How do I respond to sorrow? Why do I experience hope at one moment, and feel despair at the next? Why do I have the fears that I have? How might these fears be modified or eliminated? In what kinds of situation do I respond with anger? What is the difference between a rational and an irrational expression of anger? Asking such particular questions is the only path toward knowledge about the passions that is sufficiently concrete to provide actual help in the quest *ad finem* (§4.2).

The *ST* treats the particular passions because of its practical motive: to guide and quicken the rational creature's motion toward eternal beatitude (see 1.1.4.co). Thus Aquinas devotes a large slice of the 1a2ae to questions that might not strike contemporary philosophers as interesting. This may be taken, according to one's standpoint, as a judgment against either Aquinas or contemporary philosophy. It is not that Aquinas finds the general questions that drive recent debates (e.g. "Are we responsible for our passions?" [§4.4]) to be entirely unimportant. But they are not the questions that he privileges. Far from constituting a free-standing summary of Aquinas' thinking, the general discourse on the passions serves as a preparation for the treatment of the particular passions. Simply put, Questions 22–5 of the 1a2ae on the passions *in generali* are teleologically ordered to Questions 26–48 on the passions *in speciali*, just as the 1a2ae as a whole ("universal moral discourse") is written for the sake of the more particularized discourse that comprises the 2a2ae (see 2-2.pr.). Bearing this in mind, I wish to survey some features of Questions 26–48 as a whole, before moving to examine the treatment of love.

Table 5.1 *The particular passions in order of appearance*
in the 1a2ae

De passionibus concupiscibilis			De passionibus irascibilis		
Love	26	De ipso amore	Hope/	40	De spe et
	27	De causa amoris	despair		desperatione
	28	De effectibus amoris	Fear	41	De ipso timore
Hate	29	De odio		42	De obiecto timore
Desire	30	De concupiscentia		43	De causa timoris
Pleasure	31	De ipsa delectatione secundum se	Daring	44	De effectibus timoris
	32	De causis delectationis		45	De audacia
	33	De effectibus delectationis et de remediis eius	Anger	46	De ira secundum se
	34	De bonitate et malitia delecationum		47	De causa effectiva irae
Pain and sorrow	35	De dolore et tristitia secundum se		48	De effectibus irae
	36	De causis tristitiae			
	37	De effectibus doloris vel tristitiae			
	38	De remediis doloris, seu tristitiae			
	39	De bonitate et malitia doloris vel tristitiae			

Aquinas divides the Questions on the particular passions into two parts, according to the distinction between the concupiscible and the irascible (§2.4 and §2.5). Within each division, the passions occur roughly in the order of generation (§3.5). See table 5.1.

The division into concupiscible and irascible is not equal. There are fourteen Questions on the concupiscible passions, and nine Questions on the irascible. This inequality is not accidental; it reflects the subordination of the irascible to the concupiscible. Another revealing inequality may be seen in the number of Questions assigned to each passion. Since hate parasitically follows love (see §6.1), it receives but one Question. As the contrary of desire, aversion receives not a single Question. The radical priority of good to evil (§1.4) seems to inform the distribution of Questions on the particular passions.

Nonetheless, Aquinas assigns the largest number of Questions to sorrow. Why is this? A simple explanation would advert to Thomas's view that sorrow is "most properly" a passion, as well as the *sine qua non* for daring and anger. Despair, by contrast, does not rate a single Question, since it is a *per accidens* motion from good. Similarly, daring as a *per accidens* motion toward evil receives but one Question. Fear and anger receive four and three Questions respectively, suggesting their relative weight within the irascible. Can the assignment of not even a full Question to hope be reconciled with its status as a "principal passion"? The move strongly suggests that Aquinas means to supplant the traditional scheme of "four principal passions" with another, more complex ordering (§3.5). Another striking feature of the taxonomy is that only pleasure and sorrow receive Questions about their relation to good and evil. Pleasure and sorrow are the passions in which every other motion of the sensitive appetite (whether concupiscible or irascible) terminates. As ends of the other passions, they particularly lend themselves to moral evaluation. Any other passion, to the extent that it lies under the command of reason and will, may also be good or evil. But its moral status will derive from the character of the pleasure or sorrow toward which it moves, and which precedes it in the order of intention.

To say why some passions receive more Questions than others will require close reading. Aquinas writes as little or as much as he judges the topic to require; he is never bound to a Procrustean scheme. But, for the most part, he treats each passion according to a threefold rubric.[1] He typically begins with a treatment of the passion "in itself" (*ipsum*, or *secundum se*), introducing its formal object (§3.1). He then introduces a more explicit consideration of the passion's "cause" (*causa*). Here he shifts from what constitutes the passion (its formal cause) to the factors (whether efficient or dispositive causes) which produce the apprehension that activates the passion. Third, Aquinas concludes with a description of the passion's effects, attending to both the appetitive motion and the proportionate somatic element (§2.3). The threefold rubric appears most visibly in the Questions that "bookend" the treatment of the particular passions (26–8 on love, 46–8 on anger). Question 40 (hope/despair) and Question 45 (daring) collapse the scheme, but do not violate it. The Questions on pleasure and sorrow inflect the scheme by adding Questions *de bonitate et malitia* and (in the case of sorrow) *de remediis*. The most

---

[1] The exceptions are aversion (no Question), hate (Question 29), and concupiscence (Question 30).

singular variation may be seen in Questions 41–4 on fear. Here, as I have already observed (§3.1), Aquinas follows the tripartite scheme, but interposes a special Question on the object of fear.

In Parts 2 and 3 of this book, my aim is to provide close readings of the twenty-three Questions on the particular passions. Often, but not always, I will follow the thread of Aquinas' own thinking, proceeding Question by Question, article by article. To write about Aquinas in this manner is not typical today. A few words in its defense might be helpful. I will use a concrete example that will also serve as a transition to the next chapter.

Imagine a list of things that a philosophy teacher and her students might say in a seminar about the nature of love. The list would be quite long. Now imagine Aquinas as the teacher, posing questions of this form: "Of all the things that a pedagogically driven treatment of the passions, intended for the 'beginners' that are mentioned in the *ST*'s prologue, might say about the nature of love, which are the most crucial? How ought they to be said? At what length? In what order?" To understand what Aquinas thinks is most essential about love (or any other particular passion), some effort must be made to grasp the textual acts of inclusion and exclusion, as well as the rationale for treating the issues in the order in which they appear. To engage in this latter task means to inquire into the *ordo articulorum*, the "order of the articles" that constitutes the spine of a Question.

In the chapters that constitute Parts 2 and 3 of this book, I engage in some debate with commentators (especially Santiago Ramírez) who take this dimension of Aquinas' texts seriously. As it happens, while I think that Ramírez is often wrong in his construals of the *ordo articulorum*, engaging with his proposals is a useful stimulus to understanding why Aquinas proceeds in the manner that he does. In following Aquinas's thinking about the particular passions, I am not overly concerned to place him in dialogue with this or that debate within contemporary philosophy. Rather, my goal is to read Aquinas closely, on his own terms, attending to form and content. From time to time, I will not hesitate to use illustrations and parallels from authors and texts unknown to Aquinas (most are later, but some are earlier, e.g. the *Republic*). But the primary goal is to understand what he says about the particular passions, and why he says it. Thus the exposition begins where Thomas himself begins, with love.

5.2 LOVE AS A PASSION

Question 26 treats "love itself." Aquinas begins by inquiring into the location of *amor*, asking whether it is in the concupiscible power. He answers that love is the "principle" of the sensitive appetite's motion toward a perceived good (Article 1). But since a principle of motion is not itself a motion, how can love be a passion in the proper sense of the term? Thomas proceeds to reconcile love as a *principium motus* with love as a motion proper (Article 2). The first half of Question 26 may be read as an elucidation of the proposal that love is essentially a passion residing in the concupiscible power. The elucidation, however, does not exhaust the topic of "love itself." As it exists in human beings, love cannot simply be considered as a motion of the sensitive appetite without any reference to reason. Thus Question 26's second half begins a consideration of the relation between sensitive and rational love.[2] Aquinas asks whether *amor* is the same as *dilectio*. *Amor* names a genus, *dilectio* a species (Article 3). To throw further light on the relation between sensitive and rational love, the Question concludes with the distinction between "love of concupiscence" (*amor concupiscentiae*) and "love of friendship" (*amor amicitiae*) (Article 4).

Article 1 begins by considering what appears to be the case, that not all love belongs to the concupiscible power. The first objector draws upon Scripture to identify an *amor* that seeks a wisdom not apprehended by the senses. The second objector reads Augustine to suggest that because fear is ultimately a kind of love, love has an equal claim to be placed in the irascible. Finally, the third objector cites the "natural love" which belongs to the vegetative soul rather than the concupiscible. Why should love be uniquely located in the concupiscible? As is typical in the *ST*, the objections contain important truths that cannot be overlooked. Love is *not* uniquely in the concupiscible. Only one kind of *amor* belongs to the concupiscible power, namely *amor sensitivus*. As the first and third objectors argue, there are two other loves that correspond to other forms of appetite, natural (§1.2) and rational (§1.3). Hence the question arises: What is the ground for holding that love is most properly in the concupiscible power? Why is *amor* properly said to be of the sensitive appetite, and attributed to natural and rational appetite only by extension?

Before addressing these questions, Aquinas draws our attention to what is common to each of the three loves: "Love is something pertaining to the

---

[2] Article 3's point is to consider the *relation* between rational and sensitive love, for the sake of illuminating further the nature of *sensitive* love. Ramírez also divides this Question in half. But he thinks that Thomas abruptly shifts focus, moving to an explanation of rational love (Article 3) followed by its division (Article 4). On our reading, the *telos* of all four Questions is to understand sensitive *amor*.

appetite, since good is the object of both. Whence any difference in love occurs according to a difference of appetite" (26.1.co). In all three cases, *amor* denotes an inclination towards motion. "In each of these appetites, that which is the principle of motion (*principium motus*), tending toward an end that is loved (*finem amatum*), is called *amor*" (26.1.co). To describe this principle in the case of the natural appetite, Aquinas uses the term *connaturalitas*. He illustrates by reference to the simplest case – that of a thing possessing only natural love, such as a heavy body. The *connaturalitas* of a heavy body is its *gravitas*, its natural tendency to move downward unless acted upon by some countervailing motion. We see at once that *amor naturalis* cannot be *amor* in the proper sense of the term. Heavy bodies do not literally "love" to move downward; their *gravitas* can be called love, but only "in a way" (*quodammodo*) (26.2.co).[3] What licenses the metaphor is that any created thing, whether or not it has sensation, possesses some natural inclination to the motion that completes its form (§1.1). Although Aquinas frequently illustrates natural love through beings that lack sensation (e.g. stones and fires), one should remember that everything has *amor naturalis* (§1.2).

If the natural tendency of all beings to seek their preservation is only metaphorically spoken of as *amor*, what about the love that belongs to the rational appetite? This love, the *amor intellectivus vel rationalis* (cf. 26.1 ad 1m), seems to have a much stronger claim to *amor* in the most proper sense of the term. Aquinas delays consideration of this issue until the second half of Question 26. For now, he is content to observe that sensitive love and rational love have something in common. Each is the *connaturalitas* of a being toward a good which completes its form. Thomas specifies the *connaturalitas* with two key terms that are almost as difficult to translate as *connaturalitas*. The first is *coaptatio*, "co-adapation." Aquinas speaks of the "*coaptatio* of the sensitive appetite, or of the will, to some good." Describing love as a *coaptatio* emphasizes both its natural and its relational character. The lover is adapted to something that is fitting by nature. The second key term is *complacentia in boni*, "complacency in the good." By identifying the *coaptatio* between appetite and its object as a *complacentia*, Aquinas evokes the pleasure aroused by the appetible object. He preserves, however, the important distinction between the initial pleasure that prompts motion toward the good

---

[3] Thus Ramírez (1973): "innate or natural love, coinciding with appetite as innate or congenital appetite, is a certain kind of love, but said in an improper and loose sense, according to transference or metaphor" (p. 89).

(*complacentia*) with the pleasure that is attained when appetite rests in the good (*delectatio*).

All three types of love – natural, sensitive, rational – are unified, at least analogically, by their status as a principle of motion. Pasnau suggests that "because Aquinas extends the concept of love so broadly, he is forced at times to speak rather mechanically about it" (2002, p. 242). But what may strike a modern commentator as mechanical speech may actually reflect a subtle ear for the play of sameness and difference. Pieper observes that "a single fundamental word apparently underlies all the variety in vocabulary and binds together all special meanings" (1997b, pp. 146–7). To discern the unity among the diverse types of *amor* permits one to say precisely what the following have in common:

a stone's love of downward motion
a dog's love of his master
a young man's love of his fiancée
a woman's love of chocolate
a drinker's love of wine
a mathematician's love of calculus
a philosopher's love of wisdom

For each case, "love" names a basic inclination or adaptation of the subject toward an object that is apprehended as naturally suitable to it. In this most basic respect, language does not lie. The minimal grammar of love requires a subject (a "lover") and an object (a "beloved"). As Pieper remarks, any definition of love that fails to respect this minimal grammar is *ipso facto* suspect.[4] We experience love most palpably in cases where appetite is evidently in motion toward an appetible object. But love cannot be equated with the motion itself (i.e. desire or concupiscence), because the motion may cease and the inclination remain. Suppose that a person desires chocolate cake and eats two slices. Feeling full, her appetite is no longer in motion; she no longer desires to eat. But has she thereby ceased to love chocolate cake? Love names not the motion of the appetite, but its fundamental inclination.

To understand *amor* as a principle of motion, as the source of desire that remains constant while particular desires wax and wane, accords with human experience. It also raises a question. If love is a principle of

---

[4] Pieper notices a particularly egregious violation of this grammar in Spinoza's definition of love as "joy with the accompanying idea of an external love" (Pieper 1997b, p. 230). Cf. Spinoza, *Ethics* 3.6 (1994, p. 189).

motion, in what sense is it an act of the sensitive appetite? Can we continue to defend the idea that love is a passion, properly speaking? Article 2 confronts this difficulty, asking *utrum amor sit passio.* The first objector suggests that love would be more adequately described as a "certain power"; the second objector proposes that *amor* is a union and therefore more akin to a relation than a passion. The third objector makes the point technically: love is not a motion, but a *principium* of motion, and therefore not a passion.

What is at stake is nothing less than the character of love as a passion. If love is not a motion, then it is not, strictly speaking, a passion. In order to preserve the status of love as a passion, it must be accurately described as a motion in some sense of the term. As I have observed, Aquinas' use of *motus* is elastic (§2.3). While love is not a motion in the same respect as desire or concupiscence, it is nonetheless a motion. Love names "the *motus appetitus* whereby the appetite is changed by means of the appetible thing, so that the appetible thing might be pleasing to the appetite" (26.2 ad 3m). When we possess *amor* in its proper sense, we have it because we have been acted upon by something outside ourselves. This further clarifies why natural love can be *amor* only metaphorically. Because natural love does *not* result from another's action upon us (it is simply a feature of our created nature), it cannot be love *proprie dicta.* Sensitive love, by contrast, is a passion in the proper sense of the term, because it arises through the action of another.

Thus, because love consists in a certain *immutatio* of the appetite by the appetible object, it is manifest that love is a passion, indeed properly so called, according as it is in the concupiscible. Now it is generally a passion, and by an extension of the name, according as it is in the will. (26.2.co)

Here Aquinas implicitly raises the question of the relation between sensitive love, a passion properly speaking, and rational love, a passion only *extenso nomine.* He proceeds to confront the question explicitly in Article 3, when he asks *utrum amor sit idem quod dilectio.* Some interpreters, most notably Ramírez, see a sharp division between the two halves of Question 26. Its first half, Ramírez claims (1973, p. 87), treats sensitive love (*amor* said properly and univocally); its second half treats rational love (*amor* taken analogically but still properly). Within the second half, Article 3 provides the definition of rational love, while Article 4 specifies its proper division. This interpretation supposes that the chief aim of Article 3 is to define rational love. I will argue that this supposition is difficult to reconcile with what actually occurs in Article 3. Understanding the real aim of Article 3, I claim, suggests a radically different interpretation of Article 4.

Ramírez contends that Aquinas defines rational love as "simple willing." He astutely notes an analogy between the volitional sequence *simplex velle, intentio,* and *fruitio,* and the passional sequence *amor, desiderium,* and *delectatio* (1973, p. 97). The problem with Ramírez's reading, despite its ingenuity, is that Article 3 displays no interest in proposing a definition of rational love. Aquinas does not construct Article 3 because he wants abruptly to switch gears from sensitive love to rational love, as if he had suddenly abandoned his interest in the former. Rather, he judges that inquiry into the relation between *amor* and *dilectio* will illuminate something about the nature of *amor,* and particularly sensitive love. It may cast some light on *dilectio* and *caritas,* but only *per accidens.* The focus of Question 26 from beginning to end is *amor* as such. *Pace* Ramírez, the Question's second half is not primarily a search for the definition and division of *amor rationalis.*[5] Article 3 asks a different question about terms inherited from the tradition. Are *amor* and *dilectio* identical? If not, how should we understand their relationship? Aquinas begins by acknowledging the unity that seems to underlie traditional discourse about love. "Four names are found which, in a way, pertain to the same thing, sc. *amor, dilectio, caritas,* and *amicitia*" (26.3.co). But only "in a way" (*quodammodo*). Distinctions must be made. *Amor, dilectio, caritas,* and *amicitia* are not interchangeable terms. Thomas explains their relation:

Among these terms, *amor* is the more general, for every *dilectio* and *caritas* is an *amor,* but the converse does not hold; for *dilectio* adds beyond *amor* a preceding choice (*electio*), as the name itself echoes (*sonat*), whence *dilectio* is not in the concupiscible, but only in the will, and only in rational nature. Now *caritas* adds beyond *amor* a certain perfection of love, inasmuch as that which is loved is estimated to be of great price, as the name itself denotes. (26.3.co)

As the rational perfects the sensible, so *dilectio* and *caritas* complete *amor.* While agreeing with this conclusion, Aquinas wants to prevent certain misunderstandings. One might take the superiority of *dilectio* and *caritas*

[5] Ramírez considers another reading of Question 26's order that finds Aquinas principally concerned to explicate the teachings of Dionysius, Augustine, and other *magistri* in turn. Attributing this reading to John of St. Thomas, Ramírez (1973) protests that it is superficial, since "St. Thomas does not appear except as a mere compiler" (p. 85). However sound in principle, the criticism suggests neither the appropriateness of Ramírez's own reduction of Question 26 to a logical scheme nor the absence of a *tertium quid* (such as the one that we propose).

to justify the view that only rational love has true value for human beings, and that sensitive love is something to be neutralized or avoided. Or one might hold that one has to choose between rational love and sensitive love. These tendencies are amply attested in modern thought. To cite two examples: (1) Erich Fromm proposes that *either* love is something that requires knowledge and effort (i.e. an act of will) *or* it is a pleasant sensation that one experiences and falls into (i.e. a passion) (1956, p. 1); (2) Kant argues in the first section of the *Grundlegung* that, as the activity of the good will, true love of neighbor occurs with no regard for the inclinations. In contrast to such positions, Thomas upholds the value of sensitive love. That Aquinas understands the importance of vindicating *amor* as a passion may be gathered from the fact that his defense appears in a "gratuitous" reply to an objection. In Article 3 of Question 26, the *ad quartum* is not a response to a fourth objector (there are only three objections). Rather, it is among those comparatively rare places in the *ST* where Aquinas answers the *sed contra*. The *ad quartum* is so important for understanding Thomas's high valuation of sensitive love that it deserves to be quoted once again:

> The reason that some held that, even in the will itself, the name of *amor* is more divine (*divinius*) than the name of *dilectio*, is that *amor* conveys a certain passion, chiefly according as it is in the sensitive appetite; *dilectio*, however, presupposes the judgment of reason. But man is more able to tend toward God through *amor*, drawn passively in a way by God himself, than he can lead himself to God by means of his own reason (*ratio*), which pertains to the character (*ratio*) of *dilectio*, as said above. And on account of this, *amor* is more divine than *dilectio*. (26.3 ad 4m)[6]

Love in its most proper sense is sensitive love, because sensitive love is most passive.[7] Allowing oneself to be passively helped by God is the precondition of *dilectio*, of inclining oneself toward God by rational means. *Amor sensitivus* turns out to be the seed out of which the highest *amor rationalis* grows. This particular teaching of Aquinas may surprise us.

---

[6] Ramírez (1973) adds another reason for regarding *amor* as "more divine" than *dilectio*. Terms said "most generally" (paradigmatically, *esse*: Ramírez cites 1.13.11) are most appropriately said of God (pp. 97–8). Though this may be true enough, it seems to miss Thomas's point. *Amor* is more divine than *dilectio*, not on account of its wider scope, but on account of its greater potency to overcome sloth and propel the creature to the wholehearted love of God.

[7] To say that sensitive love is "most passive" implies that rational love, though properly a volition (and therefore active), also has a passive dimension. Ramírez correctly makes this suggestion. Identifying rational love with *simplex velle*, he writes that *amor rationalis* is the "prima immutatio passiva" of the will by the spiritual good apprehended by the intellect (1973, p. 97).

It disturbs the conventional wisdom that what is most relevant for the rational creature's motion toward her end is the love that presupposes and proceeds from an act of will. Something like this conventional wisdom underlies the usual lack of attention to the Questions on the passions in the 1a2ae. However, Thomas does not shrink from the conclusion that the most passive form of *amor* is also the most potent. Far from being collapsible into rational love, the *amor* proper to the senses has a function of its own. The power of God to draw creatures to himself by sensible means exceeds the power of human reason. *Amor sensitivus* cannot be neglected by the rational creature in its motion toward God: "The highest does not stand without the lowest."[8] Lacking the energy of the sensitive appetite, the *amor intellectualis Dei* will be weak.

5.3 'AMOR AMICITIAE' VS. 'AMOR CONCUPISCENTIAE'

Amor in its most proper sense is *amor sensitivus*, an act of the concupiscible power. In rational creatures, this can lead to an active love (aspects of which are named by *dilectio* and *caritas*) that proceeds from the will. Aquinas concludes Question 26's treatment of love in itself with an Article that asks whether love is appropriately divided into the "love of friendship" (*amor amicitiae*) and the "love of concupiscence" (*amor concupiscentiae*). Where does Article 4 fit into the order of Question 26? Some take Thomas to conclude Question 26 by treating a distinction that he knows from the tradition, but from which he distances himself. This answer is too easy. If Aquinas had judged the distinction to be trivial, he might have ignored it, especially within a highly compressed Question containing only four Articles. It is safer to suppose that Article 4 continues the path blazed by Article 3. Like the distinction between *amor* and *dilectio*, the distinction between *amor amicitiae* and *amor concupiscentiae* promises to illuminate something about love itself.

To begin with a clarification of terms. As Aquinas himself says in reply to the first objector, *amor concupiscentiae* and *amor amicitiae* are not

---

[8] Cf. Lewis (1960), pp. 20, 32. De Lubac (1987) also makes the point: "It is a great illusion to confuse desire and love, need and charity (*eros* and *agape*). It is one scarcely less great to believe that our love of God can and must break radically away from our condition as a creature, or that in the least of our natural loves, if it rise to the human, there is not something there already which from afar relates it to charity. The fundamental optimism of the Thomists and of the Salesian doctrine seems in this connection the only true one, the only one worthy of man, the only one as well which fully satisfies the data of Revelation" (pp. 137–8).

alternate terms for concupiscence and friendship.⁹ Rather, they designate two kinds of love. *Amor concupiscentiae* is the inclination that any animal – and not just rational animals, as Ramírez supposes¹⁰ – has for various objects that are distinct from the animal. It is not love in its proper sense, because it presupposes a being for whose sake the various objects are loved as means. Thus Thomas concludes that any object of *amor concupiscentiae* is loved "not simply and in itself, but for something else." *Amor amicitiae*, by contrast, is more fundamental. What is loved with the *amor amicitiae* is loved "simply and for itself (*simpliciter et per se*)" (26.4.co).

For any creature capable of loving, *amor amicitiae* is the absolute presupposition of love. It is related to *amor concupiscentiae* "as prior to posterior" (*prius et posterius*). In irrational creatures, this reduces to natural love of self. A horse loves its feed with *amor concupiscentiae*, because it desires it as a means to its own sustenance and preservation. It loves itself with the *amor amicitiae*.¹¹ Something similar holds for human beings. Objects distinct from the self are loved with *amor concupiscentiae*. We desire them instrumentally, for the sake of something else. Aquinas quotes a sentence from the *Rhetoric*: "to love (*amare*) is to will a good thing (*bonum*) to or for someone (*alicui*)." Who is the "someone" for whom the *bonum* is loved as a means? There are only two possibilities. A person loves something good (*bonum*), Aquinas says, either "for himself or for another" (26.4.co). But can we genuinely love another for her own sake, and not merely as a means to our own gratification? If the answer to this question is negative, it follows that we can love others only with *amor concupiscentiae*. We can love them only in a secondary sense, as things that we use rather than persons worthy of respect (to use the Kantian terminology). It is worth considering the possibility that we are capable of loving only ourselves for our own sake. La Rochefoucauld remarks: "The man who thinks he loves a woman for her own sake is very much mistaken" (1959, §374, p. 85). If this warning is not enough, we may quote another French moralist:

What about a person who loves someone for the sake of her beauty; does he love *her*? No, for smallpox, which will destroy beauty without destroying the person,

---

⁹ As Ramírez (1973) notes, "*Amor* is the name of an act or motion, while *amicitia* is the name of a habit" (p. 89; see also p. 98).
¹⁰ The supposition is arbitrary, in that the text of Article 4 offers no evidence on its behalf. It is intelligible, in that it is virtually determined by Ramírez's reading of Article 3.
¹¹ Cajetan (1889) grasps this point well: "Since any desired object (*concupitum*) is desired for someone, there is no *amor concupiscentiae* without *amor amicitiae* of the person for whom the object is desired" (p. 191).

will put an end to his love for her. . . . And if someone loves me for my judgment or my memory, do they love me? *me*, myself? No, for I could lose these qualities without losing my self. Where then is this self, if it is neither in the body nor the soul? And how can one love the body or the soul except for the sake of such qualities, which are not what makes up the self, since they are perishable? Would we love the substance of a person's soul, in the abstract, whatever qualities might be in it? That is not possible, and it would be wrong. Therefore we never love anyone, but only qualities. (Pascal 1966, §688, p. 245; cf. Pascal 1976, §323, p. 141)

We never love anyone, but only qualities – with the exception of ourselves (certainly we love ourselves, regardless of our qualities). Is it possible to extend this *amor amicitiae* to others? Those who wish to consider an affirmative answer to this question characteristically adopt one of two possibilities. The first is to transfer the love we naturally have for ourselves to another who is truly worthy of this love, and thereby destroy our original self-love. In certain moods Luther seems to recommend this route: "for to love is to hate oneself" (*est enim diligere seipsum odisse*).[12] From Thomas's perspective, this strategy is doomed for several reasons. To love another by hating oneself is not above nature, but utterly contrary to nature, and therefore not even a possibility for grace, "since grace does not destroy nature, but perfects it" (1.1.8 ad 2m). Second, it implies that divine love and human love are wholly disanalogous. God's free extension of his "self-love" *ad intra* in the life of the trinitarian Persons to creatures *ad extra* would not function, in any sense, as an exemplar for human beings to imitate. In loving creatures for their own sake, God does not hate himself. Third, even if humans were called to defy nature, inverting rather than imitating the divine mode of loving, it remains that self-hatred is simply impossible. (Aquinas will argue the point explicitly in Question 29; see §6.2.) Exhortations to love others by hating ourselves are bound to fail.[13]

The second possibility is for persons to accord others the *amor amicitiae* that they naturally bear toward themselves, *without* ceasing to love themselves. Nothing suggests that loving others in this way is easy or especially characteristic of human beings. That humans can say they love others with the *amor amicitiae* as they love themselves, without actually doing so, is always possible. The warnings of La Rochefoucauld and Pascal against self-deception are to the point. Moreover, the extension of *amor amicitiae*

---

[12] Cited by Pieper 1997b, p. 211, which cites its quotation in Nygren 1937, p. 533.

[13] As knowledge of others is impossible without knowledge of self, so genuine love of others is impossible without self-love. Bogliolo (1977) makes this point and adds that "love of God and neighbor would not be possible without love of oneself. There is nothing more natural than love of oneself; nothing is more secure, nothing is more evident in our daily experience" (p. 109).

to others, so that we love our neighbors as we love ourselves, may well be impossible without divine grace. Nonetheless, it is absolutely necessary. If we love only ourselves with *amor amicitiae*, we will inevitably love others as instruments to our own satisfaction. That is, we will love them only for their qualities, rather than for their own sake. Without radical self-transcendence, the perfection of love that Article 3 associates with *caritas*, such a condition may be inevitable. But is it acceptable? Frederick Wilhelmsen writes:

The attempt to love a person for his or her qualities – be they spiritual or physical, intellectual or temperamental – deteriorates into a kind of prostitution in which the person is used and valued for what he does and has. Relationships based on the mutual admiration of qualities end in disillusion and often in bitterness. (1962, p. 37; quoted in Pieper 1997b, p. 204)

Extension of the *amor amicitiae* beyond the self requires us to make the arduous effort of loving another *as a person* – that is, for her very self, rather than for the qualities that attach to that self. If this possibility is to be anything more than notional, we must recognize something about the self beyond the enumerable qualities that constitute its essence. What does this mean? Perhaps the best path to understanding is a *via negativa*. When I say that "I love you for your own sake," I mean that I do not love you for your beauty, I do not love you for your wit, I do not love you for your judgment (as considerable as all three might be). If one person loves another with *amor amicitiae*, she loves him on account of something that underlies and transcends these desirable qualities.

The treatment of love in itself culminates in the *amor amicitiae*. By structuring Question 26 in this manner, Aquinas anticipates the place of *caritas* among the theological virtues. If *amor amicitiae* is the highest kind of love, why does Thomas nonetheless maintain the primacy of love as a passion? *Amor sensitivus* constitutes the natural starting-point for love as experienced by the embodied creature. It is, as I have observed (§5.2), the soil from which rational love grows. Pieper makes a helpful distinction between the "incipient stages" of love and its ultimate actualization. Incipient love may contain a good deal of *amor concupiscentiae*. We are attracted to other persons or things because they fit into our plans. They serve our own ends. If such love is to mature into *amor amicitiae* for another, it must go beyond the realm of attributes. It must, as Pieper writes,

penetrate to the core of the person who stands behind these qualities and who "has" them, to the true subject of that unimaginable act that we call existing, to the beloved's innermost self, which *remains* even when the lovable qualities long since have vanished, those same qualities that once upon a time, far back at the beginning, may have approximated a "reason" for love. (1997b, p. 205)

Love goes beyond reasons. But in affirming this view, Aquinas does not endorse the "voluntarist" view of love as pure act of will detached from apprehension. Rational perception of the good is involved in two ways. First, it enables us to perceive attractive qualities that belong to the beloved's *essentia*. These qualities often give love its *incipit*. Second, it leads toward perceiving the other in a way that corresponds to her very being, transcending what is captured by any list of attributes. Construed as a claim about the attractive qualities that motivate incipient love, the view expressed by Pascal contains much truth. But if such love is to mature into genuine *amor amicitiae* for another, it will move beyond a person's qualities toward an affirmation of the other's being, her *esse*. As Pieper writes:

The test question . . . is *not*: Do you find the other person likeable, capable, "nice"? Rather, the question is: Are you glad for his existence, or do you have anything against it; can you honestly say, "It's good that he exists"? (1997b, p. 205)

5.4 WHAT CAUSES LOVE?

What causes love? Aquinas has already given an abbreviated answer to the question. As a passion, love is caused by a desirable thing (*appetibile*) acting upon the appetite (cf. 26.2). Aquinas immediately reaffirms this answer in the first Article of Question 27. "Properly, the cause of love is the object of love" (27.1.co). But what makes something an object of love? Thomas must expand the compressed answer that he has already given. For something to cause love, it must be a good, since appetite is the inclination toward the good which completes its possessor (Article 1). In order for the good to exert its causal power in beings with sensation, it must somehow be cognized. Thus *cognitio* is a cause of love (Article 2). Aquinas makes his own the Aristotelian doctrine that any act of cognition involves contact between things that are like one another in some respect. Thus likeness is also a cause of love (Article 3). Finally, since love names the appetite's first inclination toward the good, no other passion can be prior to love in the causal order (Article 4).

The dialectic of Question 27 begins with objectors who argue that not only good things are objects of love. The first objector argues that "evil is also loved." The second objector offers corroboration, citing Aristotle's maxim that "we love those who acknowledge their evils." Arguing from Dionysian authority, a third objector adds that beautiful things, which do not necessarily seem either good or evil, are loved by all. In the response, Thomas frontally opposes the first claim. "An evil is never loved except under the aspect of good." If one loves iniquity, Aquinas concludes, one loves it only insofar as one sees it leading to a good, such as pleasure or money (27.1 ad 1m). Aquinas quotes Augustine's *De Trinitate* in support of this claim: "Nothing is loved certainly except the good alone" (27.1.sc).[14]

Because evil in itself is nothing, it lacks any direct causal power. Insofar as it can bring about anything, it can do so only by simulating some good. If evil cannot be the *causa amoris*, what about beauty? Beauty can cause love, but not by departing from the good. The reason is that beauty does not differ essentially from the good. "The beautiful is the same as the good, differing from it only in aspect (*sola ratione*)" (27.1 ad 3m). Good calms the desire as such; good specified as beauty calms the desire by being seen or known. The objector offers Aquinas the opportunity to restate the teaching of the 1a *pars* on the relation between beauty and goodness: "that which pleases (*complacet*) the appetite simply is called *bonum*; whereas that of which the very apprehension is pleasing, is called *pulchrum*" (27.1 ad 3m). The view fits ordinary experience. We call any meal that satisfies our appetite "good" (at least in some respect). But we never speak of a meal as "beautiful" unless it is presented in such a way that its very apprehension is pleasing.

Good is the *sola causa amoris*. Rather than multiply causes of love, the subsequent Articles of Question 27 illuminate the various modes by which good exerts its causality. Article 2 considers the role of "knowledge" (*cognitio*) in the causation of love. Aquinas asserts that "the good is not the object of the appetite, except as it is apprehended" (27.2.co). What Aquinas has argued generally with respect to the relation between apprehension and appetition in Question 22 applies particularly to the passion of love. "*Amor* requires some apprehension of the good which is loved" (27.2.co). Thomas will trace the differences among the passions to the differences in their objects, which in turn are reducible not to material

---

[14] This may seem at odds with Augustine's analysis in book 2 of the *Confessions* of the incident in which he stole pears from a garden. But Aquinas would argue that Augustine's analysis does not show that his action is unintelligible. Though the act *qua* sin is nothing, it is nonetheless explainable as a perverse imitation of divine liberty, apprehended *sub ratione boni*. On the pear-stealing episode, see Vaught 2003, pp. 54–65.

differences among goods, but rather to differences among the various ways of apprehending the good (§3.1).

In grounding love in the *apprehensio boni*, Aquinas conveys a complex teaching. First, he holds that knowledge is a precondition for love. One cannot love what one does not know. This view, as expressed by the Augustinian dictum *nullus potest amare aliquid incognitum* (*De Trinitate* 10.1) in the *sed contra*, recalls a basic feature of the architecture of the *ST* itself. Before addressing the human love for God, the *ST* must begin by clarifying the human knowledge of God – even if this means knowing more what God is not than what he is (1.3.pr.). As the invocation of "negative theology" would suggest, full knowledge of a thing is not required in order to love it. This points to the second part of the complex teaching: only *some* apprehension of the good (*aliqua apprehensio boni*) is necessary. As I have already suggested by analysis of the anomalous *ad quartum* of 26.3, love outruns knowledge. Some apprehension of a thing must be present for love to be kindled. But love naturally goes beyond the qualities that we perceive in what is loved. How do we know that our love of something can exceed our knowledge of it? We might point to our love of a newborn baby, love of a spouse, or love of God. Aquinas, however, directs our attention to more mundane examples. That a thing can be loved completely, without being perfectly known, is "most evident in regard to the sciences, which some love on account of some outline knowledge (*aliquam summariam cognitionem*) of them: for instance, they know that rhetoric is a science that enables man to persuade others; and this is what they love in rhetoric" (27.2 ad 2m). This is preeminently true of philosophy, as Plato shows. What prevents someone from being a philosopher is not a lack of knowledge, but a defect in *eros*. When Thomas declares that what applies to the lover of rhetoric is "likewise to be said regarding the love of God" (27.2 ad 2m), he concurs with this Platonic and Augustinian teaching. Although one cannot know God perfectly in this life, one can love him perfectly.

Article 3 asks whether "likeness" (*similitudo*) is a cause of love. That likeness causes love is entailed by the power of *bonum* to generate love. Anything that arouses the motion of the appetite must somehow bear a likeness to the appetite. If it did not, it would not be able to make contact with the appetite. Any contact between mover and moved presumes their resemblance in some respect. Aquinas constantly reminds us of the connection: the *appetibile* is like the *appetitus*. Nonetheless, the issue is complicated. The difficulties are suggested by the inclusion of four objectors in the Article's *videtur quod*. Many particular likenesses seem to bring about hatred. Those alike in pride are contentious; potters quarrel with another. "A man loves in another that which he would not be himself: thus he loves an actor, but would not himself be an actor," says the second objector, quoting Augustine (27.3 arg. 2). We generally love what we lack, and what is hence unlike our present condition. Sick men love health; poor men love riches. Finally, the objections conclude, we love our benefactors, but our benefactors are often unlike us. In short, likeness does not seem to be a reliable cause of love. Against these objections, the argument *sed contra* appears singularly weak: "every beast loves its like" (Ecclus. 13:19; *ST* 1–2.27.3.sc).

Aquinas approaches the question by distinguishing two kinds of *similitudo*. The first arises from two things that have "the same thing in act" (*idem in actu*), as two actually white men are said to be alike. This mode of likeness, in itself, causes the *amor amicitiae*. "For from the fact that two men are alike, as though having one form, they are in a way one in that form." Those who share a common form are naturally drawn to another; each loves the other on account of the same form by which he loves himself. Thus the *amor amicitiae* arises: "The affections of one tend to the other as if in union with himself, and he wishes good to the other as he wishes it to himself" (27.3.co). Things sharing the same form are naturally inclined toward one another. Why, then, are things that are alike so often opposed to one another? Part of the answer is contained in the argument of the previous Article. If the likeness is to produce love, it must be decisive in a person's apprehension. If this condition is absent, the likeness loses its power to generate love.

The second *similitudo* arises when one thing has "in potency and in a certain inclination" (*in potentia et in quadam inclinatione*) what another thing has *in actu* (27.3.co). This kind of likeness also generates love, that is, the *amor concupiscentiae*. If Brown actually possesses what Jones wants but lacks, Jones will desire it with the *amor concupiscentiae*, as a means to his own satisfaction. This is the basis of utility and pleasure friendships. It corresponds to what C.S. Lewis calls "need-love" (1960, pp. 12–21). Need-love is not necessarily bad. "He who loves what he needs has a likeness to that which he loves, as potency is to act" (27.3 ad 2m). Need-love – that is, the *amor concupiscentiae* – is a natural aspect of any relation where one person possesses a good *in actu*, and the other *in potentia*. "One seeks a midwife for his thoughts, another someone to whom he can be a midwife: thus originates a good conversation" (Nietzsche 1966, p. 100). The same is true of a cook and diner, a husband and wife, or man and God.[15] Nonetheless, the inclination toward something possessed by another, in order to acquire what one lacks, is not the highest kind of love. It is parasitic on the *amor amicitiae*.[16]

In light of the power of both modes of *similitudo* to cause love, why does likeness seem to generate rivalry and hatred? Aquinas writes:

> A man loves himself more than another, since he is one with himself in his substance, and one with another only in the likeness of some form. And thus, if he is impeded from acquiring the good he loves by that which is like himself in the participation of a form, the result is that he becomes hateful to him. This happens not to the extent that he is like him, but to the extent that he is an impediment to acquiring his good. (27.3.co)

One woman at a party hates another woman, not because she is like her in beauty, but because she prevents her from being known as the most beautiful woman in the room. Two academics at the same conference in German philosophy hate one another – not because they both study Hegel, but because each wants to be recognized as the *Mensch* who excels others in all things Hegelian. In itself, likeness draws people together: *similitudo, propie loquendo, est causa amoris* (27.3.co). But when likeness of form prompts comparison in relation to an external good, the result may be hatred. Thus the objectors are not wrong to cite the scriptural verse that "there are contentions among the proud" (Proverbs 13:10), or Aristotle's observation that "potters quarrel among themselves." As Rousseau clearly sees, likeness breeds comparison, and comparison engenders rivalry (1987, pp. 63–4).[17] To put the point in another way: likeness *simpliciter* causes love, whereas likeness that arouses comparison with respect to a

---

[15] Writing as a spokesman for the discipline of modern academic psychology, Stanovich (1989) suggests that only those threatened by scientific progress embrace "folk psychology." "Psychology's threat to folk wisdom," he explains, "disturbs some people" (p. 31). As an example of "how psychology treats folk wisdom and treats it scientifically," Stanovich offers the following: "Here then is a message for everyone who at one time or another has stated that 'opposites attract': you were wrong. Psychologists have done much research on interpersonal attraction, and the results point strongly in one direction: 'Birds of a feather flock together'" (p. 31). Here one might recall the principle of non-contradiction: nothing can be A and ~A *in the same respect*. Aquinas can acknowledge the truth contained in both maxims. "Opposites attract": two persons, each of whom has something the other lacks but desires, are drawn together by *amor concupiscentiae*. "Birds of a feather flock together": friends bound in a different respect by *amor amicitiae* are attracted by what they have in common. Stanovich complains that modern academic psychology is the "Rodney Dangerfield of the sciences" (p. 145). If it were to acknowledge and learn from the tradition (as certain branches of it already do), it might earn more respect.

[16] The problem is not so much *amor concupiscentiae* itself, as the deceptions and obfuscations that cause people to mistake as friendship-love what is only need-love.

[17] In Aquinas' terms, the *zelus invidiae* is the inevitable result of conceptions of the good that include malevolence against one's neighbor. See 28.4 ad 2m: "from a defect of goodness, it happens that

scarce good tends to produce hatred. If two Plato scholars are interested in acquiring a deeper understanding of the *Republic*, rather than increasing their reputation, the commonality will generate an *amor amicitiae* between them. As Socrates shows in his interrogation of Thrasymachus, the just man (the only person capable of real friendship-love) does not try to get the better of his like. Only the unjust man attempts to get the better of another who resembles him (*Republic* 349b–350d).

The first three Articles elucidate a point that is fundamental for Aquinas' thinking about the passions, namely that good is the *sola causa amoris*. But if love is the cause of the other passions, it follows that good must be the cause of all the passions. Aquinas' principal *auctoritas* on the primacy of the good is Dionysius. That Dionysius is among the most important authorities for Aquinas' thinking about love (only Augustine can compete with him) is often neglected. If Question 27 on the cause of love is thoroughly Dionysian in its identification of the power of good to cause love, Question 28 on the effects of love will manifest an even greater dependence upon the Areopagite. Question 27 concludes by asking whether any other passion of the soul is a cause of love. We have already seen the basic argument in Article 2 of Question 25. That both Articles should quote the same passage from Augustine in the *sed contra* is not accidental. All the other passions presuppose love, because "every other passion of the soul suggests either motion toward something, or rest in something" (27.4.co). Love as such, however, does not presuppose any other passion. It is true, as Aquinas acknowledges, that particular loves may be generated by things that are immediately desired on account of some other passion. In this sense, "desire of one thing can be the cause whereby another thing is loved" (27.4 ad 2m). But in the background of such desire stands a prior love. As good is prior to evil (§1.4), so love is prior to the other passions. The primacy of love anticipates the status of *caritas* as the mother of all the other virtues (see 62.4.co). Thomas will reiterate this fundamental teaching as he progresses through the Questions on the passions. So, for example, in the opening Question on anger, we are reminded that "love is the first root of all the passions" (46.1.co). Here he concludes that no passion is more basic than love, because love is the

certain small goods cannot, in their entirety, be possessed by many at the same time: and from the love of such things arises the zeal of envy." This explains the transition from *superbia* to *invidia* in Dante's *Purgatorio*: the type of *eccellenza* that Oderisi reveals himself to have pursued in canto 11, line 87 (and line 91: "Oh vana gloria de l'umane posse!") naturally gives rise to the *invidia* that identifies one's own good with another's misfortune (see Dante 2003, p. 176).

first inclination toward good (§1.4). "There is no other passion of the soul which does not presuppose some love" (27.4.co; see §3.5). Love is the first root of the other passions; it is not caused (except *per accidens*) by some other passion.

If love is caused by a good, what does it cause? What does *amor* bring about? In Question 28, Thomas wants to show that love has a wide range of psychical and physical effects. They are, in order of appearance:

union (*unio*, Article 1)
mutual inhesion (*mutua inhaesio*, Article 2)
ecstasy (*extasis*, Article 3)
zeal (*zelus*, Article 4)
wounding of the lover (*laesiva amantis*, Article 5)
all things done by the lover (*omnia quae amans agit*, Article 6)

Articles 1–4 discuss the formal effects of love. The primary effect of *amor* is union, which in turn causes the complementary effects of *inhaesio* and *extasis*. *Inhaesio* describes the dwelling of the beloved in the lover; *extasis* refers to the lover's being taken out of himself when he dwells in the beloved. Since *inhaesio* and *extasis* are intense, they characteristically produce *zelus*, which may be either good or bad for the lover. In Article 5, Thomas turns to the somatic effects of *amor*. Article 6 closes by reiterating that all human action may be traced to *amor* as its cause.

First among the effects of love is union (*unio*). Union is a necessary effect of love, in terms of which the remaining effects must be understood. But in what sense are the lover and the beloved united? The objectors illuminate the nature of *amor*'s union by showing what it cannot be. Love cannot produce either union of essence or union of likeness. But what kind of union does *amor* produce? Aquinas distinguishes between two kinds of union: union "according to the thing" (*secundum rem*), and union "according to affection" (*secundum affectum*) (28.1.co). The latter is what Thomas has already described as the *complacentia* or *coaptatio* of the lover in the thing loved (§5.2). *Complacentia* indicates a positive affection of the lover toward the beloved; it is a connection of sorts. But it naturally seeks a more palpable union. Thus the *unio secundum coaptationem affectus* is not only the formal cause of *amor* ("ipse amor est talis unio vel nexus") (28.1.co), but also serves as the efficient cause of *unio secundum rem*. Union in the order of intention leads the lover to strive after union in the order of things. This may sound trivial, but consider the implications of its denial. If a person says something to the effect that "I love her, but I do not care if I am ever with her again," can he love her in any real sense? As the presence of the beloved to the lover, *unio* is not merely one possible consequence of love, but its necessary effect. Union *secundum rem* is the natural goal of union *secundum affectum.*

If realized union requires the union of affection, the union of affection presupposes something still more basic. "A certain union (*quaedam unio*) is the cause of love," says Aquinas (28.1 ad 2m). In the case of self-love, this "certain union" is substantial union. In the case of love directed to others, it is union of likeness. As we have seen from Question 27, Article 3, the union of likeness causes both *amor concupiscentiae* and *amor amicitiae.* The former is evidently reducible to self-love. But is this not any less true of friendship-love? To what extent does Thomas want to dispel this impression? Here is the response:

When someone loves a thing as by concupiscently wanting it (*concupiscens illud*), he apprehends it as belonging to his own well-being. Likewise, when someone loves a person by the *amor amicitiae*, he wishes good to that person just as he wishes good to himself, whence he apprehends him as another self, wishing him good to the extent that he wishes good to himself. (28.1.co)

Aquinas is remarkably unconcerned to dispel any fear that all love is a sublimation of self-love.[18] Love for others, proceeding from the *unio similitudinis*, is modeled on the love of self which proceeds from the *unio substantialis*. Pieper observes that, far from suggesting that self-love is an image of friendship, Aquinas intends just the opposite: "Friendship is the image and self-love is the original; we love our friends as we love ourselves" (1997b, p. 236). The ontological priority of substantial union to the union of likeness cannot be evaded or overcome. Aquinas claims that "a man loves himself more than another, because he is one with himself in substance, but one with another only in the likeness of some form" (27.3.co). This is not a state of affairs that requires some drastic reversal. It is the natural condition. As such, it may need to be transcended, but it neither can nor should be undone. Thus Aquinas unites pagan and Christian antiquity in a single sentence: "Hence a friend is said

---

[18] The fear will be felt most acutely by those who agree with Nygren (1937) that "no way, not that of sublimation either, leads from eros to agape" (p. 35; quoted in Pieper 1997b, p. 213).

to be another self, and Augustine says, in *Confessions* IV, 'Well indeed did one say to his friend, you are half my soul'" (28.1.co).[19]

Unio secundum rem surpasses union that exists only according to intention. But it is not an impossible condition in which the being of the lover is entirely submerged or lost in what he loves. Love between two subjects is always a union between things that remain essentially distinct. The union of the lover and the beloved never brings about the complete absorption of either in the other. "We're one, but we're not the same": the lyric perfectly captures the non-negotiable limit of love.[20] If the love we naturally bear ourselves is ineliminable, our love for others cannot require or result in a literal loss of self.

But what is this union, if not the total blending of two selves into a whole lacking distinct parts? The paradigm case, according to Aquinas, is "when the beloved is in the presence of the lover" (28.1.co). The lovers of Aristophanes' speech in the *Symposium*, known to Aquinas from Aristotle's report in book 2 of the *Politics*, recognize that if they were to become one according to union by essence, they would be destroyed. Since they wish their own fulfillment rather than their destruction, the union they seek is not union by essence. It is a union "which is suited for and becoming to" (28.1 ad 2m) the creature that has its own being ("God-given, certainly, but for that very reason given to us to be truly our own" [Pieper 1997b, p. 218]), and cannot avoid willing its own fulfillment.[21] Far from being a mystical loss of selfhood, the appropriate union between embodied creatures is the union of presence. Such union, Aquinas says, is typically experienced in mundane activities like "living together and speaking together" (28.1 ad 2m). We may protest that our deepest desire is to lose ourselves in the being of the other. But is not even this romantic dream grounded in the basic, non-negotiable desire for self-fulfillment?

Like faith and reason, the lover and beloved are united, but remain distinct. Neither element of each pair can be swallowed up in the other.

---

[19] In light of these reflections, one might agree (with some qualifications) with Nietzsche's blast in *Ecce Homo* against "that gruesome nonsense that love is supposed to be something 'unegoistic.' One has to sit firmly upon *oneself*, one must stand bravely on one's own two legs, otherwise one is simply *incapable* of loving. Ultimately, women know that only too well: they don't give a damn about selfless, merely objective men" (1967, p. 266). And see Larkin (1988): "The difficult part of love/Is being selfish enough,/Is having the blind persistence/To upset an existence/Just for your own sake./What cheek it must take" ("Love," p. 150).

[20] U2, "One," on *Achtung Baby* (Island Records, 1991). Compare Michelet's *L'Amour*. "Pour s'unir il faut rester deux" (1859, p. 398; quoted in Pieper 1997b, p. 246).

[21] Cf. Bogliolo (1997): "It is difficult to found a Christian ethics without the presupposition of creation" (p. 116).

Article 1 of Question 28 presents an eminently "sober" teaching on love. The next three Articles appear to qualify this teaching. After union, love produces three other effects: mutual inherence (*mutua inhaesio*), ecstasy (*extasis*), and zeal (*zelus*). In Article 2, Aquinas discovers mutual inherence to have four dimensions. Regarding both the apprehensive power and the appetitive power, the lover is said to be in the beloved, and the beloved said to be in the lover. None of these dimensions negates the distinctness of lover and beloved. But they do suggest that love, in its most intense form, includes but goes beyond the mundane activities of togetherness noted in Article 1. Thus, for example, the lover is said to be in the beloved, according to the apprehension, "to the extent that the lover is not content with a superficial apprehension of the beloved, but strives to inquire into the singular things that belong to the beloved's inmost being" (28.2.co). As we have seen from Article 2 of Question 27, love in its beginnings requires only a minimal knowledge of the loved. But it necessarily presses forward – in a manner more reminiscent of intoxication than of sobriety – to know as much as it can about the beloved, so that it may be more perfectly united with its object. Although the passions can stand in the way of knowledge, they can also be powerful forces in the service of its acquisition (§4.3).[22]

Does the lover's drive to perfect his union with the beloved result in ecstasy? As its name would suggest, *extasis* is a condition whereby the lover "stands outside himself" (*ex*, "out of" + *stare*, "to stand"). Eminently sober folk, the objectors point to familiar cases of lovers who, however much in love, are in control of themselves. Only a gauzy romanticism takes literally the notion that lovers go out of themselves into the beloved. It seems more realistic to say that the lover draws the beloved to himself. This view, moreover, coheres better with the teaching that one cannot love another more than one loves oneself. Aquinas grants these objections no small share of truth. Even in the most intense case of ecstasy, that of the appetitive power, Thomas is willing to speak only of a person "going outside himself in a certain way" (*exiens quodammodo extra seipsum*) (28.3.co).

Within this limited ecstasy of the embodied creature's appetite, Aquinas allows a distinction between two modes of outgoing. The ecstasy that is

---

[22] On the value of the passions for knowledge, La Rochefoucauld (1959) remarks: "Nature, it seems, has buried deep in our minds skill and talents of which we are unaware; the passions alone have the function of bringing them to light and thereby sometimes giving us a clearer and more comprehensive vision than ingenuity could ever do" (§404, p. 89).

an effect of the *amor concupiscentiae* is temporary and circumscribed, since the *telos* of any concupiscent motion toward a thing outside the self is always to possess the thing for oneself. Because "such affection, *in fine*, is concluded within the self," it is ecstasy "not simply, but only relatively" (*non simpliciter, sed secundum quid*) (28.3.co). Ecstasy, simply speaking, is an effect of the *amor amicitiae*. When a person loves another simply and for her own sake, she transcends her tendency to desire things merely as means to her own gratification. In this sense, she goes outside herself (*extra se exit*). Following the Dionysian habit of describing this phenomenon is useful. But Thomas is careful not to literalize the notion. Even in its purest form, going out of oneself remains tethered to the act of remaining within oneself, the union that has been described as substantial union. If a lover can love another as much as himself, can he really love her *more* than he loves himself? The third objector suggests that such a thing is plainly false ("patet esse falsum"). Aquinas can only agree. Although friendship-love generates ecstasy *simpliciter*, the lover does not will good to his friend more than he wills it to himself. Whence "it does not follow that he loves another more than he loves himself" (28.3 ad 3m).

Aquinas does not want a notion of ecstasy that opposes self-love and love of the other. Yet he does not dispense with the notion of *exstasis*. Rather, he applies it to the apprehensive as well as the appetitive power. If reason can be raised above its connatural apprehension, it can equally fall beneath it, as when overcome (*passus*) by *furia* or *amentia*. I would hazard that Thomas's deepest intention in the *ST* is to produce a rational ecstasy, an elevation of the reason beyond its connatural apprehension that does not destroy its rational character, but perfects it. Such elevation is legitimately described as ecstasy, perhaps even as divine madness, but it does not entail a loss of self. It leads to another kind of occurrence, one that Aquinas (no less than Socrates) was attested to exemplify in his own life: "intense meditation on one thing draws the mind away (*abstrahit*) from other things" (28.3.co).[23]

Article 4's treatment of "zeal" (*zelus*) completes the qualification of what initially seems to be a simply "sober" teaching on the effects of love. Zeal is the natural effect and trustworthy sign of love. Where zeal is lacking, it is probable that either no real love exists, or that the love is

---

[23] The most memorable account of Thomas's legendary *abstractio mentis* may still be Chesterton 1956, pp. 97–101. For Socrates' abstraction, see *Symposium* 220c–d.

merely the *lento amore* that lies at the heart of sloth (*Purgatorio*, canto 17, line 130; cf. Dante 2003, p. 282). If, for example, a man professes to love a woman as a friend, but consistently remains unmoved in the face of obstacles that prevent her from attaining her good, his claim to love her is doubtful. Zeal is the ordinary byproduct of love, whether this be the *amor amicitiae* or the *amor concupiscentiae*. The type of zeal present offers a clue to the character of the *amor* from which it proceeds. Our most familiar experience of zeal may correspond to the "zeal of envy" (*zelus invidiae*). A better kind of zeal, however, proceeds from the *amor amicitiae*. It is what the *Glossa ordinaria* calls the *bonus zelus*, and what Dante glosses more amply as the "righteous zeal which in due measure glows in the heart" (*il dritto zelo che misuratamente in core avvampa*) (*Purgatorio*, canto 8, lines 83–4; cf. Dante 2003, p. 130). When a person's love is rightly directed toward another's good, Aquinas says, "it causes a man to be moved against everything that opposes the friend's good." *Il dritto zelo* accompanies *amor amicitiae* in general, but especially the love of God: "Some person is said to be zealous for God (*pro Deo*), when he endeavors, according to his power (*secundum posse*), to repel those things which are contrary to the honor or will of God" (28.4.co). Both types of zeal, Aquinas emphasizes, stem from love. To the objection that the *zelus invidiae* may equally be said to arise from hatred, Thomas replies succinctly: "The very fact that someone possesses hate toward those things that oppose what he loves, proceeds from love. Whence zeal is properly set down as an effect of love rather than of hatred" (28.4 ad 3m). All the passions, even hatred, have love as their cause (§3.5, §5.4).

Articles 1–4 of Question 28 delineate the effects of love in a way that accords with experience. Article 5, similarly, takes its point of departure from lived experience, asking whether love is a wounding passion (*passio laesiva*). The sensations of faintness (*languor*), softness or melting (*liquefactio*), and intense heat (*fervor*) are familiar to lovers. Ought not they to be included among love's effects? If so, it would appear that *amor* is not only an inclination to what is suitable or perfective, but also – and more palpably – a "wounding and corruptive passion" (*passio laesiva et corruptiva*) (28.5 arg. 2). In order to do justice to both experiences – love as perfective, love as corruptive – Aquinas deploys the distinction between the material and formal element of the passions (§2.3). Formally, love is an inclination to the suitable, because it does not originate except through the apprehension of something as suitable. If the beloved is actually *conveniens*, then love can only be "perfective and better-making" (*perfectivus et meliorativus*) (28.5.co). If, however, the beloved is only apprehended as suitable, without being such, then the lover will necessarily be "wounded and impaired" (*laeditur et deterioratur*) (28.5.co). What the objectors say about love generally applies mostly to love that is misdirected or disordered. The "proximate effects" that ensue from the change in the appetite (as distinguished from any bodily organ) are *liquefactio, fruitio, languor,* and *fervor* (28.5.co). Beyond these, any number of effects proportionate to these, but caused by a change of bodily organ, can ensue. Aquinas acknowledges these effects, while being content to leave their enumeration and description to others.

Is love the cause of everything the lover does? Perhaps to underscore the importance of the doctrine, Aquinas closes the sequence of Questions on love with a final declaration of its causal power. Since he has already argued that without love no other passion would exist, he can afford to be brief. Because every agent acts for an end, the response argues, and the end is some *bonum desideratum et amatum*, it is manifest that every agent, whatever it might be (*quodcumque sit*), performs every action (*quamcumque actionem*) from some love (*aliquo amore*). The selection of adjectives recalls the universality of *amor*, the theme with which Aquinas began Question 26 on love in itself. Every agent acts from love; every action proceeds from love. Although this is true of action as such, as Aquinas makes clear in the *ad primum*, citing Dionysian authority, it is most evidently true of actions inspired by a passion. "Every action which proceeds from some passion, proceeds also from love, as from a first cause" (28.6 ad 2m).

Because *amor* is the root of the other passions, Aquinas places love at the head of his treatment. The most decisive authority for securing the primacy of love, and indeed for Questions 26–8 as a whole, is Dionysius.[24] Thus we may conclude, at least provisionally, that Aquinas' consideration of the fundamental passion, and therefore his treatment of the passions as such, has a deeply Platonic character, even as it makes use of Aristotelian materials throughout. As Pinckaers suggests, Question 28's consideration of love's effects "evokes directly the language and the experiences of Christian mysticism; the numerous citations of the *De divinis nominibus*

---

[24] This may appear to be contradicted by the fact that Aristotelian authority is cited twelve times, and Dionysian authority nine times. But this objection presupposes that the Aristotelian and the Dionysian citations in this context have the same character. For a clear and convincing argument that assessments of Thomas's handling of *auctoritates* based simply on quantity are gravely misleading, see Jordan 1992a, pp. 21–30, and especially pp. 24–5.

of Denys the Areopagite are there to confirm it" (1990, p. 382).[25] The importance of Dionysius for Aquinas is difficult to overstate. "Denys a la charité: il était en place" (Pascal 1976, §568, p. 209; cf. Pascal 1966, §762, p. 259). The primacy of love among the passions in the 1a2ae points ahead to the place of *caritas* among the theological virtues in the 2a2ae.

---

[25] In view of the importance of Dionysius for Thomas's analysis of love (and therefore every other passion), it is puzzling that Gondreau (2002) should include Dionysius among the "marginal sources" of Aquinas (p. 128). It is, of course, true that Dionysius is not cited as often as other *auctoritates*. But Gondreau himself presents the argument, citing Jordan and Lafont, that a census of citations is a poor criterion for judging the ultimate importance of a source (pp. 116–17). Mauro (1974) makes a similar mistake, omitting Dionysius altogether from his otherwise insightful review of sources (p. 27).

CHAPTER 6

Hatred and concupiscence

When he turns to the passion of hatred, Aquinas departs from his usual scheme of treating the essence of the passion first, followed by a consideration of causes and effects. Instead, he begins with the cause of hatred (§6.1), and proceeds to ask what kinds of things qualify as the objects of hatred (§6.2). After examining hatred, Aquinas moves to the passion of "desire or concupiscence." The treatment of this passion seems abbreviated, since Aquinas chooses to devote only one Question to it – and no Question at all to the passion he had earlier identified as its direct contrary, aversion. Despite its abbreviated character, the treatment of concupiscence is pivotal. After showing why concupiscence does not name the motion of the concupiscible power in general, but picks out a particular passion (§6.3), Aquinas proceeds to illuminate an important distinction between one type of concupiscence that all beings with sensation have, and another type that, while a passion in the proper sense and not a pseudopassion (see §2.2), is possible only for beings with intellect. This Aquinas calls "rational" or "non-natural" concupiscence (§6.4).

6.1 THE NON-ESSENCE OF HATRED

Aquinas devotes only one Question to hatred (*odium*), the second of the eleven primary passions. The same pattern holds for the brief treatments of concupiscence (Question 30), hope/despair (Question 40), and daring (Question 45). In the Questions on hope/despair and daring, Thomas employs the same tripartite scheme that structures the three Questions on love. He asks about (1) the passion in itself, (2) its cause, and (3) its effects. In Question 29's consideration of *odium*, by contrast, this scheme drops out. Only its second component is clearly visible. Aquinas begins Question 29 with the *causa odii*, asking about the roles of evil (Article 1) and love (Article 2) in the causality of hatred. As causes are superior to their effects, he adds, so love is stronger than hatred (Article 3). In the final half of the Question, Thomas does not directly ask about the effects of hatred. His goal, rather, is to clarify the relation of hatred to its targets and to ascertain its proper scope. One's self does not belong among the possible targets of hatred, Aquinas argues (Article 4), but particular truths may be an object of hatred, to the extent that they seem to oppose the self (Article 5). Question 29 closes with an inquiry into whether hatred can be directed toward the universal (Article 6).

Not all commentators have noticed the distinctive character of Question 29's *ordo articulorum*. Ramírez forces the treatment of hatred into the essence/cause/effect scheme, apparently convinced that if Aquinas uses the scheme for the other passions, he must do so for hatred as well. Accordingly, he begins with a commentary *de ipso odio secundum se*, subdivided into *de natura vel essentia odii* and *de divisione odii* (1973, pp. 154–5). But Thomas conspicuously lacks a treatment *de ipso odio*. This absence, we suppose, reveals something essential about hatred. Because we cannot hate a thing as such, as Thomas will argue, hatred has no "in itself" character. Thus the omission of a section on the essence of hatred is perfectly appropriate.

Like evil, hatred is not a thing with an essence of its own. Nonetheless, some account of the phenomenon must be given. Thus Aquinas begins by asking whether evil is the cause of hatred. The *sed contra* of Article 1 provides a summary statement of the key relations: as the object of love is *bonum*, so the object of hatred is *malum*. This creates the expectation that *malum* and hatred will bear the same relation to non-being as *bonum* and love bear to being. The response fulfills this expectation with a musical metaphor. Love is a "certain consonance of the appetite" (*consonantia quaedam appetitus*); hatred is a "certain dissonance of the appetite" (*dissonantia quaedam appetitus*) (29.1.co). Dissonance is not a thing in itself; it presupposes a prior harmony that has been altered or distorted. It exists, but only parasitically. Hatred is a loathing that cannot exist except in a being that loves the contrary of what is loathed. Love, by contrast, is an affinity for something that exists in itself. It does not require as a precondition the loathing of any other being.[1]

Insofar as it exists, hatred must be caused by something positive – by *bonum*. As we saw at 27.1, *bonum* is the cause of *amor* (§5.4). If there is a sense in which love causes hatred, then it follows that *bonum* as well as *malum* can be the cause of hatred. In Article 2, Aquinas asks whether love causes hatred. The response applies the logic of the previous Article,

---

[1] See Aristotle, *Categories* 11, 14a6: "In the case of contraries, it is not always necessary that if one exists the other should also exist: for if all became healthy there will be health and no disease, and again, if everything turns white, there will be white, but no black."

reiterating the comparison of love to *consonantia* and hatred to *dissonantia*. Aquinas then claims:

In any particular thing, it is necessary first to consider what is suitable to it, before considering what is repugnant to it. For something is repugnant to another, since it corrupts or impairs what is suitable to it. Whence it is necessary that love is prior to hatred, and that nothing is hated, unless it is contrary to a suitable thing that is loved. Accordingly every hatred is caused from love. (29.2.co)

Perhaps one can conceive hatred and love on equal terms, since their objects present themselves simultaneously *secundum rationem.* But in the order of things, *secundum rem,* love is prior to hatred, and therefore its cause (29.2 ad 1m). That Aquinas holds this position is clear: "love of one thing is the cause of one's hating its contrary" (29.2 ad 2m). The principle seems straightforward, and easy to illustrate. We do not hate to be poor, unless we love money. A dirty office does not bother us, unless we care about a clean workspace.

These examples, however, conceal difficult questions. Does hatred of poverty necessarily imply a corresponding lust for riches? What if I simply dislike my inability to pay the rent? Does aversion to a dirty office entail any real love for cleanliness? If the principle is not to violate our ordinary experience, it requires some interpretation. In the *Categories* (ch. 5, 3b24), Aristotle argues that one substance is not the contrary of another substance. That I love spicy food does not entail that I hate mild food, since spicy food and mild food are not contraries. They are substances, things with contrary qualities, but not themselves contrary things. I can enjoy them both. Whatever the principle means, it cannot mean that my hatred of a particular thing is caused by my love for another thing which has a quality contrary to some other quality in the thing that I hate.

The principle "Love of one thing is the cause of hating its contrary" does not apply, at least in any straightforward fashion, to a subject's relation to distinct substances. It applies more evidently to the relation between a substance and qualities that it wants to possess or not possess. If a substance desires to have one quality, it is necessarily averse to possessing its opposite: "No substance admits contrary qualities at one and the same moment" (Aristotle, *Categories,* ch. 6, 6a). If I want to be healthy, I necessarily do not want to be sick. But what about the student who generally wants to be healthy, but hopes to wake up sick on a particular day? The example suggests that a temporal index must be included within the principle. I cannot wish to be healthy and sick at the same time.

The principle may thus be restated. If a person (at a particular time) hates to possess one quality, he necessarily (at that same time) loves to possess its contrary. Thus my hatred of disease is caused by my love of health. Disease and health, according to Aristotle (*Categories*, ch. 10, 12a5), do not admit of intermediate degrees; the body is either diseased or healthy. Other contrary qualities, however, do admit of degrees, for instance good and bad. Good and bad are extreme poles on a continuum. If I hate what is extremely bad, does it follow that I love what is extremely good? Or would it be truer to say that hatred for what is bad corresponds to an inclination to what differs from the bad, but not necessarily to what is simply good? My hatred for being a cretin does not entail that I am zealous to become a saint. It seems that we have to state the principle in a way that respects the Aristotelian distinction between the two kinds of contrary qualities. If we are considering qualities that do not admit of degrees, then hatred of one simply entails the love of its contrary. But if the opposed qualities have intermediates between them, an accurate formulation of the principle is more complicated. It would run something like this:

If a person (at a particular time) hates to possess a certain quality, he necessarily loves either: (1) to have (at that same time) the contrary quality, if the quality does not admit of intermediates, or (2) to have (at the same time) either the contrary quality or a negation of that quality that approaches, but is not identical to, the contrary quality.

Thus reformulated, the principle seems more adequate to the phenomena. While hatred of being poor causes a desire to have money, it need not engender a desire to be as wealthy as possible. Our statement of the principle focuses on qualities. Aquinas' formulation of the principle, however, speaks of things rather than qualities: "Love of one thing is the cause of its contrary being hated" (29.2 ad 2m). If I love a thing, in what sense do I hate its contrary? My love for Scotch, a bitter drink, does not necessitate loathing for Thai iced tea, a sweet beverage. Indeed, to consume both in the same evening is pleasurable. When Aquinas says that "it is for the same reason that something (*aliquid*) is loved and its contrary is hated" (29.2 ad 2m), we must understand the "something" with respect to a certain quality that is judged uniquely desirable for a particular thing to have. (So sour Thai iced tea, or sweetened Scotch, would be repugnant, since either monstrosity would possess the contrary of the quality it ought to possess.) With this qualification, the principle seems to correspond to our experience.

"We never love anyone, but only qualities," Pascal says (1966, §688, p. 245). Whether or not this applies to love, it seems true of hatred. We cannot hate a thing as such. We can hate it only on account of some objectionable quality that it possesses. Moreover, we cannot even hate an objectionable quality as such. We find a quality objectionable only because it is contrary to another quality, apprehended as good, toward which we have a positive inclination. Thus the priority of love to hatred reflects the priority of good/being to evil/non-being (§1.4). As Aquinas writes:

A being (*ens*), inasmuch as it is a being, does not have the nature (*ratio*) of repelling (*repugnantia*), but rather of fittingness (*convenientia*), since all things are fitting in their being. But a being, inasmuch as it is a determinate being, has the nature of being repugnant to another determinate being. And because of this, one being is hateable to another, and is an evil – not in itself, to be sure, but through comparison to another. (29.1 ad 1m)

Things are not in themselves objects of hatred. We hate something only because it has a certain quality, which is hateful only by comparison to a contrary quality apprehended as suitable. A thing cannot be hated simply on account of its being. Being as such, *ens inquantum ens*, is *conveniens*. Aquinas refuses to begin Question 29 with a treatment *de ipso odio secundum se*, because he wants to emphasize that to the extent that *malum* is the cause of hatred, it is a product of non-being.

If hatred approaches nothingness, and exists only by the agency of a prior love, why does our experience of hatred seem more palpable, at least on occasion, than our experience of love? Thomas raises this question in Article 3, asking whether love is stronger than hatred. In the order of causality, the answer is evident. Since causes are stronger than their effects, and since turning away from evil is invariably a means to the acquisition of a perceived good, love is stronger than hatred. Ramírez nicely captures this aspect of Aquinas' thinking: "Motion toward the end is stronger in itself than motion toward the means" (1973, p. 160). Nevertheless, Aquinas is aware that our experience may suggest otherwise. He states this forthrightly: "Hatred sometimes seems to be stronger than love, for two reasons" (29.3.co).

First, Thomas acknowledges that "hatred is more sensibly experienced than love" (29.3.co). But why? He recalls that *amor* occurs first as an *immutatio*, a change in the appetite. *Amor* is most strongly felt in two phases: (1) when the appetite is acted upon, "in the very act of being immuted" (29.3.co), and (2) when it strives to obtain what it desires but does not yet have. When the appetite attains its object, love remains, but the feeling subsides. Love of an absent good, as Augustine remarks, is felt more strongly than love of a present good. But any absent good implies some obstacle that stands between the lover and the object of desire. Two passions may thus be compared: love for the desired good, and hatred for the impeding obstacle. Which is felt more strongly? Our experience of a present obstacle, staring us in the face, is more "vivid" than our experience of the absent good. If the obstacle is both present and formidable, our hatred for its existence will be felt more strongly than our love for the absent good. Thus Thomas says that our *repugnantia* for the present obstacle is "perceived more sensibly" than the *convenientia* of the absent good (29.3.co). It is true that we would not regard anything as an obstacle unless it impeded our ability to acquire something that we desire. In the order of intention, love is superior to hatred. But in the realm of felt experience, what counts is the order of execution. Here the apprehension of *repugnantia* often registers more strongly than the perception of *convenentia*, despite the fact that the former would not exist without the latter.

Aquinas gives a second reason for the appearance that hatred is stronger than love. Often we compare strong hatreds with weak loves. Think of someone who loves her reputation more than virtue, even if she professes to love both. If she thinks that acting virtuously in a particular situation will damage her reputation, she will not do what virtue requires. Her hatred for losing face is stronger than her love for virtue. What is clear in this example holds generally: "A hatred which corresponds to a greater love moves a person more (*magis movet*) than does a lesser love" (29.3.co). But the hatred draws its stronger motivational force only from the love to which it corresponds. Far from casting doubt on his position, the phenomenal experience of hatred's strength enables Aquinas to underscore its causal dependence on love.

6.2 WHAT KINDS OF THING CAN BE HATED?

In the second half of Question 29, Aquinas continues to establish the dependence of *odium* on *amor*. But he does so by shifting the focus of the inquiry. Departing once again from the essence/causes/effects scheme, he does not begin an inquiry into the effects of hatred. The decision not to include a section on the effects of hatred might be read as a means of

underscoring its ultimate impotence.[2] Instead of asking about the power
of hatred to produce effects, Aquinas seeks clarity about two of its
potential targets. Article 4 asks whether a man can hate himself; Article 5
asks whether a man can hate the truth. In the Questions on love, Thomas
has already made the argument that self-hatred constitutes a metaphysical
impossibility. Here he emphasizes the point: "It is impossible, speaking
per se, that someone should hate himself" (29.4.co). To hate oneself would
be to will evil toward ourselves, but we cannot will anything toward
ourselves unless we perceive it *sub ratione boni*. This fact can be grasped
by natural reason, as Dante's placement of the following words in the
mouth of Virgil (at *Purgatorio*, canto 17, lines 106–8; cf. Dante 2003,
p. 280) would suggest:

Now, because love can never turn its face away from the well-being of its subject,
all things are safe from self-hatred.

Here Dante captures the core of Thomas's argument. We cannot purely
and simply hate ourselves, although we can will things that are bad for us.
The extreme case would be suicide. Aquinas claims that suicide is not self-
hatred "absolutely speaking" (*per se loquendo*) (29.4.co). It cannot be, since
it is motivated by self-love. La Rochefoucauld proposes, "even those who
deliberately take their own life do not count it as cheap, for they are
startled when death comes by some other way than that of their own
planning, and resist it as strongly as everybody else" (1959, §504, p. 101).
Less aphoristically, Aquinas suggests that "those who kill themselves
apprehend death itself under the aspect of good, inasmuch as it puts an
end to some misery or pain" (29.4 ad 2m). Suicide or any other self-
inflicted evil is hatred only *per accidens*. Thomas notices two ways in
which a person may inflict evil against himself. The first is when he desires
what is good in some respect (*secundum quid*), but evil in itself (*simplic-
ter*), such as suicide. The second occurs when his love for a lower and less
human part of himself exceeds his love for what is higher and more
human. "Some persons estimate themselves as being most of all (*maxime*)
what they are according to their corporeal and sensitive nature" (29.4.co).
Driven by self-love, they act accordingly, preferring sensible goods to
intelligible goods. But because they undervalue or ignore what they really
are, they frustrate their own nature and thus hate themselves *per accidens*.

---

[2] One may contrast this reading with Ramírez's implied suggestion that Thomas is merely using the
second half of the question to "solve difficulties" (1973, p. 162).

This account of self-hatred presupposes some answer to the question: What are human beings "most of all"? Aquinas answers directly: "Man is most of all the mind of man" (*homo maxime est mens hominis*) (29.4.co). Here Thomas is not lapsing into a sharp dualism of soul and body. His thought is the antidote to angelism, since it never proceeds without considering the composite nature of the human person. But Aquinas never supposes that the elements of the composite are equal. *Mens* is the primary part of man. Any approach to life that chooses to ignore the primacy of *mens* will generate self-defeating acts, "sinning against himself, against society, and against God, the master of life," as Ramírez glosses 29.4 ad 2m (1973, p. 164). In some cases, the foolishness of such acts is so apparent that one cannot but help describe them as cases of self-loathing. "He abuses drugs because he hates himself" – statements of this form contain some truth. But such phenomena are not instances of self-hatred *simpliciter*. Rather, they are examples of human action that is motivated by false conceptions of what a person is, and thereby self-frustrating.

No matter how ultimately self-destructive, a person always chooses her acts, when she chooses them, under the aspect of good (*sub ratione boni*). Someone who hates the highest part of herself will be driven by love for another part of herself. Because such a person acts to destroy what is most proper to her being, there is some justification for regarding this syndrome as self-hatred. In *Daybreak* Nietzsche appropriately warns: "We have cause to fear him who hates himself, for we shall be the victims of his wrath and his revenge. Let us therefore see if we cannot seduce him into loving himself!" (1982, §517, p. 207). But because self-hatred *simpliciter* is not possible, we need not literally seduce a person into loving himself. He does that in any case, as Augustine observes (1958, chs. 23–6). Nietzsche's suggestion should be construed as: "let us see if we cannot seduce him into loving the more noble part of himself." From Aquinas' perspective, the question "Should we love ourselves?" is a pseudo-question. The only real question is "In what manner should we love ourselves?"[3]

Article 4 establishes that a man cannot hate himself. Can he hate what is higher than himself? Can he hate God? After denying the possibility of self-hatred, Dante has Virgil say that "because nothing can be conceived

---

[3] Augustine's way of putting the matter at *De doctrina christiana* 1.25 may be helpful: "Thus man should be instructed concerning the way of loving, that is, concerning the way of loving himself properly. To doubt that he loves himself and desires to improve himself is madness. But he must be instructed how he should love his body so that he may care for it in an ordinate and prudent way" (1958, p. 22).

as self-existent or divided from the First, every creature is cut off from hating him" (*Purgatorio*, canto 17, lines 109–111; cf. Dante 2003, p. 282). The first objector of Article 5 makes essentially the same claim: "For good, true, and being are convertible. But a man cannot hate good. Neither, therefore can he hate the truth" (29.5 arg. 1). Aquinas endorses the argument. Since all things seek the good, "good in its very nature (*bonum secundum rationem boni*) cannot be the object of hatred, neither in the universal nor in the particular" (29.5.co). The same applies, Thomas claims, to "being and truth in the universal" (*ens et verum in universali*). But descending to some particular being or truth, one finds that either can be an object of hatred, "to the extent that it has the nature (*ratio*) of the contrary and repugnant" (29.5.co). To apply this to the argument at the center of the *Purgatorio*: a person can hate some particular being or truth that she identifies with God, and thereby imagine herself to hate God. But it will never be God that she is hating. The object of her hatred can only be a simulacrum of God, satisfying at least one of three conditions identified by Aquinas under which some truth is "repugnant or contrary to the good that is loved" (29.5.co). These are: (1) when she wishes that something that is true were not true, (2) when knowledge of truth prevents her from doing as she pleases, and (3) when another learns a truth about her that she would prefer to remain unknown. But no matter how hard she tries, she will never succeed in hating God. Thus Dorothy L. Sayers: "Any appearance of hate against God or the self is one of the delusions of Hell" (1955, p. 201).

If the passion of hatred tends to be activated by some particular being (*quoddam ens*) or some particular truth (*quoddam verum*), as Article 5 seems to suggest, it may seem that hatred bears no relation to the universal. Article 6 corrects this impression. It aims to describe the manner in which the universal can also be an object of hatred. Since the object of a passion, strictly speaking, is a particular sensible thing, it appears that no motion of the sensitive appetite can have a universal as its object. It is true that sensible apprehension cannot perceive the universal as such, because the universal is formed by abstraction. Nonetheless, Aquinas wants to save the truth of a contrary appearance, indicated by Aristotle in the *Rhetoric* (2.4, 1382a): "Anger is directed to something singular, whereas hatred is also directed to a thing in general" (29.6.sc). The sheep does not hate the wolf on account of any qualities that would distinguish this wolf from that wolf. What activates the passion of hatred in the sheep is precisely its apprehension of the attributes that all wolves have in common. In this sense, it is correct to say that the sheep hates the wolf "generally" (*generaliter*) (29.6.co). But such generality does not occur through perceiving the universal "according as it stands under the intention of universality" (*secundum quod substat intentioni universalitatis*) (29.6 ad 3m). It simply requires a pattern of apprehension according to what is common to all things of the same nature (see §1.3).[4] Anger etc., by contrast, requires the agent to perceive an action as originating from an individual (see 46.7 ad 3m). Aquinas makes the point only briefly, postponing elaboration until he arrives at the Questions on anger.

I have emphasized the ontologically parasitic character of hatred. This is the key both to understanding the succession of the three Questions on love by a single Question on hatred, and to interpreting Question 29's internal architecture. Aquinas' perspective should not be confused with bad moralizing against hatred. Since rightly ordered love entails that some things (not in themselves, but insofar as they are hostile to being) are rightly apprehended as *repugnans* rather than *conveniens*, hatred is not simply an undesirable passion. Though hatred should not be cultivated as a good in itself, it is the legitimate corollary of love. The idea that hatred should be despised unconditionally belongs to sentimental retail versions of Christianity. It plays no role in the Christianity of St. Augustine and St. Thomas (or Psalm 139:21). Nietzsche exclaims: "Regard the faces of great Christians! They are the faces of great haters" (1982, §411, p. 175). As usual, Nietzsche is close to the mark. Both Nietzsche and Aquinas agree that "great Christians" are "great haters." Nietzsche even acknowledges that Christians are distinguished by "hate of sin." What, then, is the contrast between Nietzsche and Aquinas? Nietzsche judges that "a Christian who has freed himself from sin is usually afterward ruined by hate of sin." For Aquinas, by contrast, hatred of sin is a prerequisite for growing in love, and thus contributes to the perfection of the human being. If Nietzsche concludes that hatred of sin is unhealthy, he does so on the basis of a judgment that there is no sin, but only "sin."[5] In making this judgment, Nietzsche is no innovator, but the last prophet of the modern gospel according to Machiavelli and Hobbes. If the universe is devoid of

[4] As Ramírez (1973) suggests, the sheep cannot hate the wolf formally, since it lacks the capacity for abstracting logical intentions. But the sheep "materially attains the direct universal, and thus can have such hatred, as when it hates the nature of the wolf, and not only this or that wolf" (p. 166).

[5] For example, Nietzsche suggests that lust is the product of Christianity's determination to "make necessary and regularly recurring sensations into a source of inner misery" (1982, §76, p. 45). The Christian need not object to Nietzsche's statement (at the beginning of the same paragraph) that "the passions become evil and malicious if they are regarded as evil and malicious."

an ultimate end to which all things tend by their nature, then it is indeed difficult to see how there can be genuine sin. Behind the Question on hatred stands not only basic anthropological issues, but also the fundamental question, *quid sit deus?*[6]

6.3 CONCUPISCENCE AS A PASSION

The single Question on *concupiscentia* contains four Articles and any number of surprises.[7] There is not a single mention of sin, original or actual. Sexual desire is never brought forward as the paradigm case of concupiscence. Augustine is not cited once as an authority. Perhaps the biggest surprise is that Question 30 directly raises an issue which commentators tend to consider only with respect to the irascible passions. The issue may be stated as follows. Properly speaking, the passions are motions of the sensitive appetite, caused by the apprehension of a particular sensible thing. Yet the passion of concupiscence, in its distinctively human form, is not caused simply by an act of the senses. Rather, it is activated by an apprehension involving both a rational and a sensible element. A primary goal of Question 30 is to confront this issue. Thomas wants to preserve the status of *concupiscentia* as a passion in the strict sense, as a motion of the sensitive appetite (§2.2), while accounting for the role played by reason in the activation of desire.

In light of this motivation, the *ordo articulorum* of Question 30 becomes apparent. Aquinas begins by establishing the proper sense of *concupiscentia*, anchoring it in the sensitive appetite. Extended meanings of *concupiscentia* may be honored (Thomas cites Romans and the book of Wisdom), provided these are understood to denote a motion of the rational appetite (Article 1). Aquinas proceeds to show that *concupiscentia* does not name just any appetitive orientation toward the sensible good, but picks out something more particular, namely motion toward the absent good (Article 2). Thus the first half of the Question, as Ramírez observes, following Koellin's 1589 commentary, outlines the nature of concupiscence *per genus et differentiam* (1973, p. 169). The Question's second half examines the passion's primary division. Aquinas distinguishes

---

[6] Here I mean to echo the final sentence of Leo Strauss's *The City and Man* (1964, p. 241).

[7] Why does Aquinas treat the nature of *concupiscentia*, but not include any consideration of its cause or its effects? Ramírez (1973) suggests: "Thomas does not inquire into the cause and effect of desire, as he inquired into the cause and effect of love, because these things are determined with sufficient ease" (p. 169).

between natural or animal concupiscence, on the one hand, and non-natural or rational concupiscence on the other (Article 3). To illuminate the principle of this division, Aquinas asks whether there are any limits to concupiscence (Article 4).

Though my reading of Question 30's architecture largely coincides with that of Ramírez, one difference is noteworthy. Throughout his exposition, Ramírez speaks of *concupiscentia seu desiderium* (1973, pp. 167–89). Presumably Ramírez has in mind Thomas's habit in Questions 22–5 of naming the passion as *desiderium vel concupiscentia*, or simply *desiderium*. But when Aquinas arrives at Question 30, things change. He consistently uses *concupiscentia* and avoids *desiderium*. This fact is obscured by Ramírez's treatment. Its reason is suggested by 30.1 ad 2m: "*desiderium* can belong, more properly speaking, not only to the lower appetite, but also to the higher: for *desiderium* does not convey any association in concupiscible-wanting (*in concupiscendo*), as does *concupiscentia*, but a simple motion toward the *desideratum*." In the earlier Questions on the passions *in generali*, Aquinas is content to use the general term. As he moves to the consideration of the passions *in speciali*, he deliberately employs the more proper term (i.e. *concupiscentia*). Such is Thomas's thinking *in actu*, so often missed by his commentators.[8]

Before considering its distinctively human form, Aquinas establishes the notion of concupiscence that is common to animal nature. Article 1 fixes *concupiscentia* as a motion of the sensitive appetite. Improperly or metaphorically, one may speak of acts of the rational appetite as instances of concupiscence. But in the precise sense, concupiscence is a part of the irrational soul, according to Damascene (*De fide orthodoxa* 2.12) and an *appetitus delectabilis*, according to the Aristotelian definition (*Rhetoric* I.11, 1370a17). *Delectatio* is twofold, since pleasure in the intelligible good (*bonum intelligibili, quod est bonum rationis*) is not the same as pleasure in the sensible good (*bonum secundum sensum*) (30.1.co). The object of concupiscence is the latter. What activates the passion is something desired "under the aspect of the good which is pleasurable according to the senses" (30.1 ad 3m).

In specifying the object of concupiscence as the pleasant good, Aquinas raises the question about the relation of this passion to the body and the soul. As an appetite for sensible good, concupiscence might be regarded as simply a bodily thing, bearing no relation to the spirit. Against this view,

---

[8] I remain indebted to Mark Jordan for increasing my own sensitivity to these considerations.

Aquinas reminds us that what desires is not the body, but the whole person. The apprehended good is the "good of the whole composite" (*bonum totius coniuncti*) (30.1.co). To drive the point home, Thomas draws upon an etymology of the term. Concupiscence is *cupiditas* of the body together with the soul (30.1.co).[9]

The description of concupiscence's object as the *bonum delectabile secundum sensum* raises some questions. If the formal object of concupiscence is whatever is pleasurable according to the senses, the objectors of Article 2 wonder, why does *concupiscentia* pick out a specific passion? Would not the description cover what is common to every motion of the sensitive appetite? As a specific passion, *concupiscentia* must have a proper object. To make this clear, Aquinas must clarify the manner in which passions are individuated by their objects. A "material difference of the passions" (*materialem differentiam passionum*) occurs whenever there is difference in the object "according to the nature of the thing" (*secundum rei naturam*) (30.2.co). Apprehending Thursday's dinner and Friday's breakfast as instances of the pleasant good will give rise to two materially different concupiscences. We can point to distinct episodes that correspond to numerically different feelings. But there is no formal difference between the two, since both are instances of the same passion. If all the concupiscible passions were activated by objects which differed as individual things differ from one another, but were invariably apprehended under the same *ratio*, there would be only one kind of passion in the *vis concupiscibilis*. Aquinas agrees with the objectors on this point, but adds that it is possible to apprehend sensible goods (or even a single sensible good) under distinct aspects (*rationes*). Differences in *ratio*, Aquinas argues, give rise to formal differences among the objects (see §3.1).

What are the formal differences? Aquinas limits them to the ways in which the *bonum delectabile secundum sensum* can be perceived as present or absent. Apprehended as present, *bonum* produces the passion of *delectatio*. Apprehended as absent, *bonum* arouses *amor*, occurring when the appetite is initially acted upon and changed by the appetible object, and *concupiscentia*, activated by the appetite's motion toward the desired object. Similarly, the other three concupiscible passions are individuated by formal differences in the apprehended evil. Thus *tristitia* is generated

---

[9] For an expanded etymology that derives the term from *cum* and *cupere*, locating a further connection to *cuppedia* and suggesting an onomatopoeia of "*cup cup*," and "*glut glut*" (whence *glutire*, "to swallow" or "to gulp"), see Ramírez 1973, pp. 170–2.

by a present evil, while *odium* is caused by the initial apprehension of an evil as repugnant. As for the passion that is the direct contrary of *concupiscentia*, Aquinas introduces an ambiguity into his account. At 23.4 he had named it straightforwardly as *fuga vel abominatio*. Now, however, he chooses not to name it, declaring that the *passio quae directe opponitu concupiscentiae, innominata est* (30.2 ad 3m). If an absent evil is apprehended as little or nothing, it gives rise to no passion that is worth speaking about. This is literally true – Aquinas refuses to devote a single Question to the passion to which he had earlier referred by name.[10] If the absent evil is apprehended as something significant – that is, absent but threatening or impending – it gives rise to *timor* or *audacia*.

If the formal object of concupiscence is the pleasurable sensible good, how can the passion have anything to do with reason? Article 1 raises the issue in a preliminary way. Article 2 sharpens the question: by defining what is most essential about *concupiscentia*, its formal object, as sensible good, has Aquinas not precluded the involvement of reason? Article 3 confronts the question directly. It must do so, in order to draw its core distinction between natural and non-natural concupiscence. Before Aquinas elaborates this distinction, however, he locates a prior division between natural and animal concupiscence. Natural concupiscence is the desire for goods "suitable to animal nature," such as food and drink. Like natural love (§1.2), it is a function of the animal's most basic nature, not dependent upon its power of apprehension. As such, it is distinct from specifically animal concupiscence. As Ramírez suggests, it is "innate or purely ontological concupiscence, which is found in all beings" (1973, p. 177). What produces animal concupiscence is anticipated delight in obtaining goods "suitable to an animal according to its apprehension" (30.3.co). As animals, human beings possess this type of concupiscence.

---

[10] Citing a note in Corvez's translation (Thomas Aquinas 1949, p. 237), D'Arcy (2006) suggests that Aquinas does not include a Question on aversion because "it plays too trivial a part in the emotional life: one does not feel strongly about an evil which is easily avoided" (p. 131). More deeply, Ramírez (1973) proposes: "Since the means are reducible in a certain way to the extremes, which with respect to aversion are hatred and fear, the things that pertain to aversion are in a certain way contained in the things that are said of hatred and fear. Because of this, St. Thomas does not pose a special question on aversion, as he had said he would" (p. 192). Manzanedo (1987) echoes this reading – "The explication of this intermediate passion is contained in a certain way in the teaching on hatred and in the teaching on fear" – and adds that "the Thomistic terminology is variable and imprecise, such that Aquinas himself affirms that he treats an 'unnamed' passion" (pp. 229–30). The question is: *Why* does Aquinas employ imprecise terminology? Rather than suppose that he is simply careless, it seems safer to hold that Thomas deliberately moves from the imprecise mode of natural speech to the conclusion that, properly speaking, the obverse of *concupiscentia* has no precise name.

In addition, they possess another mode of concupiscence, proper to rational animals. This is what Aquinas calls "non-natural" (*non naturalis*) or "rational" (*rationalis*) concupiscence.

6.4 "NON-NATURAL" OR "RATIONAL" CONCUPISCENCE

It may seem odd, even contradictory, to describe any form of concupiscence as "rational." Here Pasnau's comment is to the point.

> There is no initial contradiction in the idea of a *rational* appetite doing things that are *foolish*. Aquinas is not at all troubled by the thought that the will regularly chooses foolishly, even irrationally. The will is not a rational appetite in the sense that it always makes the choice that is, all things considered, most rational. To identify the will as rational appetite is simply to identify the source of the will's choices. The will chooses that which reason judges to be best. So if reason can make foolish judgments, the will can make foolish choices. (2002, p. 237)[11]

To make non-natural concupiscence intelligible in a way that distinguishes it from animal concupiscence, Aquinas must identify the rational element within the apprehension that generates concupiscence, while maintaining that concupiscence remains essentially a motion of the sensitive appetite. In the 1a *pars*, Aquinas locates multiple movers of the sensitive appetite: "The sensitive appetite is naturally moved, not only by the estimative power in other animals, and in man by the cogitative power which the universal reason guides, but also by the imagination and sense" (1.81.3 ad 2m). He makes the same point explicitly in the discussion of rational concupiscence. Because man has "not only universal reason, pertaining to the intellectual power, but also particular reason pertaining to the sensitive power," it follows that "even rational concupiscence may belong to the sensitive appetite" (30.3 ad 3m). He adds that "the sensitive appetite can be moved by the universal reason also, through the medium of the particular imagination" (30.3 ad 3m). In light of these texts, one cannot responsibly attribute to Aquinas the view that the sensitive appetite is moved only by sensation (see §3.4).

To the extent that it simply cognizes abstract concepts, reason does not activate passion. Universal reason moves the sensitive appetite only

---

[11] Similarly, Murphy (1999) helpfully distinguishes between "rational" as a label for any case "in which reason has merely produced a judgment" and "rational" as an evaluation "in which reason has judged correctly" (p. 175). What Aquinas calls "non-natural concupiscence" is "rational" only in the first sense.

by means of particular reason or particular imagination. For example, consideration of the proposition "Exercising is good" may cause me to decide to go to the gym. But if I decide to go to the gym, it is by an act of will, which may occur without any accompanying passion. For the sensitive appetite to be moved, there must be more than an act of universal reason (e.g. the calculation "Health is a good to be pursued; exercising promotes health; I should exercise"). If I am to be "fired up" about exercising, where being fired up denotes a palpable motion of my sensitive appetite, something else must occur. I must perceive exercising as a good thing for me to do at this time, in this gym, around these people. It may help to imagine a certain physique and the benefits flowing therefrom as a reward for drudgery. (That exercise is a form of drudgery is confirmed by common experience and Socrates; see *Republic* 357c–d.) For there to be anything more than a volition or pseudopassion (§2.2), the apprehension of the good must be particularized, rendered in hues that are vivid and concrete.

To specify the abstractions of universal reason, so that the sensitive appetite might be aroused, is the work of the particular reason and the imagination. The activation of "rational concupiscence" provides an exemplary instance of how the powers of the soul work together in the activation of passion. Not everyone has seen that for Aquinas, the powers of the soul do work together. Roberts (for example) attributes a "resolute division to the faculties" to Aquinas (1992, p. 297), and suggests that if "reason cannot enter into sense perception," it "remains mysterious" that Aquinas would think that reason plays a role in the origination of anger (1992, pp. 297–8). What is genuinely mysterious is that Roberts would overlook the possibility that for Aquinas, reason can and does interact with sensation. As Leget observes, the perceptual acts which activate passion are for Aquinas always "part of an interchange and cooperation of various faculties of the human soul" (2003, p. 574). Similarly, Pasnau contends that for Aquinas "individual powers rarely work in isolation; the familiar operations that we call perception, thought, and choice all rest on a complexly interconnected sequence of operations" (2002, p. 255). Terruwe and Baars find that the sensitive powers are "strongly influenced by man's higher cognitive faculty, namely, the intellect. Man's intellect not only utilizes the sensory cognitive powers, but it also ennobles them by its greater penetrating power and universality" (1972, pp. 26–7). For analytical purposes, Aquinas is willing to distinguish apprehension into a sensory element and a rational element; but, as Maritain would remind us, *distinguer pour unir.*

What must be present in the apprehension for rational or non-natural concupiscence to occur? Aquinas distinguishes between two kinds of apprehension. What generates natural concupiscence is "simple apprehension" (*apprehensio absoluta*) (30.3 ad 2m). By contrast, when "something is apprehended with deliberation" (*apprehenditur aliquid cum deliberatione*), the result is non-natural or rational concupiscence (30.3 ad 2m). How to interpret the meaning of *deliberatio* in this context is not immediately evident. Aquinas follows Aristotle in suggesting that rational concupiscence is generated by "thinking out (*excogitare*) something as good and suitable, beyond what nature requires" (30.3.co). To take an example from Thomas's commentary on the *Nicomachean Ethics*, nature demands that we sleep. But does it demand that we sleep on "a bed strewn with feathers and costly coverings" (*InNE* 3.20.9; cf. Thomas Aquinas 1993, p. 202)? What generates this type of desire in someone is not natural need, but the opinion that her good requires her to go beyond the satisfaction of natural need. (One may recall Glaucon's desire for the luxurious city [*Republic* 372d–e].) In what way is the *excogitare* a *deliberatio*? Aquinas is not merely claiming that deliberation is simply consequent to passion, as when my desire for some particular pleasurable thing leads me to devise means of acquiring that thing. More interestingly, in rational concupiscence, deliberation does not merely follow the appetite, but plays a special role in the generation of the appetite itself.

To see the manner in which this occurs, consider the single example of rational concupiscence that Aquinas gives in Article 4: the desire for wealth (*divitiae*) that goes beyond what is necessary for life (30.4.co). Since what attracts the person who covets wealth cannot be reduced to the perception of particular sensible qualities, this cannot be an act of animal concupiscence. Yet, if this example is to be a genuine instance of concupiscence, wealth must be apprehended as something pleasant. How does this happen, and why must it involve *deliberatio*? One might object that those who desire non-natural goods do so not as a result of reflective deliberation, but on account of their susceptibility to the lure of socially conferred prestige. Such prestige is less a function of deliberation, the objection would continue, than advertising.

The objection contains some truth. Is there any doubt that Madison Avenue plays a far greater role than rational calculation in the generation of passions for non-natural goods, such as an appetite for fashionable clothes, or the emaciated women who model them? Aquinas' point, however, is not to deny this. It is to say that the identification of particular non-natural goods as pleasant things, far from being self-evident, requires some act of reason, however perverse. The point becomes clearer if we recall the distinction between the formal object of concupiscence, its *ratio*, and the material object. As a material object of concupiscence, wealth is desirable for the pleasure its possession brings. The "reason for the object's desirableness," the *ratio appetibilitatis* (to use the term of *QDV* 25.1) is necessarily *delectatio*. (If the thing is apprehended not as pleasant, but rather as useful or as simply good, the result is not an act of the concupiscible, but either an act of the irascible power or a volition.) But how does wealth materially satisfy this *ratio*? Wealth is not obviously or naturally pleasant. It must be *construed* as pleasant by some act of reason. This act of construing wealth as pleasant is akin to deliberation in the following sense. The person who pursues the good under the *ratio* of pleasure can be understood as (implicitly) asking the question: "Given that I want pleasure, what particular object can satisfy this desire?" He proceeds to investigate possible candidates until he finds a suitable object. (To use the language of 1.7 of the Ia2ae, he seeks the *id in quo* that matches the *ratio*.) Because the process is largely implicit, involving little if any reflective calculation, it falls short of deliberation in the full sense. (Thus Ramírez correctly refers to it as a "quasi-deliberation" [1973, p. 183].) But the act is sufficiently like deliberation to justify an analogous use of the term, since only a rational creature has the capacity to apprehend and desire something as pleasurable, regardless of whether its sensible qualities are naturally delightful.

To summarize: rational concupiscence is a motion of the sensitive appetite toward a good perceived as pleasant, where the perception of the thing as pleasant involves not only the senses, but also an operation of reason that interprets the thing as pleasant. The final Article of Question 30 expands the teaching on rational concupiscence by arguing that it is infinite. Animal concupiscence may be said to be infinite, but only "by succession" (*per successionem*) (30.4.co). An animal is hungry; it eats its food; it is hungry again; it eats once more. The desire is limited by the natural need; no animal desires infinite meat or infinite drink. Rational concupiscence, by contrast, is "altogether without limit" (30.4.co).[12] Why Aquinas holds this may seem obscure. We can easily generate examples of rational concupiscence that go beyond natural need, but nonetheless seem finite. Suppose I desire to possess a large collection of works of modern art.

---

[12] One recalls Hobbes's decision to "put for a generall inclination of all mankind, a perpetuall and restlesse desire of Power after power, that ceaseth onely in death" (1991, p. 70). What Hobbes attributes to human beings as such, Thomas refers to one division of a particular passion.

Certainly my desire is out of proportion to any need belonging to my nature. But is it thereby infinite? Or, to return to Aquinas' own example, suppose that I desire wealth in a way that clearly goes beyond the provision of natural need. Why must this desire be infinite?

Once again, the objection's answer lies in the application of the distinction between the material object of appetite and the formal *ratio* under which it is desired. Concupiscence for particular objects is typically finite. After owning so many yachts, my desire to have more of them will come to an end. When I cease to apprehend them as pleasurable, when I find that they "get old," my passion to possess them will disappear. But the *ratio* under which I desire such objects, that is, their capacity to provide pleasure, will remain intact. The *ratio appetibilitatis* can never be curbed by the limits of any finite thing, since "it belongs to reason to proceed to infinity" (30.4.co). If there are any limits to my appetite for pleasure as such, these arise only through an act of will that subordinates the lower appetite for pleasure to the higher appetite for something else that is perceived as simply good. If the will does not formally place its last end in the *bonum honestum*, it will necessarily choose either pleasure or utility, since there are no other aspects under which it can choose (§1.1). In either case, the person whose will so chooses inevitably becomes the victim of non-natural concupiscence, enjoying lesser goods for their own sake rather than making limited use of them.[13]

Is non-natural concupiscence radically disordered? It seems that it must be, since its essence is to desire every good under the *ratio* of pleasure. Such is the condition of the tyrannical man described by book 9 of the *Republic* (see especially 573a–c). In light of this, why does Aquinas seem reluctant in Question 30 to condemn concupiscence as such? Why does he stop short of holding that concupiscence is necessarily disordered? Part of the answer is contained in the distinction between natural and non-natural concupiscence. Properly directed, according to an accurate estimation of what our natural appetite requires, concupiscence for sensible things is beneficial. More positively, Aquinas acknowledges the capacity of the sensitive appetite to participate in the rational appetite. Here improper usage is not simply loose speech, but provides

---

[13] It would thus appear that only the self-indulgent man, the man who has deliberately placed his last end in pleasure, is capable of rational concupiscence in the proper sense. For anyone else, the appetite for pleasure would be limited by the will.

an important clue to the truth.[14] The Question's first objector observes that the book of Wisdom portrays *sapientia* as an object of concupiscence (30.1 arg. 1). The second objector cites the Psalmist, who suggests that "my soul has sought (*concupivit*) to desire your justifications" (30.1 arg. 2; cf. Psalm 118:20). Far from reproving either objector for improper usage, Aquinas is happy to provide its justification. There is "some likeness" (*similitudo quaedam*) between the desire for lower goods and that for higher goods. More profoundly, the higher part of the soul's desire for wisdom or other spiritual goods can be so intense that it "overflows" (*fit redundantia*) into the lower appetite (30.1 ad 1m). Thus the desire of the lower part of the soul, though properly concerned with sensible goods, can be redirected, so that it too "in its own way" (*suo modo*) (30.1 ad 1m) tends to higher goods. One might understand this process to entail the nullification of concupiscence. But Thomas suggests that it has been reoriented, perfected but not destroyed. Thus does he read Psalm 83: "My heart and my flesh have rejoiced in the living God" (30.1 ad 1m).

When Aquinas prays that he "ardently desire" (*concupiscere ardenter*) the things that are pleasing to God – as he did on a daily basis – one need not be surprised. As part of our nature, *concupiscentia*, desire for things pleasing to the senses, is in itself good. It goes wrong only when it refuses to be subordinated to the rational appetite for the immaterial good. But even here, blame lies less in the passion itself and more in the will's decision to choose the lower good as if it were the higher good. In itself, *concupiscentia* is the natural consequence of *amor* that terminates in either *tristitia* or *delectatio*.

---

[14] As Chenu (1964) observes, although Aquinas is always careful to isolate a word's proper meaning, "this does not mean that he condemns the use of a word in its other meanings, or even in the meanings that have been added to the word or which remain very general" (p. 119).

CHAPTER 7

Pleasure

*The treatment of the passion of pleasure is complex, requiring as many
Questions as Aquinas assigns to the passions in general. In considering
the nature of pleasure, Aquinas draws crucial distinctions between
pleasure and joy, bodily pleasures and spiritual pleasures, arguing in
some detail for the superiority of the latter (§7.1). After describing the
essence of pleasure, Aquinas turns to a detailed consideration of its
causes, distinguishing between the direct cause (operation) and multiple
indirect causes (§7.2). What does pleasure do to a person? What are its
effects? Aquinas considers the sense in which pleasure brings about a
kind of "expansion" or "enlargement" of the soul, whets the appetite for
more pleasure, and constitutes the completion of activities that would be
good even if they did not involve pleasure (§7.3). How are pleasures
related to the human good? Aquinas argues for a strong connection,
arguing that pleasure is not only the natural byproduct of good action,
but constitutes the criterion by which good character may be distinguished from bad (§7.4).*

7.1 THE NATURE OF PLEASURE

In Questions 31–4, Aquinas returns to the tripartite scheme that he used to
interrogate the passion of love. Asking first what pleasure is in itself
(Question 31), Aquinas proceeds to inquire about the causes of pleasure
(Question 32) and its effects (Question 33). He expands the scheme by
the inclusion of an appendix on the passion's goodness and badness
(*de bonitate et malitia*) (Question 34). Next to sorrow, the consideration
of *delectatio* is the most expansive of the 1a2ae's analyses of the passions,
containing twenty-four Articles. The distribution of Articles is unequal:
the treatment of pleasure's effects and its morality occupies a total of eight
Articles, whereas the prior determination of pleasure's essence and its
causes demands eight Articles each.

Why does Aquinas require twice as large a canvas to depict the essence
and causes of pleasure? It seems that speaking about pleasure "in itself"

presents some particular difficulties. To gain a sense of these difficulties, one may review some features of Aristotle's treatment in the *Nicomachean Ethics*. Pleasure is the typical sign of virtue: a person who does what a virtuous person would do, but habitually fails to take pleasure in such actions, is continent rather than virtuous. Pleasure is intimately connected with human nature: "in educating the young we steer them by the rudders of pleasure and pain" (*Nicomachean Ethics* 10.1, 1172a22). When presented with alternatives, Aristotle observes, we naturally tend toward what seems most pleasant. "In the theater the people who eat sweets do so most when the actors are poor" (10.5, 1175b12). But what *is* pleasure? After surveying various opinions about pleasure, Aristotle proposes to identify its nature. But does he succeed? Even some generally well disposed toward Aristotle have wondered. Thus Anscombe remarks that difficulties about the concept of pleasure, generally papered over in her view by modern moral philosophers, "reduced Aristotle to sheer babble about 'the bloom on the cheek of youth' because, for good reasons, he wanted to make it out both identical with and different from the pleasurable activity" (1981, pp. 27–8).

In Aristotle's defense, one may say that the *Ethics* accurately identifies some important characteristics of pleasure. Pleasures follow upon and complete activity; they are relative to character; they vary according to the kinds of beings; they differ even for the same person according to his condition. But none of this, as valuable as it may be, touches the question about pleasure's essence. Arguably, the *Ethics* says far more about what pleasure is not – it is not a quality, not a motion, not a becoming, not the filling of a lack, not an activity, not thought, not perception – than what it is.

Viewed against this background, the audacity of Thomas's proposal to speak *de ipsa delectatione secundum se* becomes apparent. While Aquinas preserves some important features of the *Ethics*'s analysis, he does not share its diffidence about identifying the nature of pleasure. The first two Articles of Question 31 confront the determination of pleasure's essence. It is a passion in the strict sense, and therefore a motion (Article 1), but it is also a terminus of motion and does not essentially occur in time (Article 2). After indicating the manner in which these seeming contradictions can be held together, he proceeds to consider *delectatio* according to its primary division between intellectual and bodily pleasures. If *delectatio* is related to *gaudium* as the sensitive appetite is related to the will (Article 3), the restriction of the term *delectatio* to the sensitive appetite would nonetheless be inappropriate (Article 4).

Which are greater, intelligible or bodily pleasures? Aquinas poses this question in what appears to be the Question's climax (Article 5). Thomas proceeds to inquire about the bodily pleasures, asking whether the pleasures of touch are superior to other bodily pleasures (Article 6). The determination of *delectatio secundum se* concludes with a distinction between natural and non-natural pleasures (Article 7), followed by an explanation of the mode in which one bodily pleasure can be opposed to another (Article 8).[1]

Is pleasure a passion in the proper sense? The question is deceptively simple. As the *sed contra* says (citing Augustine, *De civitate Dei* 9), *delectatio, gaudium,* and *laetitia* are included among the passions of the soul. It appears that the authority of both Augustine and our own experience confirms that pleasure is a passion. But, as Aquinas reminds us, passion properly so called names a motion of the sensitive appetite. Defining pleasure as a motion is problematic, because Thomas has already defined pleasure as the terminus of concupiscence and desire, and therefore a state of rest rather than of motion. What appears to be an innocuous query about the status of pleasure as a passion turns out to challenge Thomas's entire theoretical framework. It would seem that Aquinas has either to abandon the core definition of passion as a motion of the sensitive appetite, or to deny that pleasure is a passion.

I have already discussed (§2.3) the claim of Costantino Marmo that shortly after Aquinas' death, Giles of Rome notices precisely this tension and "implicitly accuses Thomas of incoherence" (Marmo 1991, p. 299). It may be that Aquinas leaves an unsatisfying gap between the strict definition of passion in terms of motion, and the description of *delectatio* in terms that are far removed from motion. But it cannot be said that he is unaware of the tension. He explicitly addresses the tension at 31.1 ad 2m, distinguishing the "motion of execution" from the "motion of the appetitive part." With respect to execution, pleasure corresponds to rest. But with respect to the appetitive part itself, pleasure corresponds to motion. Candace Vogler well captures this aspect of Aquinas' thought:

---

[1] As usual, Ramírez (1973) provides an elegant ordering of the Articles that depends heavily upon the application of logical distinctions. Thus Articles 1 and 2 correspond to the genus and specific difference of pleasure; Articles 3–6 concern the *per se* division of pleasure; Article 7 features a *per accidens* distinction between normal and pathological pleasures; Article 8 identifies the *proprietas* of pleasure, especially bodily pleasure (see *De passionibus animae*, p. 194). While the scheme is logically tidy, its textual justification is uncertain.

In brief, pleasure is the interminable termination for rational appetite (in Thomistic parlance). More bluntly, it is the stopping place for action that says, "Don't stop!" (2002, p. 79)

The paradox is attested by Aristotle. The *Nicomachean Ethics* appears to deny that pleasure is a motion (see 10.4, 1174a19). In the *Rhetoric*, however, Aristotle seems to leave room for the idea (1.11, 1369b33). In the *ST*, Aquinas sides with the perspective of the *Rhetoric*, quoting its dictum that "pleasure is a certain motion of the soul." The apprehension of something as sensibly good moves the appetite: "From this perception (*ex isto sensu*) is caused a certain motion (*quidam motus*) of the soul in the sensitive appetite, and this motion is pleasure" (31.1.co). Aquinas does not identify pleasure with the apprehension itself, but rather with the motion of the sensitive appetite "following upon" (*consequens*) the apprehension of having attained a suitable good.

To say that pleasure is a motion seems to imply that it involves a temporal sequence (cf. *Nicomachean Ethics* 10.4, 1174a19). In Article 2, Aquinas confronts this issue, asking "whether pleasure is in time." The first objector asks: If pleasure is a "certain motion (*quidam motus*)," how can it avoid being in time? Aquinas responds by appealing to an Aristotelian distinction between two kinds of motion. One is the transition on the part of something imperfect from potency to act. This is the transition from "first potentiality" to "first actuality," for instance a person's slow progress in acquiring a command of Greek. Such motion evidently occurs in time. Another kind of motion corresponds to the transition from "first actuality" to "second actuality," as in the case of a person who has a command of Greek and deploys this command whenever he wishes to read Aristotle. There is no temporal gap between actually possessing the command of Greek (first actuality) and actually using it to read Greek (second actuality). Application of the power to read Greek is instantaneous; it requires only an act of the will. This illuminates the sense in which *delectatio* is not in time. Although the steps taken toward the attainment of a perceived good occur in time, there is no temporal interval between the apprehension of the attained good and the pleasure that follows. Thomas allows that *per accidens*, pleasure in some temporal good will fluctuate precisely to the extent that the agent's apprehension of that good fluctuates. But as long as the attained good remains within the apprehension, pleasure follows instantaneously. Its posteriority to apprehension is logical rather than temporal. Only an alteration in the grasp of the good as suitable can affect the corresponding *delectatio*.

In showing how pleasure is a motion, but essentially atemporal, Article 2 responds to the chief difficulty that arises from Article 1's explication of the *Rhetoric*'s definition. Article 3 shifts the Question's focus to distinguishing between kinds of pleasure. If pleasure is necessarily a function of apprehension, it follows that a difference in the mode of apprehension will produce a distinction between types of pleasure. By grounding *delectatio* in apprehension, Aquinas prepares the way for the most basic distinction between two kinds of pleasure. Here I partly agree with Ramírez's reading. Article 3 introduces what he calls the "*per se seu essentialis*" distinction between pleasures, and Article 4 comments on the same distinction (1973, p. 208). What is the distinction? Aquinas reminds the reader that she has already seen a version of it in the difference between natural and rational concupiscence. Thus "some pleasures are natural, and some are not natural but are accompanied by reason" (*cum ratione*) (31.3. co). On this basis Thomas elucidates the claim made by Damascene and "Gregory of Nyssa" (i.e. Nemesius) that "certain pleasures are bodily, certain are of the soul." Pleasures of the first kind, bodily pleasures, require nothing but sensitive apprehension. They are not rightly spoken of as "joys," since "the name of joy has no place except in pleasure which follows upon reason, whence we do not attribute joy to irrational animals, but only the name of pleasure" (31.3). Rational animals, by contrast, experience both bodily pleasure (*delectatio*) and intellectual joy (*gaudium*).

Since all bodily pleasures experienced by human beings are potentially under the sway of reason, it may seem correct to use *gaudium* exclusively for the passion as it occurs in human beings, and to reserve *delectatio* for the corresponding passion in non-rational animals. But Aquinas does not permit any such separation: "Someone may feel some *delectatio* according to the body, and yet not rejoice (*gaudet*) according to reason" (31.3.co). The power for rejoicing is an essentially rational capacity, involving the consent of the will. Implicit in Aquinas' account is a distinction between two classes of "joys" (*gaudia*). The first has as its substratum the *delectationes* of animal nature, which are then desired "with the pleasure of reason" (*cum delectatione rationis*) (31.3.co). The entrance of rational choice into such pleasures, as Candace Vogler observes, "all by itself lifts even the mature human's most soundly corporeal pleasures – say, the pleasure of a good shit – above the lowly business of mollusk life" (2002, p. 84).[2] The second

---

[2] Vogler's choice of example, far from being gratuitous, is a sign of fidelity to her Anscombian exemplar. See Jane O'Grady, "Obituary: Elizabeth Anscombe," *Guardian*, January 11, 2001.

class is based on no bodily pleasure, but consists exclusively in intellectual delight. Thus "everything that we desire according to nature, we can also desire with the pleasure of reason, but the converse does not hold" (31.3.co). There are some things that are objects of rational desire, but contain no ground in natural sensitive desire. Attaining these things causes both the highest pleasures, the ones humans have in common with the angels, Thomas says at 31.4 ad 3m, and the most depraved pleasures. (Aquinas will address the latter more fully at 31.7.)

Article 4 asks whether *delectatio* is in the intellectual appetite. The need for this question is not initially apparent. The teaching of the previous Article appears straightforward: *gaudium* is in the intellectual appetite, *delectatio* in the sensitive. Why press the inquiry about the relation of *delectatio* to rational appetite? The *sed contra* suggests a scriptural motive, quoting Psalm 36:4: *Delectare in domino*. If God is essentially the object of rational appetite, what place is there for sensitive *delectatio*? Here Aquinas does not recall his earlier gloss on Psalm 83:3 (at 24.3) about the capacity of both heart and flesh to rejoice in God. Rather, he acknowledges that while a "certain pleasure (*delectatio quaedam*) follows upon reason," this pleasure is not to be confused with *delectatio corporalis*. The "pleasure which is called joy" differs from bodily pleasure in an important respect: "the *delectatio* of the sensitive appetite is accompanied by some bodily transmutation, while the *delectatio* of the intellectual appetite is nothing other than a simple motion of the will (*simplex motus voluntatis*)" (31.4.co). The latter form of pleasure is a pseudopassion (§2.2). Aquinas confirms the distinction by the authority of Augustine: "*Cupiditas* and *laetitia* are nothing other than the will to consent in those things that we will." Aristotle associates pure joy, with no bodily disturbance, with God; Dionysius attributes the same to the angels (31.4 ad 2m). The uniqueness of humans is suggested by their dual capacity for *gaudium* and *delectatio*.

Articles 1–4 build toward Article 5, the dramatic center of Question 31. Now that Aquinas has elucidated the essential division between sensible and intellectual pleasures, he is in a position to stage a direct comparison. Which are better, Article 5 asks, bodily and sensible pleasures, or spiritual and intellectual pleasures? Ramírez's construal of Article 5 as merely the first aspect of the second subdivision of pleasure's *per se* division (1973, p. 194) misses altogether the climactic character of Article 5. One indication of Article 5's centrality is the size of its *corpus*. At 481 words, it is considerably longer than the responses of any of the Question's other

Articles, none of which exceeds 300 words.[3] Despite its bulk, Article 5 is an exemplary instance of Eschmann's observation that the *ST* conveys its teaching in a "parsimonious" manner. Its dialectic requires much unpacking. What Eschmann says about the *ST* in general is particularly true in this instance: "Although giving a full account of what is in the writer's mind, and although giving this account in clear and understandable language, it refuses, nevertheless, to go into any details" (1997, p. 7).

Which are better, sensible or intelligible pleasures? Aquinas begins with what appears to be the case for most people. Evidently, sensible pleasures seem greater than intelligible pleasures. The ambiguity of "greater" (*maior*) is exploited by the three objectors. If greater means "superior" or "preferable," then it seems that bodily pleasures are greater, because more seek them (31.5 arg. 1). If "greater" means "stronger" or "more powerful," then bodily pleasures are greater, because they affect not only the soul, but both the soul and the body (31.5 arg. 2). Additionally, they are more vehement, as indicated by the need to check them (31.5 arg. 3). It seems that sensible pleasures are greater than intelligible pleasures in every sense.

Aquinas generates a counter-appearance by juxtaposing Psalm 118 with book 10 of the *Nicomachean Ethics*. The Psalmist proclaims that divine speech is sweeter to the palate than honey is to the mouth. Aristotle argues that the greatest pleasure derives from the operation of wisdom. Which is to be believed, common experience or the authority of Scripture and Aristotle? Aquinas must construct a response that, while affirming the latter, saves whatever truth is contained in the former. The response divides into three parts: (1) a simple comparison of pleasures based on actions, apart from their objects; (2) a more complex comparison of intelligible and sensible pleasures in themselves, based on their three conditions; (3) an account of the appearance that bodily pleasures are preferable to spiritual pleasures.

Aquinas sets up the simple comparison by recalling the "intransitive" character of operations proper to the soul. An intransitive action is distinguished from a transitive act that "passes into" some matter outside the agent. If I take a bite of an apple – a transitive act – my teeth perform an operation on something external to me. But the distinct act of tasting the apple does nothing to affect the fruit. It is an "intransitive" act, because its sole effect is on the agent. To the extent that intransitive acts

---

[3] The responses of the first four Articles contain (respectively) 250, 164, 168, and 101 words. The remaining Articles are similarly short, containing (respectively) 287, 258, and 49 words.

such as understanding, feeling, and willing are natural operations of the soul, they are "themselves a certain good of the agent" (31.5.co). When the agent apprehends these acts as present goods, they naturally produce pleasure. On this basis, Thomas proposes a simple comparison of the pleasures derived from intelligible acts and from sensible acts, apart from their objects. The result: "without doubt intelligible pleasures are much greater than sensible pleasures. For man takes much more pleasure when he knows something by understanding, than when he knows it by sensing" (31.5.co). Since pleasure is not simply union with some suitable good, but the effect of apprehending that union, it matters that "the intellect turns back (*reflectitur*) upon its own act more than sense" (31.5.co). The greater intensity of self-reflection produces a correspondingly greater pleasure. Even the many are capable of recognizing this. "There is no one who would not rather lack his bodily vision than his intellectual vision, in the manner by which beasts or fools lack it, as Augustine says in *De civitate Dei*" (31.5.co).[4]

Aquinas proceeds to conduct a more detailed comparison of intelligible spiritual pleasures and sensible bodily pleasures. He announces the result in advance: "In themselves and absolutely speaking (*secundum se et simpliciter loquendo*), spiritual pleasures are greater" (31.5.co). The announcement's phrasing not only emphasizes the absolute greatness of intelligible pleasures, but also leaves room for a *per accidens* sense in which bodily pleasures are greater. The superiority of intelligible pleasures emerges from considering the "three things which are required for pleasure" (31.5.co). These are (1) the "conjoined good" (*bonum coniunctum*) present to the soul; (2) "that to which the good is conjoined," that is, the power of soul united to the good; (3) "the conjunction itself," the relation between (1) and (2). Since the true cause of pleasure is neither the good nor the apprehending power, but the relation between them, we may expect that Aquinas will place the most emphasis on the *coniunctio*. He meets this expectation, but not without a prior comparison of the intelligible and sensible versions of (1) and (2). *Bonum spirituale* is better than *corporale bonum*. Why? Rather than state the cause, Aquinas offers a sign: "Men abstain from even the greatest bodily delights (*maximae corporales voluptates*), rather than lose honor, which is an intelligible good" (31.5.co). About (2), Thomas provides only this blunt declaration: "Likewise the intellectual part is far nobler, and more knowing, than the sensitive part"

---

[4] The words of Augustine are actually from *De Trinitate* xiv.14, as Ramírez (1973) observes (p. 211).

(31.5.co). Eschmann's comment that the *ST*'s teaching is "strict" and "close-fisted" (1997, p. 7) is apposite.

The fist opens ever so slightly, however, when Aquinas addresses the *coniunctio ipsa*. If one compares the conjunction of spiritual good to the intellective power with the conjunction of bodily good to the sensitive power, the former conjunction appears *magis intima, et magis perfecta, et magis firma*. Aquinas proceeds to explain each by a sentence beginning with the proper comparative form: *Intimior quidem est ... Perfectior autem est ... Est etiam firmior*. First, spiritual pleasures are "more intimate," because the intellect penetrates to the essence, not just the exterior accidents. The apprehension of *quod quid est* is intrinsically more satisfying than the sensation of a thing's external qualities. Second, spiritual pleasures are "more complete," because the conjunction is not essentially temporal. Since intelligible things are without motion, they can be apprehended instantaneously, from which the resultant pleasures "are all at once" (*sunt totae simul*). Aquinas does not mean that the embodied creature is capable of simultaneously realizing every possible intelligible pleasure. But he does identify an act of mind (in its capacity as *intellectus* rather than *ratio*) by which it perceives multiple truths in a timeless manner. Such non-temporal apprehension produces a correspondingly intense pleasure.[5] The conjunction of sense and the sensible, by contrast, necessarily involves motion. As a result, "sensible pleasures are not perceived all at once, but some part of them is passing away, while some other part is looked forward to as yet to be realized, as is manifest in pleasures of the table and in sexual pleasures." Perhaps this illuminates the element of melancholy that seems to be present in even the most intense of sensible pleasures. The admonition to "enjoy the moment" is a tacit acknowledgment that bodily pleasures are always in the process of passing away.[6] Intelligible pleasures, unlike sensible pleasures, do not seem to

---

[5] On mental activities that "do not require a temporal interval or viewpoint," Stump (2003) has some useful commentary. "Learning, reasoning, inferring take time, but knowing does not. In reply to the question 'What have you been doing for the past two hours?' it makes sense to say 'Studying logic' or 'Proving theorems,' but not 'Knowing logic.' Similarly, it makes sense to say 'I'm learning logic,' but not 'I'm knowing logic.'"

[6] Here I think that Vogler (2002), in an otherwise perceptive analysis of Aquinas' thinking about pleasure, misses an important point. Noting Aquinas' view that sensible pleasures are imperfect, Vogler writes that such pleasure "is imperfect because we cannot always get what we want (hence, acting from sense appetite is sometimes painful) and because sense appetite keeps cropping up as long as we are bound to this mortal coil. Neither 'imperfection' should be admitted as such in a secular view. Nothing requires that I find my tiramisu even faintly unsatisfying" (p. 84). Aquinas is making a deeper point. No matter how satisfying the tiramisu, the experience is fleeting and may

involve this essentially transient character. Although they are episodic, they are not determined by temporal circumstance; they are infinitely repeatable, without loss. Grasping this contrast illuminates the final point of comparison. The conjunction of spiritual good and the intellectual power is "more firm" (*firmior*) than the conjunction of sense and the sensible. "Bodily delights (*delectabilia corporalia*) are corruptible, and wane rapidly, whereas spiritual goods (*bona spiritualia*) are incorruptible" (31.5.co).

In light of the absolute superiority of spiritual pleasures to bodily delights, how can Aquinas save the appearance of common sense, which is to the contrary? He does so by distinguishing what is true *per se* from what is true "in relation to us" (*quoad nos*) (31.5.co). Aquinas supplies three reasons (everything in Article 5 comes in threes). First, sensible things are more known to us than intelligible things. Second, sensible pleasures are accompanied by a bodily motion. Third, sensible pleasures are "more felt, and as a result more welcomed" (*magis sentiuntur, et per consequens magis acceptantur*) than spiritual pleasures as remedies for sorrows. For the embodied creature, sensible pleasures provide quick relief for pains. Although spiritual pleasures can be experienced so intensely that they overflow into the sensitive appetite, and thus cause bodily delight, Aquinas suggests that this is the exception, not the rule. Nothing is more natural for a creature in pain than to seek a bodily remedy. Binx Bolling's declaration is eminently sensible: "Ten years ago I pursued beauty and gave no thought to money. I listened to the lovely tunes of Mahler and felt a sickness in my very soul. Now I pursue money and on the whole feel better" (Percy 1960, p. 172). Common sense does not err in preferring sensible pleasures as short-term remedies for pain. Limited comforts are appropriate for limited pains, as Aquinas will make clear in Question 38. The God who exists outside any genus of being cannot be made into some giant source of pain relief. It is not that God cannot decide to ease our pain here and now. But in this life, as de Lubac writes, "suffering is the thread from which the stuff of joy is woven" (1987, p. 39). If Aquinas

---

serve as an occasion for sorrowing over the transient, unenduring nature of sensitive pleasures. (Perhaps the better the tiramisu, the more apt it is to provide such an occasion.) On the next page of her book, Vogler comes some way toward acknowledging the point, though she cannot quite bring herself to accept it: "Night falls and the gardener goes indoors. Morning nears and the lovers drift off to sleep. One finishes reading the novel. The credits roll on the screen. In a sense, then, the pleasures of mortal life become faint promises of the endless delight of beatitude, and part of the work of practical reason in pleasant action becomes holding steady with an eye on this promise. The interminability of the consideration (together with the finitude of worldly pleasures) points one toward otherworldly pleasures" (pp. 85–6).

recommends the pursuit of spiritual joys over sensible pleasures, it is not because they produce an earthly life that "feels better."

Aquinas has vindicated the superiority of spiritual joys, while doing justice to bodily pleasures. In Article 6, he proceeds to compare bodily pleasures among themselves. Are the pleasures of touch greater than pleasures that follow upon the acts of the other senses? The answer is clear: if we confine ourselves to the limits of sensation, touch is unquestionably the most pleasurable of the senses. To support this claim with respect to irrational animals, Aquinas cites Aristotelian maxims about dogs and lions.[7] We may add that something similar is true for human animals whose rationality is undeveloped. Small children who see pleasurable objects will proceed to touch them, unless they are prevented from doing so. Those affected by concupiscence may require the admonition "Look but don't touch." Within the realm of sensation, tactile pleasures are the greatest. But what makes them the greatest? Aquinas answers that non-rational animals like tactile pleasures most not only because they feel best, but also because the sensible objects of touch are most closely related to what is useful for the animal's preservation. To delight in things for their own sake, apart from their relation to self-preservation, is not possible for the non-rational animal. As Aquinas argued at 30.2, irrational animals are capable only of natural concupiscence; they desire only what they need for their preservation. Thus animals pursue objects and their associated pleasures not for their own sake, but as a means to the satisfaction of need. Irrational animals "do not have pleasure following upon sense, except by reason of utility" (31.6.co).[8]

Unlike non-rational animals, human beings can experience objects as pleasurable simply by virtue of perceiving them, whether or not they are useful. Following the opening of the *Metaphysics*, Aquinas holds that the sensible act most capable of knowing and delighting in something for its own sake, without any reference to the end it serves, is the act of sight. Thus while visual pleasures remain inferior to tactile pleasures "within the limits of sensible pleasure" (31.6.co), their non-utilitarian character gives them the closest resemblance to the pleasures of intellectual apprehension. To that extent, they surpass the pleasures of touch.

---

[7] Aristotle, *Nicomachean Ethics* 3.10, 1118a33: "For dogs do not take delight in the smell of hares, but in eating them ... nor does the lion feel pleasure in the lowing of an ox, but in devouring it."

[8] Here I render *delectatio secundum sensum* as "pleasure following upon sense" rather than "pleasure according to the sense," although the latter would not be incorrect. For the meaning of *secundum* as "following after," taken from the derivation of *secundum* from *sequor*, see the illuminating note in O'Brien 1977, p. 493.

What can be learned from this comparison? One need not deny that, absolutely speaking, tactile pleasures are the greatest of bodily delights. Yet feeling is not a sure guide for which pleasures are the most choiceworthy. Rather than touch everything that looks appealing, the rational being learns to admire delightful things at a distance, subordinating tactile pleasures to the pleasures of sight. By the same logic, visual pleasures must be subordinated to spiritual pleasures. Rather than remain content with sensible pleasures, Aquinas suggests, the rational creature must develop its capacity for intellection, so that the pleasures of sight give way to the pleasures of insight. Aquinas does not understand subordination of the lower to the higher to entail the annihilation of the lower. On the contrary, sensible pleasures will surely remain, since "no one can live without some sensible and bodily pleasures" (34.1.co). But their pursuit must be governed by knowledge of the good that perfects human beings.

Which pleasures to choose? Aquinas has answered: spiritual pleasures, and bodily pleasures as ordered toward spiritual pleasures. Though the distinction between "normal and pathological" pleasures may well be a *per accidens* distinction that rounds out the treatment of the division of pleasure, as Ramírez suggests, the deeper intention of Article 7 is to confront the question: To what extent does nature function as a guide in enabling a person to distinguish between pleasures? If pleasure is the natural consequence of the act whereby something is apprehended as suitable, it would seem that all pleasures are natural. In a sense, this is true. No existent pleasure can be altogether unnatural. Yet any pleasure may be judged as more or less natural. Thus far, in both Question 30 and Question 31, Aquinas has used "natural" in its sense of "animal nature," contraposing it to "rational." Now Thomas reminds us that "natural" may also refer to "rational nature." With respect to animal nature, the most natural pleasures are those useful for bodily preservation. Those who describe the performance of opera or the study of higher mathematics as "unnatural" appeal implicitly to animal nature as the standard. But if the relevant standard is rational nature, such pleasures may be entirely natural. The pleasures most in accord with rational nature, according to Aquinas, are those which result from contemplating the truth and doing works of virtue. Article 7's analysis illuminates how we can understand a person who systematically prefers sensible pleasures to intelligible joys as acting unnaturally, even as he chooses things which in themselves are natural.

The sensible pleasures we observe in animals are natural, however unnaturally human beings choose to pursue them. But some pleasures are so far removed from either animal or rational nature that Thomas does not hesitate to describe them as "unnatural" (*innaturales*). Aquinas cites those who take pleasure from eating dirt or coals, or those who enjoy cannibalism. By their very existence, such pleasures have become connatural to those who delight in them, and are thereby natural *secundum quid.* Yet because they arise from some corruption of human nature, they remain unnatural *simpliciter loquendo.* Though they become natural *per accidens* to "this individual" (*huic individuo*), they are "against the nature of the species" (*contra naturam speciei*) (31.7.co). How does one distinguish pleasures that are unnatural and frustrate rational nature from pleasures that enhance or develop it? Pleasures in conformity with rational nature are perfective of those who experience them when they are governed by reason, Aquinas answers, whereas non-natural pleasures lack any power to complete the agent. Thus proficiency in opera singing is natural, since it actualizes a potency that is natural to the rational being, namely the intelligent and artful control of one's natural ability to modulate one's voice. Eating coals, or eating flesh, does not actualize any such potency.

The unusually short final Article of Question 31 – at forty-nine words, the response is just barely longer than the *sed contra* – asks whether one pleasure can be contrary to another pleasure. The Article may be construed as a final reminder that pleasures cannot be regarded in a democratic manner. The person who tries to have all pleasures is doomed; he seeks to instantiate a metaphysical impossibility, since some bodily pleasures necessarily exclude others. Some pleasures must be chosen and others forgone. But which ones? The question cannot profitably be asked, unless one abstracts from particular instances of pleasure and understands its essence. Such is the overarching aim of Question 31's treatment of the nature of pleasure.

7.2 WHAT CAUSES PLEASURE?

What are the causes of *delectatio*?[9] Question 32's distribution of Articles has occasioned much controversy among the commentators. The proposed causes are as follows:

---

[9] Ramírez (1973) usefully observes that between the authorship of the *Sentences* commentary in 1256 and composition of the 1a2ae, Aquinas discovers Aristotle's *Rhetoric*, and thus radically reconsiders the question of the causes of pleasure. This may constitute an important exception to Mauro's claim (generally valid) that Thomas's thinking about the passions is "substantially unaltered in its main lines" from the *Sentences* commentary to the "mature and definitive formulation" of the *ST* (1977, p. 339). Less convincing is Ramírez's claim that Question 32's aim is well described as "reducing to a system those things which are found dispersed and confused in Aristotle" (1973, p. 232).

1. Activity (*operatio*)
2. Motion
3. Hope and memory
4. Sorrow
5. Actions of others
6. Doing good to others
7. Likeness (*similitudo*)
8. Wonder (*admiratio*)

Koellin assigns the first four to interior causes, and the last four to exterior causes of pleasure. This division does not withstand scrutiny, Ramírez argues, because *similitudo* is essentially connected to interior disposition.[10] Cajetan proposes an alternative ordering (1889, pp. 223–5; see also Ramírez 1973, pp. 235–7). The basic division is between *operatio*, which Aquinas explicitly identifies as the "proper cause" (*propria causa*) of pleasure, and the other seven causes. These may in turn be divided into causes properly speaking (Articles 2–4) and factors that dispose the agent toward pleasure (Articles 5–8). Ramírez judges this distribution of Articles as superior to that of Koellin, but nonetheless proposes a different ordering. Thus he takes Articles 1–6 to locate the "immediate or perfect-ive" cause of pleasure, making Articles 7–8 into a coda on its "mediate, or remote or dispositive" causes (1973, pp. 238–40). It seems possible, and reasonable, to combine the suggestions of Cajetan and Ramírez into yet another ordering. With Cajetan, I agree that the most basic division is between Articles 1 and Articles 2–8. *Operatio* is the direct cause of pleasure; the others serve as causes only to the extent that they bring about the required *operatio*. Within the indirect causes, I agree with Ramírez that *similitudo* and *admiratio* are set apart as formal and efficient causes.

The *operatio* that stands as the "proper cause" of pleasure is twofold. It refers both to attainment of the "suitable good (*bonum conveniens*)," and to the cognition of that attainment. Aquinas is able to speak briefly in Article 1 about the *operatio* that causes pleasure, because he has already discussed it in detail in Question 31. In Article 2, he raises a more difficult problem. To what extent does such *operatio* involve motion or change? Aquinas recalls two components of the "conjunction of pleasure" (*delect-abilis*), the agent and the object, as well as the "knowledge of this

---

[10] For Koellin's disposition, see Ramírez 1973, p. 234. Although he finds Koellin's ordering "subtle and beautiful," he doubts "whether it is grounded in the text."

conjunction" (32.2.co). With respect to our own natures, motion seems to contribute to pleasure. Because our natures do not remain constant (we enjoy fire in the winter but not in the summer), we tend to derive pleasure from operations that change in proportion to our inconstant nature. If one looks at the matter *ex parte obiecti*, motion similarly seems to cause pleasure. Aquinas observes that whenever anything gives us pleasure, it does so because it is present in a certain measure. When that measure is exceeded, the thing no longer provides pleasure. The restoration of pleasure in such a case can only come about by a change, namely the removal of the thing whose measure has been exceeded. Finally, knowledge of the conjunction provides pleasure, and such knowledge necessarily changes when the thing cannot be known simultaneously. When something "cannot be apprehended all at once" (*non poterunt apprehendi tota simul*), but can to some extent be known successively, the change involved in discursive motion causes pleasure (32.2.co).

The presence of change with regard to subject, object, and conjunction is typical for humans. But Aquinas does not leave the matter at this. He compares the ordinary human experience of pleasure with another case. An agent who is unchangeable possesses a natural mode of being that cannot be exceeded by the continued presence of a good. Because such an agent would "intuit simultaneously" the entire object of its delight, Aquinas says that change cannot in this case be a cause of pleasure. To the extent that human operation approximates these conditions, the corresponding pleasures "can be made more continuous" (32.2.co). Thus Aquinas reiterates the superiority of spiritual to bodily pleasures. Motion causes pleasure, but less and less as one ascends toward union with the highest, unchanging cause of pleasure.

In Article 3, Aquinas asks whether hope (*spes*) and memory (*memoria*) can cause pleasure. Once again, reflection on the nature of the "conjunction" between the person and the object is fundamental. The most pleasurable conjunction involves actual union, *coniunctio secundum rem* (§5.5). Short of this, however, there may be a "conjunction of likeness" (*coniunctio secundum similitudinem*), which Aquinas describes as a union existing in the mind of one who contemplates a suitable good (32.3.co). Though not present *secundum rem*, the pleasurable thing may be considered by the mind as present, and thereby cause pleasure. Though such pleasure pales in comparison to that which flows from real union, it is not negligible. Within the "conjunction according to likeness," Aquinas distinguishes between objects existing in the past, brought before the mind simply by an act of memory, and future objects made present to the mind "according to our faculty or power to attain the good that provides pleasure" (*secundum facultatem vel potestatem adipiscendi bonum quod delectat*) (32.3.co). The latter pleasures require not only memory, but both hope and memory, and are more potent than the pleasures requiring only memory.

Activity (*operatio*) is the "proper cause" of pleasure. Hope and memory produce pleasure by inducing the mind to perform an activity (namely, bringing the future or past good before the mind as present) that causes pleasure. The other passion that causes pleasure is sorrow (*tristitia*). Yet, as the objectors of Article 4 observe, the connection between sorrow and hope is attenuated. Whereas the object of hope or memory can of itself produce pleasure, the object of sorrow cannot. Actual sorrow in a person's soul always corresponds to the deprivation of some good. But if that person should begin thinking about the good whose absence causes sorrow, he brings it to mind as present, a circumstance that may cause one to experience pleasure. For example, a father is sad because his son has died. The absence of his son causes sorrow. Sorrow may prompt him to think about his son, which proceeds to give him pleasure. Thus does sorrow *in actu* cause pleasure. Greater pleasure, however, is caused by the recollection of sorrow *in memoria*. The immediate effect of recollecting past sorrows, Aquinas argues, is to apprehend one's present freedom from the past evil which caused the sorrow as a good. This apprehension of present good causes pleasure. But, as Aquinas reminds us, it is only a *per accidens* cause of pleasure. In itself, sorrow causes pain.

Articles 5 and 6 shift the focus from passion to action. Article 5 asks whether the actions of others can be a cause of pleasure to us. That others can act in ways that please us seems evident. But in what manner does the act of another give us pleasure? We cannot love another person or take pleasure in his actions unless there is some identifiable connection to our own good. Aquinas names three forms such a connection can take: (1) Another's action might enable us to obtain a good of our own. Thus when my banker lowers the interest rate, I can assume a loan and derive pleasure. (2) Another's action causes us to know or appreciate our own good. A student's positive evaluation leads me to think highly of my status as a teacher, from which pleasure follows. But if she turns out to be merely a flatterer, the ability of her testimony to bring me pleasure is compromised, since "a stronger evaluation is generated from the testimony of the good and the wise" (32.5.co). (3) Friendship-love prompts me to regard the good of another as my own. Suppose my colleague receives a $200,000 award for excellent teaching. If I regard my colleague as a friend, and not simply a competitor for a scarce good, I take pleasure in his good as though it were my own. (Nonetheless, I may ask him to buy the next few lunches.)

If we receive pleasure from the actions of others, can our own acts of good toward others bring us pleasure? In Article 6, Aquinas answers that they can, but only by virtue of the connection between another's good and our own good. That another's good could bring us pleasure, without bearing any connection to our own good, Aquinas does not consider as a real possibility. In genuine friendship, when I do good to a friend, I do myself good, and thus take pleasure in the action. Something similar applies to friendships based on utility. The crucial difference is that I do not value the other's good as simply my own, but as a means to a distinct good I will obtain in exchange for doing my friend good. Similar results follow from analysis of the "origin" (*principium*) of an action. Doing good to another may arouse in a man "an imagination of abundant good existing in him, from which he can share with others. And thus men take pleasure in their children, and in their own works, as things by which they share their own good" (32.6.co). Furthermore, doing good to another is pleasurable when it becomes habitual. The distinctive sign of the person who possesses the virtue of generosity is that he does not apprehend the act of benefiting another as a sacrifice of his own good, required by duty. Rather, he perceives the act as an instance of his own good.

Articles 7 and 8 complete the treatment of the causes of pleasure. Against both Koellin and Cajetan, Ramírez proposes that *similitudo* functions as an objective formal cause of pleasure, whereas *admiratio* serves as an efficient cause of pleasure on the side of the subject who experiences it. Why is likeness a cause of pleasure? Since we are substantially one with ourselves, we love ourselves most. Therefore, we are essentially drawn to what is like ourselves, and take pleasure when we attain it. Apparent exceptions are plentiful: one athlete may despise another athlete. But this occurs not in virtue of likeness *per se*, but because the likeness serves to hinder the attainment of some good. "A potter dislikes other potters, not because they are potters, but because they deprive him of his own excellence, or rather his own lucre, which he seeks as his own good" (32.7). In itself, however, likeness is a formal cause of love and the pleasure that comes from attaining the good. (The reasoning here is similar to 27.3's argument that likeness is a cause of love [§5.4].)

If *similitudo* is a formal cause of pleasure, *admiratio* comes nearer to being an efficient cause that motivates the agent. The immediate effect of *admiratio* ("wonder," "astonishment," "marvel") is not pleasure, but the desire to know. What causes pleasure is the conjunction of this desire with the hope that the object of desire can be attained. Thus Aquinas says that wonder, if it is to function as a cause of pleasure, includes "hope of acquiring the knowledge which one desires to have" (32.8.co). The response concludes by attending to another way in which *admiratio* causes pleasure. We may be struck by spectacles that in themselves are sorrowful. Augustine tells us that he loved to be made sad at the theater (*Confessions* 3.2). Aquinas provides a persuasive account of such phenomena:

All wonderful things (*mirabilia*) are pleasant, as those things which are rare, as are all representations of things, even of those which are not pleasant in themselves. For the soul rejoices in the collation (*in collatione*) of one thing with another, because to compare (*conferre*) one thing with another is the proper and connatural act of the reason, as the Philosopher says in his *Poetics*. And this is why "it is more pleasant to be liberated from great dangers, because it is something wonderful," as is said in the first book of the *Rhetoric*. (32.8.co)[11]

Though we naturally love contemplating known truth, and often prefer it to the arduous search for what is unknown, we may sometimes find the latter more pleasant, if our desire is sufficiently great. Aquinas' declaration that "greater desire is awakened (*excitatur*) from a perception of our ignorance" (32.8 ad 2m) arouses our own *admiratio*. Among other things, this declaration suggests why Thomas does not hesitate in the 3a *pars* of the *ST* to describe Socrates as a teacher of great excellence (3.42.4.co). Rather than merely supply a review of truths already known, Thomas writes the *ST* as a *manuductio* designed to increase our wonder, and thereby lead us to long for what we do not know.[12]

7.3 THE EFFECTS OF PLEASURE

What does pleasure bring about? Aquinas offers a short consideration of its primary effects in Question 33. Ramírez proposes that Articles 1–3 describe the effects of pleasure when it functions as an efficient cause, and Article 4 considers the results of pleasure taken as a final cause. This may be generally correct, but his neat assignment of "physiological" effects to Article 1 and "psychological" effects to Article 2 (1973, pp. 255–6) does not bear scrutiny. Rather than apply a logical scheme, I propose an ordering

[11] Cf. Aristotle, *Poetics* 4, 1148b9, and *Rhetoric* 1.11, 1371b9. The citation of the *Poetics* by Aquinas is quite rare.
[12] For an enlightening treatment of *manuductio* in Thomas, see Candler 2006.

that begins from the following textual observation: the first two Articles of Question 33 contain not a single reference to Aristotle, whereas the final two Articles mention or quote him eleven times. Thus my division of the Question is as follows: Aquinas begins by proposing a non-Aristotelian view of the primary effects of pleasure. These are *dilatatio* ("expansion" or "enlargement") (Article 1) and desire for more pleasure (Article 2). With the treatment of the primary effects in place, Thomas turns to questions that arise particularly from the Aristotelian texts. These are the relation of pleasure to reason (Article 3) and its role in completing activity (Article 4).

Things are often named for their effects, as Aquinas observes throughout the *ST*. Hence a near synonym for *delectatio* is *laetitia* ("gladness"), related to *latus* ("wide," "spacious") and *latitudo*. The conjunction of the intensive prefix *de* with *latitudo* leads to *dilatatio*, the first effect of pleasure (see Ramírez 1973, p. 256). Why Ramírez would be tempted to describe this as a "physiological or organic" effect is easy to see. Aquinas defines *dilatatio* as a "kind of motion towards breadth (*latitudo*)." Since *latitudo* is a dimension of body, Aquinas holds that "in the affections of the soul, it is not said except according to a metaphor" (33.1.co). But the inference that Article 1 intends primarily to describe *dilatatio* as a physiological effect, rather than the real psychological effect named metaphorically by the term, is misleading. Aquinas holds that the apprehensive and the appetitive powers of the soul are enlarged by pleasure. When a person apprehends himself as united to the suitable good, he perceives himself to have attained a certain perfection. This perfection is a "spiritual magnitude" (*spiritualis magnitudo*) (33.1.co). Because the magnitude is spiritual, Aquinas concludes, "the mind of man (*animus hominis*) is said to have been magnified or enlarged by pleasure" (*per delectationem magnificari, seu dilatari*) (33.1.co). Similarly, the *dilatatio* of the appetitive power is a spiritual event. When the appetitive power rests in the good, "the affections (*affectus*) of man are enlarged by pleasure" (33.1.co).

Though Aquinas acknowledges the correlative somatic effects caused by pleasure, including a literal expansion of the heart, Article 1 is not primarily interested in the physical event. The term "heart" in the verse from Isaiah quoted *sed contra* ("Thou shalt see and abound, thy heart shall wonder and be enlarged") does not refer to a physical organ. The aim of Article 1 is not (*pace* Ramírez) to identify the "physiological or organic" effect of pleasure. On the contrary, Aquinas wants to evoke its spiritual effect with a biological metaphor. Other spiritual writers do the same. When Catherine of Siena says that suffering born of love does not shrivel up the soul, but "makes her grow fat" (1980, p. 30), she uses essentially the same figure. Why is expansion of the heart so important? In order to attain the ultimate end, the enjoyment of God, our heart must be opened: "A person opens his heart, so that he may perfectly enjoy that in which he takes pleasure" (33.1 ad 3m). According to Aquinas, the most powerful agent for opening the heart's doors is *gaudium.* By expanding the affections, spiritual joys from this life prepare the heart to receive still greater pleasures in the next.

Joy brings about *dilatatio. Dilatatio* opens the heart to receive more joy. Article 2 makes this explicit, asking whether pleasure causes desire or thirst for itself. The response is built on a distinction between pleasure *in actu* and pleasure *in memoria.* The latter case is the simplest: when a person finds herself in a frame of mind that corresponds to some remembered pleasure, she naturally desires to experience it again. More complex is the handling of pleasure *in actu.* Aquinas begins by marking the difference between *desiderium* in its proper sense, as denoting an appetite for a thing not yet possessed, and a wider sense where it simply suggests the "exclusion of distaste" (*exclusionem fastidii*). In its proper sense, as rest in the good attained, pleasure does not *per se* cause desire for itself. But if the present good is only incompletely possessed, then the pleasure generated by partial attainment of the good will generate desire for the additional pleasure that is promised by a fuller possession of the thing. Strictly speaking (and contrary to Ramírez's analysis) "desire for itself" is not a *per se* effect of pleasure. But since our attainment of the good is typically successive, it happens *per accidens* that our actual experience of pleasure causes desire for itself. This may be due either to the nature of the object itself, such as a piece of music that can only be experienced in time, or it may be due to something about the person. Aquinas gives an illuminating example. While the last end is perfect in itself, our possession of it is successive and incomplete: "One does not have it immediately (*statim*), but acquires it little by little (*paulatim*)" (33.2.co). The pleasure generated by partial possession leads to a desire for more pleasure. In this world, Aquinas concludes, "we take pleasure in perceiving something incomplete with respect to divine knowledge; and this very pleasure excites thirst or desire for complete knowledge" (33.2.co).

If *desiderium* is taken in a wider sense, as simply indicating the exclusion of distaste, the same conclusion follows. Bodily pleasures cause no desire for themselves, once their natural limit has been reached. Spiritual pleasures, by contrast, "never grow beyond the natural condition, but rather perfect nature" (33.2.co). A person who experiences genuine contemplative pleasure will thirst for more of the same. To underscore the point, Thomas quotes the same verse of Scripture twice in the response: "They that drink me shall yet thirst." This applies, he adds, even to the angels, who know and delight God perfectly, but still "desire to look at" him (1 Peter 1:12).

Articles 1 and 2 establish the role of spiritual pleasure in preparing the heart to receive God. In Articles 3 and 4, Aquinas turns to problems that are suggested by Aristotle. Article 3 asks whether pleasure impedes the use of reason. As we have seen, the power of contemplative pleasures to quicken further desire for themselves promotes the activity of reason. Article 3 adds that spiritual pleasure "does not hinder the act of reason, but helps it; because we are more attentive in doing that which gives us pleasure, and attention helps activity (*operatio*)" (33.3.co). Bodily pleasures, however, interfere with reason "in a threefold manner" (*triplici ratione*) (33.3.co).[13] The three *rationes* by which pleasure distracts *ratio* are: (1) "by reason of distraction" (*ratione distractionis*); (2) "by reason of contrariety" (*ratione contrarietatis*); (3) "according to a certain binding" (*secundum quandam ligationem*). In binding the reason, bodily pleasure causes an extreme physiological alteration, "greater even than in other passions." The first two cases admit of the possibility that reason can be redirected toward its proper object. If reason is distracted, it is not necessarily bound (the first case). If the judgment of prudence is lost, the speculative act of reason remains intact (the second case). But with respect to the third case, the act of reason is entirely destroyed. This occurs in drunkenness, which Aquinas seems to regard as the paradigm case of *ligatio*. (Hobbes's decision in the *De cive* to regard drunkenness as contrary to the law of nature might be seen as a surviving fragment of this perspective.)

Clarity about the modes in which bodily pleasures can distract reason is important, not least because it plays an indispensable role in the account of incontinence that Aquinas gives later in the 1a2ae. Article 3 of Question 33 seems to prepare the ground for 77.2, where Thomas asks whether every sin can be traced back to ignorance. The answer that Aquinas develops begins with the acknowledgment that Socrates was "somewhat right" (77.2). The will cannot be moved by an object, unless

---

[13] That Aquinas would select the term *ratio* to indicate these ways suggests that pleasures can impede reason only by imitation, that is, by a certain *ratio*. Another example of this sense of humor may be found very early in the *ST*: "Respondeo dicendum sacram doctrinam esse scientiam. Sed sciendum est quod duplex est scientiarum genus" (1.1.2.co).

that object appears good to the reason in some respect. But how can something that a person knows to be bad nonetheless appear good to the reason? The hinge of Aquinas' answer to this question turns on the three ways identified by 33.3 in which passion impedes reason by substituting an alternate *ratio*. Passion does not impede reason by simply negating it, but rather by moving it to act under a surrogate *ratio*, a *ratio* contrary to what reason knows when not distracted or bound by pleasure.

Bodily pleasure is dangerous. It causes those who know better to fall into sin. But Aquinas does not want to end Question 33 on this note. However harmful they might be when not conformed to the order of reason, bodily pleasures are in themselves good. Aquinas certifies the essential goodness of pleasure by attending to the way in which pleasure, taken as a final cause, perfects operation.[14] By saying that pleasure completes operation, Aquinas denies that pleasure is something entirely independent of activity. *Delectatio* names not some free-floating thing, but the motion of the appetite that occurs upon the successful completion of activity. It is thus distinct from, yet dependent upon, the activities that it completes. As we have seen, Anscombe acknowledges "good reasons" for making pleasure "both identical with and different from the pleasurable activity," but faults Aristotle for engaging in "sheer babble about 'the bloom on the cheek of youth'" (1981, pp. 27–8). Aquinas' own perspective on this question may be close to Anscombe's. He makes no particular use of the Aristotelian image, but simply declares that "pleasure perfects activity by way of final cause." A person is drawn to an activity by perceiving that it is desirable in some respect. This perception is first registered in the appetite as *complacentia* (the change in the appetite associated with *amor* [§5.2]). Such pleasure serves as the final cause of the activity which (if successful) leads to *delectatio*.

Do human acts necessarily require pleasure as a final cause? It seems not; the rational creature is capable of choosing courses of action that seem to involve no joy. But, in the Aristotelian phrase quoted by Aquinas, "appropriate pleasures increase activity" (see *Nicomachean Ethics* 10.5, 1175a36). Pleasure's capacity to distract the reason is matched by its power to increase the intensity of its operation. If the object of pleasure coincides with the object of reason, the activity in pursuit of that object will be especially intense. Moreover, we will perform the activity better.

---

[14] As Ramírez (1973) observes, it may also be taken as a formal cause. "Since pleasure formally has the character of an end, one may say derivatively that its final effect is in reality the same as its formal effect" (p. 256).

Departing from logical schemata just long enough to attend to what "experience establishes," Ramírez offers this suggestion: "What we do with pleasure and freely, we do better: thus pleasure in eating and drinking completes good digestion; pleasure in sexual intercourse produces better generation" (1973, p. 263). Similarly, he adds, activities of the spirit improve when they are done with pleasure. With respect to the highest goods, spiritual intensity is not an option, but a necessity. If joyless activity is possible, intense joyless activity is rarely so. Without the *delectatio* that completes *operatio*, sliding back into the pursuit of lesser goods in which one does take pleasure is virtually inevitable.

7.4 GOOD AND EVIL PLEASURES

Aquinas has already considered good and evil with respect to the passions in general (Question 24). What makes it necessary to supply a treatment of good and evil in relation to any of the particular passions? Why does Aquinas choose pleasure and sorrow as the only targets of such a treatment? Cajetan gives one plausible answer to the question. Because the other passions terminate in pleasure and sorrow, and are regulated by them in a certain way, it is appropriate to reserve the treatment of morality for pleasure and sorrow (1889, p. 236). Candace Vogler gives a more colorful answer, also worth consideration:

Whether our focus is on the pallid pleasures of abstract contemplation, the thrill of morally satisfying reading, the darker business of debauchery, or the loose delights of sense appetite's pursuits, there is something about pleasure that is potentially at odds with ethics and potentially an enemy to efficiency. (2002, p. 76)

Aquinas structures Question 34 *de bonitate et malitia delectationum* as a commentary on the doctrines of the ancient schools. The Stoic view that all pleasures are evil is both intellectually unsupportable and contrary to lived experience (Article 1). But the same may be said of the diametrically opposed "Epicurean" view that all pleasures are good (Article 2). Both Stoics and Epicureans may be corrected by the "Platonic" view that some pleasures are good and some are not. But Plato erroneously infers that no pleasure can be the highest good (Article 3). Not only does a certain pleasure rigorously correspond to the human attainment of the highest good, Aquinas concludes, but pleasure itself is the supreme rule for judging moral good and evil (Article 4). One may be tempted to conclude that the serial correction of the Stoics, the Epicureans, and Plato culminates in the affirmation of Aristotle. But Thomas's own teaching is more subtle than this. As the *sed contra* would suggest, he concludes the Question on the good and evil of pleasure with a careful harmonization of Aristotle and Augustine.

Are all pleasures evil? The Stoic view suggests they are. But Scripture denies this; once again Thomas quotes Psalm 36 in the *sed contra*: "*delectare in Domino*" (34.1.sc; cf. 31.4.sc). As he did at 24.2, Aquinas numbers the Stoics among the *antiqui philosophi* who fail to distinguish between the sensible and the intelligible. This distinction alone suffices to resist the claim that all pleasures are bad, since spiritual pleasures are good. Yet this may suggest that while intelligible pleasures are good, sensible pleasures are evil. Aquinas rejects this view in no uncertain terms. Before supplying the theoretical basis for its rejection, he gently observes the hypocrisy of those who would teach it. "Since no one can live without some sensible and bodily pleasure, if those who teach that all pleasures are evil are caught in the act of experiencing some pleasures, men will be more inclined to pleasure by the example of their works, overlooking the teaching of their words" (34.1.co). In human actions and passions, Aquinas observes, men are "more moved by examples than words" (34.1.co).

Experentia plurimum valet. Humans are not wrong to have this view. But Aquinas does not leave the matter at common sense. He proceeds to explain how we may distinguish between sensible pleasures that are good and those that are evil. Pleasure is the rest of the appetitive power in some good, attained by some operation. To evaluate any pleasure as good or evil, we must examine both the operation and the good. Good and evil in moral matters depend upon the relation of the attained good to reason. If the attained good "agrees with reason" (*convenit rationi*), the resulting pleasure will be good. If it is "discordant with it" (*discordat ab ea*), the corresponding pleasure will not be good (34.1.co). While knowing what agrees with reason in any particular case may not always be easy, and requires the virtue of prudence, it seems easier to know what is discordant with reason. This is because, in any evil pleasure, the appetite rests "in that which is discordant with reason, and with the law of God" (34.1.co). Whatever is contrary to divine law necessarily contradicts reason, since reason and divine law have the same root. While moving toward the good can hardly be reduced to rule-following, observing the negative prohibitions of the law enables the reliable avoidance of evil pleasures.

If agreement with reason is the principle of good sensible pleasures, what of those pleasures that are essentially irrational? We have seen that Aquinas regards drunkenness as a paradigmatic case of the capacity for pleasure to fetter the reason. In the *ad primum* of this Article, Thomas expands the teaching on the "binding of reason" (*ligatio rationis*). Although sexual intercourse is not intrinsically at odds with reason, he observes, the bodily alteration that it produces normally fetters the reason. It might seem that sexual intercourse would thus be evil, for the same reason that drunkenness is evil. But Aquinas denies this appearance, citing the case of sleep, in which reason is fettered without the act's being morally evil. It would appear that the "binding of reason" is not evil in itself. But what explains the difference between drunkenness, on the one hand, and sleep and sexual intercourse, on the other? Why not assimilate drunkenness to sleep and intercourse? Aquinas declares that "reason itself has this property, that the use of reason be interrupted at times" (34.1 ad 1m). Drunkenness would not qualify as one of these times, since a drunk person achieves no good that is not more effectively (and less riskily) achieved by one who is sober. Sleep and sexual intercourse, by contrast, attain goods that cannot be achieved in any other way, and hence remove the evil that would otherwise be involved in the fettering of reason. Despite the "binding of reason" that it produces, conjugal intercourse is not, according to Aquinas, either a mortal or a venial sin. As he says later in the *ST*: "The abundance of pleasure which is in the sexual act that is ordered according to reason is not contrary to the mean of virtue" (2.2.153.2 ad 2m).[15]

Some will hold that, owing to Augustinian baggage, Aquinas unfortunately stops short of a full-bodied affirmation of the goodness of the conjugal act. He appears to do this when he adds that the *ligatio* "originates from a certain moral malice, namely from the sin of our first parents, since it did not exist in the state of innocence" (34.1 ad 1m). It is superficial, however, to conclude that Aquinas is unable to affirm the goodness of sexual intercourse. The simple acknowledgment that some things are the effects of original sin does not make the underlying acts sinful. The pain of childbirth, for example, is an effect of original sin. But childbirth itself is not a sin. Similarly, Aquinas is perfectly consistent in holding that the binding of reason involved in a normal sex act is an effect of original sin, without suggesting that the act of sexual intercourse is sinful.[16]

---

[15] Williams (1974) calls attention to this passage (p. 257).

[16] In his analysis of the sense in which Christ's passions are "defects," Gondreau (2002) distinguishes between an "ontological defect" and a "moral defect" (p. 231). A parallel distinction may apply here.

Against the "Stoic" doctrine that all pleasures are evil, we find the extreme opposite view that all pleasures are good. This is the view that Aquinas attributes to the Epicureans.[17] The view contains a kernel of truth: since all pleasurable things are pursued as goods, they must in some respect be good. But to say that something is good in some respect is not to judge it as simply good. We must distinguish what is "simply good" (*bonum simpliciter*) from what is "good to a particular person (*bonum quoad hunc*)" (34.2.co). If an agent apprehends as good something that is not simply good, he does so for one of two reasons. First, he may have a non-natural disposition which causes something that is not ordinarily good to be suitable in his particular case. Aquinas cites the example of a leper for whom eating something poisonous happens to be good. Second, and more commonly, a person may estimate something as suitable which is not in fact suitable (34.2.co). The causes of mistaken estimation are various, but they always lead to an action that results in an evil pleasure. If by contrast one chooses what is simply good, the result is pleasure simply (*simpliciter delectatio*).

Rejection of both the "Stoic" and "Epicurean" extremes leads Aquinas to a more nuanced position. Some pleasures are evil, some pleasures are good. Aquinas finds Plato to teach this view, but indicts him for a more subtle error about the nature of pleasure. Because Plato associates all pleasure with the process of attaining a good, and holds that the greatest good involves no process or motion, he concludes that no pleasure can be the greatest good. The first of two faults in his argument, according to Aquinas, lies in the assumption that all pleasure involves a temporal process. Although bodily pleasures are imperfect and involve motion, spiritual pleasures as such do not. Aquinas has already described the sense in which spiritual pleasures are out of time. He does not repeat the teaching here in detail, but simply points out the lacuna in the Platonic claim. The second fault of Plato's argument, according to Aquinas, is that it overlooks the legitimate multiplicity of ways of speaking about the greatest good. If by greatest good we mean the *summum bonum simpliciter*, then something as human as pleasure cannot be the greatest good. The *summum bonum simpliciter* is God. But Aquinas observes that "we are speaking of the greatest good in human things" (34.3.co). The vocabulary

---

[17] Plé (Thomas Aquinas 1994–6) is no doubt right to suggest that "St Thomas has not understood Epicurus except in a manner quite incomplete and deformed by the calumnies spread by the Stoics, and more or less repeated by the Christian tradition. Epicurus's position on pleasure is quite different" (p. 235n8).

that describes human appropriation of the good is richly varied; the response speaks of *usus, possessio,* and *fruitio*. For the rational creature, the enjoyment of God "conveys a certain pleasure in the ultimate end" (34.3.co). Thus Aquinas concludes that there is a pleasure that corresponds to the greatest good.

Closing the entire treatment of *delectatio*, Article 4 asks whether pleasure is the measure or rule according to which good and evil in moral things is judged. All three objectors draw from Aristotle. It seems that pleasure cannot be the rule of moral good and evil, for three reasons: it is posterior to love and desire, it is too protean in its nature to function as a stable criterion, and its status as an effect of operation, rather than a cause, compromises its ability to serve as a rule for judging good and evil. The response to the objections is to fix more securely the role of pleasure as an end of operation. Aquinas begins by harmonizing Aristotle and Augustine in the *sed contra*. Commenting on Psalm 7, Augustine says that "the end of care and cognition is the pleasure which each person aims at achieving" (34.4.sc). Similarly, Aristotle holds that "pleasure is the architectonic end."[18]

When Aquinas argues that pleasure is the rule by which moral good and evil is to be judged, he does not have particular acts in mind. As the quotations from the *sed contra* suggest, *delectatio* is proposed as a criterion by which a *person* may be judged. The response makes this clear: "According to the pleasure of the human will, a man is primarily judged to be good or evil" (34.4.co). When Thomas speaks of the "pleasure of the human will," he does not include sensible pleasures. Whether sweets act upon one's palate in a manner that produces a motion of the sensitive appetite is not relevant to character assessment. But whether one takes pleasure in the choice of eating a large amount of sweets may be morally decisive, at least with respect to the virtue of temperance. No matter how pleasing the sensation of tasting chocolate pie, a temperate person is repulsed by the idea of eating the whole pie at a single sitting. She would not will such a thing; such a volition would bring her no pleasure. The self-indulgent man, by contrast, takes pleasure in doing such things. It is not that he enjoys the taste of the pie more than the temperate person does. (In fact, due to years of excess that dull the senses, he probably enjoys it less.) What he takes pleasure in is the decision to eat more than what the rational mean prescribes. Does the self-indulgent man act under

---

[18] Aristotle, *Nicomachean Ethics* 7.11, 1152b. Here Thomas slightly misquotes Aristotle; the "architect of the end" in Aristotle's text appears to be the political thinker, not pleasure.

the *ratio* of willfully defying the rational mean? Not necessarily – it is more likely that he has come to estimate what reason knows to be destructive as somehow suitable for himself. Typically this involves no small degree of rationalization and self-deception. Rather than choose excess under the description "Overeating is unsuitable, but I will do it anyway," he is more likely to tell himself a story, such as "My repressive parents never let me eat as much as I wanted. Now that I am liberated from their tyranny, I can do whatever I please." One sign that a person is vicious (and not merely incontinent) is that he habitually takes pleasure in actions that are contrary to reason, and fails to recognize these actions as contrary to reason.

"The good and virtuous person is he who rejoices (*gaudet*) in works of virtue, the evil person is he who rejoices in evil works" (34.4.co). The choice of verb reinforces the point that Aquinas has moved from sensible *delectationes* to spiritual joys. Taking pleasure in things contrary to reason is the culmination of the process that begins with disordered *amor* and proceeds through non-natural *concupiscentia*. According to the *via generationis*, love and desire precede pleasure. But in the order of intention, *secundum rationem finis*, pleasure comes first. Here one sees clearly the link between intended pleasure and the change of the appetite that Aquinas describes as *complacentia* in Question 26 (see §5.2).[19] The treatment of the concupiscible passions directed toward the apprehended good has come full circle. What we love prompts the motion of the appetite. But what we take pleasure in shapes our affections, and thus serves as the ultimate *regula* by which our characters may be judged.

[19] Thus D'Arcy (2006) is wide of the mark when he says that "one must not translate [*complacentia*] with a word that suggests pleasure, since that belongs to the third, not the first, stage of the orectic process" (p. xxvi). What is first in the order of intention – pleasure – prompts what is first in the order of execution, the *amor* that is *complacentia*. As Manzanedo (1989) comments, "Pleasure also includes love, completing or 'consummating' it with the possession of what is loved" (p. 128). The "suggestion of *placere* in the word *complacentia*" captures this perfectly. See also Terruwe and Baars 1972, p. 34n8.

CHAPTER 8

Sorrow

Of all the discussions of the particular passions, the treatment of sorrow is the longest, taking five Questions. Aquinas begins by distinguishing sorrow in the proper sense from pain, whether "interior" or "exterior," and notes multiple species of sorrow (§8.1). Whatever causes the apprehension of something as a present evil is capable of generating sorrow. Aquinas reduces to four the factors that bring about the required apprehension (§8.2). In light of his view that sorrow is a passion in the most proper sense of the term, whereby a person is acted upon for the worse, one might expect Aquinas to dwell upon the negative effects of sorrow. But this is not his emphasis. On the contrary, Aquinas stresses that when regulated by reason, sorrow is a natural passion that can deepen the soul and prepare it for the gift of true humility (§8.3). Even so, it is appropriate to seek "remedies" for pain and sorrow. These range from the most cerebral (contemplation) to the most earthly (sleep and warm baths) (§8.4). Though the prolonged experience of sorrow does not befit the nature of the human person, Aquinas does not think that sorrow ought to be eliminated in this life. He concludes the treatment of sorrow by clarifying the difference between "moderate" and "immoderate" sorrow (§8.5).

8.1 THE NATURE OF PAIN AND SORROW

Of all the passions, sorrow or sadness (*tristitia*) is "most properly" said to be a passion (22.1.co; compare 41.1.co). Perhaps because the soul is most violently acted upon (*pati*) when it suffers, the phenomena denoted by "sorrow" and "suffering" overlap considerably.[1] The close connection between *pati* and sorrowing/suffering may explain why Aquinas devotes

---

[1] Thus (for example), while a majority of English translators render the title of Goethe's *Die Leiden des Jungen Werther* as *The Sorrows of Young Werther*, a minority (with equal correctness) opt for *The Sufferings of Young Werther*. In Latin, the distinction is perhaps more visible. As Ramírez (1973) reminds us, Cicero in the *Tusculan Disputations* (see 2.15.35) locates a distinction between *dolor* and *labor*, *labor* afflicts mind and body, whereas *dolor* is more narrowly focused on the body (pp. 292–3). Yet, as Cicero notes, the two are close neighbors (*sunt finitima omnino*).

more Questions to *tristitia* than to any other passion. Another explanation of the treatment's comparative length would recall the complexity of the historical conversation. Taking the passages *sed contra* in Question 35 alone, we find citations of Virgil, the Old Testament, Paul, Augustine, Pseudo-Dionysius, Nemesius, and Damascene. From this profusion of *auctoritates*, we may infer that Aquinas intends to make his own contribution to a many-sided discussion. But what is his distinctive contribution? What is at stake? To grasp Thomas's intention, one must undertake an attentive reading of each of the five Questions about "pain and sorrow" (*dolor et tristitia*) (35.1.pr.).[2]

When Aquinas proposes to consider a passion "in itself" (*secundum se*), he typically does four things. First, he seeks the precise characteristic that makes the thing a passion, rather than a habit, an act, a sensation, or some other kind of motion. Second, he considers the "animal" passion in relation to its "rational" counterpart. The joint consideration of *dolor* and *tristitia* parallels the treatment of *amor* and *dilectio*, *concupiscentia* and *desiderium*, *delectatio* and *gaudium*. Third, he considers the passion in relation to its contraries. Fourth, he considers the passion in relation to divisions attested by the tradition. Treating *de dolore et tristitia secundum se*, Aquinas structures Question 35 accordingly. He begins by determining what makes pain a passion (Article 1) and proceeds to query the relation between *dolor* and *tristitia* (Article 2). In the midsection of the Question, Thomas treats the relations between sorrow and pleasure (Articles 3–6). Like any serious psychologist,[3] Aquinas acknowledges both their evident opposition and their intimate connections. In the Question's last part, Aquinas addresses two prominent divisions. The first concerns the relation between "exterior" and "interior" pain (Article 7). The second concerns the historically attested species of sorrow (Article 8).[4] Following "Gregory" (i.e. Nemesius) and John of Damascus, Thomas identifies

---

[2] Throughout I uniformly translate *dolor* by "pain" and *tristitia* by "sorrow." Both terms may bear alternative translations; my aim is simply to maintain consistency with Thomas's own terminology.

[3] The comparison of Aquinas to a psychologist is appropriate. Stagnitta (1979) emphasizes the parallels, finding a correspondence between Thomas's perspective and modern trends in psychology which, "without prescinding from behaviorism, aim to give it a less alienating and more human face" (p. 8). While Aquinas' treatment of the passions cannot be reduced to behaviorism with a human face, Stagnitta is surely correct to suggest that his approach anticipates, or is open to, many particular observations of empirical psychology.

[4] The reading of Question 35's *ordo articulorum* offered by Ramírez (1973) is not too far removed from the one I give. The main difference is that he groups together Articles 2–7 and restricts the account of *divisio* to Article 8 (p. 291), whereas I take the *divisio* to embrace Articles 7 and 8 on *dolor* and *tristitia* respectively.

these as pity (*misericordia*), envy (*invidia*), anxiety (*anxietas/angustia*), and torpor (*acedia*).

In Article 1 of Question 35, Aquinas asks whether pain (*dolor*) is a "passion of the soul" (*passio animae*). The question is surprisingly difficult. We spontaneously tend to associate pain with the body and sorrow with the soul. Some, in fact, have not hesitated to map the difference between pain (*dolor*) and sorrow (*tristitia*) onto the distinction between body and soul. Aquinas gives some justification for such a reading in the *De veritate*. There he identifies one kind of passion that "begins with the body" (*incipit a corpore*) and proceeds to affect the soul *per accidens*, such is "a kind of bodily passion" (*quaedam passio corporalis*) (*QDV* 26.2.co). Another kind of passion "begins with the soul (*incipit ab anima*)" and proceeds to affect the body with a proportionate *corporis transmutatio*: "this is called a *passio animalis*" (*QDV* 26.2.co). On the basis of this distinction, it seems plausible to speak of "the distinction between a *passio corporalis* and a *passio animalis/animae* as exemplified here in the distinction between pain and sorrow" (Loughlin 2005, p. 763).[5] Can this be reconciled with Article 1's conclusion that pain is a genuine *passio animae*? Aquinas emphasizes that "perception" (*perceptio*) of a thing "under the aspect of evil (*sub ratione mali*)" is required for pain to ensue (35.1.co). Since *perceptio* necessarily involves the apprehensive power and causes appetitive motion, it follows that "pain, like pleasure, is in the intellectual or the sensitive appetite," and is thus "most properly called a *passio animae*" (35.1.co). As a passion of the soul, *dolor* is categorically distinct from physical sensations or "bodily ailments" (*molestiae corporales*) that are "properly called *passiones corporis*" (35.1.co).

The distinction between *dolor* and *tristitia*, as deployed in the *Summa*, does not correspond neatly to the distinction between *corpus* and *animus*. It is true that pain is "said to be of the body, since the cause of pain is in the body, as when we suffer some harm to the body." But, Aquinas continues, "the motion of pain is always in the soul: for 'the body cannot

---

[5] While Loughlin intends his account of the *dolor/tristitia* distinction as a reading of the *Summa*'s treatment, it appears to be informed by *QDV* 26.2. These accounts are not necessarily identical; they may even be in some tension with each other. Gondreau (2002) notices a "development" of Thomas's thought on this point from the *Sentences* commentary and *QDV* to the *Summa* (p. 391; see also pp. 208 and 380–2). From a different point of view, Italo Sciuito finds that "the *De veritate* underscores . . . a distinction which is passed over in silence in the *Summa*" (Sciuito, *Le passioni dell'anima nel pensiero di Tommaso d'Aquino*, p. 78, quoted in Galeazzi [2004], p. 557). This suggests the possibility that the *ST*'s presentation is motivated by pedagogical abbreviation rather than an authentic development in Thomas's thinking.

feel pain unless the soul is in pain,' as Augustine says" (35.1 ad 1m; see Augustine, *Ennarationes in Psalmos* [*PL* 37, 1110]). Thomas is aware of the tradition of regarding pain as a kind of bodily sickness, noting that Augustine himself often calls pain *aegritudo*.[6] While it may be legitimate to speak of pain metaphorically as a sickness, Aquinas insists that by its nature *dolor* is a passion of the soul, no less than *tristitia*. The reason is that both pain and sorrow require the perception of an actual "conjunction with some evil" (*coniunctio alicuius mali*). If evil is non-being, one may wonder, how there can be an actual conjunction with it? Aquinas anticipates the question. The thing with which one is conjoined is in itself good, but evil to the extent that it "deprives one of some good (*quia privat aliquo bono*)." Aquinas draws the following inference: if a thing is not perceived as depriving a person of some good, it will be incapable of causing pain or sorrow. In order to cause either, it must be perceived *sub ratione mali*.

Tristitia and *dolor* are both passions of the soul. Are they different names for the same passion, or do they denote different passions? In Article 2, Aquinas addresses this question. In its narrowest sense, *dolor* refers to the passion caused by the apprehension of the exterior senses, while the passion named by *tristitia* is necessarily caused by the interior senses. Because anything apprehended by the exterior senses can become an object of the interior apprehension, but not vice versa, it follows that sorrow extends to more things than pain does. Thomas affirms this consequence of the argument, but proceeds to notice a wider sense of *dolor*. In this sense, all things experienced as unpleasant may be described as painful, and only some of them are rightly said to cause sorrow. Sorrow is thus redescribed as a species of pain: "If *dolor* be taken in a wide sense (*communiter*), then it is the genus of sorrow" (35.2 ad 3m). Recalling the parallel argument of 31.3, Aquinas concludes that "*tristitia* is a certain species of *dolor*, just as *gaudium* is a species of *delectatio*" (35.2.co).

The parallel conceals an important asymmetry between the treatments of *delectatio/gaudium* and *dolor/tristitia*. In Questions 31–4, Thomas places the most emphasis on the generic term, *delectatio*, experienced by irrational and rational animals alike. But in Questions 35–9, he devotes significantly less attention to *dolor* than to *tristitia*. While bodily pains are better known than spiritual pains, as Thomas acknowledges (35.2 ad 1m),

---

[6] Here Augustine's exemplar is Cicero, who uses *aegritudo* to name the chief perturbation from which the *sapiens* is free. See Cicero, *Tusculan Disputations* 3.6.12 and *passim*.

his principal objective is to understand the latter. Aquinas writes as a psychologist, not a healer of physical ailments. Behind pain there are nerve endings; "behind sorrow there is always a soul" (Wilde 1999, p. 88). For the spiritual life, the interior event is of greater importance than the exterior. Why did this very fact not lead Aquinas to stress *gaudium* over *delectatio*? One explanation is that *gaudium* is only ambiguously a *passio animae*. In its pure form, *gaudium* is an affection of the will, a pseudopassion (§2.2, §7.1). *Tristitia*, though in one sense the rational correlate of *gaudium*, stands as the paradigmatic case of *pati*, "being acted upon." That one is more violently acted upon by *tristitia* than *dolor* is evident. One may experience bodily pains or ailments without being significantly affected by them. Precisely because sorrows are caused by interior apprehension, they act upon the soul more deeply, striking the spirit at its root.

Tristitia is more properly a passion than either *gaudium* or *dolor*. Therefore, it receives the most attention in Questions 35–9. Article 3 begins a series of four Articles in which Thomas wants to affirm both formal opposition and material connections between *tristitia* and *delectatio*. The formal opposition is straightforward. Perceived *sub ratione boni*, as the "present good" (*bonum praesens*), a thing becomes the object of pleasure and joy. Perceived *sub ratione mali*, as the "present evil" (*malum praesens*), a thing becomes the object of pain and sorrow (35.3.co). Since contrary formal objects of the apprehension produce contrary motions of the appetite, pain and pleasure are contrary passions. Materially, however, sorrow and pleasure may be connected in any number of ways. As Aquinas says:

Nothing prevents one contrary from being the *per accidens* cause of the other. Thus can sorrow be the cause of pleasure, in one way, insofar as sorrow about the absence of some thing, or about the presence of its contrary, inspires one to seek more keenly the thing in which one takes pleasure. Thus a man thirsting seeks more keenly the pleasure of drink as a remedy against the sorrow which he suffers. (35.3 ad 1m)

These considerations adumbrate the contention that receives more technical elaboration in Article 4 – that not every sorrow is contrary to every pleasure. Article 5 poses a more difficult question. Is there any sorrow that is contrary to the pleasure of contemplation? That Aquinas considers the question unusually difficult is indicated by the appearance of five objectors in the Article. Most pleasant actions are not unalloyed, but come with contrary pains. This is true of not only the pleasures that

Augustine describes in book 2 of the *Confessions*,[7] but also any pleasures that are subject to time. Contemplation, however, is the exception, precisely because it is the locus of human participation in divine timelessness. Of all the pleasures of which humans are capable, it alone involves no sorrow. But how can this be? Sorrow appears inextricably bound up with contemplation. This seems true from reflection on the object of contemplation, as the first three objectors argue. Sorrow seems to be the natural result of contemplating anything that inspires penance (35.5 arg. 1), anything contrary to what gives pleasure (35.5 arg. 2), or any evil at all (35.5 arg. 3). An analysis of the activity seems to yield the same conclusion. Sorrow ensues when the act is hindered, as it inevitably is (35.5 arg. 4), or when it produces "affliction of the flesh," which Sirach suggests is the usual result of *frequens meditatio* (35.5 arg. 5).

In the appearance *sed contra*, Thomas significantly chooses a scriptural authority. The exaltation of contemplation as the single pleasure that involves no sorrow is not motivated simply by a desire to vindicate Aristotle's teaching. It is inspired by a thoroughly scriptural understanding of wisdom. The *sed contra* quotes and briefly comments upon chapter 8 of the book of Wisdom: "Her conversation hath no bitterness nor her company any tediousness; but joy and gladness" (35.5.sc). Aquinas comments: "Now the conversation and company of wisdom are found in contemplation. Therefore there is no sorrow contrary to the pleasure of contemplation" (35.5.sc).

How can a doctrine so seemingly contrary to the facts of human experience be defended? Aquinas' strategy is to distinguish two senses of the *delectatio contemplationis*. If the pleasure refers to the object contemplated, it is certainly possible to think about something harmful and sorrowful. But if the focus is on the activity of contemplation itself, then sorrow cannot enter into the picture. Here Thomas cites not only Aristotle, but also "Gregory" (i.e. Nemesius), in order to strengthen the impression that when he exalts the contemplative act to a height that sorrow cannot touch, he is simply affirming the teaching of the tradition as a whole. The premise is that "sorrow *per se* is contrary to the pleasure which regards a contrary object" (35.5.co). For every bodily pleasure, there will be a contrary pain, as the pleasure of heat is contrary to the pain in cold, because heat and cold are contraries. But nothing in reality is contrary to the "good of the intellect" (*bonum intellectus*) (35.5 ad 3m),

---

[7] "You were always by me, mercifully hard upon me, and besprinkling all my illicit pleasures with certain elements of bitterness, to draw me on to seek for pleasures in which no bitterness should be" (Augustine 1993, p. 24).

since falsehood is a privation of truth, not its really existing contrary. If contrary passions require contrary objects, and if the rejection of Manicheanism entails that nothing is contrary to the *obiectio contemplationis*, then "there cannot be, speaking *per se*, any contrary sorrow to the pleasure which occurs in contemplating" (35.5.co). Bodily pleasures derive their character as palliatives against contrary ills. The spiritual pleasure that attends contemplative activity is no mere *medicina* – Aquinas' restriction of the term to bodily pleasures may be a judgment against Cicero's conception of philosophy as *animi medicina* (*Tusculan Disputations* 3.3.6) – but pleasurable in itself. Thomas reiterates the argument of Question 31: contemplative activity is not a temporal becoming, but a perfect operation.

In itself, the act that thinks in eternity contains no contrary sorrow. What produces the appearance that sorrow is mingled with contemplation is the mind's use of the sensitive powers, whose objects and acts occur within time, and thus admit of contrary sorrows. But these sorrows "have no place in the mind's contemplation, since the mind has no corporeal organ" (35.5.co). Any pains that appear connected with contemplation are side-effects, related to the act only *per accidens*.[8]

Contemplating the highest good is incompatible with sorrow, because the highest good has no positive contrary. This priority of the good (see §1.4) underlies the contention of Article 6, that the desire for pleasure, caused by a suitable good, is more eager than the avoidance of sorrow. Just as evil is always a privation, so sorrow is inevitably "partial" (*secundum partem*) (35.6.co). This is the first of two arguments that Aquinas gives in the response of Article 6. The second argument is based on the same premise. Because good exists in itself, and is therefore stronger than evil (which must counterfeit the good in order to exist), the inclination to seek good is naturally stronger than the inclination to seek evil. The Augustinian and Dionysian premise of the argument is evident; the *sed contra* cites Dionysius explicitly. Once again, the problem is to account for apparently contrary appearances. Aquinas cites Augustine: "love is felt more keenly, when we lack that which we love" (*De Trinitate* 10.12). We do not feel sorrow for a thing that we lack – indeed, we do not

---

[8] Thus Keats (2002) on contemplation: "It enjoys light and shade; it lives in gusto, be it foul or fair, high or low, rich or poor, mean or elevated – It has as much delight in conceiving an Iago as an Imogen. What shocks the virtuous philosopher, delights the camelion Poet. It does no harm from its relish of the dark side of things any more than from its taste for the bright one; because they both end in speculation" (Letter to Woodhouse, October 27, 1818, p. 195). What Keats attributes to the poet may be equally attributable to the speculative theologian, if not the "virtuous philosopher."

perceive it as a lack – unless we love that thing. A person who has no love of stamps is not sad about his present lack of a stamp collection. But if that same person has a love of recorded music, he will grieve when his stereo malfunctions. Sorrow presupposes love and desire; love of the good is stronger than avoidance of evil. If human beings expend a large amount of energy avoiding evils, they do so in the name of goods which they care about. The intensity with which a person avoids an evil is a function of the intensity with which that person loves the contrary good.

In different ways, Articles 5 and 6 ask whether good is stronger than evil. Article 7 continues the inquiry about strength, but shifts the focus to a division between two kinds of pain. Which is greater, outward or inward pain? Interestingly, Aquinas does not deploy the distinction established in Article 2 between *dolor* and *tristitia*. Instead, he speaks of *dolor exterior* and *dolor interior*. The implication is that *dolor interior* cannot be identified with *tristitia*.[9] Outward pain is caused by sensory apprehension, primarily touch, whereas inward pain is caused by "interior apprehension," whether by the imagination or the reason (35.7.co). Irrational animals can feel inward pain; their powers of imagination and memory suffice to make something painful, even if it does not directly touch them. They cannot, however, feel *tristitia*, or what the *sed contra* (quoting Sirach) identifies as *tristitia cordis*, "sorrow of the heart" (35.7.sc). *Interior dolor* refers to pain that is felt by any being with an imagination; *tristitia* captures the kind of inward pain that is peculiarly experienced by human beings. This explains why Article 7 is something more than a rehash of Article 2's distinction between *tristitia* and *dolor*. Non-rational animals may experience a kind of pain that is not directly caused by sensation, but this should not be confused with the passion of sorrow as experienced by rational creatures.

Is *tristitia*, the sorrow proper to the rational creature, a passion in the strict sense? Why not claim that *tristitia*, insofar as it is caused by intellectual apprehension, is an affection of the will? Aquinas does not exclude the possibility of a purely rational correlate to the passion, that is, a pseudopassion (see §2.2). But what is true of rational concupiscence applies to *tristitia*. Both are caused by reason, and are possible only for rational creatures. Yet they are truly passions, in the proper sense of the term, because they are motions of the sensitive appetite. Thus Aquinas

---

[9] Contrary to Manzanedo's claim that *dolor interior* can be identified with *tristitia* (1991, p. 64). The two may be related as genus to species. So while all *tristitia* is *interior dolor* (hence the appearance of *interior dolor* as a near equivalent of *tristitia* in the discussion of remedies at 38.2.co), not all *interior dolor* is properly *tristitia*.

remains faithful to his intention to describe the acts common to humans and other animals, while focusing on what is particular to human beings.

To summarize, Thomas uses four key terms for pain and sorrow:

1. *Dolor* in the generic sense – any kind of pain or sorrow.
2. *Dolor exterior* – pain caused by any of the immediate proper senses.
3. *Dolor interior* – pain caused by the imagination, felt by irrational as well as rational creatures.
4. *Tristitia* – pain caused by rational apprehension, but involving a motion of the sensitive appetite.

The first seven Articles of Question 35 provide a gradual expansion of the vocabulary necessary for describing pain and sorrow in themselves. One may suspect that Aquinas has overlooked other emotional phenomena that are closely related to pain and sorrow. The final Article of Question 35 may serve to allay this suspicion. Here Thomas adverts to the "four species of sorrow" named by both "Gregory" (i.e. Nemesius) and John of Damascene: pity (*misericordia*), envy (*invidia*), anxiety (*anxietas/angustia*), and torpor (*acedia*). Aquinas does not allow these "four species of sorrow" to inform the controlling taxonomy, and for good reason. The essential species of pain must be distinguished according to the mode of apprehending their cause, not by something "foreign to the notion conveyed by the genus" (35.8.co). Yet Thomas is sanguine about admitting the four species into an account of sorrow's associated phenomena. Adding these four species to the consideration of *dolor et tristitia* contributes to the sense that Aquinas provides a full (though necessarily brief) treatment of how we experience sorrow. Unlike bodily pain, which concerns present evils exclusively, sorrow extends to evils of the past, present, and future. Sorrow is capable of this extension, because its cause lies in the reflective act of the interior cognitive power. Reflecting on his own "Symphony of Sorrow," Wilde writes in *De profundis*:

Suffering – curious as it may sound to you – is the means by which we exist, because it is the only means by which we become conscious of existing; and the remembrance of suffering in the past is necessary to us as the warrant, the evidence, of our continued identity. (1999, p. 18)

In a similar way, Aquinas regards the capacity to feel sorrow as a condition of being human. This explains, at least, in part, why Christ assumes the "defect of soul" constituted by *tristitia* (see 3.15.6).[10]

---

[10] For insightful commentary on Christ's sorrow, see Gondreau 2002, pp. 388–403.

8.2 WHAT CAUSES SORROW?

What produces sorrow? Aquinas has already identified the basic cause of sorrow, namely the apprehension of a present evil (36.2.co). Why, then, does he choose to devote an entire Question to the cause of sorrow? One reason is that Aquinas has not clarified the relation between the principle that evil is a privation of good and the notion that what causes sorrow is not simply a privation of good but the apprehension of evil as such. There is another reason for giving the "causes of sorrow" their own Question. Even if one agrees that sorrow's direct cause is the apprehension of a present evil, one still wants to know more about what prompts the mind to apprehend things as evils. In the case of bodily good, this may be obvious ("it hurts"). But what leads us to perceive things as evils, even when they cause no bodily pain? Rather than proceed solely from facts about the mind, or from properties that inhere in things themselves, Aquinas approaches the matter both *ex parte obiecti* and *ex parte subiecti*. Articles 1–3 consider primarily subjective causes of sorrow: the perception of something as an evil (Article 1), the presence of concupiscence (Article 2), and the desire for unity (Article 3). In Article 4, Thomas shifts to an "objective" cause, isolating the conditions under which an irresistible power outside the self produces sorrow.[11]

Aquinas begins Question 36 with an ear to conflicting voices from the tradition. He wants to reconcile Augustine's claim that sorrow is caused by the loss of temporal goods with Damascene's contention that a present evil causes sorrow. If being and knowing were exactly the same, he comments, the question would be of no moment (36.1.co). In the order of things, there is no difference between the privation of good and the presence of evil. But the order of things is not the same as the order of apprehension. If a person has lost a genuine good, something bad has happened to him. But to apprehend the loss of the good as an evil requires an additional step. It is possible that he does not see the loss of the good as a loss, or that while he sees it as a loss, he judges it to be compensated by the acquisition of a greater good. In either case, he will not perceive the loss of a good as an evil. This fact makes sorrow less likely to ensue. If, however, a person both loses a good and apprehends that loss as an

---

[11] Ramírez (1973) also makes a division between Articles 1–3 and Article 4, but glosses it as a *per se* and *per accidens* distinction (p. 305). This cannot be correct, since the only *per se* cause of sorrow is the apprehension of something as *malum praesens*. *Concupiscentia* and *appetitus unitatis* are contributing factors, causing sorrow only to the extent that they bring about the perception of something as a present evil.

evil, the passion of sorrow necessarily follows. Because apprehension of the lost good as an evil is required for the production of sorrow, Thomas concludes that "the cause of sorrow or pain is more properly the conjoined evil than the lost good" (36.1.co).

With this distinction, Aquinas is able to take into account both the "objective" and "subjective" factors that lead a person to apprehend something as evil. He saves the phenomenon noted by Augustine – the production of sorrow by the loss of temporal goods – and reconciles it to the authority of Damascene, who emphasizes the necessity of perceived evil in sorrow's causation. Missing from this reconciliation is Aristotle. If Aristotle generally has little to say about pain and sorrow, he has virtually nothing to say about the topics of Question 36. Each of the next three Articles quotes Augustine in the passages *sed contra*. Article 2 asks whether *concupiscentia* is a cause of sorrow. Thomas begins by considering *concupiscentia* not in its proper sense, but in its wider sense as *amor*, the first motion of the appetite towards a suitable good. Love causes sorrow not through being its immediate object, but as the presupposition necessary for regarding a thing as evil. To perceive something as evil requires a basic inclination of the appetite against it, which Thomas has already described as "hate." But hate itself requires love, since nothing can be hated unless its contrary is loved, as Aquinas argued in Question 29 (§6.1). Because there is no pain without hate, and no hate without love, it follows that *amor* is a "universal cause of pain" (36.2.co).

Is *concupiscentia* in its proper sense a cause of sorrow? The quotation from Augustine in the passage *sed contra* suggests an obvious way in which this is true. *Concupiscentia noxiarum*, the desire for hurtful things, inevitably leads to pain. A person who desires to drink heavily may proceed to do so. If he does, he will feel no small amount of pain. Rather than dwell upon this scenario, Aquinas considers two other possibilities. When a person wants a good but finds himself unable to obtain it, he will be frustrated. As long as hope for attaining the thing is present, such frustration will not turn into sorrow. But when "hope is removed through the present of an impediment, then concupiscence causes pain" (36.2 ad 3m). Such pain is real enough. But it pales in comparison to the sorrow produced in a person who has successfully obtained and enjoyed a good, but proceeds to lose it. "We sorrow more about the withdrawal of a present good, in which we have already taken pleasure, than about a future good that we desire to have" (36.2.co). The pain felt by a couple who want children but cannot have them, while far from illusory, does not compare to the sorrow of parents who have lost their children to death.

In each of these three ways – wanting hurtful things, wanting good things but never attaining them, and wanting and obtaining good things but losing them – desire causes sorrow. But is there a form of desire that is particularly connected to the production of sorrow? Article 3 suggests an answer this question. Among the appetites that cause sorrow, the "appetite for unity" (*appetitus unitatis*) seems especially potent. The desire for good is, in the long run, a desire for unity, because we desire by nature to be united with the good that perfects us. Just as love or desire for good is a cause of sorrow, Aquinas concludes, so also is the love or appetite for unity. What produces sorrow is our recognition of the gap between the condition we desire – to be in union with all other goods, insofar as they complete our natures – and the condition in which we actually find ourselves, described by terms like "fragmentation" and "alienation." Insofar as we perceive the condition as a present evil, sorrow will result. (If we have no hope in overcoming the evil, the sorrow will be magnified.)

In Article 4, Aquinas asks whether a power that "cannot be resisted" (see 36 pr.) can be a cause of sorrow. Once again, the impetus of the Article is Augustine. The *sed contra* quotes Augustine's *De natura boni* 20: "Sorrow in the soul is caused by the will resisting a stronger power, while pain in the body is caused by sense resisting a stronger body" (*PL* 42, 557). Aquinas provides a brief account of the reason underlying this doctrine: "It is against the inclination of the appetite, that it cling to a thing that it presently experiences as evil. Now what is against a thing's inclination never occurs except through the action of some stronger thing. Whence Augustine takes the cause of sorrow to be a greater power" (36.4.co). Yet Aquinas restricts the application of this doctrine. The "greater power" functions as a cause of sorrow only as long as the inclination of the appetite against which the greater power acts is able to remain in existence. If the greater power succeeds in eliminating the inclination, resistance is broken and sorrow disappears.[12]

8.3 THE VALUE OF MODERATE SORROW

What does sorrow bring about? Question 37 addresses the matter, treating the characteristic "effects of pain or sorrow." A cursory inspection of

[12] For example: a decent lawyer forced to submit as a condition of employment to the unethical billing practices of his partners will experience sorrow. But if the power of his peers manages to alter his inclinations, such that he comes to perceive his firm's practice as normal and even natural, acceptance will take the place of sorrow.

Question 37 reveals its apparently negative tone. Sorrow and pain eliminate the capacity to learn (Article 1), depress the soul (Article 2), weaken all
activity (Article 3), and harm the body more than the other *passiones
animae* (Article 4).[13] It would seem that Aquinas considers sorrow to be
bad for the human person. Yet a more subtle reading suggests that, like all
the passions, sorrow is natural to the rational creature. As such, it has
considerable value when it is rightly used.

Aquinas begins with the bad effects of pain, opening the Question with
an inquiry into pain's power to "remove the power to learn" (37.1). Pain
destroys the faculty of learning, because learning requires a total concentration of the soul's *intentio*, and pain distracts it. Quoting Proverbs 2,
Thomas suggests that were humans to devote the same amount of energy
to seeking wisdom as they do to money-making, they might become
wiser. Because learning requires the total concentration of mind upon
its object, physical pain necessarily hinders it. Aquinas observes that pain
prevents a person not only from learning new things, but even from
attending to what he already knows. Anyone who has attempted to follow
a complex argument, give a coherent lecture, or write an essay while
feeling ill knows what he means. Augustine's report of his toothache
at Cassiciacum, quoted by Aquinas in the *sed contra*, represents the
experience of many.[14]

But notice that the emphasis is on *dolor* rather than *tristitia*. What is
evidently true of pain cannot be attributed to sorrow without qualification. "Moderate sorrow" (*tristitia moderata*) (37.1 ad 1m), as long as it
excludes the mind's wandering, can enhance learning, especially when a
person wants to learn more about what lies beyond sorrow. As an
example, consider Pascal's famous "image de la condition des hommes"
(1976, §199, p. 109; cf. 1966, §434, p. 137). Those who encounter this
image for the first time typically find it depressing. But contemplation of
the image may focus our attention more keenly upon the power of grace.
Tristitia moderata is a necessary condition for ascent.

---

[13] Superficially, Articles 1–3 treat sorrow's psychological effects, and Article 4 its physiological effects.
Ramírez (1973) makes this suggestion (p. 312). The suggestion is not confirmed by the text, since
Thomas explicitly adverts in Article 2 to paralysis as a somatic corollary of the *aggravatio animi*
caused by sorrow.

[14] But not everyone. Collingwood (1939) reports that "whether luckily or unluckily, I have never
known any illness to interfere with my power of thinking and writing, or with the quality of what
I think and write. When I am unwell, I have only to begin work on some piece of philosophical
thinking, and all my ailments are forgotten until I leave off. But this does not cure them. If they are
due to overwork, it may aggravate them" (p. 117). As for Augustine's report of his toothache, see
Confessions 9.4.

To be sure, Aquinas holds that moderate sorrow contributes only *per accidens* "to the facility of learning, insofar as it takes away a super-abundance of pleasure" (37.1 ad 2m). But this contribution, even if *per accidens*, is not trivial. Few things are more effective in preventing a person from acquiring the habit of contemplation than immersion in frivolous pleasures. The experience of sorrow is a salutary counter-weight to such diversions; it serves as an antidote to the supreme vice of shallowness. In *De profundis*, Wilde reports that he used to live entirely for pleasure, shunning sorrow and suffering of every kind. Only after experiencing genuine sorrow was he able to transcend himself, learning not just about suffering, but about the love that stands as its cause:

Now it seems to me that Love of some kind is the only possible explanation of the extraordinary amount of suffering that there is in the world. I cannot conceive any other explanation. I am convinced that there is no other, and that if the worlds have indeed, as I have said, been built out of Sorrow, it has been by the hands of Love, because in no other way could the Soul of man for whom the worlds are made reach the full stature of its perfection. Pleasure for the beautiful body, but Pain for the beautiful Soul. (1999, pp. 66–7)

Like the other passions, sorrow in moderation contributes to the perfection of the human person (§4.2).

In Article 2, Aquinas turns to a more familiar effect of pain and sorrow, the *aggravatio animi*. In the condition, the soul is "weighed down" (*aggravatio* derives from *aggravare*, i.e. *ad + gravare*), in a manner that may recall the contemporary metaphor of "depression." That sorrow can burden the soul is evident. More interestingly, Thomas notices three kinds of depression. The least pernicious form of *aggravatio*, which we might think of as "mild depression," hinders the motion of the soul, but does not paralyze it completely. To the extent that it retains hope, the soul preserves its natural ability to repulse the evil that weighs it down. If the soul has altogether lost hope to repel the afflicting evil, it suffers from a more intense *aggravatio*, which might correspond to "serious depression." But seriously depressed persons are able to maintain the external appearances of human functioning, even if they are moving toward *la seconda morte*.[15] Last on the continuum would be the case of those who are so

---

[15] On *la seconda morte*, see especially Dante, *Inferno*, canto 1, line 117, as well as Revelation 20:14. See also Rieff (1973 and 2006), who exploits the category of the "second death" in a virtually unparalleled way. I am indebted to Sebastian Miner for calling my attention to the phrase in St. Francis's "Canticle of the Sun" (St. Francis 1982, p. 39).

depressed as to be entirely functionless. For these persons, "even the external motion of the body is impaired, so that a man becomes stupefied" (37.2.co). In its acute forms, depression causes the soul to be "withdrawn into itself and, as it were, constricted into itself (*quasi in seipso constrictus*)" (37.2 ad 2m). This type of self-enclosure is a fault and requires spiritual therapy. But Aquinas does not condemn depression out of hand. Mild depression may be a natural and proper effect of what Thomas calls the "sorrow which is according to God" (*tristitia quae est secundum Deum*) (37.2 ad 1m). This sorrow ought not to be eliminated or narcoticized; it is a condition of spiritual growth.

In the next Article, Aquinas appears to hold that sorrow or pain weakens all activity. This reading of Article 3, however, is superficial, as may be seen from the handling of the *videtur quod*. The objectors make the case for the view that sorrow can promote activity. Sorrow produces carefulness, which in turn conduces to good work; sorrow causes desire, and therefore leads to intense action; sorrow quickens activities to which it is naturally suited, such as mourning the dead. If the *respondeo dicendum* were simply to deny these arguments, our interpretation of Article 2 would be difficult to sustain. But Aquinas does not simply negate the objections. In the response he distinguishes two ways in which action may be related to sorrow. If action is sorrow's object, that action will be hindered: "We never do that which we do with sorrow so well as that which we do with pleasure, or without sorrow" (37.3.co). But action may also be related to sorrow as its principle and cause. In this case, Aquinas claims, sorrow does not weaken operation, but actually serves to promote it. "The more one sorrows on account of a certain thing, the more one strives to drive sorrow away, provided there is a hope of driving it out" (37.3.co). Entirely hopeless sorrow is enervating, but sorrow mixed with hope can be energizing. Because the objections are substantially true, Aquinas does not provide an explicit answer to them. The response is sufficient; *per hoc patet responsio ad obiecta*.

In the final Article of Question 37, Aquinas concludes that immoderate sorrow is more harmful to the body than any of the other *passiones animae*. Immoderate sorrow does not merely exceed the body's natural motion according to some measure; it is repugnant to vital motion by its very nature. The conclusion of Question 37 stands as a reminder that sorrow can be dangerous, not least because it can lead to *acedia*. But does sorrow necessarily have this effect? What is true of immoderate sorrow applies neither to sorrow in moderation nor to *tristitia quae est secundum Deum*. Wilde is neither wrong nor anti-Thomist when he declares that "where there is Sorrow there is holy ground" (1999, p. 47). Out of sorrow's depths, Wilde discovers the elements of a *vita nuova*: "sorrow remarries us to God" (p. 63).[16] Through the experience of sorrow,

one discerns things that one never discerned before. One approaches the whole of history from a different standpoint. What one had felt dimly through instinct, about Art, is intellectually and emotionally realised with perfect clearness of vision and absolute intensity of apprehension. (1999, p. 65)

Does sorrow have this value for Aquinas? He writes:

Present griefs (*luctus praesens*) lead to the consolation of a future life, because by the very fact that man should mourn for his sins or for the delay of glory, he merits the consolation of eternity. Similarly a person merits it when he does not run away from sufferings and straits in order to draw near it. (35.3 ad 1m)

This perspective finds later expression by another Dominican. Dwelling in the cell of self-knowledge requires us to embrace sorrow, according to Catherine of Siena. Catherine proposes that "suffering and sorrow increase in proportion to love. When love grows, so does sorrow" (1980, p. 33). For both Thomas and Catherine, sorrow flows from the human capacity to love. It is not something to medicate out of existence, although it is natural and appropriate to seek remedies.

8.4 REMEDIES FOR PAIN AND SORROW

In Question 38, Aquinas considers five remedies for pain and sorrow. He begins with pleasure, the most basic remedy for sorrow (Article 1), and proceeds to identify three activities that bring about the replacement of sorrow by pleasure. These are, in order of intensity, tears and groans (Article 2), the sympathy of friends (Article 3), and contemplation of the truth (Article 4). If contemplating truth does not avail, we learn in the Question's denouement, sleep and baths may be appropriate (Article 5).

Pleasure is *the* remedy for sorrow. "Any pleasure offers a remedy for the mitigation of any sorrow, no matter where it comes from" (38.1.co). The particular pleasure need not be specifically contrary to the particular sorrow. In the long term, the pleasure may be worse for the person than the sorrow it mitigates. Nonetheless, pleasures are always effective while

[16] Wilde attributes the line to Dante, but I cannot find that it occurs in Dante's texts in precisely this form.

they last. When Augustine first grieves over the death of his friend, he is unable to recognize his deepest pathology, namely the disordering of his affections that causes him to love another person as though he were more than a person. Yet the relief of his immediate sorrows does not require this recognition. Why not? Aquinas explains:

Perception (*sensus*) of the present moves more strongly than memory of the past, and love of self remains longer than love of another – hence it is that pleasure finally drives out sorrow. Whence a little further on (*Confessions* 4.8) Augustine adds that his "sorrow yielded to his former pleasures." (38.1 ad 3m)

Time may not heal all wounds, but it reliably corresponds to a decrease in pain. In Article 2, Aquinas continues to draw upon book 4 of the *Confessions*. When Augustine mourned the death of a friend, "in groans and in tears alone did he find some little refreshment" (38.2.sc). Why do tears and groans mitigate sorrow? Thomas gives two reasons.

First, because any noxious thing enclosed interiorly hurts more, since the soul's intention regarding that thing is multiplied all the more. But when it is diffused toward exterior things, then the soul's intention is dispersed in some way toward exterior things, and thus interior pain (*interior dolor*) is diminished. And because of this, when men in sorrow outwardly manifest their sorrow by tears or groans, or even by words, their sorrow is mitigated. (38.2.co)

Outward expression of inner turmoil provides relief; keeping emotions bottled up is unhealthy. As Burton declares, "grief concealed strangles the soul" (1927, p. 471). Aquinas supplies a second reason why tears mitigate sorrow. "Tears and groans are actions befitting a man who is in sorrow or pain; and consequently they become pleasant to him." Because "every pleasure in some way mitigates sorrow or pain, as was stated, it follows that sorrow is mitigated by lamentation and groaning" (38.2.co). Anything suitable by nature is pleasant, and therefore an antidote to sorrow.

Article 3 considers the capacity of sympathetic friends to mitigate pain and sorrow. Sorrow burdens the soul; talking with compassionate friends lightens the load. As Johnson says, the man who talks for fame can never be pleasing, but "the man who talks to unburthen his mind is the man to delight you" (1934, vol. III, p. 247). In a similar vein, St. Francis de Sales writes: "The heart finds relief in telling its troubles to another, just as the body when suffering from persistent fever finds relief from bleeding" (2002, p. 204). Why is discourse with friends particularly effective in assuaging sorrow? Aquinas draws two reasons from book 9 of the *Nicomachean Ethics*. He describes the first as follows:

When someone sees others saddened by his own sorrow, a certain fancy (*quaedam imaginatio*), as it were (*quasi*), occurs to him. It seems that others are bearing the burden with him, striving, as it were (*quasi*), to make the burden lighter. And thence the burden of sorrow becomes light, as happens also in carrying corporeal burdens. (38.3.co)

The double use of *quasi*, as well as *quaedam imaginatio*, suggests that Aquinas wishes to place some distance between this account and his own thinking. Thomas proceeds to identify a "second, and better reason."

When a person's friends are sorrowful for him (*contristantur ei*), he perceives that he is loved by them. This is pleasurable, as was said above. Whence, since every pleasure mitigates sorrow, just as was said above, it follows that a sympathetic friend (*amicus condolens*) mitigates sorrow. (38.3.co)

This "second reason" is better precisely because it secures the connection that Aquinas wants to make between the provision of pleasure and the mitigation of sorrow.[17]

If tears and talk are temporary palliatives, is there a more durable remedy that involves a more intense pleasure? Article 4 answers the question affirmatively. The contemplation of truth is a superior remedy for sorrow. This is clear from Aquinas' prior argument that the greatest of pleasures arises from the contemplation of truth. But he recognizes the possibility of scepticism on the point. As one objector argues:

The remedy for an ailment should be applied to the part which ails. But contemplation of truth is in the intellect. Therefore it does not assuage bodily pain, which is in the senses. (38.4 arg. 3)

The objection has some validity. Those unable or unwilling to develop their natural capacity for contemplation will not find it a useful remedy for pain and sorrow. But the "more perfectly someone is a lover of wisdom" (*perfectius aliquis est amator sapientiae*) (38.4.co), the more potent a remedy contemplation becomes. "In the powers of the soul an overflow occurs (*fit redundantia*) from the higher to the lower. And accordingly, the pleasure of contemplation, which is in the higher part,

---

[17] At *Nicomachean Ethics* 9.11, 1171a30, Aristotle raises the question about which of these two reasons is nearer the truth, while hesitating to answer it. Aquinas does not hesitate; the second reason is better. The first reason falls short because "the other does not take on himself a part of the same numerical sorrow which someone feels, so that his sorrow may be lessened" (*InNE*, 9.13.6). Cf. Thomas Aquinas 1993, p. 583: "The second reason is better and belongs to the sorrow itself." It is worth remarking that although Aristotle dismisses the question, Thomas is unusually insistent in his commentary about the power of sympathetic friends to mitigate sorrows: "What we have described certainly happens."

overflows (*redundat*) in order to mitigate even that pain which is in the senses" (38.4 ad 3m). Here Aquinas is thinking not of the sighing philosopher, but of the saint. Quoting the Dominican breviary, Thomas recalls that the "martyr Tiburtius, when he was walking barefoot on the burning coals, said: 'It seems to me that I walk on roses, in the name of Jesus Christ'" (38.4.co).

Of the multiple pleasures accessible to human beings, contemplation is the highest. Because it is most pleasurable, it is best suited to enable the human being to transcend pain and sorrow. Yet Aquinas does not conclude the Question on this note. As if to remind us that human beings are embodied intellects, for whom no contemplative activity is entirely continuous, he returns in Article 5 to more earthly remedies. Sleep and baths give pleasure that relieves sorrow. Article 5's *sed contra* cites Augustine's quotation of Ambrose's hymn: "Sleep restores wearied limbs to toil, refreshes the weary mind, and dissolves anxious griefs."[18] By restoring the body to its natural and normal state, sleep and baths produce pleasures that mitigate sorrow. What holds for sleep and baths applies to all "bodily remedies" (*remedia corporalia*) (38.5.co).

On our reading, the climax of Question 38 occurs in Article 4. *Contemplatio veritatis* is the most potent remedy for sorrow, precisely because it is the most intense form of pleasure available to *amatores sapientiae*. Yet, as if to allay any suspicion that he offers an exclusively "intellectualist" approach to the melioration of sorrow, Thomas surrounds the climax with Articles that acknowledge the power of other remedies to produce pleasure and thereby mitigate sorrow. Ramírez divides Question 38 into a treatment of *remedia directa et immediata* (Articles 1–3) and *remedia indirecta et mediata* (Articles 4–5) (1973, pp. 317–18). This is not plausible, since the only "direct" remedy is *delectatio*. All the other remedies are "indirect"; their capacity to mitigate sorrow is strictly correlated with their ability to cause pleasure. The key to the elimination of sorrow is *delectatio*.

---

[18] In book 9 of the *Confessions*, after the death of Monica, Augustine says that it occurred to him to bathe, "for I had heard that the bath – which the Greeks call *balaneion* – is so called because it drives anxiety from the mind" (1993, p. 168; Sheed's transcription of the Greek corrected). The passage is significant for two reasons. First, it contains the only explicit invocation of a Greek term within the *Confessions*, and thus perfectly counter-balances the distaste for the Greek language recorded more famously in book 1. (I owe this point to discussion with Michael Foley.) Second, it suggests the source for Aquinas' thinking about the power of *remedia corporalia*. Augustine makes it clear that "he was the same man after as before. The bitterness of grief had not sweated out of my heart" (p. 168). Yet when he woke up the next day, his sorrow was somewhat relieved. Similarly, the placement of Article 5 as a coda to Article 4 suggests that one should neither overrate nor underrate bodily remedies.

Aquinas affirms this psychological truth without any suggestion that sorrow invariably requires remediation. On the contrary, in light of sorrow's power to transform trivial voluptuaries into noble lovers of wisdom, not all sorrows should be eliminated.

8.5 SORROW IN RELATION TO GOOD AND EVIL

Which sorrows ought to be remedied? Which should be preserved and even cherished? Such questions lead naturally to the consideration *de bonitate et malitia doloris vel tristitiae*.[19] Article 1 of Question 39 establishes that not all sorrow is evil. The next two Articles develop the positive value of sorrow, exhibiting its capacity to participate in two of the three kinds of *bonum* (§1.1). Article 2 links sorrow to the *bonum honestum*; Article 3 connects it to the *bonum utile*. Aquinas concludes the treatment of sorrow in Article 4 with the declaration that sorrow cannot be the "supreme evil for man."

Sorrow is unpleasant by its very nature. But is it thereby evil? The *sed contra* of Article 1 provides the simplest reason for denying that *tristitia* is absolutely evil: sorrow for evil is itself good. The response is more nuanced. Aquinas wants to accommodate the notion that there is something inherently bad about sorrow, but without denying its positive relation to the good.[20] To accomplish the first objective, he acknowledges that if sorrow is considered *simpliciter et secundum se*, then "every sorrow is a certain evil" (*omnis tristitia est quoddam malum*) (39.1.co). By *malum*, Aquinas does not mean what contemporary ethicists sometimes mean by "moral evil." His argument is that, taken in abstraction, sorrow has the aspect of evil, the *ratio mali*. This is because according to its nature, sorrow impedes the rest (*quies*) of the appetite in the good that it seeks. The entirely formal character of the argument is evident. Whether any particular sorrow is good or evil remains an open question, the answer to which depends wholly on the specific *bonum* in which the appetite is unable to rest. Thomas provides an analogy to shame (*verecundia*),

---

[19] In his reading of this Question, Ramírez (1973) emphasizes the difference between Thomas's standpoint and the error "of the Stoics who say that all sorrow is bad and ignoble" (p. 323). While the departure from the Stoics is pronounced and bears reflection (Ramírez correctly notes that Aquinas follows in the footsteps of Augustine), it is nonetheless striking that Question 39 does not contain a single mention of the Stoics.

[20] As Gondreau (2002) remarks, the "balanced appraisal of the passion of sorrow forges the foundation not only for Thomas' response to the Stoic objection that sorrow has no place in the life of virtue, but also for his eventual defense of the presence of sorrow in Christ that will take place in the *Tertia Pars*" (p. 393).

a passion he had earlier glossed as evil in its species (24.4.co). In the abstract, shame may be bad. But if shame is felt "on the supposition of some evil act committed" (39.1.co), the opposite is true. The same logic holds for sorrow. Thomas concludes: "It belongs to goodness that, on the supposition of a present evil, sorrow and pain should follow" (39.1.co).

Sorrow is formally evil, but materially either good or evil. Which ought to be emphasized? One might think that what is true in itself, independent of what holds only *ex suppositione*, should be given the last word. But Thomas clearly rejects this view of the matter. "Because moral discourses are directed to particulars, and actions (*operationes*) are of particulars, that which is good *ex suppositione* ought to be judged as good" (39.1.co). However bad sorrow may appear in the abstract, the moral perspective is obliged to view the passion "materially," in the concrete. It cannot possibly judge whether any particular *tristitia* is good or bad without seeing it in relation to its surroundings.[21] The dictum of "Gregory" (i.e. Nemesius) that *omnis tristitia malum est, sui ipsius natura* must be read as a statement that sorrow, as constituted by the perception of a present evil, is necessarily repugnant. "All flee sorrow, insofar as they flee evil," Thomas holds, "but they do not flee the sensation and rejection of evil" (39.1 ad 1m).

By affirming the doctrine that sorrow is *malum* by its very nature, but nonetheless placing the doctrine under the severest of qualifications, Aquinas has cleared the way for exhibiting the participation of *tristitia* in the good. Article 2 asks whether sorrow can be a *bonum honestum*. Thomas answers by noting that an evil may be rightly perceived as evil by the reason, and rightly detested by the will. Any sorrow that results from the rectitude of the will is necessarily an instance of the *bonum honestum*. The transition from Article 1 to Article 2 is remarkable. Article 1 began with the assertion that sorrow "has the aspect of evil" (*rationem mali habet*). In Article 2, Thomas concludes that "it is manifest that *tristitia* can have the aspect of the *bonum honestum*" (*manifestum est quod tristitia potest habere rationem boni honesti*) (39.2.co). Article 1 limited itself to the conclusion that what is formally bad may be materially good. Article 2 transforms this conclusion: by issuing from the rectitude of the

---

[21] A comment of Dorothy L. Sayers, put into the mouth of Helen de Vine (the scholar's scholar of *Gaudy Night*), is apposite. "I entirely agree that a historian ought to be precise in detail; but unless you take all the characters and circumstances concerned into account, you are reckoning without the facts. The proportions and relations of things are just as much facts as the things themselves; and if you get those wrong, you falsify the picture really seriously" (1936, p. 19).

reason and the will, sorrow acquires the *ratio* of the highest good. It is difficult to imagine a more thorough "rehabilitation" of *tristitia* from its earlier status as formally evil.[22]

If sorrow can attain to the dignity of the *bonum honestum*, it seems evident that it would be able to participate in the less exalted *bonum utile*. As obvious as this seems, the objectors usefully recall a feature of common experience, quoting Sirach 30:25: "Sorrow has killed many, and there is no profit in it" (39.3 arg. 1). To persist in feeling sorrow, especially when it impedes positive action, seems useless. Aquinas acknowledges the substantial degree of truth in the objection, but holds that it applies to "immoderate sorrow, which absorbs the mind" (39.3 ad 1m). In Article 2, Aquinas identifies *immoderata tristitia* as a particular case of passion unregulated "according to the rule of reason, which is the root of the *bonum honestum*" (39.2 ad 1m). Now he emphasizes that not all sorrow, but only immoderate sorrow, "immobilizes the mind, and impedes the flight from evil" (39.3 ad 1m).

To identify the uselessness of immoderate sorrow is one thing. A Stoic would be in full agreement with Aquinas on the point. More difficult is to establish the utility of moderate sorrow. How can sorrow, even if governed by the *regula rationis*, be positively useful? It is not as if sorrow itself can help to expel the present evil. As Aquinas observes, once the evil is present, sorrow is the necessary result, and *id quod est praesens, non potest non esse praesens* (39.3.co). To put this another way: sorrow's utility cannot consist in its own elimination. No passion, least of all sorrow, has that power. Sorrow is useful, rather, because it can provide some assistance in the avoidance of two kinds of actions: those which are occasions of evil, and those which are bad in themselves. With respect to the first kind of action, Aquinas credits sorrow with the ability to remind us that attachment to temporal goods will lead the soul to evil. By nature, we perceive temporal goods as instances of the *bonum delectabile*, and pursue them accordingly. Our experience of sorrow is a useful check on the tendency to succumb to this pursuit of superficially attractive goods. Regarding the second kind of action (things bad in themselves that should always be avoided), Aquinas observes that "sorrow for sin is useful so that man can avoid sin" (39.3.co). It is not, of course, that sorrow should be

---

[22] This may be the most striking confirmation of Sweeney's proposal (1999) that, from an apparently pessimistic starting point, Thomas progresses toward a "vision of the passions as forces for good, moving away from seeing them as a detriment or something to be merely tolerated or controlled" (p. 220). (See the discussion at §4.4.)

the principal motive for avoiding evils. One should avoid adultery because it offends God, and not because one dreads the emotional guilt that may ensue. Nonetheless, sorrow for sin is useful, since it "doubles the cause for avoiding it" (*geminatur fugiendi causa*) (39.3.co). Many have difficulty avoiding sin for the sake of avoiding sin. But sorrow, according to its own nature, is a cause of aversion.

For as evil itself according to its own nature is to be avoided, everyone avoids sorrow itself according to its own nature, just as all desire good, and pleasure in the good. Therefore just as pleasure in the good causes the good to be sought more avidly, so sorrow for evil causes evil to be avoided more vehemently. (39.3.co)

The final Article of Question 39 asks whether bodily pain is the greatest evil. For some, it is simply obvious that if Achilles or Socrates were to act shamefully, he would commit an evil far worse than any bodily pain he might suffer. Others find heroism which endures bodily pain for the sake of a greater good more or less unintelligible. Apparently impervious to the Greek tradition from Homer and Plato, they suppose that bodily pain really is the greatest evil. Can Aquinas convince anyone who does not already see the point? Is he able to succeed where the literary charm of Homer and Plato (or the example of St. Thomas More) fails? It is difficult to say. Aquinas' strategy is to provide an argument against the identification of not only bodily pain, but any pain whatever, as the greatest evil. He distinguishes two kinds of evil, real and apparent. Sorrow for real evils cannot be the greatest evil, "for there is something worse, namely, either not to judge as evil that which is truly evil, or not to reject it" (39.4.co). Sorrow for apparent evils cannot be the greatest evil, "for it would be worse to be alienated entirely from the true good" (39.4.co). Therefore, no pain or sorrow can be man's greatest evil.

The negative thesis that sorrow cannot be the *summum hominis malum* suggests a positive corollary: every sorrow contains some good. Here the asymmetry between pleasure and sorrow emerges. Every sorrow contains some good, Aquinas says in the *ad primum*, but not every pleasure contains some evil. The asymmetry between pleasure and pain reflects the priority of good to evil (§1.4), a priority that informs Thomas's entire treatment of pain and sorrow. Like any other passion, sorrow must consent to the rule of reason. That sorrow can be misdirected, immobilizing, and positively harmful is evident. Loughlin writes that "Thomas considers a moral approach as that which most appropriately addresses sorrow at its very roots, and hopes to eliminate it" (2005, pp. 776–7).

But does Aquinas in fact propose the radical elimination of *tristitia*, or of any other passion? Both the concept and the metaphor of extirpation (literally, "tearing out from the roots") belong to Stoicism.[23] In according sorrow a positive value – most explicitly in the Articles showing that it can be a *bonum honestum* and a *bonum utile*, but throughout the previous Questions as well – Aquinas applies the insight that the passions are natural to man. When governed by reason, they serve the good of the human person. The purpose of Question 39 is not to provide a radical treatment that eliminates sorrow where the mitigating remedies of Question 38 fall short. It is to provide an evaluation of sorrow according to its *bonitas* and *malitia*. Thus does Thomas exhibit the capacity of *tristitia*, when brought under the politic rule of reason, to promote the motion of the rational creature *ad finem* (§4.2).[24]

---

[23] "Extirpation" derives from *exstirpo*, "to tear out from the roots" (*stirpes*). See, for example, *Tusculan Disputations* 3.34.84 and (even more dramatically) 4.26.57.

[24] Cf. 59.3 ad 3m: "Tristitia immoderata est animae aegritudo, tristitia autem moderata ad bonam habitudinem animae pertinet, secundum statum praesentis vitae."

PART 3

Particular passions:
the irascible passions

CHAPTER 9

Hope and despair

Aquinas begins the consideration of the irascible passions by treating hope and despair in a single Question. Aquinas is not treating the theological virtue of hope, or the sin of despair, but the passions that take the same names (§9.1). The causes of hope are multiple. Attending to concrete experience, as he does throughout the Treatise, Aquinas identifies both experience and inexperience as causes of hope, along with alcoholic intoxication (§9.2). Since hope's object is the possible but difficult future good, a person can never be certain that she will attain what she hopes for. This fact, however, has no tendency for Aquinas to undermine the important distinction between "false hope" and hope that is rational (§9.3). Aquinas concludes Question 40 by treating the effects of hope, identifying "love" as the principal interior effect and "activity" (operatio) as the principal exterior effect (§9.4). Though hope and despair, considered as passions, are distinct from the corresponding virtue and sin, the two are related, since the virtues are habits that perfect the powers of the soul, including the powers whose acts are the passions (§9.5).

9.1 HOPE AND DESPAIR AS PASSIONS

Aquinas devotes only one Question to the passion of hope. Strictly speaking, he does not give hope a full Question. The topic of Question 40 is not *spes*, but *spes et desperatio*. Why the lack of detailed treatment? Three possibilities suggest themselves. First, the treatments of love and desire already contain much of what can be said about the common object of hope. (Recall the Prologue's complaint about *frequens repetitio*.) Second, the passion of hope seems to raise fewer questions than the corresponding theological virtue, which Aquinas treats in the 2a2ae. Third, the historical conversation about hope as a passion is not nearly as complex as the conversations about love, sorrow, and pleasure. In the Questions on those passions, Thomas faces the challenge of reconciling diverse *auctoritates*. This challenge seems less formidable with respect to the passion of hope. If there are multiple voices that have spoken about hope, most have concerned themselves with the theological virtue rather than the passion.[1]

Despite its compressed character, the analysis of hope does not differ structurally from the treatment of the other passions. In a single Question, Aquinas considers the nature of hope in itself, the causes of hope, and its effects. Articles 1–4 are equivalent to a treatment of hope *secundum se*. Articles 5–6 consider the causes of hope, relating them to both experience and its lack. Articles 7–8 argue that the two chief effects of hope are love (*amor*) and activity (*operatio*).[2]

Aquinas' decision to begin the treatment of the irascible passions with hope is not accidental. Of the irascible passions, hope bears the simplest and most direct relation to the good. The other irascible passions have a less direct relation to good: despair regards the good as impossible; fear and daring are responses to evil; anger aims for a good, but only when it perceives something else as evil. Because hope bears a direct relation to the good, it comes first in the sequence of the irascible passions. As Eileen Sweeney observes:

> Love and hope are placed first in each category because the object of passion in general is simply the good; all passion is in some way reducible to the tendency of things to seek what is suitable to their nature, all are movements which presuppose a likeness or aptness to that toward which they tend. (1999, pp. 220–1)

Article 1 of Question 40 asks whether hope is the same as desire or cupidity (*desiderium sive cupiditas*). The question arises naturally from the tradition. As the first objector notices, Augustine (in book 14 of *De civitate Dei*) names *cupiditas* rather than *spes* as one of the four principal passions. In a sense, hope and desire appear to run together. "John hopes for a pay raise" and "John wants a pay raise" seem to express the same thing, namely desire for a future good (as the second objector observes). Finally, the third objector argues that even if hope differs from desire by the fact that hope's object is possible, whereas desire's object might be either possible or impossible ("John wants a pay raise, but he has no hope of

---

[1] As Manzanedo (1993) remarks, "Among the names of the different passions, the name of 'hope' is more apt for signifying a 'virtue' (a good operative habit)" (p. 397). This suggests one explanation for the comparative lack of studies of hope as a passion.

[2] Though my placement of the divisions corresponds to that proposed by Ramírez (1973, p. 363), I do not find that Articles 5–6 treat the causes of both hope and despair (*causae communes spei et desperationes*). The emphasis throughout is on the cause of hope; the cause of despair gets short shrift.

getting one"), this difference is not sufficient to generate a specific distinction between hope and desire.

Each of these objections contains something true. The object of hope cannot simply be other than the object of desire. As Aquinas argues, nothing can be the object of hope unless it first be desired. Thus "hope presupposes desire, just as all the irascible passions presuppose the concupiscible passions" (40.1.co). But the converse is not true. One may desire something without having any hope for it. This is precisely what occurs in despair: "Despair presupposes desire, just as hope does, since for that which does not fall under our desire, we have neither hope nor despair" (40.4 ad 4m). To become an object of hope in its proper sense, Aquinas says, a thing must meet "four conditions" (*quator conditiones*) (40.1.co):

1. It must be perceived as a good.
2. Its attainment must lie in the future. Hope always concerns the "not yet."
3. It must be apprehended as a difficult and arduous good.
4. It must be seen as possible to attain.

Whereas desire requires only the first two conditions, hope demands all four. What distinguishes hope from desire is the character of hope's object as "an arduous thing, attainable with difficulty" (*aliquid arduum cum difficultate adipiscibile*) (40.1.co). One may object that we hope for things that are not intrinsically difficult to obtain. I walk into the house after mowing the lawn: "I hope there is Diet Coke in the fridge." But this example actually confirms Thomas's point. If we use language correctly, we do not express our hope that Diet Coke is in the refrigerator, unless we have some doubt about the matter. The presence of doubt suffices to introduce some difficulty in the attainment of the desired good, and thereby to make the thing an object of hope in its proper sense. Despite its triviality, the example is useful in suggesting that what makes something an object of hope is not simply related to some intrinsic attribute of the thing. No less important is the manner in which we perceive the thing's relation to our present situation. "Someone is not said to hope for some trifling thing, which is immediately in his power to have" (40.1.co). If we apprehend a good as easily attainable, we are not moved by the passion of hope. This remains true even if we continue to use "hope" interchangeably with "want" and "desire."

What immediately determines whether the passion of hope will be activated is not the actual difficulty of attaining the good, but the apprehension of this difficulty. In reality, it may happen that the good is either easily obtainable, or impossible to obtain. But as long as the

future good is perceived under the *ratio* of "the difficult" or "the arduous,"
hope will ensue, regardless of how things stand. Here "difficult" is elliptical
for "difficult to attain, but not impossible." Aquinas makes this point in
specifying the last of hope's *quator conditiones*. If the first three conditions
are satisfied, but the good is apprehended as impossible to attain, the
result is *desperatio*. For any hope to be present, the object must be
apprehended as somehow possible (even if just barely possible) to attain.
Aquinas' insistence on this point is salutary, not least because it exposes
the silliness of the idea that one can hope for things whose attainment is
consciously perceived to be impossible. Suggesting (with no evidence) that
"most literary giants seem convinced that life is intolerable without
positive illusions," Lazarus and Lazarus recommend that people cultivate
hope, even if the notion that one can attain the hoped-for good is an
illusion (1996, p. 74). Aquinas would have none of this. If the thing is
simultaneously apprehended as a future arduous good and impossible to
attain, despair is the necessary result. Asking people to hope regardless is
not so much cruel as metaphysically impossible.

Whether a person experiences hope is determined entirely by the object
as apprehended, the formal object (§3.1). But, as the *sed contra* of Article 2
argues, hope is not itself in the apprehensive power, since its object is
good, which is the object of the appetitive power. Although hope (like all
the passions) requires a logically prior apprehension, it does not consist in
this apprehension. Hope is a motion of the appetite, which Thomas
describes as a "certain stretching out of the appetite toward the good"
(*extensionem quandam appetitus in bonum*) (40.2.co). If the *extensio* is of
the sensitive appetite – that is, if one experiences hope as a passion in the
proper sense of the term – a corresponding bodily effect will occur. This
accounts for the peculiar sensation of elevation and anxiety experienced by
those who suffer the passion of hope.[3]

As we have seen from our examination of *amor* and *dilectio*, *delectatio*
and *gaudium*, and *dolor* and *tristitia*, Aquinas often distinguishes between
the passion common to men and other animals, and an affection proper
to beings with intellect. In the case of hope, there is no explicit terminological differentiation. Yet Article 3 suggests the possibility of a distinction
between two forms of *spes*. Asking whether hope is in dumb animals,
Thomas answers that it is, drawing upon the empirical observation of

---

[3] "Stretching out of the appetite" translates *extensio appetitus* more faithfully than "tendency of an
appetite" (the Blackfriars translation; see Thomas Aquinas [2006h]), and evokes more vividly the
feeling that often accompanies the passion of hope.

animal behavior: "If a dog sees a hare, or a hawk sees a bird, too far in the distance, it is not moved toward it, as though having no hope to catch it. But if it be near, the dog is moved, as though in hope of catching it." (40.3.co). Although it does not use concepts, the animal's *vis estimativa* (here Aquinas simply names a *quoddam instinctus naturale*) can in a sense judge particular things as either possible or impossible to attain (§3.3). The *ad primum* makes clear that the instinctual judgment of brutes is teleologically guided: "Although brute animals do not know the future, yet an animal is moved by natural instinct to something future, as though it foresaw the future. For an instinct is planted (*inditus*) in them by the divine intellect that foresees (*praevidente*) the future" (40.3 ad 1m). Human beings, by contrast, have no such assurances. Snap judgments about the possibility or impossibility of attaining difficult goods are likely to be erroneous. In its basic form, human hope does not differ essentially from animal hope. But for human hope to be rational, the apprehension of something as possible or impossible requires deliberation.

If a difficult future good is apprehended as impossible to attain, despair is the result. Article 4 asks whether hope and despair are contraries.[4] The *sed contra* gives the obvious etymological argument: *desperatio* simply means an absence of *spes*. In the response, Aquinas deploys the distinction between two kinds of contrariety that he first made in Question 23 (see §2.5). In each of the contrary concupiscible passions, the contrast is between motion toward a perceived good, on the one hand, and motion away from a perceived evil, on the other. Love, desire, and pleasure are directed toward good; hate, aversion, and sorrow are repulsions from evil. Both the direction of motion ("toward" and "from") and the term of motion (good and evil) are contrary. In the case of despair, the term is the same as that of hope, that is, a good. Only the direction of motion is contrary: hope is movement toward an arduous good; despair is movement away from that good, perceived as impossible to attain.[5] What gives

---

[4] Ramírez (1973) construes this as the occasion for a treatment *de ipsa desperatione* (p. 363). As he suggests, it appears that the consideration of *spes* has been "interrupted" in a manner not characteristic of Thomas, so that "this question does not seem well ordered with respect to all of its parts." Ramírez himself rejects this appearance, supplying three possible justifications for Thomas's order and expressing his own preference for the view that Article 4 constitutes the point at which Thomas begins to treat hope and despair in tandem. We agree with Ramírez that Question 40 is not poorly ordered. But rather than explain away the appearance of an interruption, it may be safer to hold that Thomas deliberately structures the Question to underscore the epiphenomenal character of despair.

[5] White (2002) gives a succinct and insightful formulation. "The range of response in appetite," he writes, "is symmetrically complex: whereas the concupiscible appetite inclines simply toward good

despair its particular character is that the person in despair continues to perceive a thing as good, even as she turns away from that thing. If a person is in love but finds himself rejected, he may attend to (or manufacture) negative qualities of the beloved, and come to apprehend her as an evil to be avoided. Success in this enterprise will ensure that where desire and hope were, aversion will be. The luckless lover will no longer want the previously desired good, because he no longer perceives it as good. But the unrequited lover is different. He will continue to perceive the object of desire as an attractive good, but come to regard his prospects of attainment as simply impossible. When this apprehension occurs, the result is despair.

Is despair necessarily a bad thing? Annotating the text of 45.2, J. P. Reid comments:

> Daring and despair have something paradoxical about them; both are apparent violations of the natural reaction of appetite to specific objects. The first pursues the disagreeable while the second turns away from the agreeable. The former may be called for by the circumstances, but the latter is never appropriate or gratifying. (Thomas Aquinas 2006h, p. 76)

This conclusion is too strong. While despair is not "gratifying," it may be appropriate in some circumstances. In Article 3, Aquinas argues that non-rational animals experience *desperatio*, and suggests that such despair is healthy and natural. When the dog pursuing the hare finally gives up the chase, it acts according to nature. Similarly, the passion of despair in human beings may signal the advisability of giving up when the arduous good proves impossible to obtain. Rather than suppress despair, we should acknowledge that our efforts might be more profitably spent seeking a good that we can attain.[6] With regard to the attainment of any particular, finite good, it is always possible that despair is a legitimate response. If this sounds odd, it is because we tend to equate "despair" with despair about God. But Question 40's proper subject is not despair regarding the universal good, but hope and despair in relation to particular goods. Despair about union with God is not a passion, but a perverse act of will caused by sin (especially *acedia*). In a treatment of the passions, detailed analysis of this sort of despair would be out of place.

---

and away from evil, the irascible may either approach a promising difficult good *as* good, in hope, or fall away from it *as* unreachable, in despair. Furthermore, it may either shrink from a menacing difficult *as* evil, in fear, or attack it *as* a conquerable difficulty, in daring" (p. 109).

[6] Whence the moral acceptability (in some cases) of discontinuing medical treatment, which does nothing to imply the legitimacy of direct killing.

9.2 WHAT CAUSES HOPE?

In Articles 5 and 6, Aquinas considers the causes of hope. As we have seen in the Questions on the other passions, Thomas leads the reader from a concise description of the passion's formal cause (given in the consideration of the passion *secundum se*) toward a more ample inquiry. The formal cause of hope is the apprehension of a future good as difficult but possible to attain. But what prompts us to apprehend future goods as either possible or impossible? Article 5 provides an analysis of the role of experience (*experientia*) in generating hope. Aquinas distinguishes two ways in which something might cause hope: "either because it makes something possible to a man, or because it makes him think (*existimare*) something possible" (40.5.co). In the first way, experience causes hope exclusively. By *experientia*, Aquinas means the repeated performance of actions that creates a power or capacity for performing a certain kind of action. "Through experience man acquires the faculty of doing something easily, and from this hope ensues" (40.5.co). If Annie improves her command of ancient Greek through experience, the despair she once felt about reading Greek yields to hope.[7] After a certain point, she will no longer need hope to read Greek, since she will no longer perceive that good as something arduous. But the hope generated by the experience does not disappear. It may provide her with confidence to attempt the arduous good of acquiring other languages. The example illustrates the importance of hope as a passion. If a person simply wants things, but lacks the energy to seek the goods which she (correctly) perceives as arduous, she will not get what she wants. "Fine things are difficult," the ancient Greek proverb reminds us. Without the passion of hope (never mind the virtue), the accomplishment of fine and difficult things would be impossible.

The second way in which experience causes hope, according to Aquinas, is by causing a person to think something possible. Such experience is generated not by the repetition of virtue-building acts, but through "teaching and persuasion" (*doctrina et persuasio*) (40.5.co). To see how this is true, consider the large number of hopes instilled by what others say about a person's chances for attaining elusive goods, for instance by

---

[7] The point also applies to fear. See 42.5 ad 1m: "The things that increase a man's power are given by nature (*nata*) to increase hope, and, for the same reason, to diminish fear, since fear concerns an evil that cannot easily be resisted. Since, therefore, experience makes a man more powerful for the sake of operation, it happens that just as it increases hope, so it diminishes fear."

parents who tell their children that they can become a great athlete or the President of the United States. The cause of the child's hope, which may well carry into adulthood, is the teaching of his mother or father. Similarly, a mother who routinely tells her son that he is "not college material" (perhaps because he seems intellectually inferior to his older sister) will probably succeed in generating despair with respect to scholastic achievement. Many particular hopes and despairs can be traced to the persuasions of parents, teachers, priests, coaches, and other figures, whether or not their estimations have anything to do with reality. To an extent, such hopes and despairs can be undone by contrary experiences. A person may discover, regardless of what his mother may have told him, that he is actually quite adept at reading. In this case, experience will generate in a person's soul an "opinion (*existimatio*) that something is possible for him, which he used to consider (*repubat*) impossible" (40.5.co). But the contrary may also occur. Experience can lead a person to regard something as impossible which he previously thought possible. If the person continues to perceive the impossible thing as a good, despair will replace hope.

Experience causes both hope and despair. This is the safe conclusion to draw. Aquinas endorses the safe conclusion, but he does not want to emphasize it. He ends the response of Article 5 with this declaration: "Experience is a cause of hope in two ways, but a cause of a deficiency of hope in one way. Because of this, we are able to say more that experience is a cause of hope" (40.5.co). Thomas does not think, however, that experience is the sole cause of hope. Inexperience must be given its due, as Article 6 makes clear in its acknowledgment that hope abounds in young men and drunkards.[8] The inclusion of this Article is funny in more than one sense. The *ad tertium* of Article 5 has already identified *stultitia et inexperientia* as accidental causes of hope. Why does Aquinas choose to underscore the point with a reflection on the hope of young men and drunkards? Three reasons come to mind. First, it provides a simple way for him to ensure that the Question includes eight articles. Thomas is partial to the number eight and its factors, especially in the Questions on the passions.[9] Second, it furnishes an occasion to bring Aristotle (who has

---

[8] Ramírez (1973) understands the relation between Article 5 and Article 6 as a division between the "psychological" and the "physiological" causes of hope (p. 363). But this fails to get at the center of Aquinas' intention. In Article 6, Thomas is not mainly concerned to exhibit the physiological causes of hope. His primary aim is to deepen the reflection on inexperience as a cause of foolish hope; he does so by providing concrete instances of the *stultitia et inexperientia* mentioned at 40.5 ad 3m.

[9] The number of Articles in nineteen of the twenty-three questions (82 percent) on the particular passions is eight or one of its factors. Questions 31, 32, 35, 40, and 46 have exactly eight Articles each.

gone missing for some time) back into the picture. The *sed contra* quotes the passage from the *Ethics* that "drunken men are hopeful" (3.8, 1117a14), as well as the *Rhetoric*'s claim that "the young are full of hope" (2.12, 1389a19). Third, it enables him to reinforce the point that "false hope" does exist.

9.3 FALSE HOPE VS. GOOD HOPE

It has become fashionable to deny the existence of "false hope" as a category. Lazarus and Lazarus provide one specimen of such a denial. They quote the words of Seymour Epstein, whom they describe as a "distinguished research psychologist":

> Some physicians object to a psychological approach because they fear it will produce "false hope." I have never quite understood what false hope is. All hope is "false" in the sense that what is hoped for may not materialize. At the time of hoping one cannot know the outcome. (1996, p. 71)

"We find what Seymour Epstein says here unassailable," they add. If one desires an argument *sed contra*, here is Augustine:

> There are two things that kill the soul: despair and false hope.[10]

Which *auctoritas* is nearer the truth, Seymour Epstein or St. Augustine? To decide this question, I want to consider why the former has "never quite understood what false hope is." Epstein assumes that people who employ the category of "false hope" understand its opposite to consist in hoping for things whose attainment is certain. But Aquinas would not conflate truth and certainty in this manner. The genuinely hopeful person is rarely, if ever, certain that she will attain a difficult good. She is fully aware that it "may not materialize." This knowledge is no small part of what leads her to apprehend the good as arduous or difficult. But she must perceive the future difficult good as *possible* to attain. "Since the prospects of attaining a difficult good are uncertain, all hope is equally true or false" – this is a *non sequitur*.

But what is false hope? Article 6 provides two clear instances: the hope of drunkards, and the hope of young men. The drunk person at a party who hopes to jump from the eighth floor to the ground without injury has false hope, as does his drunken buddy who hopes to charm the girl who has always found him repulsive. Both hope to achieve a difficult good, but

---

[10] Augustine, *Sermones* 87.8, quoted by Pieper (1997a), p. 113.

their hope is not governed by reason. Even if it is possible, in some sense, to attain the good, the drunkard's belief that he, in these circumstances, can achieve this goal is irrational. Because the belief is irrational, it leads to false hope. Even while sober, the young hold opinions about the possible and impossible that are scarcely more realistic than those of the drunkard. Aquinas supplies the reason: they falsely judge both their own limitations and the strength of the obstacles (if they are aware of the obstacles to begin with). If this verdict seems harsh, we suggest (recalling the first book of Aristotle's *Ethics*) that the young are not necessarily the chronologically young. Thomas suggests as much when he concludes that "all fools, without using deliberation, attempt everything and are of good hope" (40.6.co).

False hope, described ironically as *bona spes* in the case of youths and drunkards, derives from an apprehension of something as possible, precisely when a person more aware of his own powers, the nature of the desired object, and the relation between the two, would perceive it as impossible. With respect to a finite good, *desperatio* may be preferable to *spes*. What makes hope rational is not the fact that attainment of the good is certain or probable, but the rationality of the belief that it is wise for this person to seek this good at this time. The view espoused by Aquinas in no way restricts hope to goods whose attainment is probable. A soldier who attempts to win a battle in which he is outnumbered does not have false hope. Fighting against the odds, knowing that shame is an evil worse than death, belongs to the essence of an excellent soldier. But a general who has the option of improving his position by waiting and gathering additional armies, yet sends his troops into a disastrous situation, is simply thoughtless. If he pleads that, despite the odds, he was motivated by the hope of victory, he does not remove the stain of guilt. He merely shows that (like Seymour Epstein) he does not know the difference between true hope and false hope.

The simple fact of probability does nothing to distinguish true hope from false hope. What matters is a more nuanced judgment concerning what is rational and appropriate to the particular case – "a comparison between one's own forces and the object's difficulty," in the apt phrase of White (2002, p. 109). Consider a person who nourishes the hope that his body will live forever in its earthly state. Such a person, even more than a drunkard or a young person, possesses false hope. His hope is based on a belief that is not only unattested, but directly contradicted, by the universal experience of the race. But a person who expresses the hope that her soul will survive the body's death cannot be accused of false hope.

Experience does nothing to contradict the survival of the soul. Reason may be able to make powerful arguments for the soul's immortality, or at least dispel the pretensions of those who claim to know that the soul dies with the body. Thus Socrates tells Simmias in the *Phaedo* (67c) that his journey to the next world is full of "good hope" (*elpis agathos*). The entire argument of the *Phaedo*, and any assertion of good hope whatever, would be absolutely meaningless, were there no such thing as bad hope.

9.4 "INTERIOR" AND "EXTERIOR" EFFECTS OF HOPE

Articles 1–4 treat hope in itself. Articles 5–6 consider its causes. Aquinas concludes Question 40 with two Articles that describe the principal effects of hope, love (*amor*) and activity (*operatio*). Each of the objectors of Article 7 argues that love precedes hope, not vice versa. Love is the first of the passions (arg. 1); love precedes desire, desire precedes hope; therefore love precedes hope (arg. 2); hope causes pleasure, but pleasure pertains to the good that is loved (arg. 3). The objections are essentially correct; they condense what has been argued at length in prior Questions. But Aquinas must somehow accommodate the notion that love not only causes hope, but also results from hope. His immediate motivation is suggested by the passage *sed contra*:

The gloss commenting on Matthew 1:2, "Abraham begot Isaac, and Isaac begot Jacob," says "faith begets hope, and hope begets charity." But charity is love. Therefore love is caused by hope. (40.7.sc)

How can Thomas reconcile the drift of his previous analysis with the scriptural gloss? This question drives the response of Article 7. Up to this point of the analysis, Aquinas has proceeded as if the only relevant factors were the individual who hopes, and the good that he hopes to attain. Now Thomas corrects this abstraction, observing that "it happens that sometimes what is arduous becomes possible to us, not through ourselves but through others" (40.7.co). This "communitarian" adjustment of the picture shows that hope regards not only the arduous good, but also "that by which something becomes possible to us." With regard to the arduous good, the objectors are absolutely correct: hope is caused by love, "since hope does not exist, except with respect to the desired and loved good" (40.7.co). But if we consider the person through whom the hoped-for thing becomes possible to attain, the reverse is true. "Insofar as hope regards one through whom something becomes possible to us, love is caused by hope, and not conversely" (40.7.co).

Aquinas' analysis has practical implications, the drawing out of which he leaves to the reader. If another person makes something possible for us, she causes us to hope. Because she has given us a good (that is, hope), we proceed to love her as we did not love her before. In this sense, hope causes love. For those whose goal is to be loved by others, the analysis bears immediate fruit. To make the point as a maxim: if you want another person to love you, do something that gives him hope. A base way to accomplish this, consistent with the analysis of *doctrina et persuasio* as a primary cause of hope, is to flatter someone. To flatter a person means to downplay his limitations and make impossible goods appear possible. A more noble example would be to introduce a person to the sacraments, and thereby give her hope of leading a spiritually richer life. In either case, *amor* is an effect of *spes*. Which should be preferred? Aside from the inherent superiority of the noble to the base, we may notice that the base strategy contains a particular danger. If you flatter someone and give him false hope, you may gain his love in the short term. But if the victim discovers that he has been duped, and that his hope is false, what will happen? Probably he will despair in relation to the good, and hate the person whom he previously regarded as a source of hope.

Article 7, as Ramírez observes, considers the "interior" effect of hope (1973, pp. 387–8). Article 8 treats its principal "exterior" effect, *operatio*. Once again, the objections contain acute observations. To consider the first objection: if hope generates security, it can lead to smugness and diminish action. This can happen, Aquinas acknowledges. He adds, however, that if *securitas* causes us to perceive the good as easy to attain, it proportionally diminishes the character of hope. Its place would be taken by false hope. To look upon union with God as not an arduous good, but a good of which one is assured (whether through bogus subjective certainty that one has been "saved," or through a misguided belief that God owes us salvation in exchange for the performance of particular works), is dangerous. But if *securitas* protects us from being paralyzed by fear, without obscuring our perception of the highest good as difficult to attain, it has no negative impact on either hope or *operatio*.

In itself, Aquinas argues, hope promotes activity. He gives two reasons. First, the perception of the good as arduous serves to "excite the attention" (*excitat attentionem*) (40.8.co). Those who have observed a gifted child in the classroom can confirm this. If the assignments are too easy, the child will get bored and decrease her level of activity. But if she perceives the work as challenging, she will rise to the occasion, becoming more focused and working harder. Again, the practical implications of Thomas's analysis are clear. An executive who wants to increase the productivity of his personnel ought to increase expectations, taking care to stop just short of the point at which his employees perceive the difficult good as impossible. The second reason that hope promotes *operatio* is that hope causes pleasure (as Aquinas argued at 32.3), and pleasure quickens activity.

9.5 HOPE AS PASSION VS. HOPE AS THEOLOGICAL VIRTUE

As natural passions, hope and despair are directed to the attainment of particular goods. When hope and despair regard the universal good, they cease to be passions. In relation to God, hope is a theological virtue, and despair a sin. Because Question 40 is concerned with hope as a passion, it says little about hope and despair in relation to God. Nonetheless, the question about the relation between the passion of hope and the corresponding theological virtue is inescapable. In Questions 17–22 of the 2a2ae, Aquinas considers the theological virtue of hope, as well as its associated gifts, opposed vices, and relevant precepts. The first Article of Question 17 contends that the passion and the virtue have the same "formal" object, the future good that is difficult but possible to attain. Materially, however, the objects differ as finite and infinite. "God is the principal object of hope" (2-2.17.5.co).

One might suppose that hope, as a theological virtue, is the perfection of hope as a passion. The relation between the two, however, is not so direct. What perfects the passion of hope is not the theological virtue, but the acquired virtue of magnanimity (2-2.129.2 ad 2m).[11] Acquisition of this virtue, in itself, does not cause one to possess the theological virtue of hope, which comes by divine infusion. Superficially, the perfection of natural hope and the possession of theological hope may appear to be in tension. As Aquinas writes:

Magnanimity tends to the arduous in the hope of attaining something that is in one's power. Whence it properly concerns the doing of great things. But hope, according as it is a theological virtue, concerns something arduous, to be obtained by the help of another. (2-2.17.5 ad 4m)

The self-reliance characteristic of the great-souled man seems at odds with the humility that comes through acknowledging one's dependence on

---

[11] See also Pieper 1997a, p. 101. The definition of hope as an *extensio appetitus*, and magnanimity as an *extensio animi*, is a sign of their close connection.

another.[12] Those who want the theological virtue, while dispensing with the effort involved in perfecting the passion, may be inclined to take some comfort in this. But such hope, akin to what Bonhoeffer calls cheap grace, brings dangers of its own. Why should we suppose that persons who lack the habit of aiming for the arduous good in earthly matters are nonetheless well prepared to attempt the most difficult of goods? There may be no logical impossibility. God *can* infuse the virtue of hope even in souls that have no prior discipline in aiming for the difficult good.[13] But in the usual order of things, the order ruled by God's *potentia ordinata* rather than *potentia absoluta*, things do not happen in this manner. Souls indifferent to the achievement of human things cannot be expected to exert themselves in divine things.

In Question 20 of the 2a2ae, Thomas explains why. Those with flat souls will often be unable to discern goods beyond the most obvious of bodily pleasures. Because they are "infected with love of bodily pleasures, among which sexual pleasures are primary" (2-2.20.4.co), they perceive spiritual goods as tasteless or insignificant. Such perception leads naturally to despair; it leaves no room in the soul for the virtue of hope. That those consumed by lust are generally unaware of their despair does not make it any less real.[14] In another type of case, both bodily and spiritual pleasures have lost their savor. Without the virtue of magnanimity, such a person will be particularly susceptible to the opinion that he can accomplish nothing. The name for this condition is "sloth" (*acedia*). "Since *acedia* is a sorrow (*tristitia*) that casts down the spirit, in this manner despair is generated out of *acedia*" (2-2.20.4.co). When a person does not even attempt to cultivate the virtue of magnanimity, she exponentially increases her vulnerability to either lust or *acedia*, both of which are primary causes of despair.

The virtue of magnanimity is the perfection of natural hope. Precisely as a virtue, it requires humility, so that it truthfully estimates its own possibilities, rather than exaggerate them. The proper ordering of natural hope, as Pieper observes, is born from "the interaction of magnanimity and humility" (1997a, p. 102). In itself, magnanimity is neither necessary

[12] See 2-2.129.3.co: "Magnanimity and humility are not contrary to one another, although they appear to tend in contrary directions, because they proceed according to different considerations."

[13] It is not that prior discipline entails full qualifications. As Jeffrey (1996) reminds us, none of the prophets called by God is "qualified" for his position (pp. 23–5).

[14] In *The Sickness unto Death*, Kierkegaard (1980) writes: "It makes no difference whether the person in despair is ignorant that his condition is despair – he is in despair just the same" (p. 44). More dramatically, "to be ignorant of being in despair is the specific feature of despair" (p. 45).

nor sufficient for the theological virtue of hope. But to suppose no connection between the two would be a mistake. Magnanimity prepares the soul for the theological virtue, not least by dispelling the obstacles that naturally inhibit its reception. By causing its possessor to perceive accurately the difference between what is possible and impossible for him, the virtue of magnanimity perfects the passion of hope. If the failure to possess this virtue does not generate despair, in the ways we have indicated, it will likely lead to presumption, the "sorte de glorie, qui est une trop bonne opinion que nous concevons de notre valeur" (Montaigne 1930, p. 599). If we have an excess of the quality that in moderation constitutes magnanimity (see 2-2.130.2), we will habitually regard ourselves as capable of attaining through our own powers things that in fact are impossible without help from others.[15] Untruthfully exaggerating our own capacities ("une affection inconsidérée, de quoi nous nous chérissons, qui nous représente à nous-mêmes autres que nous ne sommes" [Montaigne 1930, p. 599]), we render ourselves unlikely (if not unable) to lean on the help of God. Such leaning, as Aquinas says (see 2-2.17.1), belongs to the essence of theological hope. Without it, one cannot possess the virtue.

Another type of presumption occurs in a person who makes the bogus claim to rely on the power of God. What makes the claim bogus is his presumption that God would (or can) accomplish what is repugnant to his nature. Aquinas gives the example of a man "who tends to some good as possible by the strength and mercy of God, which is not in fact possible, as when someone hopes to obtain pardon without penance, or glory without merits" (2–2-21.1.co). A person guilty of this kind of presumption abdicates his responsibility. He attempts to justify his abdication by falsely hoping in the power of God to accomplish what is neither good nor possible. Such presumption, as Aquinas concludes, removes or despises the aid of the Holy Spirit.

The human enterprise of perfecting the passions, without divine grace, is not sufficient for those who aspire to a supernatural goal. But to scorn this enterprise, presuming that divine grace magically relieves human beings of any need to order their passions, is dangerous. Thomas shows this to be the case in his analysis of hope. As a passion, hope must be governed by reason in order to perform its natural function. A woman once wrote Samuel Johnson, requesting that he use his influence with

---

[15] At 2-2.130.2.co, Aquinas explicitly identifies the opposition of magnanimity by excess as presumption.

the Archbishop of Canterbury to gain her son's admission to Cambridge. Dr. Johnson replied:

Hope is itself a species of happiness, and, perhaps, the chief happiness which this world affords: but, like all other pleasures immoderately enjoyed, the excesses of hope must be expiated by pain; and expectations improperly indulged, must end in disappointment. If it be asked, what is the improper expectation which it is dangerous to indulge, experience will quickly answer, that it is such expectation as is dictated not by reason, but by desire; expectation raised, not by the common occurrences of life, but by the wants of the expectant; an expectation that requires the common course of things to be changed, and the general rules of action to be broken.[16]

Deprived of rational governance, hope is bound to degenerate into illusion. Aquinas would agree with Freud's sense that a person who adheres to anything that he recognizes as an illusion is not so much pious as morally corrupt.[17] While we may reject Freud's particular claim to have exposed religious belief as an illusion, nothing prevents us from acknowledging the relevance of psychoanalysis to the rational cultivation of hope and the other passions. As Alasdair MacIntyre writes:

We need to learn how to understand our desires rightly and how to direct them rightly. But the question, for each of us, of how in our everyday relationships and activities to direct our desires rightly is central to our moral lives, and the questions of how to understand our desires rightly and of what it is towards which they should be directed are central to ethics and politics. And this suggests both that any moral or political philosophy that is uninformed by psychoanalytic insight will be seriously defective and that any psychoanalytic understanding of human nature that is not integrated into and complemented by a moral and political philosophy will be seriously incomplete. (2004, p. 27)

Does Aquinas himself provide the psychoanalytic insight that MacIntyre takes to be necessary? It is possible that Thomas's texts contain a greater number of particular psychological insights than has been customarily recognized. It is also the case that the work of Freud (and some of his successors) contains insights that have no precedent in Aquinas. One may hope to acquire from the 1a2ae not only particular insights about human nature, but also a framework in which the requisite integration between "moral or political philosophy" and the "psychoanalytic understanding of human nature" may occur.

---

[16] Samuel Johnson, letter of 8 June 1762; see Boswell (1934), vol. 1, p. 368.
[17] "Il y a peu de vrais Chrétiens, je dis même pour la foi. Il y en a bien qui croient, mais par superstition" (Pascal 1976, §256, p. 124; cf. Pascal 1966, §179, p. 184).

CHAPTER 10

Fear

After sorrow, fear is most evidently a passion in the strict sense. In explaining fear's status as a passion, Aquinas provides a useful review of what makes something a passion. Distinguishing between natural and unnatural fear, he provides a fine-grained analysis of the emotional phenomena that constitute the species of fear (§10.1). Every passion has its own formal object. But only in the treatment of fear does Aquinas devote a separate Question to the passion's object. Identifying the precise conditions under which a thing inspires fear, rather than sorrow, daring, or anger, is a delicate task, requiring careful attention to both time and modality (§10.2). Clarity about fear's formal object does not for Aquinas exhaust the question about its cause. The proof is that he proceeds to discuss the cause of fear in a separate Question that contains only two Articles (§10.3). What does fear do to a person? In approaching this question, Aquinas attends not only to the formal element of fear, but also to the corresponding somatic effects, such as knees that knock, lips that quiver, bowels that loosen. By disturbing the reason, fear clouds the judgment and can produce panic. It would seem that fear's effect is typically negative. Nonetheless, Aquinas ends the consideration on a more positive note, not only by using Aristotle and Augustine to temper the Stoics, but also by citing the Pauline exhortation to work out your salvation with fear and trembling (§10.4).

10.1 FEAR ITSELF

Next to sorrow, fear most clearly exemplifies the character of passion. As Burton writes in his typically florid manner: "Cousin-german to *sorrow* is *fear*, or rather a sister, a faithful squire, and continual companion, an assistant and a principal agent in procuring of this mischief, a cause and symptom as the other" (1927, p. 227). Aquinas makes the point more calmly, noting that fear regards future rather than present evil, and thus participates only slightly less in the *ratio* of passion (41.1.co).

Aquinas devotes four Questions to fear. These address fear in itself (Question 41), its object (Question 42), its cause (Question 43), and its effects (Question 44). Uniquely, the consideration of fear contains a Question devoted entirely to the passion's *obiectum*. It is typical for Aquinas to treat the passion *secundum se* in one Question, and its cause in another. But he does not ordinarily interpose a separate Question on a passion's object. Why does he do so in this case? What about fear's object demands that it be treated in a different manner? After examining Aquinas' thinking about the nature of fear itself, I will address these questions.

Question 41 considers fear itself (*de ipso timore*). Aquinas identifies what makes fear a passion of the soul (Article 1), explains why fear names a particular passion, rather than any kind of flight (Article 2), asks whether fear is natural in any sense (Article 3), and considers the six species of fear as delineated by "Gregory" (i.e. Nemesius) and Damascene (Article 4). Ramírez plausibly reads the Question's first half as a definition *per genus et differentiam* (1973, p. 391). The genus of fear is "passion"; the specific difference is "caused by a future evil, difficult to resist." In the Question's second half, according to Ramírez, Thomas treats the division of fear (1973, p. 399). This reading is less plausible. Certainly both Articles 3 and 4 contain distinctions. But in asking whether natural fear exists, Thomas is not providing a canonical division of the passion. Rather, he continues the ongoing dialogue with Damascene, who has made six appearances in the Question's first half. While the six species of *timor* identified by Damascene is a division or sorts, it does not mean to be a comprehensive classification of the kinds of fear. Article 4 is more plausibly read as the culmination of Question 41's dialogue with Damascene, where Aquinas vindicates the placement of emotions like "shame" (*verecundia*) and "astonishment" (*admiratio*) within a genus to which they may not seem to belong.

What makes fear a passion of the soul? That fear is a passion is clear, as attested by book 14 of the *De civitate Dei* (cited at 41.1.sc) and common experience. In Article 1, Aquinas reviews the essential characteristics of a passion and notes the presence of each in fear. First, fear belongs to the appetitive power, which regards good and evil. Second, it pertains to the sensitive appetite in particular, as we know from the somatic reactions that accompany fear.[1] Third, it involves our being acted upon in the most palpable sense; we experience ourselves at the mercy of a future evil. Though the evil is in the future, Aquinas acknowledges that it must be

---

[1] Can there be a purely intellectual fear, with no somatic element at all? As far as I can tell, Aquinas neither adverts to nor eliminates the possibility of a corresponding pseudopassion (see §2.2).

present in some sense in order to activate a passion. The evil is present to the imagination "according to the apprehension of the soul" (41.1 ad 2m). (If the evil were to become materially present, the result would be not fear but sorrow.)

In Article 2, Aquinas asks what makes fear a *passio specialis*. The procedure he follows is similar to that of 30.2, which asks why *concupiscentia* names a particular passion, rather than the desire for any kind of good. *Timor* does not name any kind of flight, but picks out a particular kind of avoidance. At 30.2 Thomas had postulated that passions differ specifically according to formal differences in the object. In 41.2, he gives the same teaching a slightly different reformulation:

Passions of the soul receive their species from their objects. Whence any particular passion (*specialis passio*) is that which has its own object (*speciale obiectum*). Now fear has its own object, as does hope. For just as the object of hope is to attain the future arduous possible good, so the object of fear is the future difficult evil which cannot be resisted (*malum futurum difficile cui resisti non potest*). Whence fear is a particular passion. (41.2.co)

Since Aquinas has already chosen to devote the next Question to the articulation of fear's object, he does not linger on the formula's meaning. He does, however, argue that a proper understanding of fear will locate the passion squarely in the irascible power. To make this argument, he must correct certain readings of Aristotle and Damascene. Aristotle, according to the third objector, conflates fear and sorrow: "Fear is a kind of sorrow," he says in the *Rhetoric* (2.5, 1382a21). If this were true, then fear would be in the concupiscible. From a different angle, the objection continues, Damascene's labeling of fear as a "desiring power" (*virtus desiderativa*) also implies that fear resides in the concupiscible (*De fide orthodoxa* 3.23; see *PG* 94, 1088). Aquinas corrects Aristotle with the observation that while the object of fear is involved in the causal chain that leads to sorrow (when the future evil becomes the present evil), the object of fear itself is a future difficult evil, and thus belongs to the irascible. Damascene correctly holds that what generates the flight from the evil characteristic of fear is the desire for good. But this implies that the "desiring power" (i.e. the concupiscible) is a cause of fear, not that it is the same as fear.

Is there a certain kind of natural fear? Aquinas' decision to pose this question in Article 3 cannot be explained (*pace* Ramírez) by attributing to him a desire to construct a general taxonomy of fear. Rather, Aquinas wants to continue the conversation with Damascene. If desire is natural, it would seem that fear is equally natural. This is the appearance of Article 3's *videtur quod*, generated directly by the logic of Article 2. But, *sed contra*, "Those things which are natural, are commonly found in both animate and inanimate things. Therefore fear is not natural" (41.3.sc.). The resolution of the question depends on what is meant by "natural." "Natural" may mean "anything that is part of a created being's nature," regardless of whether that being has an apprehensive power. This is the sense taken by "natural" in 26.1's discussion of *amor naturalis*. In this sense, natural fear is impossible. A heavy body, when it is not acted upon violently, will move toward the center of the earth; it thereby may be said to have an *amor naturalis* for downward motion. But to ascribe fear to it is unintelligible, even metaphorically. This is because fear is essentially the product of apprehension, whereas love, desire, aversion, hatred, and hope may be attributed (if only metaphorically) to beings that lack the power of apprehension, but possess natural inclinations. Like pleasure and sorrow, the capacity of apprehension is a *conditio sine qua non* of fear.[2]

In one sense, nature seems alien to the concept of fear. But Thomas does not affirm the *sed contra*'s blunt declaration that "fear is not natural." Nature, he argues, inclines the apprehensive power to function in certain ways. When animals apprehend things in their environment as "corruptive evils," as things that threaten to tear them apart and end their existence, fear is generated. Such fear is rightly termed "natural," because it corresponds to the natural inclination for self-preservation. But only objects that directly threaten a being's existence, Aquinas holds, have the ability to cause natural fear. Though it is natural to prefer pleasure to pain, it does not follow that fear of "painful evils," such as a visit to the dentist, is natural in the same sense as fear of evils that threaten one's being.[3] The former evils, Aquinas concludes, are "repugnant not to nature, but to the desire of the appetite" (41.3.co).

The final Article of Question 41 considers the six species of fear according to Damascene and "Gregory" (i.e. Nemesius). About the species of sorrow

---

[2] This is not to deny the possibility of innate fear. As Dave Barry observes, "All of us are born with a set of instinctive fears – of falling, of the dark, of lobsters, of falling on lobsters in the dark, or speaking before a Rotary Club, and of the words 'Some Assembly Required.'" The capacity for fearing some things may indeed be hard-wired (the sheep fears the wolf from instinct). But the activation of the passion cannot occur without an act of apprehension, whether this be a perception of the external world, or an act of the imagination.

[3] "Natural fear" in this sense has no necessary reference to pain at all. One naturally fears an act imagined as capable of bringing about death, even if the act that causes death (or the death itself) involves no pain at all. This connection of fear to what is dangerous, though not necessarily painful, reaffirms the distinction between the irascible and the concupiscible (§2.4).

given by these two *auctoritates*, Aquinas had expressed reservations, finding them to name diverse effects of sorrow rather than its essence. In this Article, by contrast, Aquinas holds that the six species of fear "are grasped according to the proper division of the object of fear itself" (41.4 ad 1m). Though Aquinas affirms the six species, he recognizes that the list involves some difficulties, as indicated by the presence of five objectors.[4] The six species of fear are "sloth" (*segnities*), "blushing" (*erubescentia*), "shame" (*verecundia*), "astonishment" (*admiratio*), "stupefaction" (*stupor*), and "anxiety" (*agonia*).[5] The list is carefully constructed. The principle informing its construction is revealed by the description of fear's object: "Fear is of the future evil which surpasses the power of one who fears, so that it cannot be resisted by him" (41.4.co.) Corresponding to the first part of the description, the first three species derive from a person's apprehension of his own acts and capacities. The latter three species are generated by three modes in which a person imagines things outside himself to surpass his power of resistance.

Segnities (sluggishness) is the fear of someone who "runs away from work because he fears excessive hardship" (41.4.co).[6] It is not simply disinclination to work; it denotes the feeling of anxiety experienced by anyone confronted by an unavoidable labor that surpasses his inclination, for instance the dread of a university faculty member who has never desired to write for publication, because he has nothing to say, but suddenly finds himself obliged to do so.[7] The second species, *erubescentia* or "shamefacedness," differs from sluggishness, in that it bears an essential relation to what others think. It arises from the anticipation of a "disgrace that wounds one's reputation" (*turpitudo laedens opinionem*). As the term suggests, its most evident symptom is reddening of the face. When Plato

---

[4] For the *ST* as a whole, and particularly the Questions on the passions, five is an unusually large number of objections. Of the 132 Articles devoted to the passions, only one other Article (35.5) contains five objections.

[5] The list's history is of some interest. Aquinas derives the list from Damascene and Nemesius, but its origin may go back to Cicero, who names the following as species of *metus: pigritia, terror, timor, pavor, examinatio, conturbatio, formido* (*Tusculan Disputations* 4.7). As to the relation between Cicero's generic term, *metus*, and the term that comes to be privileged, *timor*, Ramírez (1973) offers this conjecture: "*Timor* is drawn from *timendo*. For *timere* and *metuere* perhaps bear the same origin and form, though with different pronunciation on account of a metathesis of syllables" (p. 394).

[6] A near equivalent is Cicero's *pigritia* (*Tusculan Disputations* 4.8). Aquinas himself speaks of "*pigritia, sive segnities*" at 44.4 arg. 3.

[7] "I already knew that there are two reasons why people refrain from writing books: either they are conscious that they have nothing to say, or they are conscious that they are unable to say it; and that if they give any other reason than these it is to throw dust in other people's eyes or their own" (Collingwood 1939, pp. 19–20).

has Thrasymachus or Dionysodorus blush, he signals to the reader that they are afraid, because their ignorance is about to be exposed (see *Republic* 350d and *Euthydemus* 297a). Both *erubescentia* and the third species of fear, *verecundia*, may be assimilated to the general category of "shame."[8] But they differ subtly. *Erubescentia* pertains to an act committed in the present, or about to be committed in the future, whereas *verecundia* arises from disgrace over a *fait accompli*. Since both are caused by the perception of one's own actions as an arduous evil, both are reckoned species of fear. Each of the first three species of fear arises from a perception of the self, rather than anything outside the self. This is especially true of shame. As Collingwood writes: "What a man is ashamed of is always at bottom himself; and he is ashamed of himself at bottom always for being afraid" (1942, p. 71).

In the second part of 41.4's response, Aquinas considers the final three species of fear. Confronted by a great evil, a person may find himself unable to think rationally about outcomes, paralyzed by the fear that Thomas calls "astonishment" (*admiratio*). Aquinas has already discussed *admiratio* as a cause of pleasure (32.8). What is the relation between *admiratio* as a cause of pleasure and *admiratio* as a species of fear?[9] The question is difficult; two objectors attack the inclusion of *admiratio* among the species of fear. Thomas agrees that not every instance of wonder is fear. For *admiratio* to be *timor*, something must be perceived as a difficult evil (41.4 ad 4m). This happens particularly, Aquinas says, when the wonder from which philosophical study arises leads to fear that one may unavoidably fall short of the truth (41.4 ad 5m). The fifth species of fear, "stupefaction," results from apprehending a thing under the aspect of "the unaccustomed." Here the evil may be relatively small in itself. But since it violates our established habits of perception, we perceive it as something great. The fear described by stupefaction occurs "from the imagination thrown out of its groove" (*ex insolita imaginatione*) (41.4.co). *Admiratio* causes a person to shrink from immediate judgment, but it does not exclude subsequent inquiry. *Stupor*, by contrast, entirely prevents its victim from engaging in either judgment or inquiry. One is taken aback, thrown off one's mount by the unexpected perception of an evil. The last

---

[8] For a more detailed account of *verecundia* and *erubescentia*, see 2-2.144, where Thomas discusses *verecundia* as an integral part of temperance.

[9] It may be true, as Gondreau (2002) concludes, that "wonder as a desire for knowledge of an unknown cause differs considerably from the passion of wonder as fear" (p. 418). But that Thomas does not use the term in a purely equivocal manner suggests the appropriateness of looking for an analogical connection between *admiratio* as a cause of pleasure and *admiratio* as a species of fear.

species of fear is "anxiety" (*agonia*). Like *segnities, agonia* is a kind of anxiety or dread. *Agonia* names the fear that arises when a person perceives a difficult evil under the *ratio* of "unforeseeability" (*improvisio*). It corresponds to what St. Francis de Sales calls "anxiety of mind." Such anxiety, Francis writes, "is not so much an abstract temptation, as the source whence various temptations arise" (2002, p. 202). Echoing Aquinas, Francis holds that "it is natural to us all to desire good, and shun that which we hold to be evil." But anxiety differs fundamentally from sorrow. It is the result of seeking deliverance from sorrow "as though all depended more upon himself than upon God." When someone in the condition of *agonia* "does not find what he wants, he becomes exceedingly impatient and troubled, which does not mend matters, but on the contrary makes them worse, and so he gets into an unreasonable state of anxiety and distress, till he begins to fancy that there is no cure for his trouble" (p. 202). Of the six species of fear that Aquinas names, *agonia* is the most spiritually dangerous. "This unresting anxiety is the greatest evil which can happen to the soul, sin only excepted" (Francis 2002, p. 202).

10.2 WHAT IS THE OBJECT OF FEAR?

What is the object of fear? Aquinas has already given a summary description: "The object of fear is the future difficult evil which cannot be resisted" (*obiectum timoris est malum futurum difficile cui resisti non potest*) (41.2.co). The summary description stands in need of elaboration. It leaves open certain questions, such as: What attributes are required for any particular thing to attain the status of such an evil? What kinds of thing are evils, but not necessarily feared evils? When Aquinas says that the evil "cannot be resisted" (*resisti non potest*), does he intend to say that resistance is literally impossible, or simply difficult? In Question 42, Thomas addresses these issues. Minimally, for anything to qualify as the object of fear, it must be perceived as an evil (Article 1), and specifically a "threatening evil" (*malum imminens*) (Article 2). Voluntary actions are thereby excluded (Article 3), but fear itself can be construed as an extrinsically caused threatening evil, and thereby feared (Article 4). Among the factors that make an evil more terrible, especially prominent are sudden and unexpected arrival (Article 5) and lack of remedies (Article 6).

In Article 1, Aquinas argues that the proper object of fear is necessarily an evil (*malum*). The objectors play an important role by providing apparent counter-examples. We fear the loss of good things (arg. 1); we apprehend power as something good, and yet fear it as well (arg. 2);

we regard God as good, but we fear him as well (arg. 3). None of these objections denies that we fear evil; they simply claim that we also fear the *bonum*. It seems that restricting the object of fear to the *malum* is arbitrary. In responding to these objections, Aquinas does not compromise the doctrine that fear's proper object is future evil. By its very nature, fear involves a recoiling or flight (*fuga*) of the appetite. Since the appetite flees what the apprehension perceives as evil, it follows that the proper object of fear, "first and in itself" (*primo et per se*), is evil (42.1.co). Yet how does one account for the fact that a person's appetite can recoil from what he perceives as good? Aquinas answers that good may "bear some relation to evil" (42.1.co). We do not fear good things in themselves; we fear the loss of good things, when we perceive such loss as an evil. This answers the first objection. In reply to the other two objectors, Aquinas observes that good may be the cause of things that we perceive as evils, and thus lead to fear. We do not fear the power of men, strictly speaking; we fear it insofar as it threatens us. We do not fear God in himself. We fear him as one who inflicts punishments, when we perceive those punishments as evil.

Any material object of fear is necessarily apprehended under the formality of future evil in some respect. The subsequent Articles of Question 42 proceed to describe the object of fear in more detail. In Article 2, Aquinas asks whether the "evil of nature" (*malum naturae*) is an object of fear. The response begins with a contrast between evils arising from natural causes (e.g. natural death) and those arising from non-natural causes (e.g. violent death inflicted by an assailant). In modern political philosophy, the distinction is crucial; as Strauss observes, Hobbes founds the commonwealth not on the fear of death generally, but on the particular fear of sudden and untimely death (1952, pp. 15–18). Aquinas recognizes the distinction, but does not accord it the same importance. In line with ordinary experience, he suggests that both natural and non-natural death may be feared. What matters is not the thing's naturalness, but only whether it is apprehended as a future evil.

What is meant by "future evil"? Does the "distance" of a thing in the future significantly affect its status as an object of fear? The evidence suggests that it does. To use Aquinas' own example: if death is perceived as an event occurring in the distant future, it is feared little, if at all. Most people imagine death as something far away, and hence are not gripped by the fear of death. On the other extreme, if death is perceived as virtually present, fear diminishes as well. "Those who are already on the scaffold, are not afraid," Aquinas quotes book 2 of the *Rhetoric* (2.5, 1383a5), since (Aristotle continues) "for a man to be afraid, there must be some hope of escape for him" (42.2.co). This suggests why Thomas describes the "future evil" more precisely as the "threatening evil (*imminens malum*)." In Question 41, the phrase *imminens malum* is utterly absent. In Question 42, *imminens malum* appears as the key term, replacing *futurum malum*. By specifying the future evil as the threatening evil, Thomas distinguishes the proper object of fear from the wider class of things that cause aversion or sorrow. Like the object of a photographer's lens that comes into focus, the threatening evil can be neither too close nor too far away.[10] What makes something threatening, however, is not simply related to time. The presence or absence of hope is a crucial variable. If no hope of escape exists, the evil loses its threatening character; it is perceived as virtually present, even if some time must pass before its actual arrival. But if evil is near at hand, "and yet with some hope of avoidance, then it will be feared" (42.2.co).

Article 1 argues that the formal object of fear is evil. Article 2 specifies the character of the evil: it is the future evil that is perceived as "threatening." Article 3 further specifies the evil by excluding particular evils that can be chosen by the will, the "evil of fault" (*malum culpae*) associated with sin. The object of fear is "the difficult future evil which cannot be avoided easily (*de facili*)" (42.3.co). Anything that can be avoided *de facili* is not an object of fear. While avoiding sin may not seem easy, Aquinas regards any act that is "altogether subject to our power and will" as an instance of what can be avoided *de facili*.[11] Opposed to evils that can be avoided by an act of will are those which have the "nature of the terrible" (*ratio terribilis*) (42.3.co). Such things are terrible because they are not under the will's power; they have an "extrinsic cause" (42.3. co). Because sin is necessarily an act of will, and violence cannot be done to the will (cf. 1.81.1; 1.106.2; 1.111.1), the "evil of fault" arising from sin cannot have the *ratio terribilis*. Against this somewhat technical argument, one might protest that we are nonetheless capable of fearing to commit sin.

---

[10] An inadequate grasp of this point leads Meyer (1994) to suppose that Thomas vacillates between describing the *obiectum timoris* as nearby and distant. Appropriately, Aquinas sometimes emphasizes the nearness of fear's object (its "impending" character), while at other times stressing its status as a future evil, in order to distinguish it from the present evil that activates sorrow. On the fundamental point that if a thing is to inspire fear, it must be perceived as neither too close nor too far away, Aquinas is entirely consistent. Meyer's sense that "Saint Thomas semble s'opposer à lui-même" (1994, p. 368) is a product of his own confused exegesis, which proceeds by quoting texts at random, without appropriate attention to sequential order.

[11] "Easily" translates *de facili* with only some accuracy. For Aquinas, the category of what can be avoided *de facili* is not purely subjective, as if it were simply a matter of what an individual happens to find easy or challenging.

Aquinas accounts for the appearance by noting the power of an extrinsic cause to incline, without necessitating, the will toward sin. If the cause's power to incline the will is strong, we may fear its power, and thereby fear derivatively that we will sin. But properly speaking "a man fears the seduction (*seductio*), rather than the fault (*culpa*) according to its proper nature (*ratio*) – that is, insofar as it is voluntary, it cannot be feared" (42.3.co).

Articles 1 through 3 show that the object of fear is the future evil that is threatening and non-voluntary. Article 4 asks (somewhat in advance of FDR, as Eileen Sweeney observes [1999, p. 229]) whether fear itself can be feared. In the response, Aquinas reiterates that only extrinsically caused evils can be feared. Fear is due to an extrinsic cause, inasmuch as it is a "certain passion following upon an imagination of threatening evil" (42.4. co). Because we have the power of imagining a future state of affairs in which we fall victim to a great evil, of which we will be afraid, we are able to fear fear. The future state of affairs becomes an object of fear, but only if we imagine it as threatening. It is not that fear of the future state of affairs coming to pass is identical to the fear of the dreaded thing itself. My fear that, according to the law of averages, I will someday be a victim of car-jacking, though genuine, is not the same passion as the fear generated when I see a menacing shape approach my car with knife in hand.[12] Both are instances of fear, but they are not the same fear. Aquinas shows his own firm grasp of these distinctions in the replies. "Not every fear is the same fear; rather, there are diverse fears according to the diverse things which are feared" (42.4 ad 1m). "The fear by which the threatening evil is feared is one thing; the fear by which fear itself of a threatening evil is feared is quite another" (42.4 ad 2m).[13]

The remaining two Articles of Question 42 clear up an important ambiguity in Aquinas' initial brief description of the *obiectum timoris*.

---

[12] Citing 42.4.co, Roberts (1992) suggests that for Aquinas, nothing like the first example would count as an instance of fear, since Aquinas (allegedly) thinks that "the object of fear must be present to sense or imagination" (p. 291). But this is not what Aquinas holds at 42.4. When Aquinas claims that the object of fear cannot be what is voluntary, but must rather be extrinsic to the will, he is not denying that something perceived by rational apprehension can be an object of fear. Roberts attributes to Aquinas the view that "since the passions belong to the sensory appetite, instances of fear that do not take sense-objects are therefore not passions," citing 22.3 ad 1m and 3m (p. 291). As I have shown, when Aquinas claims that acts of rational appetite which bear a likeness to acts of the sensitive appetite are not *passiones*, he is not denying their status as *affectiones* or "pseudopassions" (§2.2).

[13] Implicit in Thomas's account is a distinction between first-order and second-order fears. Just as desiring to desire health is not the same as desiring health, so fearing that one will someday fear a particular object is really and logically distinct from presently fearing that object. The most influential contemporary account of the distinction between "first-order" and "second-order" desires remains Frankfurt 1971.

In Question 41, Thomas defined the object of fear as the "future difficult evil which cannot be resisted" (*malum futurum difficile cui resisti non potest*) (41.2.co). What exactly does "cannot be resisted" mean? Does Aquinas mean that resistance is perceived as literally impossible? Or does he intend to suggest that the evil, while certainly difficult to resist (as it must be, if it is to correspond to a passion within the irascible), is not literally impossible to resist? The question is important, since the distinction between the difficult and the impossible is not trivial. As Question 40 makes clear, it marks the difference between hope and despair (§9.1). A narrow construal of "*resisti non potest*" would suggest that resistance is impossible. But this is not Aquinas' view. If evils avoided *de facili* are not objects of fear, one may infer, then evils that are objects of fear are avoided *de difficili* rather than *de impossibili*. (Hence in the next Question, Aquinas redescribes the fear's object as the future evil "which cannot be resisted *de facili*" [43.1.co].) Articles 5 and 6 confirm this interpretation. In Article 5, Aquinas asks whether "unexpected and sudden things" (*insolita et repentina*) are "more terrifying" (*magis terribilia*). They are, he answers, because what makes an evil difficult to avoid comes from both "the greatness of the evil and the weakness of the one who fears" (42.5.co). Why should the suddenness of an evil change the perception of its inescapability? In answering this question, Aquinas explicitly draws upon Cicero's analysis in the *Tusculan Disputations*. Evils can appear smaller, Cicero says, if we have time to consider and anticipate them. When they arrive unexpectedly, they are perceived as great, since there is no time to prepare for them.[14] This fact not only increases the perceived magnitude of the evil, Aquinas adds, but contributes to the sense of weakness felt by the person who fears, subtracting as it does from the remedies that he might use to ward it off.

Evils generally appear worse when their arrival is sudden. But, as Aquinas notices, there are exceptions. In the *ad tertium*, he illustrates both the typical case and the exception. The typical case is exemplified by a rich man who suddenly loses all his money. His poverty is felt more deeply than it would be if there had been time for him to grow accustomed to it. Such cases suggest that "sudden evil is feared more, because it seems more to be evil" (42.5 ad 3m). But in the exceptional case, the reverse is true. It may happen that "the greatness of some evil is hidden, for example when

---

[14] Cicero endorses, with some reservations, the *praemeditatio futurorum malorum* (which he associates with the Cyrenaics) as a palliative to misfortunes (see *Tusculan Disputations* 3.14).

an enemy hides himself in ambush. And then it is true that the evil becomes more terrible (*terribilius*) through careful consideration" (42.5 ad 3m).

Because Aquinas takes the trouble to specify the conditions under which feared evils become more or less difficult to avoid, it seems clear that one should not opt for a narrow construal of 41.2's formula that the object of fear is an evil "which cannot be resisted." Article 6 specifies an additional factor that makes a threatening evil something terrible – the apparent lack of any remedy. One might suppose the contrary. As the first objector argues, if there are no remedies, the evil is inevitable. Inevitable evils do not inspire fear, but a sense of resignation that diminishes or eliminates fear. Aquinas agrees that if someone perceives that an evil is coming and sees that he can do nothing to prevent it, both hope and fear come to an end. But he has a different case in mind. Suppose that one can act to prevent an evil from coming, but that one also knows that, after a certain point, there are absolutely no remedies against it. Chemical warfare and nuclear warfare provide relevant instances. We simultaneously fear these evils and hope to prevent them (an arduous but worthwhile good). But what makes the evil particularly terrible is precisely the fact that, if a chemical or nuclear attack should occur, there are virtually no remedies for them. Even worse, the effect of such an attack is not sudden death, but pain and suffering that may last for many years. In arguing that circumstances have the power to increase an evil, Aquinas comments that "long, or even perpetual duration" (42.6.co) is especially effective in augmenting the terrible character of a feared evil.

Question 42 specifies the *obiectum timoris* with precision. For a particular thing to become feared, it has to be a future evil that is perceived as both threatening and out of the control of one's will. If fear itself meets these conditions, it too can be feared. Feared evils are necessarily difficult to avoid, but not necessarily impossible. Something becomes more difficult to avoid, and thus inspires more fear, if its arrival is sudden and unexpected, or if it appears that no remedies are available. Having thus delineated the object of fear, Aquinas proceeds to consider its cause.

10.3 THE CAUSE OF FEAR

What is the distinction between the object of fear and the cause of fear? That Aquinas should find some significant difference between them is implied by his decision to devote one Question to the *obiectum* of fear, and another to its *causa*. One might explain the decision thus: Aquinas has so much to say about fear's object and cause that a single Question would be inadequate. But this would be to argue *suppositio falsi*, since Questions 41 and 42 contain only six Articles between them. A better explanation for the decision is that Aquinas knows what Wittgenstein will rediscover eight centuries later:

We should distinguish between the object of fear and the cause of fear. Thus a face which inspires fear or delight (the object of fear or delight), is not on that account its cause, but – one might say – its target. (1953, §476, p. 125)[15]

That Aquinas would distinguish between fear's object and its cause might be surprising. In previous Questions, Thomas appears to identify a passion's cause with its object (see §3.1).[16] For example, "passions differ according to their *activa* (*differunt secundum activa*), which are the objects (*obiecta*) of the passions of the soul" (23.4.co). In the spirit of Wittgenstein, one might gloss *activum* as the material object or particular target of the passion. So the delight I experience upon seeing Maria's face would have her face as its *activum* or target. But what causes the delight that occurs when I see her face? What causes me to apprehend her face as something that inspires pleasure? The answer to this question cannot simply be "the face." To answer this question properly would be to identify the cause of the passion.

Aquinas' own approach is informed by this distinction. As we have seen, the aim of Question 42's inquiry into fear's *obiectum* is to specify the properties that formally belong to any target capable of activating fear. Question 43 on fear's cause has a different goal. Its purpose is to identify the things that dispose a person to construe something as possessing features that inspire fear, that is, to perceive the thing as an *obiectum timoris*. As Ramírez suggests, Question 43 considers the cause of fear "in genere causae quasi materalis et *dispositivae*" (1973, p. 415; emphasis in original). Following this suggestion, one may say that Aquinas identifies two dispositional causes of fear: *amor* (Article 1) and *defectus* (Article 2).

---

[15] Kenny (1963) calls attention to this passage (p. 71). See also his discussion of the formal objects of passions (pp. 187–202).

[16] This impression may be intensified by Shapcote's over-translation of an important passage from 23.1.co: "The object of the concupiscible power is sensible good or evil, simply apprehended as such, which causes pleasure or pain." But Aquinas simply says: "Obiectum potentiae concupiscibilis est bonum vel malum sensibile simpliciter acceptum, quod est delectabile vel dolorosum." It is true, as I have argued in §3.1, that objects activate the passions, and in this sense function as their causes (cf. 23.1.co; 23.4.co; 30.2.co; 31.8 ad 3m; 35.4.co; 36.4 ad 3m; 40.1.co; 40.2.co). But when Aquinas inquires into the *causa* of the passion, he does not suppose "cause" to have the meaning taken by *activum* in 23.4.co.

In what sense is love a cause of fear? The *sed contra* cites Augustine, the *auctoritas* most frequently invoked by Aquinas when he wants to assert the priority of *amor*. Augustine writes: "There can be no doubt that there is no cause for fear except the loss of what we love, when we possess it, or the failure to obtain what we hope for" (*On Eighty-three Different Questions*, Question 33). Aquinas glosses the passage: "Therefore every fear is caused by this – that we love something. Thus love is a cause of fear" (43.1.sc).

In the body of the Article, Aquinas makes a more technical argument, stipulating that the objects of passions bear the same relation to the passions themselves as forms bear to the things (*res*) they inform. He deploys this analogy as follows:

Just as whatever is a cause of the form, is a cause of the *res* constituted by that form, so whatever is a cause, in any manner at all, of the object, is a cause of the passion. (43.1.co)

If love is a cause of the *obiectum timoris*, then love is also a cause of fear itself. But in what manner does love cause the object of fear? To answer this question, Aquinas makes another distinction. A thing may be the cause of an object either "through the mode of an efficient cause" (*per modum causae efficientis*) or "through the mode of material disposition" (*per dispositionis materialis*) (43.1.co). Love cannot cause the object of fear, the threatening evil, in the first mode, since love efficiently causes an agent to apprehend something under the aspect of good. But love does cause fear in the second mode; it stands as the dispositional cause of fear. *Amor* not only inclines a person toward the *bonum conveniens*, but also inclines him away from what he perceives as contrary to the suitable good. In this way, love makes a person "so disposed that a thing is such an evil to him" (43.1.co). Therefore love is the "cause of fear, and of its object, through the mode of material disposition" (43.1).

By disposing a person to apprehend some things as goods, and consequently other things as evils, love causes fear. But is the converse possible? Can fear be the cause of love? The first objector poses this question. Aquinas acknowledges that fear can, at least *per accidens*, give rise to love. His example: "Through fear of being punished by God, man keeps his commandments, and thus begins to hope, and hope brings (*introducit*) love" (43.1. ad 1m). The analysis may be expanded. A salesman, for example, may fear that others will not perceive him as successful unless he drives a certain kind of car, with which he proceeds to fall in love. Or a woman may fear that if she does not keep up with the latest styles, her friends will laugh at her; hence she develops an attachment to certain fashions. Certainly fear can generate love in this manner. But, Aquinas would add, such examples do not make sense except against the background of some loved good. Only the woman who craves the esteem of her friends fears their rejection. Only the salesman who cares about success fears the opinions of those who think he drives the wrong car. Marketers cannot successfully play upon the fears of their targets unless they know the loves that feed and inspire their fears. Politicians cannot take advantage of the fear of terrorism to win votes unless they have a keen appreciation for the loves threatened by terrorism. These examples confirm Aquinas' analysis: fear, like the other passions, profoundly depends on love (§1.4, §3.5, §5.2). It is not inconsistent to say that fear is also caused by hate: "The fact that we anticipate evil from someone provokes hatred of him rather than love" (43.1 arg. 2). But since hate itself is caused by love, this only reinforces the teaching that love causes fear: "the good, to which the feared evil is contrary, was loved from the beginning" (43.1 ad 2m).

In Article 2, Aquinas proposes "deficiency" (*defectus*) as the second dispositive cause of fear.[17] Once again, the distinction between efficient causality and material disposition is crucial. With respect to the mode of material disposition, "deficiency, speaking *per se*, is a cause of fear, for out of some lack of power (*defectu virtutis*) it happens that someone cannot easily (*de facili*) repel the threatening evil" (43.2.co). A thing is an object of fear to the degree that it is a threatening evil. It threatens us, because we perceive ourselves to be powerless against it. Such impotence is a primary example of the *defectus* that stands as the second dispositive cause of fear.

From the standpoint of efficient causality, *defectus* is not essentially a cause of fear. Aquinas acknowledges, however, that *defectus* may accidentally generate fear in another. A tyrant is properly feared on account of his power: "Might and strength, speaking *per se*, cause fear, for it is from this that something which is apprehended as harmful is powerful, whence it happens that its effects cannot be repelled" (43.2.co). But a tyrant's *defectus*, for instance injustice, may be regarded as a *per accidens* cause of fear. His injustice is only a *per accidens* cause of fear, however, because injustice must be accompanied by a positive wish to harm another. If the

---

[17] Ramírez (1973) takes this Article to be a treatment of the "physiological cause of fear," following Article 1's treatment of the "psychological cause of fear" (pp. 416–18). I do not find this reading confirmed by the text; nowhere in Question 43 does Aquinas suggest that *defectus* is to be understood in primarily physiological terms. In fact, the presumption is to the contrary; the *defectus potentiae* on account of which the weak are not confident of victory (cf. 43.2 ad 3m) is not necessarily a lack of physical strength.

Machiavellian prince is to be capable of inspiring fear (and not simply
hatred), he must be regarded not only as unjust, but also as threatening.
Should he fail to cultivate a reputation for eliminating obstacles in his
path, he will not be properly feared, though he may be hated.[18]

10.4 WHAT FEAR DOES TO A PERSON

As a composite of form and matter, any passion involves not only a
motion of the appetite, but also a correlative set of physiological symptoms (§2.3). This claim, made by Aquinas throughout, informs Question 44's
consideration of fear's effects. Aquinas identifies four effects of fear:
contraction (Article 1), susceptibility to counsel (Article 2), trembling
(Article 3), and hindrance to operation (Article 4). Why does Aquinas
dispose the material in this manner? There does not appear to be any
obvious sequential relation between these effects. Ramírez's claim that
Articles 1 and 2 consider fear's effects as interior events of the soul, and
that Articles 3 and 4 treat exterior events of the body, is not persuasive,
since (as Ramírez himself observes) *contractio* is a "physio-psychological"
effect (1973, p. 422). A more adequate interpretation of the Question's
ordo articulorum will attend to the authorities in the passages *sed contra*.
In sequential order, these are Damascene, Aristotle, Cicero, and Paul. As
an alternative to Ramírez's "systematic" ordering,[19] I propose the following
interpretation:

> Article 1: Aquinas lays down an anchor, establishing the essentially
> hylomorphic character of fear. He makes use of Damascene, the
> *auctoritas* whom he typically prefers when grounding the basic
> definition of passion.[20]
> Article 2: With this anchor in place, Aquinas takes up a question raised
> by book 2 of Aristotle's *Rhetoric*. The proper *determinatio* of the
> question suggests the manner in which the passions can serve reason.
> Article 3: But the passions can also disturb reason. That Cicero should
> appear as the only authority in the *sed contra* (for the first and only

---

[18] Thus a prince should avoid a reputation for liberality, since "among all the things that a prince
should guard against is being contemptible and hated, and liberality leads you to both"
(Machiavelli 1998, p. 65).

[19] Ramírez (1973) introduces the second paragraph of his exposition with this remark: "If one wishes
to reduce these four effects to a system . . ." The imperative is strictly hypothetical.

[20] Here I follow a trail marked by Jordan (1986), who writes that "John Damascene's definitions of
the passions anchor each of the major discussions" (p. 74).

time in Questions 22–48[21]) indicates Aquinas' willingness to do justice to the position historically opposed to the Aristotelian standpoint.

Article 4: Having rehearsed the debate between the Peripatetics and the Stoics, Aquinas draws upon Pauline authority. He thus uses Scripture to mediate between the two preeminent pagan schools, following the example of Augustine.

Article 1 asks whether fear produces contraction. The objectors argue that the particular motions of the vital spirits which cause contraction lead not to fear, but to daring (44.1 arg. 1) or pain (44.2 arg. 2). Both the physiological theories of the objectors and Aquinas' careful replies to those theories may lead a contemporary reader to write off his perspective as hopelessly dated. This would be a mistake. Aquinas does not suppose that the passions are reducible to physiology. But he does think that common expressions like "His blood ran hot with anger" and "Her blood went cold in fear" contain something worth preserving. If the motion of vital spirits from the exterior to the interior parts of the body is somehow connected with both fear and anger, there must be some distinction within this motion that corresponds to the difference between the passions themselves. The difference, Aquinas claims, is that the vital spirits associated with anger move inward and upward, just as heat rises, whereas those connected with fear move inward and downward, on account of condensation caused by cold. As a piece of natural science, Aquinas' claim is dated. But the conviction that motivates it retains its validity. The conviction is that different motions of the sensitive appetite will produce correspondingly different somatic effects. Feeling hot with anger and cold with fear are experiences grounded in nature. While the *explanans* may change as natural science changes, the *explanandum* will remain the same.

Distinct events within the soul produce distinct bodily events. But precisely because Aquinas regards the body and soul as fundamentally integrated, the distinction is not a separation. There will always be an ordered connection between them. The connection is one of formal rather than efficient causality. For every passion, Aquinas argues, there is a formal and a material aspect (§2.3). "Just as the formal aspect (*formale*) is the very motion of the appetitive power (*ipse motus appetitivae potentiae*),

---

[21] He also appears at 46.1.sc, where he is mentioned in conjunction with Damascene to argue that anger is a *specialis passio*. Interestingly, *perturbare* and cognate terms (favored by Cicero in descriptions of the emotions) appear nowhere in the other Questions on fear, but seven times in Question 44.

so is the bodily change (*transmutatio corporalis*) the material aspect (*materiale*), of which one is proportioned to the other (*quorum unum alteri proportinatur*)" (44.1.co). To describe the connection between the soul-event and the body-event as a proportion, Aquinas argues, is to imply a resemblance between the two. "According to the likeness and character (*similitudo et ratio*) of the appetitive motion, the bodily change follows" (44.1.co).

With this argument in place, Aquinas explains the relation between the *passio animae* of fear and the somatic effect of *contractio*. Because it responds to the apprehension of a threatening evil difficult to repel, combined with a sense of one's own powerless, fear implies an inward shrinking, a "contraction in the appetite" (*contractio in appetitu*). Aquinas substantiates this claim with two different examples: nature withdraws inwardly in a dying person who lacks power; urban dwellers struck by fear flee to the middle of the city. Thomas chooses two examples that appear unrelated, because he wants to drive home the point that *contractio* as a response to fear is rooted in nature. It does not depend on variations of circumstance.

The "contraction in the appetite" described by Aquinas is mirrored by a bodily contraction. Thomas does not describe the contraction at length; his intent is not to supply a detailed physiological description of common experience. His objective, rather, is to emphasize the relation of original to image. The motion of the sensitive appetite is the original; the bodily contraction occurs "according to the likeness" of the contraction in the soul. What happens *ex parte corporis* – the local motion of vital spirits *ad interiora* – imitates what occurs *ex parte animae* in the motion of the sensitive appetite. Some who have noticed this parallel have wondered whether Aquinas is equivocating on "motion," or else engaging in an illegitimate transition from the bodily to the spiritual. "All emotions involve internal physical movements, but Aquinas did not refer to them in explaining why emotions are movements," Knuuttila writes, as if this were an objection to Thomas (2004, p. 251).[22] For good reason, Aquinas does not use local motion to *explain* the act of the sensitive appetite. This would be to explain the original by the likeness, something that Aquinas would (rightly) not do. If the objection is that Aquinas uses the same word to designate distinct phenomena, the response is to observe that Aquinas is

---

[22] Gondreau (2002) relevantly observes: "By defining passion as a 'movement' of the sensitive appetite, or by affirming that affectivity is characterized by a movement 'towards things,' Thomas of course does not have 'local motion' in mind, i.e., physical displacement in time and place, as may *prima facie* be understood by the modern reader" (p. 209).

following Aristotelian usage. "Motion" can denote a change in quantity, a change in quality, or a change from one place to another (see §2.3). In describing the somatic effects of passions as "likenesses" of the proper act of sensitive appetite, Aquinas is drawing upon a complex metaphysics that traces multiple relations between soul and body, act and potency, form and matter, original and likeness. An objection to Aquinas that wants to persuade cannot merely assert that he is "unclear." It must attempt (as Descartes, Hobbes, Spinoza, and Hume do) to articulate an alternative metaphysics and a correspondingly different theory of the passions. When Knuuttila detects "terminological vacillation" in the *ST*, he is pointing to what Aquinas would understand as analogical predication.

In Article 2, Thomas asks whether fear produces persons inclined toward deliberation. The *sed contra* quotes Aristotle's *Rhetoric*: "Fear produces deliberative persons" (2.5, 1383a6). When we are afraid, we lack confidence in our own ability to repel the threatening evil, and therefore seek counsel all the more eagerly. "Most of all do men seek counsel when they are afraid" (44.2.co). If seeking counsel is generally good, and fear inspires us to seek counsel, then fear is good. To this extent, the passion is healthy. In the response's second part, Aquinas shifts the emphasis. Those under the influence of fear may be eager to seek counsel, but they do not themselves make wise counselors. The power of deliberating well requires the ability to see things as they are. "To a man affected according to some passion, a thing seems greater or smaller than it is according to the truth of the thing – as what is loved seems better to a person in love, and what is feared seems more terrifying to the person who is afraid" (44.2.co). When it is governed by reason, a passion can be utilized for the sake of good (§4.3). But when a person is "affected" by it – when she is possessed by the passion rather than possessing it – her perspective is inevitably distorted. A parent possessed by fear, for example, will waste psychic energy worrying about things that are not ultimately dangerous.

Aquinas' frank admission that fear distorts the perspectives of those affected by it recalls the argument of the Stoics. In book 3 of the *Tusculan Disputations* (3.11.25), Cicero defines fear (*metus*) as "the opinion of a great impending evil" (*opinio magni mali impendentis*). Book 4 expands this to "the opinion of an impending evil, which seems to be intolerable" (4.7.14). The similarity of these definitions to Damascene's formula is not accidental, as Cicero may be its indirect source. The result of fear, Cicero claims, is "a certain withdrawal and flight of the soul" (*recessum quendam animi et fugam*) (4.7.15). As if to confirm his intention to engage the Stoic argument, Aquinas has the second objector quote Cicero: fear "drives away all thought and dislocates the mind" (44.2 arg. 2).[23] In reply, Aquinas does not deny the objection's force. In the extreme case of panic fear, a man's thoughts are so disturbed that he is incapable of receiving any counsel at all. Only when his fear is "small" (*parvus*) is a man able to receive counsel. Fear is small, Thomas argues, when it "does not much disturb the reason" (*nec multum rationem conturbet*) (44.2 ad 2m). Aquinas' emphasis on the helpfulness of fear seems to contrast sharply with the Stoic doctrine that fear is simply bad, to be avoided by the *sapiens* at all costs. But the contrast is superficial. Cicero himself acknowledges the existence of an emotion, *cautio*, that resembles fear, but is amenable to reason (*Tusculan Disputations* 4.6.13). To observe a deeper convergence between Aquinas and the Stoics is congruent with Thomas's own view (itself an echo of Augustine) that the debate between the Stoics and the Peripatetics is largely verbal: while the difference "appears great in words, it is nevertheless in reality none at all, or but little, if we consider the intent of either school" (24.2.co). Against this Augustinian background, we see why Aquinas wants both to affirm the Aristotelian claim that "fear produces deliberative persons" and to agree with Cicero that the fear is distortive and dangerous if not governed by reason.

Before Aquinas offers a final word on this debate, he considers another somatic effect of fear. Article 3 asks whether fear produces "trembling" (*tremor*). Since ordinary experience seems to provide a clear answer to this question, one may wonder what is at issue. Three possible explanations may be given. First, by introducing "trembling" into the discussion, Thomas prepares the reader for the Pauline *sed contra* ("with fear and trembling work out your salvation") that closes the Question. Second, Article 3 is the only Article within the entire sequence of Questions devoted to the passions in which Cicero appears by himself in the *sed contra*. The use of Cicero in the *sed contra* continues the dialectic initiated by the last Article. It also suggests that Aquinas considers Cicero a valuable observer of the effects of the passions, even if his basic anthropology is too crude, failing as it does to distinguish the intellectual appetite from the sensitive appetite. Third, Aquinas may be commenting ironically on sophistic attempts to use the latest scientific theories to prove that fear

---

[23] "Timor est *excutiens cogitata, et mentem a suo loco removet, ut Tullius dicit, in IV de Tusculanis quaest.*" The exact words quoted by Aquinas do not appear in the text of book 4 of the *Tusculan Disputations*. The quotation appears to be a conflation of the description of *conturbatio* as "*metum excutientem cogitata*" and that of *pavor* as "*metum mentem loco moventem*" (4.8.19). It is likely that Aquinas is not quoting from the text directly, but from a florilegium whose extracts may be corrupt.

does not cause trembling. Against sophistic enlightenment, Aquinas thinks in accord with both tradition and experience. That fear produces trembling is evident. In the replies to the objections, Thomas provides some particularly vivid reminders. Those in a fearful state tremble in their speech; their lower lip and jaw quiver; their arms and hands shake; their knees knock (44.4 ad 2m). More drastically, but equally attested by experience, fear can prompt a "loosening of the bowels and a discharge of urine, and sometimes even of semen (*solutio ventris et urinae emisso, et quandoque etiam seminis*)" (44.4 ad 1m). In the modern idiom, a person can be scared shitless.

When brought under the sway of reason, fear can be useful. But fear left unchecked will cause panic. In the final Article, Thomas takes account of both truths, asking whether fear impairs activity (*operatio*). When fear "increases so much that it perturbs reason (*rationem perturbet*), it impairs activity even (*etiam*) on the part of the soul" (44.4.co). The drama implicit in the *etiam* finds more colorful expression in Collingwood: "A man really frightened can neither syllogize nor plan. His mind goes numb" (1942, p. 68). (Collingwood makes the point against rationalistic accounts of the passions given by Hobbes and Spinoza.) Yet "if fear is moderate, not perturbing the reason much, it conduces to good activity, inasmuch as it causes a certain solicitude, and makes a man more attentive to deliberation and operation" (44.4.co).[24] What assurance is there that fear can be governed? Would minimizing or eliminating fear be safer than projects that aim at its moderation? On this question, Aquinas gives the last word to neither Aristotle nor the Stoics, but to Paul. "With fear and trembling work out your salvation," he says, quoting the exhortation to the Philippians (2:12; 44.4.sc). He adds that if fear were necessarily hostile to *bona operatio*, Paul would not have said these words. Thus does Aquinas employ Scripture as an aid to his own mediation of the debate between the Peripatetics and the Stoics.

---

[24] Aquinas' perspective on fear is characteristically nuanced, in contrast to some others in the tradition that will succeed him. For example, Burton (1927) breathlessly describes the negative effects of fear, without troubling to take account of the good that can arise from what Aquinas calls "moderate fear" (*timor moderatus*) (44.4.co). "They that live in fear are never free, resolute, secure, never merry, but in continual pain: that, as Vives truly said, *Nulla est miseria major quam metus*, no greater misery, no rack, no torture like unto it; ever suspicious, anxious, solicitous, they are childishly drooping without reason, without judgement, 'especially if some terrible object be offered,' as Plutarch hath it. It causeth oftentimes sudden madness, and almost all manner of diseases . . . Fear makes our imagination conceive what it list, invites the devil to come over us, as Agrippa and Cardan avouch, and tyrannizeth over our phantasy more than all other affections, especially in the dark" (pp. 227–8).

CHAPTER II

Daring

The consideration of daring is compressed, receiving but a single Question. Aquinas spends little time on daring's formal object because he has already covered much of the ground in the discussion of fear. Like fear, daring is a response to something perceived as a threatening evil. But if this is true, how does something become an object of daring rather than fear? Aquinas addresses this problem by isolating the "contrariety" of daring and fear (§11.1). After he distinguishes daring from fear, Aquinas determines that the primary cause of daring is hope. He locates various privations (e.g. drunkenness) as accidental causes (§11.2). How is daring related to courage? They are not the same, but Aquinas thinks that courage may include daring in its exercise. He also acknowledges, however, that daring can be the product of foolhardiness. Everything depends on the passion's relation to reason (§11.3). Thinking about daring's relation to reason provokes a first objection. If daring originates not simply from the perception of a threatening evil, but more nearly from a judgment that it can be overcome, does not the origination of daring in an act of reason disqualify it from being a passion in the proper sense? From another angle, it may be objected that daring is virtually indistinguishable from anger, since both involve the same pattern of rising up against a perceived threatening evil for the sake of victory over that evil. Why does Aquinas distinguish daring and anger as passions different in kind? I consider both objections, for their own sake and as a preparation for the following chapter on anger (§11.4).

11.1 DARING AS THE CONTRARY OF FEAR

Question 45 on *audacia* is the shortest Question to appear in the treatment of the passions. A casual reader might suppose that Aquinas regards daring as comparatively unimportant. The correlation between intrinsic importance and expansiveness of treatment, however, is far from exact.[1]

---

[1] On the other hand, it is difficult not to suppose *some* correlation, especially in view of Aquinas' conclusion in *De veritate* that "sic ergo principalissimae passiones sunt gaudium et tristitia" (*QDV* 26.5.co).

Thomas devotes only one Question in the 1a2ae to natural law, yet few have dared to infer its insignificance from that fact. But why does Aquinas reserve so little space for *audacia*? Two things may be said. First, the irascible passions generally receive more compressed treatment than their concupiscible counterparts. This is not accidental, but reflects the causal dependence of the irascible on the concupiscible. Second, of the irascible passions, *audacia* is the most evidently dependent on the other irascible passions. Much of what needs to be said about the cause of daring has already been said in the treatment of hope. Both of these considerations suggest that Thomas does not want to belabor essential points about daring. They do not imply that *audacia* is an unimportant passion.

In Question 45, Aquinas follows his usual order, addressing the nature of daring, its cause, and its effects. Aquinas considers daring in itself, by situating it as the proper contrary of fear (Article 1). The next two Articles concern the cause of daring, asking about its relation to hope (Article 2) and querying the sense in which "defect" (*defectus*) is and is not a cause of daring (Article 3).[2] What impact does daring have on those who are in danger, or about to face danger? In considering daring's effect (Article 4), Thomas addresses this question.

What is daring? Article 1 approaches this question by asking whether *audacia* is contrary to *timor*. Thomas has already identified fear as the contrary of hope. How can fear also be the contrary of daring? Aquinas reminds us that (as argued at 23.2) the irascible passions exhibit two kinds of contrariety:

The irascible passions have a twofold *contrarietas*, one according to the opposition of good and evil, and thus fear is the contrary of hope; the other is according to the opposition of approach and withdrawal, and thus daring is contrary to fear, and despair to hope. (45.1 ad 2m)

Quoting this passage, Michel Meyer asks: "But is it thus clear that hope is opposed to fear, and despair to daring?" (1994, p. 367).[3] Though Aquinas never directly asserts the contrariety of daring to despair, Meyer rightly sees that, like hope and fear, despair and daring are contrary with respect to both term and direction of motion (despair is a withdrawal from

---

[2] Ramírez (1973) assigns the treatment of daring's essence to Articles 1 and 2, and restricts its cause to Article 3 (p. 427). This is probably meant to correspond to the Prologue's suggestion that Article 2 concerns "quomodo audacia se habeat ad spem" and Article 3 treats "de causa audaciae" (45 pr.). But since *spes* is related to *audacia* as cause to effect, it is more reasonable to hold that Article 2 concerns daring's *per se* cause, followed by Article 3's treatment of *defectus* as a *per accidens* cause.

[3] Cf. Meyer (1994): "Mais est-ce si évident que l'espoir s'oppose à la crainte, et le désespoir à l'audace?" (p. 367).

perceived good; daring is an approach to perceived evil). Meyer attempts to cast serious doubt on the implied contrariety of despair and daring. He writes:

The approach of a good puts evil at a distance, and inversely the evil that approaches suggests the correlative withdrawal of the associated good. Thus one is tempted to say that the more one despairs with respect to the good that withdraws, the more one must have some courage to confront the evil, which is imminent. (1994, p. 368)[4]

Meyer is tempted to say this, because he does not understand Aquinas' thinking about the relation of daring to despair. Despair occurs when one has abandoned any hope of vanquishing the evil that stands in the way of attaining a difficult good (§9.1). Meyer is mistaken when he supposes that despair might create a space where "one must have some courage to confront the evil, which is imminent." On the contrary, daring yields to despair precisely when the possibility of this space has been eliminated. Despair and daring cannot coexist in the way that Meyer's scenario imagines, since "despair follows upon fear, for someone despairs because he fears the difficulty which surrounds the good to be hoped for" (45.2.co).[5] In short, when despair results, daring is no longer possible.

Though daring and despair are contraries in a sense, it is important to remember that Aquinas himself does not assert their contrariety. This is not an oversight, but an acknowledgment that daring and despair do not directly compete with each other.[6] The strict contrary of daring is not despair, but fear. As distinct passions, daring and fear cannot have the same formal object. But wherein do their formal objects differ? The question

---

[4] Cf. Meyer (1994): "L'approche d'un bien met à distance le mal, et inversement le mal qui s'approche représente l'éloignment corrélatif du bien associé. Ainsi est-on tenté de dire que plus on est désespéré à l'égard d'un bien qui fuit, plus on devra avoir du courage pour affronter le mal, qui est imminent" (p. 368).

[5] Aquinas does not deny that when fear is present in a certain measure, it may coexist with hope, without producing despair. His view is that when fear triumphs over hope, so as to eliminate it, despair will ensue. Ramírez (1973) makes the necessary qualification: "Fear is the cause of despair, not indeed imperfect and moderate fear, which may co-exist with hope – but perfect and complete fear, to the point of panic and agony. In that case, the impending evils appear irremediable and insuperable; consequently, hope for attaining the end becomes impossible, from which the motion of despair immediately follows" (p. 432).

[6] On the relation between despair and daring, Aquinas writes: "Despair entails withdrawal from good, which is as it were *per accidens*, and daring entails approach toward evil, which is also as it were *per accidens*" (25.4 ad 3m). Here his aim is not to emphasize the contrariety, but to show what they have in common, viz. that both are *per accidens* motions toward evil or away from good. It is not that Aquinas would necessarily deny that despair and daring are contraries. As Ramírez (1973) observes, the two passions appear to bear a "certain analogy based on opposition."

arises naturally, because Aquinas often emphasizes the features shared by the objects of daring and fear:

Hope is opposed to fear on the part of the object, since hope concerns good and fear concerns evil. But daring is about the same object, and is opposed to fear according to approach. (25.3.co)

And later in the 1a2ae: "Daring and fear are directed to some great danger" (60.4.co; see also 2.2.123.3 ad 3m). Both fear and daring appear to have a common object, the "threatening evil (*malum imminens*)." This would partly explain why Aquinas does not include a detailed description of daring's object, since he has already elucidated the notion of the *malum imminens* in Question 42 (§10.2). Yet the formal object of daring cannot be identical with that of fear, if passions differ by their formal objects, and daring is a passion distinct from fear. To see the *differentia* that specifies the general object common to fear and daring, one must focus not only on the term of appetite (§1.1), but also on the agent's relation to that term. The formal object of fear is not simply the threatening evil, but the threatening evil apprehended as difficult to resist in a way that surpasses our power (without yet being judged absolutely impossible). Daring's formal object, by contrast, is the threatening evil that is difficult to resist, yet within our power to overcome (if just barely). Fear and daring, Aquinas says in the *De veritate*, are contraries "according to whether the evil surpasses or does not surpass our capacity" (*QDV* 26.4.co).[7]

This is the primary point of Article 1. Fear, not despair, is the proper contrary of daring. Daring "stands furthest" (*maxime distat*) from fear, according to Aquinas, because it has the same term, but differs in the direction of its motion. Both passions concern "harm about to come" (*nocumentum futurum*). The difference is that

fear turns back from (*refugit*) the harm about to come on account of its victory over the one in fear, but daring attacks (*aggreditur*) the imminent danger (*periculum imminens*), on account of its own victory over that very danger. Whence manifestly daring is contrary to fear. (45.1.co)

Daring does not approach the evil for its own sake, since evil cannot attract anything by its own power (§1.4). It approaches the evil in order to

---

[7] Ramírez's explanation of this point may be helpful. Whereas hope and fear are opposed according to a difference in the term, "daring is opposed to fear by a formal contrary opposition, that is from the side of the motivating object or reason of motion, since fear entails a motion of withdrawal away from the arduous evil, whereas daring names a motion of approach toward the same arduous evil *on account of contrary reasons*" (1973, p. 430; emphasis in original).

overcome it. The notion of victory is of the first importance to the irascible passions in general, and to daring in particular. The contrary motions of fear and daring reflect opposed estimations about victory over the *malum imminens*. That either the agent or the threatening evil will prevail is certain. The only question is: Which one? As passions, daring and fear are not judgments arrived at through deliberation. Rather, they reflect one's sense of the prospects for victory prior to deliberation. The provision of an initial sense of things that is prior to reasoning may account, at least in part, for why Aquinas accords the passions the importance that he does. Nussbaum proposes that the emotions are "intelligent parts of our ethical agency, responsive to the workings of deliberation and essential to its completion" (1990, p. 41). Aquinas would agree (§4.3), adding that the passions may provide an important clue to our initial estimation of situations, an estimation that precedes deliberation altogether.

11.2 HOPE AS THE PRINCIPAL CAUSE OF DARING

If daring does not arise from a deliberative process, what causes it? Article 2 suggests an answer to this question, asking whether daring follows from hope. Earlier, Aquinas had suggested that "hope and despair are the reason for fear and daring: because daring arises from the hope of victory, and fear arises from the despair of overcoming" (25.3.co). He now provides a metaphysical explanation. Good is pursued *per se*; evil can be pursued only *per accidens*, on account of some annexed good. Correlatively, good cannot be avoided *per se*, but only *per accidens*, on account of some annexed evil. As what is *per se* is prior to what is *per accidens*, so (1) essential pursuit of good is prior to (2) accidental pursuit of evil, and (3) essential withdrawal from evil is prior to (4) accidental withdrawal from good. Aquinas adds:

These four things pertain to the four passions, for pursuit (*prosecutio*) of good pertains to hope, withdrawal from evil pertains to fear, motion toward the terrible evil (*insecutio mali terribilis*) belongs to daring, and withdrawal from good pertains to despair. Whence it follows (*sequitur*) that daring is consequent upon (*consequitur*) hope, for it is thus that someone hopes to overcome a terrible threatening thing (*terribile imminens*), and thereby attacks boldly (*audacter insequitur*). (45.2.co)

Daring follows upon hope. Aquinas argues this metaphysically (the priority of 1 to 2) and reinforces it rhetorically (the repetition of forms of *sequor*).

To say that *per se* withdrawal from evil is prior to *per accidens* withdrawal from good (the relation of 3 and 4 above) is a way of saying that fear is prior to despair. And Aquinas says just this in Question 45:

> Despair follows upon fear, for someone despairs because he fears the difficulty which surrounds the good to be hoped for. (45.2.co)

This conclusion follows from the metaphysical priority of *per se* avoidance of evil to *per accidens* avoidance of good. But can it be reconciled with what Aquinas said earlier in the 1a2ae about the order of the passions?

> That hope and despair are naturally prior to fear and daring is manifest from this – that, just as the appetite for good is the *ratio* by which evil is avoided, so also hope and despair are the *ratio* of fear and daring, for daring follows upon the hope of victory, and fear follows upon the despair of overcoming. (25.3.co)[8]

Which view do we attribute to Aquinas? Does despair generate fear, or does fear generate despair? It appears that by the time Aquinas arrives at Question 40, he has reconsidered the problem. If he had wanted to elaborate Question 25's claim that despair is the *ratio* of fear, he might have done so in Question 40, or else in a separate Question devoted specifically to despair. Thomas's decision not to make this argument suggests that he has rethought the matter *in actu*.[9] His reply to Article 2's second objector confirms this:

> Although good simply is prior to evil, yet withdrawal from evil must be prior to withdrawal from good, as the pursuit of good is prior to the pursuit of evil. And thence just as hope is prior to daring, so fear is prior to despair. (45.2 ad 2m)

It is not that hope and fear necessarily cause daring and despair. Aquinas adds that daring arises from hope only when the hope is particularly *vehemens*. Likewise, not every case of fear generates despair; the fear must be especially *intensus* (45.2 ad 2m). When an object is regarded as a threatening evil, but the hope for victory is more intense than the accompanying fear, the

---

[8] Manzanedo (1994) takes 25.3 to prove that "the proper cause of fear is despair, since despair of victory moves one to flee the threatening evil" (p. 448). But in light of the explicit argument found at 45.2.co, 45.2 ad 2m, and 45.2 ad 3m, not to mention the total silence with respect to *desperatio* as a cause of fear in Question 43, can we draw this conclusion so confidently? Cajetan (1889) notices the problem: "Here in particular a doubt is raised, since the author is at odds with himself. For above, at 25.3, he expressly said that despair is prior to fear, and that fear follows despair of victory, just as daring follows hope of victory. But here he plainly wants to say that despair is an effect of fear, just as daring is an effect of hope" (p. 289).

[9] Another possible motive for asserting the priority of fear to despair is that whereas fear is one of the four principal passions, despair is not. Maintaining the priority of despair over fear would make it difficult to say this.

result is daring. If the fear increases to the point that hope for victory is obliterated, the result is *desperatio*. Thus, "properly speaking, daring is not a part of hope, but its effect, just as despair is not a part of fear, but its effect" (45.2 ad 3m).[10]

That daring is generated by hope seems clear enough. Michel Meyer, however, tries to show that Aquinas cannot but contradict himself in making the argument. First, he quotes a French translation of 45.1 (Thomas Aquinas 1994–6, p. 282) in order to show that Aquinas takes fear to regard a distant evil ("mal à venir"), whereas daring as its contrary must regard a proximate evil ("le péril imminent"). He then alleges that Aquinas is committed to the opposite view, that is, because fear can also regard a nearby evil, "daring, in being opposed to fear, would be a reaction to a distant evil" (1994, p. 372).[11] And yet Aquinas cannot consistently hold the latter position, Meyer continues, because he holds that an evil's danger corresponds to its nearness, implying that the strongest form of daring would be a reaction to a proximate evil. Meyer quotes Aquinas, citing 45.4:

But the arduous is the object of daring. Therefore whenever the arduous is increased, so daring is increased. But a danger becomes more arduous and difficult when it is present. Therefore, it must be when danger is present that daring is greatest.[12]

In his zeal to exhibit that which "constitue le noeud des contradictions thomistes," Meyer has quoted neither the response nor the replies of 45.4, but the Article's second objection! In light of this elementary failure of *explication de texte*, it is difficult to take seriously Meyer's conclusion that "la question qui se pose maintenant est de savoir pourquoi Saint Thomas s'abandonne à telle confusion" (1994, p. 372). The confusion belongs to

---

[10] Aquinas presses the conclusion that fear causes despair. But might something be said for 25.3's claim that despair is the *ratio* of fear? Cajetan (1889) argues that despair causes fear "from the side of the object," and that fear causes despair "from the side of the mode of attaining the object." Correctly, he observes that while "the object of fear always has some taste of the object of despair," not all despair causes (or is caused by) fear: "If we think something impossible to attain, we may despair over that, but we do not fear" (p. 289). Ramírez (1973) observes: "Despair recedes from the end, while fear recedes from the means" (p. 431).

[11] Cf. Meyer (1994): "Le courage, en étant l'opposé de la crainte, serait la réaction à un mal lointain" (p. 372).

[12] I have translated the passage (from 45.4 arg. 2) directly from Aquinas' Latin. The edition from which Meyer quotes (Thomas Aquinas 1994–6) runs as follows: "Mais l'audace a pour objet la difficulté. Elle grandit donc avec elle. Mais le danger devient plus rude et plus difficile quand en présent. C'est donc alors que l'audace doit se déployer davantage."

Meyer – and not simply because he cannot tell the difference between an objection and a reply.[13] Meyer holds that for Aquinas despair should cause daring, since the withdrawal of a good that induces despair produces the approach of an evil, which if faced generates daring. Meyer then adds: "Curiously, St. Thomas still defends the idea that it is hope which produces daring, as if the good that approaches were to require some daring while the correlative evil is still distant" (1994, p. 371).[14] But Aquinas does not suppose that simply any hope causes daring.[15] On the contrary, he speaks precisely:

Daring cannot be a principal passion, for it arises from evil *per accidens*, since it regards evil by way of attacking it. For the daring man attacks evil, insofar as he estimates victory over, and expulsion of, evil to be a certain good, and from such good hope, daring arises. And thus, subtly considered, hope is found to be prior to daring, for hope of victory, or at least of escaping the danger, causes daring. (*QDV* 26.5 ad 2m)[16]

Meyer's claim that "Saint Thomas semble s'opposer à lui-même" (1994, p. 368) may be dismissed. Aquinas does not collapse at the first touch of Meyer's problematological finger.[17]

---

[13] No one is immune from the possibility of committing such a blunder. To quote the maxim of La Rochefoucauld that appears on the dedicatory page of Meyer (1991): "Qui vit sans folie n'est pas si sage qu'il croit."

[14] Cf. Meyer (1994): "Curieusement, Saint Thomas défend alors l'idée que c'est l'espoir qui produit le courage, comme si le bien qui est proche requérait du courage alors que le mal corrélatif est encore loin" (p. 371).

[15] Part of Meyer's puzzlement may stem from his failure to understand that for Aquinas, *audacia* necessarily regards a means to an end (i.e. vanquishing the evil for the sake of obtaining a good), and therefore presupposes the prior intention of an end. Manzanedo (1994) rightly comments that because daring is an "intermediate act," it is "posterior to hope in the order of intention," although he questionably adds that "in the order of generation or execution, daring is (in a way) prior to hope" (p. 439). The addition is questionable because while attainment of the hoped-for good follows daring in the order of execution, the passion of hope precedes daring in both orders (as 25.3 makes clear with respect to the order of execution specifically).

[16] As Manzanedo (1994) comments: "In the last analysis daring arises from hope, and is finally ordered toward joy (to the attainment of the hoped-for good). For it cannot be a principal passion" (p. 446).

[17] Meyer's assurance that Aquinas grossly contradicts himself throughout seems to derive from a general view about the nature of premodern philosophy. According to Meyer, all thought in the Platonic or Aristotelian tradition substitutes the "analysis of propositions" for the "radical questioning" that is essential to philosophy (1995, p. 6). However dubious Meyer's own application of this claim to philosophers who write dialogues, or to theologians who think in terms of *quaestiones*, there is much to say for the view that philosophical texts are essentially answers to questions, and that accurate construction of the latter is a condition of philosophic understanding. Curiously, Meyer does not acknowledge the classic formulation of the view in R. G. Collingwood's "logic of question and answer." See Collingwood 1939, pp. 29–43, 55, 122; Collingwood 1940, pp. 21–48; Collingwood 1942, pp. 253–6; Collingwood 1956, pp. 269–74.

After establishing that hope is the principal cause of daring, Aquinas asks whether "some defect" is the cause of daring. In itself, *defectus* cannot cause daring, since it is a privation. The only *per se* cause of daring is whatever provokes hope or excludes fear. But *per accidens*, a defect may cause daring, "in one manner, with respect to appetitive motion; in another manner, with respect to bodily transmutation" (45.3.co). Considering the first manner, Aquinas provides a brief catalog of "things which make us estimate that it is possible to attain victory" (45.3.co). The catalog distinguishes between what is possible according to our own power and what is possible through the power of others. Examples of the first: bodily courage, experience of dangers, a multitude of riches. Examples of the second: a multitude of friends, trust in divine help. To explain the latter, Thomas does not cite obvious scriptural loci, but quotes Aristotle's *Rhetoric*, as if to suggest that even natural reason knows that belief in divine help is a source of hope. In addition to hope, the elimination of fear "through the removal of threatening terrors" (*per remotionem terribilium appropinquantium*) may cause daring. Aquinas' single example: a person with no enemies has little reason to fear, and is thus more inclined to daring than one paralyzed with fear because a wrong move will prompt his enemies to quick action against him. Machiavelli would agree. Those who have attained power and want to preserve it, but who have acquired multiple enemies, are rarely capable of bold action (cf. Machiavelli 1998, p. 72).

The second half of Article 3's body considers the capacity of physiological changes to generate daring. Drawing upon Aristotle, Aquinas asserts that an increase in the amount of heat around the heart produces daring. This aspect of Thomas's treatment may seem scarcely worth noting, since it depends upon thoroughly antiquated science. Certainly the particulars of the Aristotelian biology are beyond saving. But Aquinas' core insight that a passion may be caused by either another passion or physiological changes (or both) remains valid. Modern natural science does not falsify Aquinas' claim that wine may enlarge the heart and thereby produce hope, which in turn leads to daring. Aquinas locates drunkenness as a *per accidens* cause of daring. "Drunkenness causes daring, not through being a defect, but through dilating the heart: and again through making a man think greatly of himself" (45.3 ad 1m). Similarly, lack of experience indirectly causes daring. The inexperienced "do not know their own failings, nor the dangers that threaten. Whence the removal of the cause of fear gives rise to daring" (45.3 ad 2m). Finally, Article 3 concludes, while the suffering of wrongdoing is a privation that cannot of itself cause daring, it may be accompanied by the opinion that God helps those who suffer unjustly. To the extent that it raises hope, the opinion is able to cause daring.

11.3 DARING AND COURAGE

In Question 45's final Article, Thomas considers the effect of daring. Article 4 asks whether the daring are more eager prior to danger than they are in its midst. As a passion, daring has a property akin to that which Socrates in the *Meno* associates with "true opinion" (98a). It makes its subjects bold, but only as long as it lasts. The *sed contra* quotes Aristotle's observation that "the daring are precipitate and full of eagerness before the dangers, and yet scatter when the dangers are present" (45.4.sc). Thomas elaborates:

Daring, since it is a certain motion of the sensitive appetite, follows an apprehension of a sensitive power. But a sensitive power is not collative (*collativa*), nor does it inquire into particulars surrounding a matter, but rather passes instant judgment. Now it happens sometimes that not everything which causes difficulty in some distressing situation can be known according to an instantaneous apprehension, whence arises the motion of daring for the sake of attacking the danger. Whence at the moment they experience the danger itself, they sense that the difficulty is greater than they had estimated. And thus they fall short. (45.4.co)

When a quick response is demanded, with no time for analysis, daring is useful.[18] But when a danger can be foreseen, Aquinas adds, it is far more rational to face the danger with deliberation. If a person is able to engage in a rational assessment of the dangers at hand, his attempt to defeat a difficult evil will be far more stable than one that emanates solely from the sensitive appetite. In contrast to sensation,

reason is aware (*discussiva*) of everything which causes difficulty in a distressing situation. And thus strong men (*fortes*), who attack dangers from the judgment of reason, appear slack in the beginning, since they are not acted upon (*passi*), but attack with due deliberation. Yet when they are in the midst of dangers, they do not experience some unforeseen thing, but sometimes the difficulties are smaller than they had anticipated. And thus they persist more. (45.4.co)

In any particular case, it can be difficult to tell the difference between the merely audacious and the genuinely courageous. One has to look beyond

---

[18] On the necessity for quick action in particular circumstances, as well as a lament of the damage caused by the view that prudent action can issue only from labored deliberation, see Vico 1971, p. 799.

the exterior act to the interior motivation. Those with fortitude will "attack dangers on account of the good of virtue," no matter how great the dangers may be, whereas "men of daring" (*audaces*) will be motivated "only on account of an estimation that creates hope and excludes fear" (45.4.co).

In itself, the passion of daring is no sin. Thomas has distinguished the vice of daring from the passion: "Anger and daring, and the names of all the passions, can be taken in two ways. In one manner, according as they denote absolutely a motion of the sensitive appetite in some object, good or bad, and thus they are the names of passions. In another manner, according as they denote, together with this motion, a withdrawal from the order of reason, and thus they are the names of vices" (45.1 ad 1m). Under what conditions does the passion of daring become a vice? Beyond the affirmation that daring becomes vicious when there is a *recessus ab ordine rationis*, Aquinas says little about this question in the 1a2ae. In the 2a2ae, however, he argues more fully that the vice of daring is opposed to the virtue of fortitude (see 2.127.2). What causes a person's departure from the order of reason, Aquinas claims, is his presumption that he is capable of achieving more than a truthful assessment of his powers would allow.

II.4 TWO OBJECTIONS

For the passion of daring to be aroused, a person must perceive or imagine a threatening evil. She must also perceive the evil as conquerable, albeit with difficulty. If daring requires the latter condition, Robert Roberts wonders what entitles Aquinas to locate daring as a motion of the sensitive appetite. Roberts distinguishes between (1) acts that seem to belong to the sensitive appetite, e.g. "bodily-based urges of a sex- and food-orientation, which may then be *modified* by considerations" (1992, p. 292) and (2) emotions that do not seem to be based in bodily appetites. Hunger is an example of (1); anger is a paradigm case of (2). Anger is questionably an act of the sensitive appetite, Roberts claims, because unlike hunger "anger is not based on any such given bodily 'appetite' which may then be modified by reasons; it *originates in its reasons*" (1992, p. 292; emphasis in original). Similarly, daring would be an instance of (2). Thus Roberts adds that "we can make the point about the need for rational determination of emotional perception using Aquinas' analysis of audacia" (1992, p. 292).

In analyzing the activation of sensitive appetite by particular reason (§3.4), and especially the activation of "rational" or "non-natural" concupiscence (§6.4), I have shown that the presence of conceptualization and judgment in the apprehension displays no tendency to show that the corresponding appetition cannot belong to sensitive appetite. This would hold if rational apprehension were capable of moving solely the rational appetite, but Aquinas does not take this view. It may be helpful, however, to subject Roberts's particular argument about daring to closer analysis. Roberts quotes Aquinas in a loose translation: "Daring [the emotion *audacia*] is properly concerned with what is disagreeable but this is accompanied by the boon of victory in the eyes of one who dares" (1992, p. 292).[19] A more accurate translation of the passage runs:

It is right to hold that daring concerns evil, to which is conjoined the good of victory according to the estimation of the daring man. But daring regards the evil, whereas it is hope that regards the conjoined good. (45.2 ad 3m)

Perhaps because he has cited only a fragment of the text, Roberts fails to notice that in the quoted passage, Aquinas subjects the claim that "daring concerns the good of victory" to an important qualification. Though daring may be said to regard both a threatening evil and the good of victory, it is hope that properly concerns the latter. Roberts glosses the fragment as follows:

The idea is that what the person experiencing daring sees with his eyes is a danger, and perhaps one to which he has an instinctual avoidance response (thus requiring nothing beyond what animals have in the way of perceptual apparatus); yet this perception is qualified by some thoughts, in particular the thought that he can overcome this danger and some of his reasons for thinking he can overcome it. (1992, p. 292)

The emphasis on "what the person experiencing daring sees with his eyes" is an artifact of the translation. Specifically visual perception is not accorded a prominent place in the analysis of daring's causality. It is true that some perception reducible to the form "This is a threatening evil, but it can be overcome," is necessary for the activation of daring. Roberts confidently assimilates what I am cautiously describing as "some perception" to the presence of "some thoughts" and "reasons for thinking" that the danger can be overcome. But Aquinas conspicuously avoids speaking of "thoughts" and "reasons" in this context. He speaks more prudently of the "*bonum victoriae secundum aestimationem audacis*" (the good of victory according to the estimation of the daring man) (45.2 ad 3m). To estimate

---

[19] The translation is from Thomas Aquinas 2006h. Roberts acknowledges that "to aid my interpretation I have occasionally made my own translation" (1992, p. 303).

that the environment contains something threatening, but that it should be resisted rather than fled, is an act of the type that Aquinas attributes to the "natural estimative power" in non-rational animals, the apprehensive power responsible for activating the irascible. Having explicit "thoughts" or "judgments" is not a necessary condition for the irascible power's activation (see §3.3).

It is true that for rational animals, intellectual considerations and judgments enter into the particular reason, and shape the agent's perception of a threatening evil as either conquerable or impossible to resist. But Aquinas has made it clear that the apprehension which activates the passion of daring in human beings, while likely to involve some conceptualization, is not essentially a product of deliberation (§11.1). Roberts has Aquinas say that "the hope which arouses daring is produced by whatever can persuade us of the possibility of success" (1992, p. 292). A more accurate rendition of the passage from 45.3.co – "the hope that causes daring is provoked by those things which make us estimate that it is possible that victory be attained" – shows that *aestimare* is a key term. Aquinas speaks of "estimating," because he is *not* talking about any quasi-deliberative process whereby rational considerations are adduced and "persuade us" that S is P. He is assuming that his readers have understood the capacity of the natural estimative power to assess a limited class of things as useful or dangerous, in abstraction from their character as pleasant or painful (§2.4 and §2.5). Roberts proposes that "since what is agreeable about the object of audacia is not (typically at any rate) something that can be grasped with the senses, it looks as though daring involves a perception that is not merely sense perception, but is determined by reason" (1992, p. 292). For Aquinas, this is the postulation of a false dichotomy. The significance of the estimative power is to account for how animals do (at least some of the time) have responses that go beyond the field of immediate sense perception (see 1.78.4 and §3.3), while lacking an immaterial intellect capable of abstracting universal concepts from sensed particulars.

Because Roberts assumes that animals are either fully cognitive beings or have no estimative powers at all, he is driven to the implausible conclusion that "most of the emotions that humans experience are never experienced by animals, and do not, therefore, belong to a non-rational appetite" (1992, p. 292). For Aquinas, by contrast, the passions do not lose their character as acts that humans share in common with other animals, though the mode in which the sensitive appetite finds itself acted upon is often influenced by reason, sometimes significantly. Here much depends on both the particular occurrence of the passion as well as the type of passion. Natural or animal concupiscence, for example, is minimally influenced by reason, whereas the distinctively human experience of anger seems impossible to imagine without some act of reason. Aquinas' account is able to accommodate both of these extremes and the intermediate cases.

From a different standpoint, Anna A. Terruwe and Conrad M. Baars object to Aquinas' treatment of daring. Though they acknowledge their profound debt to Aquinas as clinical psychiatrists, they judge that when Aquinas distinguishes *audacia* from *ira*, he is on shaky ground. They present two objections. Here is the first:

> It is not clear to us why *ira* or anger has to be differentiated as a separate emotion . . . First, according to the prevailing theory, *ira* always presupposes a present or past evil (cf. *ST* 1a2ae 23.2). Yet, the way we understand it, it is also possible for a threatening danger to bring about all the symptoms of anger and rage. And when the manifestations are the same, one should assume that the emotions are one and the same. (1972, p. 37n10)

One might try a quick response. Even if the manifestations of two passions coincide, this is merely a contingent fact. All that is required for the passions to differ is a distinction between their formal objects. If the formal object of *audacia* is not the same as that of *ira*, the passions differ, even though the somatic effects may be similar (as they can be, but are not invariably). But Aquinas himself makes this line of argument more difficult than it might seem at first. The initial description of daring's formal object emphasizes its character as a threatening evil, together with the hope of victory. But near the end of Question 45, Aquinas proposes a somewhat different characterization: "The object of daring is a composite of good and evil" (*obiectum audaciae est compositum ex bono et malo*) (45.4 ad 2m). (Cajetan notices that between 45.2 ad 3m and 45.4 ad 2m, "auctor varie loqui videtur" [1889, p. 287].) This is suspiciously similar to the formal object of anger, which Aquinas also describes as containing both a perceived good and a perceived evil. A fully adequate response to the objection would have shown that the formal object of anger genuinely differs from that of daring. There is a real difference, I think, if only because the evil present in anger's object is not simply a "threatening evil." The evil proper to the object of anger has an irreducibly personal character. It is not merely apprehended as a harm, either to be resisted or succumbed to, but more profoundly as an injury that slights, and means to slight, its target. Likewise, the good sought by anger is not simply victory, but a specific kind of triumph – that is, vindication. It seems that many things capable of activating daring would fail to arouse anger, despite the difficulty of distinguishing the phenomenological manifestations in some (many?) particular cases.[20]

The second objection advanced by Terruwe and Baars runs as follows:

St. Thomas defines *ira* as a reaction to injustice with a view to revenge (cf. *ST* qq. 46–7). For St. Thomas, therefore *ira* is also an emotion, but obviously one which is accompanied by an act of reason. When animals experience *ira*, it is because they have a natural instinct given to them by the divine reason, in virtue of which they are gifted with movements, both internal and external, similar to rational movements (cf. *ST* 46.4 ad 2m). It seems strange to us that an emotion which in essence is purely sensory would derive its distinguishing characteristic from the *ratio*, while it would occur in the animal more or less by accident, having some resemblance to that of man. Moreover, we would like to know how rage in an animal could ever have anything to do with revenge. Rather, it appears to us, an animal's rage constitutes a defense against further threatening evil. (1972, p. 37n10)

There is much to ponder (and perhaps accept) in this objection. It may be that for animals, the *audacia/ira* distinction comes close to breaking down. The analogue to human anger possessed by animals (at 46.4, Aquinas seems to argue that it only resembles genuine anger) may be difficult to distinguish from daring. One way of preserving the distinction in the animal case would begin by observing that at least some animals not only have the capacity to attack threatening evils for the sake of their own preservation ("daring"), but also seem capable of singling out individuals as particular sources of harm, and directing their aggression at those individuals ("anger"). Nonetheless, Terruwe and Baars may be correct to hold that the attribution of "vindication" or "revenge" to non-rational animals is

---

[20] Terruwe and Baars's core assumption that "when the manifestations are the same, one should assume that the emotions are the same" (1972, p. 37n10) would be challenged by Roberts (2004), who speaks of the "dubiousness of the inference of sameness of expression to sameness of emotion" (p. 588). It may be, as Roberts says, that the same smile can "express many different emotions, in contexts – not only variants of joy, say (gratitude, hopefulness, pleasant surprise, *Schadenfreude*, rapture, amusement, pride, and so on), but rather different ones such as fondness, thrill, and embarrassment" (p. 588). I wonder whether (1) neurologically, it is in fact the "same smile"; (2) this misses the deeper point of Terruwe and Baars's objection. Terruwe and Baars do not think that if the expressions of daring and anger are the same, there would be *no* difference between the two. Rather, the sameness of manifestation would point to a less significant difference than is present among passions that genuinely differ in species. The project of locating specifically different emotions, and discerning the subspecies within the basic passions, is not incompatible with attending to relevant distinctions between emotions, despite the prejudice of some against the very idea of isolating "basic passions." If daring and anger do have the "same manifestations," then "it would be necessary to reduce [anger's] manifestations to expressions of *audacia*, often modified by expression of hatred" (p. 37n10).

difficult, if not impossible. If they are right about this, I do not think
that the consequence is the utter collapse of the *audacia/ira* distinction.
Rather, the distinction would apply to the human case, even as it is
questionable in the case of non-rational animals. However this may be,
it is clear for Aquinas that reason plays a decisive role in the causation of
anger in human beings. It is equally clear that the role played by reason
does not make it any less of a passion. It may be right to attribute to God
and the angels (and perhaps to human beings in some cases) a pseudopassion corresponding to anger that involves judgment and an act of will,
but with no corresponding motion of the sensitive appetite (see §2.2).
But anger itself, as ordinarily experienced, involves an identifiable set of
characteristic somatic events. As such, it qualifies as a passion in the strict
sense. To that passion I now turn.

CHAPTER 12

Anger

Aquinas begins the consideration of anger by asking what makes it a passion. Understanding the precise nature of anger as a passion is crucial, lest it be confused with the sin that bears the same name. Aquinas asks why anger is a specific passion, rather than the general act of the irascible (as its name might suggest), and isolates the formal object of anger (§12.1). In the course of treating anger itself, Aquinas positively connects anger to reason, nature, and justice. Though anger may distort our perception of what is required by each of these things, its primal connection to these things is divinely intended and, as such, good. Or so Aquinas holds in what, I argue, amounts to a qualified defense of the passion of anger (§12.2). What causes anger? Aquinas addresses this question by identifying and explaining the efficient and dispositive causes of anger: an act of slight or contempt directed against a person, the superiority of the person who is angered, a lack or defect on the part of the person who does the slighting (§12.3). As for anger's effects, Aquinas (perhaps surprisingly) holds that pleasure is necessarily a consequence of anger. Imagining vindication generates some pleasure; achieving vindication produces even more. Other effects include fervor, the impairment of reason, and taciturnity. While attentive to the negative and destructive effects of immoderate anger, Aquinas emphasizes that anger, like the other passions, is part of human nature and has an appropriate role to play in the human pursuit of good when directed by reason. That Aquinas takes this view of the matter is confirmed by examining the treatment of Christ's anger in the 3a pars (§12.4).

12.1 DEFINING ANGER AS A PASSION

The structure of the consideration of anger initially appears straightforward. According to the Prologue, Aquinas aims to consider anger in itself (Question 46), its causes and remedies (Question 47) and its effects (Question 48). But a question arises at once. Why does Aquinas say so little about the remedies of anger in Question 47? Did he simply forget to include a Question on the topic? Or does he suppose that to speak about anger's cause *is* to address the topic, as if to know the cause of anger is to know its remedy? Ramírez suggests this reading: "Putavit satis esse videre causas irae ut remedium eius appareat" (1973, p. 438). There is a third possibility. Aquinas may avoid explicit speech about anger's remedy because his primary aim is to exhibit anger as a worthy passion. In itself, anger is natural and promotes the flourishing of the human person.[1] When anger ceases to be useful, it becomes a sin – in fact, a capital sin – and requires correction that goes beyond the palliative care implied by the term *remedia*.

Question 46 treats anger in itself. After an opening argument that anger is indeed a specific passion, and not merely another name for the irascible power in general (Article 1), Aquinas moves directly to the discussion of anger's object (Article 2). Perhaps because he so clearly connects anger with desire for the good, Aquinas anticipates that some will ask whether it should be located in the concupiscible. To address this suspicion, and to reinforce the distinction between the concupiscible and the irascible, Aquinas argues that anger's object contains the notion of the arduous (Article 3). The middle section of Question 46 may be read as an *apologia pro ira*, a defense of anger against a series of accusations.[2] Far from being simply irrational, anger requires an act of reason (Article 4). Anger is not confined to those who are maladjusted, or consumed by hatred. No less than desire itself, anger is natural to the human person (Article 5). It bears a stronger relation to the good than hatred (Article 6) and reflects the

---

[1] This is a minority report within the tradition. Stoics and Epicureans, as well as any number of Christian theologians, regard anger as something to be eliminated. Burton (1927) recapitulates the tradition's dominant voice. Anger is a "perturbation" and "temporary madness"; it "will make a Devil of a Saint"; "there is no difference betwixt a mad man and an angry man in the time of his fit"; "anger, as Lactantius describes it, is a cruel tempest of the mind *making his eyes sparkle fire, and stare, teeth gnash in his head, his tongue stutter, his face pale or red, and what more filthy imitation can be of a mad man?*" He continues: angry men are "void of reason, inexorable, blind, like beasts & monsters of the time, say and do they know not what, curse, swear, rail, fight and what not." He concludes: "Look into our Histories, and you shall meet with no other subject, but what a company of hare-brains have done in their rage! We may do well therefore, to put this in our litany amongst the rest: *From all blindness of heart, from pride, vain-glory, and hypocrisy, from envy, hatred, and malice, anger and all such pestiferous perturbations, Good Lord, deliver us!*" (pp. 233–5). Note that Burton (and the tradition he recapitulates) is condemning not only the sin of anger (such as Dante describes in *Purgatorio*, cantos 15–17), but even the passion. As Gondreau (2002) remarks, "To pen his remarks on Christ's anger, Aquinas had to contend with the weight of Scripture, Stoic philosophy, and certain patristic authorities (especially Gregory the Great), not to mention common human experience, all of which come down severely on the passion of anger because of its entanglement with sin" (p. 439).

[2] See Pieper 1991: "Sensuality is good (so much so that Thomas calls 'unsensuality' not merely a defect, but a *vitium*, a moral deficiency); anger is good; sexuality is good" (p. 122).

natural desire for justice (Article 7). The Question concludes with an assessment of the species of anger inherited from Damascene and Nemesius (Article 8).

Why does *ira* name a specific passion, rather than the irascible as such? Aquinas has already posed a parallel question about *concupiscentia* and its relation to the concupiscible, arguing from particular attributes of concupiscence's formal object to its status as a specific passion (see 30.2). The argument *de ira* is different. Thomas wants to delay the discussion of anger's formal object, perhaps because it is significantly more complex than that of concupiscence. The response of Article 1 identifies two ways in which something is said to be "general" (*generale*), arguing that *ira* cannot be general in either way. First, *ira* cannot be general as a generic term (e.g. "animal"), since "anger" is not predicated of passions as "animal" is predicated of its species. Second, a thing may be general as a *causa generalis*, that is, by producing a diversity of effects (46.1.co). It is true (as Aquinas will argue later) that anger can play some role in the generation of other passions, especially daring and hatred. But anger is primarily the effect of other passions. "The motion of anger does not arise except on account of some sorrow inflicted, and unless there be desire and hope of taking revenge (*spes ulciscendi*)" (46.1.co).

Anger can neither arise nor be understood without the passions of desire, hope, and sorrow. Since these passions themselves presuppose love – "Love is the first root of all the passions," Aquinas reminds us (46.1.co) – one may say that anger requires no fewer than four passions as prerequisites: love, desire, hope, and sorrow. (Hatred, interestingly, is not a precondition for anger.) In light of anger's dependence on the other passions, one sees why Aquinas has chosen to analyze the other passions before considering anger.[3] Nowhere is the link between Aquinas' ordering of the passions and their sequential occurrence more evident than in his treatment of *ira*. The motions of the irascible power, Aquinas says, "terminate in anger" (46.1 ad 1m). Correspondingly, the Questions on the passions themselves terminate in anger. It is not that *ira* is an absolute terminus. Anger always leads to something beyond itself: "The irascible passions both arise from and terminate in the passions of the concupiscible power" (25.1.co; cf. §3.3).

Another distinctive aspect of anger is its lack of contraries. Unlike any of the other passions, anger has no contrary.

---

[3] Lazarus and Lazarus (1996), by contrast, dispense with any such preliminary analysis. They begin their book with a chapter on anger, labeling it as one of the "nasty emotions" (pp. 13–27).

From the very fact that anger is caused from contrary passions, sc. from hope, which is of good, and from sorrow, which is of evil, it includes in itself *contrarietas*, and thus it has no contrary outside itself. In the same way, no *contrarietas* is found in mixed colors, except that of the simple colors from which they are caused. (46.1 ad 2m)

One may wonder: is "calm" not the contrary of anger? Aquinas replies (following the precedent at Aristotle, *Rhetoric* 2.3, 1380a5) that calm is anger's privation, but not its contrary (see 23.3). As we have seen, a *passio* is not an inert state of the soul, but an appetitive motion toward some good or away from some evil. Since calm corresponds to a lack of motion in the sensitive appetite, it is not properly a passion (and therefore not the contrary of anger), although it may be an "emotion" in a wider sense.

Article 1 establishes that anger is a specific passion. Article 2 considers its formal object. Anger's object is complex, aiming at vindication itself (*vindicta ipsa*), but always with reference to a person against whom vindication is sought (*ille de quo quaerit vindictam*) (46.2.co). Anyone moved by anger, Aquinas observes, necessarily perceives vindication as a good. If I am angry, I am positively attracted to the prospect of vindication, of "setting things right." I will take some pleasure anticipating vindication, and even more pleasure when I gain it. That *vindicta* is necessarily apprehended as a good is emphasized by the use of two arguments *sed contra*, a rare event in the Questions on the passions (and the *ST* as a whole). The first argument cites Augustine, *Confessions* 2.6: "anger seeks vindication" (*ira appetit vindictam*). It claims that the "*appetitus vindictae* is an appetite for the good, since *vindicta* belongs to justice" (46.2.sc). The second argument *sed contra* derives from Aristotle. Anger causes pleasure; the object of pleasure is good; therefore anger must have good for its object. *Vindicta* does not mean "revenge" or even necessarily "vengeance," as the term is often translated. When Aquinas wants to convey what English-speakers usually mean by "revenge," he will use a form of *ulciscor*. The appetite for revenge is one mode of seeking vindication, but *vindicta ipsa* cannot be reduced to revenge. Anger is fundamentally rooted in desire for the good.

If anger is impossible without apprehending vindication as a good, it also requires that we perceive the person against whom we seek vindication as an evil, as something "contrary and harmful" (46.2.co). Aquinas does not claim that someone moved by anger necessarily hates the other person; he knows that a person can be angry with those whom he loves. (Having been imprisoned by his own family, he probably knows this better than most [see Torrell 1996, pp. 8–12].) But if someone is to be moved to anger, he must perceive the other person as noxious or hurtful in some respect. One may wonder: Why must the object of anger be an individual? Cannot something more general, such as a class of persons, cause anger? And must anger be caused by a person? Is it not the case that an animal (the dog that bites you without apparent provocation) or even a thing (the printer that never works and sends inscrutable messages such as "PC Load Letter") can make us angry?

Aquinas is aware of such questions. Before addressing them, he wants to secure anger's place in the irascible. Article 3 asks whether *ira* is in the concupiscible. It is not, Aquinas argues, because the good and evil present in the object of anger is not good or evil absolutely (*absolute*), but "with a certain elevation or arduousness" (*cum quadam elevatione vel arduitate*) (46.3.co). Many things can be desired or sorrowed for. But such things are not initially objects of anger. I can regret that a valued colleague has decided to take a position at another university. But something else has to happen if I am to become angry. My colleague's action must rise to the level of a personal slight. Without this "elevation," I will not be angry, although I may be sorrowful. Similarly, a colleague may say something that I know to be directed against me personally. The remark will not, however, necessarily activate an appetite for vindication; it may be quite trivial. The motion of anger does not arise "unless there be some magnitude (*aliqua magnitudine*)" (46.3.co) about the object. Because something must be added to the object of sorrow and desire to make it an object of anger, Aquinas concludes that the passion is rightly assigned to the irascible.

In the final Article of Question 46, Aquinas considers Damascene's division of anger into three species. The Article constitutes the last of Thomas's three engagements with the taxonomies he inherits from Damascene and Nemesius. While Aquinas always wants to affirm that, in some sense, the traditional classifications are valid, the manner of his affirmation may vary. So at 35.8, Aquinas endorses Damascene's fourfold division of sorrow, but adds that the division is improper, depending on sorrow's effects rather than its essence. At 41.4, by contrast, Aquinas not only accepts the six species of fear named by Damascene, but adds that they are "derived from the proper division of the object of fear itself." What stance does Aquinas adopt toward Damascene's division of anger? The question is surprisingly difficult. If wrath, ill-will, and rancor are names for anger's beginning, its continuation, and its final phase, then it appears that Damascene divides the genus into species only "according to some accident" (*secundum aliquod accidens*), as the first objector argues. The division appears to be taken from the moments of a temporal sequence, rather than from the notion of anger itself. In reply, Aquinas holds that since anger receives "some perfection" (*aliquam perfectionem*) from these moments, their relation to anger is "not altogether *per accidens*," and so "nothing hinders" the division of anger into these particular species (46.8 ad 1m). While this may seem to be a lukewarm affirmation of Damascene's taxonomy, it is not quite as weak as the corresponding affirmation of the species of sorrow.[4] It is not merely a division according to the passion's effects, unlike Gregory the Great's threefold division of anger *sine voce, cum voce*, and *cum verbo expresso* ("You fool!"). Damascene's division takes place "according to the diverse perfection of the very motion of anger" (46.8 ad 3m).

Two points emerge from a consideration of Aquinas' engagement with the traditional divisions of passions into their species. First, each contains some truth that needs to be recognized. Aquinas underscores the appropriateness of Damascene's division of anger by exhibiting its harmony with Aristotle's use of "choleric" (*acutus*) to identify the easily angered, "bitter" (*amarus*) to identify those who retain their anger for a long time, and "ill-tempered" (*difficilis*) to describe those who never rest until they exact punishment (see *Nicomachean Ethics* 4.5, 1268a18). Second, not every division into species ought to be granted the same significance. Crucially important is the relation of the *differentia* employed by the proposed division to the passion's object.

The historical divisions of anger are complex, because the passion itself is complex. As Farrell remarks, anger may be the strangest of the passions. Because its object is essentially composite, he observes, "its strangeness is the strangeness of the hybrid or the mongrel; it has a little of everything in it, but is a very individual thing" (1942, p. 148).[5] As Aquinas has argued, anger has deep roots in our rational nature. Nonetheless, what causes anger may be any number of factors that are irrational or extra-rational.

12.2 AN 'APOLOGIA PRO IRA'?

In Article 4 of Question 46, Aquinas begins what amounts to a defense of anger against a series of charges that are often leveled against it. What is

[4] Cajetan (1889) is similarly hesitant on the question. Judging that Aquinas does not disclose his view about the true species of anger at 45.8 ad 1m, he adds: "Perhaps it can be said that these are not the true species *ex parte obiecti*, according to their *per se* differences taken from the differences of the passions, however much they appear distinguished specifically *ex parte subiecti*. Thus I do not see anything except accidental differences, granting that they are not entirely accidental" (p. 299).

[5] Similarly, Gondreau (2002) finds that "there hangs over the passion of anger . . . a distinctly paradoxical air" (p. 433).

the relation of anger to reason? The objectors make the case that there is nothing rational about anger. Against this, Aquinas argues that anyone who is angry makes a judgment, and therefore exercises his reason in some fashion. Any act of anger requires a judgment of the form "A wrong has been committed and steps must be taken to set it right." Only reason is capable of making such a judgment. (Aquinas notes the appearance of angry movements in brute animals, but describes these as merely "like" rational motions and attributes them to instinct; cf. §11.4.) There are two modes in which reason may judge that a wrong has been committed, and that vindication is both possible and desirable. (1) Reason "commands" the will to act. The sensitive appetite is moved to anger, but remains subject to reason. (2) Reason "denounces" the evil. If reason simply denounces the wrong, refusing to look for and weigh contrary evidence, the passions (especially sorrow, desire, and hope) will distract reason (cf. 33.3 and §7.3), leading it to inflate the magnitude of the wrong committed. In such a case, as Aquinas says regarding the effects of fear (44.2; cf. §10.4), a person is "affected" by the passion, so that something "seems greater or smaller than it is according to the truth of the thing" (44.2.co). The problem with a person "affected" by a passion in this sense, Letterio Mauro observes,

does not reside in the object of the passion, but in the fact that the passional point of view is a partial, limited point of view, one that imposes its proper object in an exclusive fashion, thereby narrowing the person's field of consideration. (1977, p. 342)

Immoderate anger leads a person to take a partial, distorted view of the situation, and thus to contemplate means of vindication that he would renounce in a cool hour. The agent "does not observe the rule of reason in weighing vindication" (46.4 ad 3m) but ignores circumstances that if heeded would alter the character of his anger. While he makes a judgment, and thus performs an act of reason, he uses his reason poorly because he attends only to some of the relevant facts, ignoring others. Aquinas emphasizes that the use of reason, however distortedly, is a precondition of anger. "Those who are very drunk, so as not to have any judgment of reason, do not get angry," he observes with Aristotle.[6] "But when they are slightly drunk, they do get angry, since they have the judgment of reason, albeit impaired" (46.4 ad 3m).

---

[6] Or, more precisely, Pseudo-Aristotle. See *Problemata* 23.2.27 (871a8, 875a29).

Is anger natural? Article 5 continues the qualified defense of anger against its cultured despisers. Because man is by nature "gentle" (*mansuetus*), the first objector argues, the disposition of anger is unnatural. The argument is not unfamiliar. Those who tend to show their anger often hear that if only some combination of their family life, educational background, and sexual experiences had been different, they would not be so angry. The assumption is that a disposition toward displaying anger can originate only from questionable, contingent circumstances. Aquinas rejects this. Even if some particular manifestations of anger are unnatural, the passion itself is firmly grounded in human nature. This may not be evident, he observes, if we confine our attention to passions *ex parte obiecti*. Because the pleasures of food and sex are more natural to man than vengeance, the concupiscible passions are in a sense more natural than anger. But if we examine the matter *ex parte subiecti*, another judgment is appropriate. "If we consider the nature of man from the side of the species, viz. insofar as he is rational, then anger is more natural to man than concupiscence, inasmuch as anger is more accompanied by reason than is concupiscence" (46.5.co). What is true with respect to generic animality does not hold once the *differentia* of rationality is introduced. If one moves from a consideration of the essence to the temperament of a particular person, the naturalness of anger becomes even clearer. Some individuals are naturally prone to anger. Their anger may be destructive and counter-productive. But to describe the passion itself as "unnatural" is neither true nor conducive to sound therapy.

Articles 4 and 5 consider the positive relation of anger to reason and nature. Articles 6 and 7 continue the *apologia pro ira* by connecting it with justice. Article 6 asks whether anger is "more grave" (*gravior*) than hatred. Aquinas draws upon both Augustinian and Aristotelian authority to show the inadvisability of confusing anger with hatred.[7] Both passions have a common object, namely a thing apprehended under the aspect of evil. But the angry person, unlike the hater, wishes evil to the person for the sake of attaining a genuine good – that is, vindication. Anger aims for "evil under the aspect of the just" (*malum sub ratione iusti*), whereas hatred directs "evil to someone simply" (*malum alicuius simpliciter*) (46.6.co). If the evil is inflicted "according to the virtue of justice," with the guidance of reason, there is no problem. Even when it rejects the direction of reason, its basic desire to set things right is not mistaken. Aquinas says that anger

---

[7] The comparison, as Cajetan (1889) notices, is not between *ira* and *odium abominationis* (the passion discussed at Question 29), but rather between *ira* and *odium imimicitiae* (p. 297).

"fails only in this, that it does not obey the guidance of reason in taking revenge" (*ira in hoc solum deficit, quod non obedit rationis praecepto in ulciscendo*) (46.6.co). The switch from *vindicare* to *ulciscor* underscores the point. When a person transgresses the limits of reason, what he seeks is not merely vindication, but revenge. Yet even in this case, the evil is sought under the aspect of justice. Hatred, by contrast, seeks evil *simpliciter*. Thus Thomas concludes that "hatred is worse and more grave than anger" (46.6.co).

Aquinas elaborates the contrast between hatred and anger in the Article's *ad secundum*. The character of punishment is threefold: it must be against the will (*contraria voluntati*), painful (*afflicitiva*), and for some particular wrong (*pro aliqua culpa*) (46.6 ad 2m). The desire of the angry person corresponds precisely to these three characteristics. He wants his target to perceive his punishment, to be in pain (*doleat*), and to be aware that it originates on account of an injury done to himself. The hater, by contrast, "cares not at all about this, since he seeks evil to the other as such." In the *ad tertium*, Aquinas adds that because anger arises from the perception of a specific wrong done to a man, it "passes more quickly" than hatred, which is a "disposition or habit" (*dispositio vel habitus*) (46.6 ad 3m). Nonetheless, Aquinas does not advise a lax attitude toward episodes of irrational anger; he knows that prolonged anger can produce the disposition of hatred. His aim is to pay due regard to the connection between anger and hatred, without conflating them.

In Article 7, Aquinas strengthens the link between anger and justice. He does so by defending the Aristotelian proposition that anger is directed only toward those to whom justice is due. The defense must account for three appearances to the contrary. It seems that anger is also directed toward irrational beings, toward oneself, and toward communities rather than persons. Regarding the first, Aquinas distinguishes two ways in which a person may become angry. When the imagination arouses anger by denouncing an injury, it is irrelevant whether the perpetrator of the injury is rational or irrational, animate or inanimate. But anger caused in this way, Thomas argues, is not properly human anger, since it is indistinguishable from the type of anger that brute animals experience. Properly human anger is intrinsically rational. Aquinas quotes Aristotle: "It is impossible to be angry with insensitive things, or with the dead" (*Rhetoric* 2.3, 1380b24). This may appear to be an arbitrary move designed to save the position from the objection that one can be angered by irrational beings. In fact, Aquinas is simply consistent with the previous Article's analysis of what the angry person desires. Someone who is angry wants the offending party to feel pain not for its own sake, but precisely as vindication for a harm that was inflicted. The possibility of vindication, and therefore anger in its proper sense, does not exist with respect to insensible things or the dead. As Thomas remarks, they feel no pain and can do us no harm.

Why cannot a person be angered with himself? Aquinas grants the second objector that, metaphorically, we can be angry at ourselves. From the standpoint of book 4 of the *Republic*, this might appear as anger's paradigmatic case. Socrates tells Glaucon that even as Leontius indulged his desire to gaze at a group of dead bodies, his *thumos* reproached him for doing so. ("Take your fill of the sight, you damned wretches!" [440a].) Aquinas is familiar, at least indirectly, with this analysis. He acknowledges that insofar as reason rules the irascible and concupiscible powers of the soul, a man can attain vindication with respect to himself. That is, the irascible or concupiscible powers lead a person to perform a certain act that reason perceives to be wrong and wants to set right. But "properly and *per se*, it does not happen that someone is angry with himself" (46.7 ad 2m). Perhaps this "sounds like an obstinate refusal to grant the conclusion of a cogent argument – an unwillingness or perhaps an incapacity to see the obvious."[8] But Aquinas insists that we cannot be angry with ourselves *per se*. Why not? The reason is that anger requires the perception of an object *sub ratione mali*. We are incapable of apprehending ourselves as simply evil; we can only perceive ourselves as evil in some respect. Aquinas' denial that we can be angry with ourselves in the proper sense is a corollary of the claim that no man can hate himself (see 29.4 and §6.2).

Can one be angry only with an individual person? Why cannot anger be directed toward an entire class? An Irishman might assert his right to be angry with the English as a whole. Aquinas would claim that such "anger" is more properly described as hatred – that is, a disposition or tendency to perceive something as repugnant. Properly, according to Thomas, anger is "caused when someone wounds us by his own action" (46.7 ad 3m). The Irishman might persist: "The English have injured me and my countrymen." But in such a case, Aquinas replies, "the English" are conceived not as a disparate class, but as a social person, a unified agent that acts with a determinate purpose. "When the whole state (*tota civitas*) wounds us, the whole state is reckoned as one individual (*unum singulare*)" (46.7 ad 3m).

---

[8] As Mackey (1997) says about Thomas in another context (p. 112).

Aquinas has no interest in denying that nations and institutions are capable of arousing anger. But he would maintain that whenever anger is provoked by something other than a particular individual, the thing is perceived as a voluntary agent capable of doing injustice – that is, as a person. Thus Aristotle is right to say that "hatred may be felt toward a class, as we hate the entire class of thieves, whereas anger is directed only toward an individual" (*Rhetoric* 2.4, 1382a4).

Something similar applies to the possibility of directing anger toward non-humans. To the extent that we know that the dog that bites us, or the printer that malfunctions, lacks a will, and therefore ought not to be held responsible for its actions, our anger will cease, or else be redirected toward a genuinely voluntary agent (for example, toward the owner who let his vicious canine roam, or the manufacturer of the errant printer). What about the young man who is simply angry with the world? Here, too, the adolescent cannot help but think of the world as a malevolent agent that has willfully done something to him. When he outgrows this perception, his anger will abate or find another target.

12.3 WHAT CAUSES ANGER?

What is the cause of anger? To describe the formal object of anger is to identify one dimension of its total cause. Anger is caused by a perception of someone else as harmful to ourselves, along with a desire for vindication. Both elements are necessary conditions of anger. But what makes us angry? Question 47 considers the efficient cause of anger, understood as the "cause of becoming angered" (*causa irascendi*) (see 47.2 ad 1m). Aquinas proposes to treat *de causa effectiva irae, et de remediis eius.* To the extent that one knows the efficient cause of anger, Aquinas may be suggesting, one learns how to moderate the passion.

Question 47 contains four Articles. In the first two Articles, a form of *vindicta* occurs eight times. In the final two Articles, the term occurs not at all. This lexical fact suggests that Aquinas divides his treatment of the *causa effectiva irae* into two halves. The first half focuses on acts, the second half on persons. The act must be targeted toward the one who is angered (Article 1), and it must be perceived under the *ratio* of slight or contempt (Article 2). Aquinas divides the Question's second half into an analysis "from the side of the angry person" (*ex parte irascentis*) and "from the side of the person against whom one is angry" (*ex parte eius contra quem aliquis irascitur*). Thus a person's "excellence" (*excellentia*) disposes him to anger (Article 3), as does "deficiency" (*defectus*) on the part of the person who slights him (Article 4).

Article 1 asks whether someone who is angered is always made angry on account of something done against himself. Of the sixteen Articles in the treatment of anger, 47.1 is unique, being the only Article to feature four objectors. The first objector argues that although we cannot injure God, God can nonetheless be angered. The reply is straightforward. Reiterating an argument made early in the 1a *pars* (see 1.3.2 ad 2m), Aquinas observes that anger is attributed to God only metaphorically. The other three objectors argue for types of actions that cause anger, yet seem not to involve any essential reference to the person who is angered. In each case, the form of Thomas's reply is the same. A connection can invariably be traced between the action and the person who is aroused to anger.

The details of Aquinas' analysis in all three cases merit comment. The second objector claims that someone can desire vindication even against harmful acts done to others. Aquinas replies: in fact, we are angered by those who harm others only if they "pertain to us in some manner" (*aliquo modo ad nos pertinent*) (47.1 ad 2m). When someone insults our mother, we react with anger. When someone insults a colleague, we may deplore the insult as unjust, but we will not necessarily feel anger, unless that particular colleague "belongs to us" as a friend. How can this analysis account for those who feel genuine anger about injustices done to people across the world whom they will never know? Aquinas anticipates the question. For such an act to produce anger, one must perceive some connection between the victim's evil and one's own evil. Those who feel a strong sense of solidarity with their fellow man will become angry when someone unknown to them suffers a wrong that should be set right. Thus Aquinas allows that the person must be related to us "by some affinity, whether by friendship, or at least by the sharing of a common nature" (47.1 ad 2m). By contrast, the person who perceives no community between himself and another who suffers injustice will not feel anger, even if he can abstractly recognize that the other has been wronged. Perhaps such a person lacks empathy; he might be rightly judged as callous. But his extreme opposite would err in the other direction. Consider the person who is so sensitive to the sufferings of others, no matter how remote his actual relation to them, that he is in a perpetual state of anger, always desiring vindication for wrongs which are not his responsibility. Finding the mean between these two extremes is the work of the virtue of prudence.

The third objector quotes Aristotle's observation that a person can become angry with those who despise the things that interest him. "Men who study philosophy are angry with those who despise philosophy," as the *Rhetoric* notes (2.2, 1379a33). The empirical fact is indisputable. At times we do become angry with those who display contempt for our favorite pursuits, regardless of whether they intend a personal slight. Aquinas supplies the reason. When "we are especially keen" (*maxime studemus*) on something, we "take it to be our own good" (*reputamus esse bonum nostrum*) (47.1 ad 3m). Our investment in the particular good leads us, rightly or wrongly, to construe another's contempt for that good as contempt for ourselves. Without this construal, we might feel sorrow or contempt for the person who despises what we judge to be good, but we will not experience anger.

The fourth objector argues that when a person is silent, he does not wrong us personally, yet we may nonetheless become angry. According to the objector, this proves that things other than slight are capable of causing anger. Aquinas suggests that the objector's understanding of silence is superficial. Silence may in fact be a form of contempt. Machiavelli, for example, expresses his contempt for Thomas by never once mentioning him or his writings. Those who want to slight someone will accomplish their goal efficiently by ignoring everything he says. If one person wishes to minimize contact with another, but in a manner that will avoid arousing her anger, he will not refuse to speak to her. Rather, he will say just enough to allay any suspicion that she is the object of scorn. Silence can be a more potent cause of anger than language that expressly intends to inflict pain.

Article 1's analysis of human experience prepares the way for the next Article's claim that the sole motive of anger is slight or contempt (*parvipensio vel despectio*). Here Aquinas is uncompromising. Slight – and nothing but slight – is the efficient cause of anger. Why is Aquinas so apparently reductionistic? The answer can only be that he perceives a genuine unity behind the disparate phenomena that provoke anger. The third objector presses the case by suggesting that Aristotle himself identifies causes of anger other than slight. Any of the following actions by others can arouse our anger: forgetting about us, taking pleasure in our misfortunes (*exultatio in infortuniis*, i.e. *Schadenfreude*), talking about our evils, preventing us from following our will. Aquinas replies: "All of these causes may be reduced to some kind of slight." Is this anything more than a blunt assertion? He continues:

For forgetfulness is an evident sign of slight, since those things which we estimate to be great, we fix all the more in our memory. Likewise it is out of a certain kind of slight that someone does not hesitate to inflict pain upon another, by threatening him with some sorrow. Moreover, a person who shows signs of cheer in the misfortunes of another seems to care little about his good or evil. Likewise he who prevents someone from acting according to his purpose, but not on account of any advantage to himself, seems not to care much about his friendship. And thus all such things, to the extent that they are signs of contempt, are provocative of anger. (47.2 ad 3m)

By our own experience, Aquinas suggests, we may confirm the reduction of anger's efficient cause to slight.

In Articles 3 and 4, Aquinas shifts the focus from the object of anger to the disposition of the person angered. In Article 3, he asks whether the "excellence" (*excellentia*) of someone is a cause of anger. *Excellentia* is a difficult term to translate. It denotes significant accomplishment in a particular area, but in a manner that is not simply identical to moral virtue. Why does *excellentia* increase one's susceptibility to anger? The first two objectors argue that "deficiency" (*defectus*) rather than excellence causes anger; the third observes that excellent men are characteristically agreeable and hopeful, and therefore less liable to anger. Aquinas acknowledges the partial truth of the objections. Deficiency is closely linked to anger, insofar as it renders one more vulnerable to sorrow. But with respect to the "motive of anger," *excellentia* disposes a man to anger because "the more excellent (*excellentior*) someone is, the more unjustly he is slighted in that in which he excels" (47.3.co). A man who excels in riches is more likely be offended by someone who scorns his riches than by someone who questions his taste. An orator with a reputation for speaking persuasively will become indignant at the suggestion that he does not even know what rhetoric is (for an exemplary case, see *Gorgias* 449a–461b).

One may object: Would not the truly accomplished person be so confident in his *excellentia* that his despisers would be simply unable to make him angry? Aquinas quotes Aristotle (*Rhetoric* 2.9, 1368b12) in the *sed contra*: "Men are made angry (*indignantur*) on account of their *excellentia*" (47.3.sc). Why not hold that men are made angry by their insecurity rather than their excellence? The question underscores the importance of properly construing *excellentia*. When accompanied by the moral virtues, *excellentia* is predicable of the person who possesses the virtue of magnanimity. The great-souled man does not easily become angry with his inferiors. What Aquinas envisages in Article 3, however, is not magnanimity, but *excellentia* in abstraction from the moral virtues. Thus we may account for the odd (but very real) susceptibility to anger displayed by talented artists, musicians, writers, actors, and athletes who lack the moral virtues. Insofar as *excellentia* does not reside in a great soul, it increases the likelihood that its possessor will be made angry by those who scorn him in precisely the respect in which he excels.

Article 4 considers the cause of anger from the side of the person who provokes anger. Here deficiency, not excellence, increases the likelihood that anger will be aroused. Again, one may wonder why small-souled men, those characterized by *defectus vel parvitas*, should have the power to make their superiors angry. Aquinas reminds us that what provokes anger is not simply any negative judgment, but undeserved contempt. The person who can take criticism from an equal may well be angered by the same criticism when it comes from someone whom he deems inferior. "Just as the greater someone is, the less worthily (*indignius*) he is despised, so the smaller someone is, the less worthily he despises." Here Aquinas restates the teaching of the last Article, but from a different angle: "Noblemen become angry if they are insulted by peasants; wise men, by fools; masters, by slaves" (47.4.co). Other examples spring to mind – children and parents, students and teachers, younger and older colleagues. In each case, the relative deficiency of the former increases the capacity for anger on the part of the latter – but only if the former is perceived as slighting the latter. If the inferior party is penitent, however, the reverse is the case. "They seem not to despise, but rather think greatly of those before whom they humble themselves" (47.4.co).

12.4 ANGER'S EFFECTS

In Question 48, the final Question of the Treatise, Aquinas identifies four effects of anger. These are pleasure (Article 1), fervor (Article 2), the impairment of reason (Article 3), and silence (Article 4). One might think of the treatment as moving from effects that are "more necessary" to those that are "less necessary"; to see this, we may trace the *ordo articulorum* in reverse. Silence is least of all a necessary consequence of anger. Anger can often make a person more vocal than he would be otherwise. Not every instance of anger involves the impairment of reason, although we may primarily experience anger as a passion that clouds judgment. Fervor and similar physiological effects typically accompany anger, but some instances of anger may involve minimal (if any) physiological disturbance. Is there anything that qualifies as a *necessary* effect of anger? There is, Aquinas answers in the first Article of Question 48. It is *delectatio*.

The claim may seem perverse, even scandalous. Stoics and Epicureans deny any necessary link between anger and pleasure. The wise man will not redress wrongs in a manner that involves passion. Though he is not indifferent to injustice, he will take no joy in performing the actions required to set the wrong right. Vindication is a sober duty, not an occasion for pleasure. Aristotle, by contrast, approvingly quotes the Homeric saying that anger is "sweeter to the soul than honey is to the taste" (*Rhetoric* 2.2, 1378b6; cf. *Iliad* 18, lines 109–10). Aquinas does not regard this passage (quoted at 48.1.sc) as merely a contingent fact about the way some people feel. He judges it to express a necessary truth about the human soul, one that is grounded in human nature.

Why does Aquinas make this judgment? When a person imagines a wrong to have been committed against himself, he experiences sorrow. Anger is aroused when, in addition to the perception of an unmerited slight, there is also hope for vindication. To vindicate is to set things right, to mitigate or remove the hurt or sorrow that lies behind the anger. Sorrow *qua* sorrow, as we have seen, is perceived as an evil. The removal of that evil is necessarily experienced as pleasurable. Aquinas illustrates with a simple comparison. To eliminate one's thirst by the act of drinking cannot be anything but pleasurable. It is simply natural, Aquinas thinks, that humans should enjoy the elimination of afflictions. Therefore, if anger involves vindication, and if vindication entails the removal of an evil, then pleasure necessarily follows from anger. One may agree with *Republic* 9's argument that the kind of pleasure that depends upon the removal of an undesirable bodily condition is not the only kind of pleasure, let alone the highest kind. But the Platonic teaching confirms Aquinas' view that when an evil is mitigated or removed, *delectatio* is the natural consequence.

How much pleasure can vindication be expected to produce? Aquinas distinguishes two scenarios. When vindication is "really present" (*praesens realiter*), pleasure is "complete" (*perfecta*), since it "excludes sorrow altogether, and thereby brings the motion of anger to rest" (48.1.co). In the other scenario, "before vindication is really present," the angry man gleans a certain amount of pleasure from the anticipation of vengeance. This happens, Aquinas says, in two ways. The first stems from the angry man's hope (*spes*) of vindication. The second proceeds "according to continual thought." Aquinas explains: "To anyone who desires a thing, it is pleasurable to dwell in thought (*immorari in cogitatione*) upon those things which he desires, which is why even the fancies of dreams are pleasant" (48.1.co). Dreaming of vindication is itself pleasant, to the extent that one focuses on the desired good rather than one's distance from it. Both hope and contemplation of vindication produce pleasure in the angry man. But because both are instances of future good, rather than present good, they do not furnish the "complete pleasure which destroys sorrow, and consequently anger" (48.1.co).

Article 2 turns to the bodily aspect of *ira*, the *corporalis transmutatio* that is proportioned to the motion of the appetite. Formally, anger is the perception of injury combined with the hope for vindication. Materially, anger is the experience of a set of somatic effects. By selecting "fervor in the heart" (*fervor in corde*) as the emblem for the range of feelings associated with anger, Aquinas honors a tradition that goes back to Homer. While he may not fully recognize the essentially metaphorical nature of statements like "Her blood was boiling," he nevertheless avoids any crude reduction of the physiological effects of *ira* to hot-bloodedness. Thomas notices a range of symptoms, quoting at 48.2.co the following passage from Gregory's *Moralia in Job*:

The heart that is inflamed with the stings of its own anger beats quick, the body trembles, the tongue stammers, the countenance takes fire, the eyes grow fierce, they that are well known are not recognized. With the mouth indeed he shapes a sound, but the understanding knows not what it says. (*Moralia* 5.45; cf. *PL* 75, 724)

Articles 1 and 2 trace the primary effects of anger. The apprehension of vindication as a desired good produces pleasure. The perception of an unmerited slight that must be repelled leads to "great vehemence and impetuosity" (*magna vehementia et impetuositas*) in the motion of anger. Articles 3 and 4 treat of effects that are often, but not always, associated with anger. That anger can "impair reason" (*impediat rationem*) is evident from ordinary experience. The interest of Article 3 lies in the claim that what impedes reason is not anger as such, but solely its material element. In its proper act, "mind or reason" (*mens vel ratio*) makes no use of a bodily organ. But because it requires sensitive powers to execute its act, and such powers are impaired by the body when perturbed, "it is necessary that bodily perturbations (*perturbationes corporales*) impair even the judgment of reason, as is clear in drunkenness and sleep" (48.3.co). Anger listens to reason, but it "preoccupies the complete judgment of reason as if not completely listening to reason" (48.3 ad 1m). What prevents anger from listening better? Aquinas continues: "On account of the agitation of the heat (*commotionem caloris*) urging quick action, which agitation is the material aspect of anger" (48.3 ad 1m).

Article 3's location of anger's ability to impair reason in the material element of the passion confirms that Aquinas thinks of anger as essentially natural, and therefore good. Though anger may often transgress the boundaries of reason, it does not do so on account of its form or essence. It is true that "anger, among all the passions, most manifestly (*manifestius*) impairs the judgment of reason" (48.3.co). Anger provides the most familiar occasion for the clouding of judgment. But does anger as such have this effect? I have argued that, according to Aquinas, it does not. My reading is confirmed by the treatment of Christ's anger in the 3a *pars*.[9] There Thomas identifies *ira* as one of the "defects of soul" that Christ assumed. How could Christ assume *ira*, if anger necessarily produces a bodily *perturbatio* that clouds judgment? One might expect Aquinas to hold that attributions of anger to Christ are metaphorical rather than proper, or else that Christ possessed anger only as a pseudopassion (see §2.2). But Aquinas does not do this. Anger is properly "a passion composed of sorrow and the desire for vindication," he says (3.15.9.co), explicitly recalling the analysis of the 1a2ae. Because Christ possesses sorrow, he also possesses anger in the proper sense. What Christ cannot possess is any desire for vindication that goes beyond the order of reason, that is, a desire for revenge that is accompanied by sin. But desiring vindication according to justice – what Aquinas calls "zealous anger" – is entirely compatible with Christ's sinless human nature.[10]

Bodily *perturbatio* and the consequent impairment of reason are typical effects of anger in the fallen nature. Nonetheless, it is not an essential effect of the passion. Aquinas concludes Question 48 by treating another *per accidens* effect of anger, silence (*taciturnitas*). Both reason and the impairment of reason may lead those who are angry to be silent. Aquinas addresses the first possibility by noting that angry persons sometimes judge that they will attain vindication more effectively if they hold their tongue. He confirms the second possibility by attending to the impact of bodily *perturbationes* on particular organs, especially the tongue. "Therefore

---

[9] Gondreau (2002) observes that Christ's anger receives minimal attention "in the history of Christological thought, despite the fact that it represents the passion that the Gospels most attribute to Jesus" (p. 427). Gondreau locates five "explicit references" to Christ's anger in the Gospels (Mark 3:5 [twice]; 10:14; John 11:33, 38) and twenty-five other passages in the Gospels (Mark 7:6; 8:17, 33 [twice]; 9:42; 11:15–19; Matthew 7:5; 12:34; 15:7; 16:8–11, 23; 17:17; 18:6–7; 21:12–17; 22:18; 23:13–33; Mark 9:19; Luke 6:42; 9:41, 55; 11:37–54; 12:56; 13:15; 17:1–2; John 2:13–16) in which anger is implied "in the emotional experience of Jesus" (p. 37n7). If Christ's assumption of the passion of *ira* were better known, the popular images of Jesus as Mister Rogers (or some other version of the world's nicest guy) might lose their grip on us.

[10] Another way to make the point is to note that Christ possesses the virtue of meekness (see 2-2.157). As Gondreau (2002) notes, the virtue of meekness "involves *not* the total absence of anger (the extreme of defect), but instead the *mean* of anger, i.e., anger ordered to reason" (p. 430). The exemplar is Christ himself, the "model in whom moral excellence and human affectivity converge in a perfectly ordered way" (p. 261).

there can be such a great *perturbatio* of anger, that the tongue is altogether impaired from the use of speech. And thereupon follows silence" (48.4.co). Aquinas is eager to emphasize the power of anger to produce *taciturnitas*. Inspection of the *auctoritates* suggests that he is keen to incorporate Gregory's observations, which emphasize the connection between burning anger and taciturnity. Nonetheless, Aquinas is also willing to acknowledge the power of anger to loosen the tongue. Each of the three objectors quotes scriptural passages that seem to attest to this power. In his exceptionally brief replies, Aquinas does not disagree with any of their readings. He gives no reason to contest La Rochefoucauld's observation that the passions are the most voluble of orators (1959, §8, p. 38).

Anger in itself – anger as a passion – is not a sin. It becomes a sin only if it disturbs the sensitive powers and prevents a person from fully listening to the judgment of reason. Robert Solomon suggests that anger is "neither a 'good' nor a 'bad' emotion, neither 'positive' nor 'negative,' but depends, in any particular case, upon the circumstances and the individual, the nature of the 'offense' and its background" (1983, p. 284). In one sense, this judgment actually serves to undervalue anger. Anger is not merely neutral. It is a natural part of human nature, and hence good in itself. Solomon contrasts his own judgment with his understanding of what the tradition says about anger: "It is, however, listed as one of the 'seven deadly sins' in Christian mythology" (1983, p. 284). Solomon seems to have overlooked the distinction between anger as a passion and anger as a sin; he is probably unaware that Aquinas explicitly argues that the *lack* of anger can be sinful.[11] As Alasdair MacIntyre observes, "To be too angry about unimportant matters or not angry enough about what deserves anger" is a failure in practical rationality (2004, p. 16). Far from being inherently sinful, *ira* is a positive good when directed by reason. If this were not the case, "the sensitive appetite in man would be in vain, but nature does nothing in vain" (2-2.158.8 ad 2m).

---

[11] Gondreau (2002) cites both 2-2.158.8 and *De malo* 12.1 ad 4m as evidence that "*not* being angry at times may, given the correct circumstances, constitute a sin" (p. 434n161). See also the balanced observations in Roberts 2003, p. 221.

Epilogue:
The passions, the virtues, and happiness

The inquiry into the passions in the 1a2ae is lengthy and detailed. Pinckaers observes that while Aquinas addresses the passions in multiple texts, only in the *ST* does he give "free play to his genius," considering each passion with the care that it deserves (1990, p. 379). Nevertheless, Aquinas does not write Questions 22–48 as though thinking about the passions were an end in itself. The whole treatment precedes the consideration of virtue. Knowing about the passions, in some detail, is necessary for any serious ethics. As Gondreau observes, "Accurate moral theory . . . must take the passions into strict account" (2002, p. 265). But the overriding aim, as the Prologue of the 1a2ae reminds us, is to promote the motion of the rational creature *ad finem* (§4.2). Such motion is impossible without the virtues. Aquinas devotes such a large amount of space to the passions, because he does not think that adequate knowledge of the virtues is possible without a prior grasp of the passions.

What does one learn about the virtues by considering their relation to the passions? What more does one learn about the passions by attending to the role they play in the 1a2ae's treatment of the virtues? In Question 55, the first Question on the virtues as such, Aquinas fixes some basic terms that are crucial for understanding his approach. As an accident, virtue has no "matter out of which" (*materia ex qua*) it is formed. But it does have "matter about which" (*materia circa quam*) it is, as well as "matter in which" (*materia in qua*) it resides (55.4.co). *Materia circa quam* corresponds to the virtue's object (*obiectum*); the *materia in qua* the virtue exists is equivalent to its subject (*subiectum*). Because virtue is an accident, it cannot be free-floating; it must be seated or "subjected" in something that is not an accident.

Clarity about these terms is important. Otherwise one will confuse what Thomas takes care to distinguish. Gondreau writes that Aquinas "sees in the movements of passions the subject of moral virtue, or that of which the moral virtues are constituted" (2002, p. 267). This formulation contains a double error. First, it supposes that there is some matter out of which virtue is constituted, whereas Aquinas expressly denies that there is any "matter out of which" (*materia ex qua*) virtue is made. (Hence the total absence of the term *passio* from Question 63's treatment *de causa virtutum*.) Second, the passions are not, strictly speaking, the subject of virtue. Rather, they correspond to the "matter about which" (*materia circa quam*), which Aquinas identifies explicitly as their object. The *subiectum* of the virtues, the "matter in which" (*materia in qua*) they are seated, is a more complicated topic that requires separate consideration: hence Question 56, *de subiecto virtutis*. When Gondreau describes a passion as a virtue's "subject matter" (2002, p. 430), he probably intends the phrase as shorthand for *materia circa quam*, the field or domain to which the virtue applies. But Thomas never describes *materia circa quam* as the "subject" of a virtue. On the contrary, in both Question 55 and Question 60, Thomas compares *materia circa quam* to the virtue's *obiectum*, reserving *subiectum* for the power of the soul in which the virtue is seated.

What is the subject of the moral virtues? In Question 56, Aquinas begins by establishing that it cannot be the soul's essence, but only its multiple "powers" (*potentiae*). After clarifying the manner in which the powers of intellect and will can be subjects of virtue (56.3), he asks whether the irascible and concupiscible powers can also be subjects of virtue. They can, he argues, but only for human beings. Though non-rational animals have sensitive appetites (and thus the irascible and concupiscible), these powers are not in them the subjects of virtue, because they are not amenable to perfection. (Virtue is essentially a "perfection of a power" [*perfectio potentiae*], as 55.1, 55.2, and 55.3 make clear.) But in human beings, the irascible and concupiscible can be perfected, according to their capacity to participate in reason. Because they can participate in reason, they are fit to serve as subjects of moral virtues. Any moral virtue that is subjected in the irascible or concupiscible, Thomas concludes, is "nothing other than a certain habitual conformity of either of these powers to reason" (56.4.co).

Aquinas' analysis is precise. Chenu errs when he speaks of the passions as being "properly the subjects of the virtues" and as their "seat" (1974, pp. 12–13).[1] Passions cannot be the subjects of virtues, because they are the

---

[1] For protection against the danger of confusing acts and powers, it may be helpful to bear in mind Dr. Johnson's comment on Pope: he "has formed his theory with so little skill that, in the examples by which he illustrates and confirms it, he has confounded passions, appetites, and habits" (1905, pp. 174–5).

particular acts of the sensitive appetite's powers.[2] Only the *potentiae*, not the *actus*, can serve as the subjects of virtue. The sensitive appetite is perfected when the passions accept the politic rule of reason – that is, when they acknowledge the right of reason to command, while contributing something of their own that follows upon reason. Rather than being the subjects of virtue, passions are the acts whose regular, prompt occurrence according to the judgment of reason constitutes the perfection of the power from which they proceed. Without the passions, there is no prospect of perfecting the powers, since to perfect the powers of the sensitive appetite simply means to ensure that the right acts characteristically flow from those powers. But since a virtue simply is the habitual perfection of a power, the moral virtues associated with the sensitive appetite require the passions as the condition of their possibility.

With this framework in mind, one may turn directly to Question 59's treatment of the "relation" (*comparatio*) of virtue to the passions, undertaken for the sake of determining the mutual relations between the moral virtues.[3] Question 59 illumines the *comparatio* in five carefully ordered Articles. Moral virtue is not itself the same as passion; to conflate the two would violate the distinction between a habit and an act (Article 1).

---

[2] To say that the passions are *actus* is to distinguish them, in an important sense, not only from "powers" of acts, but also from "principles." Stump (2003) claims that "passions, virtues and vices are all intrinsic principles or sources, of human acts" (p. 25). Here she appears to have confused the lines along which Aquinas structures the 1a2ae. Aquinas begins with the *finis* (Questions 1–5), moves to the *actus* (Questions 6–48), and concludes with the *principia* (Questions 49–114). The acts are subdivided into those which are properly human, the acts of the will and their relation to good and evil (Questions 6–21), and those which humans have in common with other animals, the passions (Questions 22–48). Aquinas proceeds to discuss the *principia* or sources of acts, distinguishing them as intrinsic or extrinsic. After a preliminary discussion of "habits in general" (Questions 49–54), Aquinas considers particular intrinsic principles – that is, the virtues (Questions 55–67), the gifts (Questions 68–70), and sins (Questions 71–89). The extrinsic principles are law and grace (Questions 90–114). In some sense a passion may stand as the "principle" of a human act – I am angry, I yell; my anger is the principle of my yelling. Something like this may lead Stump to lump the passions with the virtues and the vices in the category of "intrinsic principles, or sources, of human acts" (p. 25). But when Aquinas divides Questions 6–114 of the 1a2ae according to a distinction between human acts and their principles, he strictly includes passions within the former category. If the passions are principles, they are not principles *simpliciter*, but only *secundum quid*. For both volitions and passions as *actus*, see 6.pr.; for the distinction between intrinsic and extrinsic principles, see 49.pr., which begins: "Post actus et passiones, considerandum est de principiis humanorum actuum. Et primo, de principiis intrinsecis; secundo, de principiis extrinsecis."

[3] The *prooemia* of 1-2.59 and 1-2.60 begin identically: "Deinde considerandum est de distinctione virtutum moralium ad invicem." How to explain this rare occurrence? In Question 59, Aquinas describes the immediate task: "considerare comparationem virtutis ad passionem" (59 pr.). Having done this, Thomas will be able to treat the differences between the moral virtues more directly in the following Question, a task that turns out to be identical to clarifying the "distinctionem moralium virtutum secundum passiones" (60 pr.).

But moral virtue can be accompanied by passion. The Stoic view that moral virtue can exist only if passion is obliterated cannot be sustained, Aquinas argues, explicitly recalling Augustine's mediation of the debate between the Stoics and the Peripatetics (Article 2). The capacity of the moral virtues to exist *cum passio* is true even with respect to sorrow, the most proper passion (Article 3). The dialectical motion of the next two Articles must be followed closely. In Article 4, Aquinas warns against universalizing a conclusion that might appear to be sanctioned by Articles 2 and 3. Not every moral virtue directly requires passion.[4] Justice is seated in the will; it perfects the power of the rational appetite, without having any immediate relation to acts of the sensitive appetite. But if Aquinas rejects the thesis that all moral virtues require passion in order to exist, he does not want to say that passions generally bear an extrinsic relation to virtue. On the contrary, the moral virtues of temperance and fortitude are seated in the two powers of the sensitive appetite (*not* the two appetites; cf. §2.4). These virtues directly require the passions, since to speak of the perfection of these powers without their acts is meaningless. Thus "it is plain that the moral virtues which are about the passions as about their proper matter (*circa propria materia*) cannot exist without passions" (59.5.co).

Aquinas emphasizes this conclusion by considering the implications of its denial. If the perfection of the sensitive appetite were to entail the elimination of its acts – that is, the extirpation of the passions – the sensitive appetite would be destroyed rather than perfected. It would literally be inactive, "entirely unemployed" (*omnino otiosum*) (59.5.co). Since the sensitive appetite is part of man's integral nature, and not an effect of the Fall, its perfection cannot consist in its elimination. The moral virtues that are the habitual perfection of its powers require the passions. But the moral virtues "which are not about the passions, but about operations, can exist without the passions" (59.5). Since the *materia circa quam* of justice is not passion but operation, justice does not require

---

[4] Not the moral virtues *simpliciter*, but only the moral virtues "quae sunt circa passiones sicut circa propriam materiam," are unable to exist without the passions. In light of the care that Aquinas takes to limit the scope of his claim, Gondreau's conclusion that "there is simply *no* moral virtue without passion" (emphasis in original) seems too blunt (2002, p. 267). Gondreau does note that justice is the "sole" exception. The exception is not exactly marginal, since by "justice" Aquinas means the master virtue that regulates the rational appetite, and thus has multiple parts. For the subjective parts, see 2-2.61–2; for the quasi-integral parts, see 2-2.79; for the quasi-potential parts (omitting the acts and the opposed vices), see 2-2.80–1 (*religio*), 101 (*pietas*), 102 (*observantia*), 106 (*gratia sive gratitudo*), 108 (*vindicatio*), 109 (*veritas*), 114 (*amicitia seu affabilitas*), 117 (*liberalitas*), 120 (*epieikeia*).

passion as a condition of its existence. Yet it does not follow that the absence of passion characterizes the most excellent acts of justice. On the contrary, "joy follows from the act of justice" (59.5). If such joy may be a pseudopassion rather than a passion in the proper sense (§2.2, §7.1), it may remain in the will without having any effect on the sensitive appetite. But "should this joy be multiplied by the perfection of justice, it will at every point overflow into the sensitive appetite, according as inferior powers follow the motion of superior powers" (59.5.co). Even when passion is not strictly required for moral virtue, its presence indicates the flourishing of that virtue. "And thus through this kind of overflow, the more perfect a virtue is, the more it causes passion" (59.5.co).

Question 59 establishes a general relation between the moral virtues and passions. But which passions are connected with which moral virtues? Question 60 proposes to discern the links between the various moral virtues by clarifying "the distinction of moral virtues according to the passions."[5] In the fourth Article of this Question, Aquinas distinguishes the moral virtues whose *subiectum* is the concupiscible from those that are seated in the irascible. Although the concupiscible has six distinct acts (i.e. the passions of love, hatred, desire, aversion, pleasure, sorrow), Aquinas finds one virtue to rule them all, *temperantia*. Why is no more than a single virtue necessary?

The diverse passions of the concupiscible do not pertain to diverse moral virtues, because their motions are consequent upon one another according to a certain order, inasmuch as they are ordered to the same thing, viz. to the pursuit of good, or the flight from evil. Thus from love proceeds concupiscence, and from concupiscence one arrives at pleasure. (60.4.co)

At every stage, temperance regulates the concupiscible passions, ensuring that its possessor experiences love and hate, desire and aversion, pleasure and sorrow according to the rational mean. The irascible presents a more complicated case. Because its object is more complex than that of the concupiscible, its five acts require three moral virtues. About the irascible passions, Thomas explains that they

are not of a single order, but are ordered toward diverse things, for daring and fear are ordered toward some great danger; hope and despair toward some arduous good; and anger toward overcoming something contrary that has inflicted harm. (60.4.co)

---

[5] This is the task assigned to Question 60 at 59 pr.

Thus fear and daring are the matter of *fortitudo*; hope and despair the matter of *magnanimitas*; and anger the matter of *mansuetudo*. Though Gondreau is right to stress this point, his gloss that "without fear, one can experience no fortitude; without the pleasures afforded by sex, there can be no practice of chastity, etc." (2002, p. 267) must be qualified. To exercise fortitude (one does not "experience" a virtue) means to experience fear when it is rational to do so, in the right measure, and not to experience fear when doing so would be contrary to reason. During any particular exercise of fortitude, it may be the case that the agent experiences no fear at all. (According to Aristotle, this is the situation of the genuinely brave warrior who goes into battle with joy, or least with no pain; cf. *Nicomachean Ethics* 2.3, 1104b5–10.) Aquinas' point is this: without a field of objects that have the potency for activating the passions of fear and daring, the virtue of fortitude would have nothing to be about – no *materia circa quam* – and would therefore not exist. But the concrete application of the virtue to the matter never requires that the agent experience fear in order to exercise fortitude, or pleasure in order to practice chastity.

Is it sufficient to assign temperance to the concupiscible passions, great-souledness to hope and despair, fortitude to fear and daring, and meekness to anger? One might think so. Aquinas, however, insists upon a finer-grained differentiation. Question 60 concludes by asking whether the moral virtues may be distinguished not simply according to the passions that constitute their matter, but according to the "objects of the passions" (*obiecta passionum*). Are the objects that formally distinguish passions from one another also capable of distinguishing the moral virtues? Aquinas answers in the affirmative: "The objects cause different species of passions, according as they are diversely related to the sensitive appetite, and they cause different species of virtues, as they are related to reason" (60.5.co). Because the two relations are not identical, the moral virtues will not exhibit a one-to-one correspondence with the passions. Nonetheless, the moral virtues (except for justice) are grounded in the *obiecta passionum* no less securely than the passions themselves. At the end of the unusually long response of Article 5, Aquinas draws the following conclusion:

Thus it is clear that, according to Aristotle, there are ten moral virtues about the passions, viz. fortitude, temperance, liberality, magnificence, great-souledness, love of honor, meekness, friendship, truthfulness, and playfulness. And these are distinguished according to the diverse matters or according to diverse passions, or according to diverse objects. (60.5.co)

The particular correspondences located by Aquinas may be summarized in table Ep. 1. In this way, Aquinas systematically connects each of the moral virtues named by Aristotle (except for justice) with the objects of the passions.[6]

Is each moral virtue of equal rank? The first objection of the next Question argues that they are, since each equally divides the genus of virtue (61.1 obj. 1). But Aquinas denies this claim. The denial is reflected in his decision to follow the "Aristotelian" division of the genus with a Question on the four cardinal virtues. In the arguments *sed contra* within each of Question 61's four Articles, Thomas cites Ambrose, Gregory, Cicero, and Augustine. Each *auctoritas* agrees with the claim that "we know that there are four cardinal virtues" (61.1.sc).

How can Question 60's scheme, represented in table Ep. 1, be reconciled to the framework of the four cardinal virtues? In Article 2, Aquinas identifies two ways in which the primacy of four virtues may be seen. First, the "formal principle" of the virtues (i.e. the good of reason) requires not only prudence and justice, but also temperance and fortitude, so that we may "put the order of reason into the passions" (61.2.co). Why does the sensitive appetite require only temperance and fortitude as cardinal virtues? Aquinas answers by referring to the previous Question's distinction between the *bonum absolute* and the *bonum cum aliqua arduitate* (60.5.co). Passions directed toward the good considered absolutely are moderated by one type of virtue, whereas passions that regard good as involving something arduous are governed by another type of virtue. In relation to the sensitive appetite, the "formal principle" of the virtues licenses these two (and only these two) cardinal virtues. The same result, Aquinas argues, can be attained by considering the subjects of the cardinal virtues: the intellect, the will, the concupiscible, and the irascible. Thomas does not suppose that the coincidence is adventitious. Rather, it shows that the location of two cardinal virtues in relation to the passions arises from the nature of the passions themselves, considered according to the difference between the *bonum absolute* and the *bonum cum aliqua arduitate* that grounds the irascible/concupiscible distinction (§2.4). Aquinas thus shows that *both* the "Aristotelian" differentiation of ten moral virtues and the

---

[6] Gondreau (2002) fears that Aquinas follows Aristotle "perhaps too narrowly in this area" (pp. 267–8). The fear would be justified if Aquinas intended the dialectic to stop with Question 59. But the subsequent Questions indicate that with respect to classifying the virtues, Thomas has little interest in following any single *auctoritas*.

Table Ep.1 *Moral virtues in relation to the objects of the passions*

Moral virtue	Corresponding object of the passions
Fortitude	Good as arduous
Temperance	Good discerned by touch
	Good discerned by inner power
Liberality	—considered absolutely
Magnificence	—considered as arduous
	Good of honor
Love of honor (*philotimia*)	—considered absolutely
Great-souledness	—considered as arduous
Meekness	Good of vindication
	Good in relation to others in serious matters
Friendship	—pleasant speech and deeds
Truthfulness	—truthful words and deeds
Playfulness	Good in relation to others in playful matters

distinction between the "four cardinal virtues" are grounded in reflection on the passions and their objects.

The grounding of the moral virtues in the passions illuminates the structure of the 1a2ae. Aquinas places the twenty-seven Questions on the passions before the Questions on the virtues, because understanding the former is a precondition of grasping the latter. Understanding the passions in relation to their subjects also throws light upon the ordering of the 2a2ae. That part of the *ST* moves from a treatment of the theological virtues (2-2.1–46) to a consideration of the four cardinal virtues. Aquinas treats prudence (2-2.47–56), justice (2-2.57–122), fortitude (2-2.123–40) and temperance (2-2.141–70). Why does he adopt this particular order? A passage from Question 66 of the 1a2ae is suggestive:

The cause and root of human good is reason. And thus prudence, which perfects reason, is superior in goodness to the other moral virtues that perfect the appetitive power insofar as it participates in reason. And in these things, one is better than another, to the extent that it comes nearer to reason. Whence justice, which is in the will, is superior to the other moral virtues, and fortitude, which is in the irascible, is superior to temperance, which is in the concupiscible and participates less in reason. (66.1.co)

Without a prior knowledge of the powers of the soul and their acts, Aquinas suggests, it is not possible to have orderly thinking about the virtues. This conviction, so important for the architecture of the 1a2ae, lies at the heart of the entire *pars moralis* of the *ST*.

Aquinas' detailed discussion of the passions, embracing both general considerations (Questions 22–5) and the particular passions (Questions 26–48), serves as a necessary prologue to the treatment of the virtues. Since exercising the virtues is partly constitutive of happiness, locating the passions in relation to virtue is one way to exhibit their place within the whole of the 1a2ae. Happiness involves the acquisition and exercise of the full range of moral virtues. Without an adequate knowledge of the passions, one cannot possess the virtues in their amplitude, since temperance and fortitude are the perfections of those powers whose acts are the passions. Moreover, if temperance and fortitude require the appropriate cultivation of the passions, and the other moral virtues require temperance and fortitude, it follows that possession of the moral virtues as such requires the passions.

Is there a more direct way to connect knowledge of the passions with the attainment of happiness? There is, if one reflects that each of the eleven basic passions, including those that moralists of a certain stripe have been quick to reject, has something vital to contribute to human flourishing. When experienced in the appropriate manner, hatred, sorrow, fear, and anger are useful. Even the passion of despair (as distinguished from the sin) has its proper role to play. A sense of the fundamental naturalness of the passions emerges from a close reading of the texts. Thomas devotes such a large portion of the 1a2ae to the acts of the sensitive appetite because he thinks that without an adequate grasp of the passions, we can neither know what happiness is nor attain it.

What makes knowledge of the passions necessary for beatitude? Pinckaers proposes that for Aquinas the passions enable our first glimpse of spiritual happiness: "Sensibility supplies man with a first image and a fundamental vocabulary for the expression of spiritual realities" (1990, p. 382). Sensitive love and pleasure function as images of their spiritual originals. Without the experience of *delectatio*, it would be difficult to have any grasp of what Aquinas means by *gaudium* and *fruitio*, associated with the last end. As composites of form and matter, the passions lie at the boundary of the sensible and the spiritual. Thus Pinckaers suggests that "the passions are a parable of the motions of the spirit in its access to the world and to God" (1990, p. 383).

The passions constitute a first image of a beatitude that transcends the passions. This does not, however, imply that the passions are solely a means to happiness, conceived as an end existing separately from the means. At the very least, the passions are partly constitutive of the happiness available in this life. Asking about the relation of happiness to the practical intellect, Aquinas concludes:

Imperfect happiness, such as can be had here, consists first and principally in contemplation, and secondarily in the operation of the practical intellect ordering human actions and passions, as is said in book 10 of the *Ethics*. (3.5.co)

Considered as a person's total perfection, happiness cannot be limited to the actualization of a part. It must include the whole of her basic powers and appetites. A person who somehow manages to avoid particular sinful volitions, but neglects her passions, cannot be described as flourishing. To feel the right things in the right time in the right way – that is, to love, hate, desire, avoid, delight, sorrow, hope, despair, fear, dare, and feel anger according to the rational mean – belongs to a person's interior happiness. Since the full notion of happiness includes the well-being of the sensitive appetite, the attainment of happiness requires a knowledge of the passions. To be acted upon in such a way that our passions are in a perpetual state of disorder is incompatible with happiness.

Right reason is required to perfect the acts of the sensitive appetite. One implication is that reason must know the passions, in order to direct them, just as those who govern must understand the nature of the governed. Luigi Bogliolo takes Aquinas to hold that "the fundamental struggle of man in this life is for man to love himself *secundum rationem* and not *secundum passionem*" (1977, p. 118). This accurately captures one part of Thomas's view. But Eileen Sweeney is no less correct to maintain that Aquinas does not "express any fundamental distrust of the passions" or "engage in any heavy-handed appeals to the need for rational control of the passions" (1999, p. 222). As Sweeney discerns, it is one-sided to hold that the passions need the guidance of reason, without adverting to the complementary sense in which reason needs the passions (see §4.4).

Lacking the cooperation of the passions, it is impossible for the will habitually to choose what is good. Aquinas acknowledges that a person may in some cases choose the good in spite of his passions. This is precisely the situation of the person who is continent rather than virtuous. Aquinas does not regard continence, characterized by a struggle of the lower appetite against the higher appetite, as a stable condition. In order to choose the good easily and promptly, the active cooperation of the passions is required. Without this cooperation, a person will simply be divided against herself, dominated by the unproductive state of soul that Plato calls *stasis* (see *Republic* 252a and 440b). What is the remedy for *stasis*? Letterio Mauro writes: "The task of man is not that of developing one power to the detriment of the others, but of developing all his powers in a harmonious manner" (1974, p. 8). Mauro's formulation of Aquinas' point captures what is crucially lacking in it by descriptions of the reason/ passion relation that confine themselves to the metaphor of control. As a constitutive part of happiness, the harmonious development of the soul's powers is not simply a matter of control over the lower by the higher. On the contrary, the passions must be positively cultivated. Without the genuine support (as distinguished from sullen obedience) of the sensitive appetite, the will is feeble, unable to accomplish its own act with any kind of assurance. Approaches to morals which appear to exalt reason and will by proposing a brutal domination of the passions are not, in fact, well designed to promote the flourishing of the rational appetite. On the contrary, the likely result is the production of "men without chests," persons who lack the thumotic energy required to choose the difficult good (Lewis 1947, ch. 1). Without appropriate knowledge and cultivation of the passions, the prospects for genuine happiness are dim. The higher cannot stand without the lower (Lewis 1960, pp. 20, 32).

In showing the link between happiness and cultivation of the passions, I have placed the accent on imperfect happiness. With regard to the happiness attainable in this life, Aquinas says, "we proceed from the perfection of the lower part to the perfection of the higher part" (3.3 ad 3m). Though the sensitive appetite does not enter directly into contemplation, its right disposition is necessary for the full actualization of the higher powers. Aquinas makes the point explicitly when he asserts that sensitive *amor* is "more divine" than rational *dilectio*, since it has more power to propel the human person toward the loving contemplation of God (26.3 ad 4m; see §5.2). The most intense love of God involves the full cooperation of the sensitive appetite. What is true of this particular case holds generally. "The will cannot be moved to anything intensely (*intese*), without a passion being aroused in the sensitive appetite" (77.6.co).

Despite their crucial place within imperfect happiness, the passions may finally seem irrelevant for attaining complete happiness. There is something to this appearance. The "attainment or possession" of perfect happiness (3.1.co) consists essentially in an *operatio* of the (supernaturally elevated) speculative intellect (3.5; see also 1.12.2 on the *lumen gloriae* and 109.1 on the *lumen gratiae*). Because this is true, perfect happiness does not bear exactly the same relation to the passions as imperfect happiness does. Yet Aquinas explicitly rejects the view that in perfect happiness the passions are left behind. On the contrary, because pleasure follows upon the intellect's *operatio*, the passions belong to

perfect happiness "consequently" (3.3.co). Perfect happiness does not
focus narrowly upon the intellect, neglecting the actualization of the other
powers of the soul. "In perfect happiness the whole man is perfected, but
in the lower part by an overflow from the higher" (3.3 ad 3m). Even after
this life, the human person does not discard the passions, as if they had
simply exhausted their usefulness.

Knowledge of happiness, whether theoretical or practical, requires the
appropriate cultivation of the sensitive appetite. This conviction animates
Aquinas' decision to devote more than one quarter of the 1a2ae to an
extended treatment of the passions. Why does he insist on the level of
detail that he does? What is gained by knowing the passions in particular?
Aquinas takes seriously the notion that it is possible for a person to
acquire insight into the multiple ways in which she is acted upon, and
even (with the help of divine grace) change those ways, should they lead
her away from beatitude. If a person is sufficiently aware of her fears,
and senses that something is wrong, she may be led to pose a question of
the form: "How do I become the kind of person who is not dominated by
fear and anxiety?" For her to achieve understanding of why she fears in the
manner she does, she must know what fear is, what it comes from, and
what it does to her. With this knowledge, it may become possible to
harmonize the judgment of her universal reason with the judgment of
particular reason (§3.4). The first step for her is to recognize that she
characteristically apprehends certain things under the formal object of
fear, even if they do not actually possess those features. The example may
be generalized. Those who seek to change the ways in which they experience the passions of love, hate, concupiscence, aversion, pleasure, sorrow,
hope, despair, daring, or anger, so that these passions may become
contributors (rather than obstacles) to beatitude, require a particularized
knowledge of the passions.

Aquinas does not think that the practical problem of the passions
admits of any "one size fits all" solution. Thus he composes a cluster of
Questions on the particular passions. To know the conditions under
which happiness is attainable, a person must understand each of the
primary passions in its nature, its causes, and its effects. Yet Thomas does
not suppose that inquiry can proceed as though the passions were discon-
nected atoms with no relation to one another. On the contrary, knowledge of the passions is inseparable from knowledge of the order among
them (§3.5). Grasping this order requires constant recurrence to love, "the
first root of all the passions" (46.1.co). While the 1a2ae devotes separate
Questions to the particular passions, it adverts throughout to their common

root in love. "It belongs to the wise to preserve due order in all things" (*InNE* 4.8.3).[7] Preserving the right order requires Thomas to trace every passion back to the non-negotiable desire for the good.

The design of the 1a2ae is meant to provide a knowledge of the passions that promotes the ascent toward beatitude. As such, it treats the passions with the requisite particularity. Yet it remains that in the 1a2ae, Aquinas approaches morals *in universali*.[8] Despite its relative detail, the treatment of the passions stops well short of the particular knowledge required for individual cases. Acquisition of such knowledge may require both a different form of discourse (e.g. the treatment of morals *in particulari* that constitutes the 2a2ae) and the practical discernment to which any written discourse can only be a prologue. The account of the 1a2ae is geared to provide illumination of what is necessary for beatitude, without making extravagant claims for its own sufficiency. It points at once toward other texts, and toward what lies beyond all texts.

---

[7] This might well apply to Aquinas' own disposition of *sacra doctrina*. Since Thomas is genuinely humble, he would not consider himself a *sapiens*. (But neither would he underestimate his own deserts, since true humility excludes pusillanimity.)

[8] Gondreau's claim that in the 1a2ae's treatment of the passions, "Thomas leaves no stone unturned and spares no painstaking effort in his endeavor to explain the complex reality of human affectivity in as satisfactory a manner as possible" (2002, p. 105), is slightly exaggerated. There are many simplifications and abbreviations in the treatment, as one would expect of the *ST*, and of the 1a2ae in particular. Yet Gondreau is certainly correct to suggest that Thomas is "not content with a generalized discussion on human passion only" (p. 211).

Bibliography

Amis, Kingsley (1954). *Lucky Jim* (London: Penguin Books).

Anscombe, Elizabeth (1981). "Modern Moral Philosophy," in *The Collected Philosophical Papers of G. E. M. Anscombe*, III: *Ethics, Religion and Politics* (Oxford: Basil Blackwell), pp. 26–42.

Aristotle (1984). *The Complete Works of Aristotle: The Revised Oxford Translation*, ed. J. Barnes (Princeton: Princeton University Press).

Augustine (1958). *On Christian Doctrine*, tr. D. W. Robertson Jr. (New York: Prentice Hall).

(1984). *City of God*, tr. H. Bettenson (London: Penguin Books).

(1993). *Confessions*, tr. F. J. Sheed (Indianapolis and Cambridge, Mass.: Hackett Publishing).

(1998). *The Trinity*, tr. E. Hill (New York: New City Press).

Avicenna (1972). *Liber de anima seu Sextus de naturalibus*, ed. S. van Riet (Leiden: Brill).

Barad, Judith (1991). "Aquinas on the Role of Emotion in Moral Judgment and Activity," *Thomist* 55, pp. 397–413.

Blanco, G. (1948). "El concepto de pasión en Santo Tomás," *Sapientia* 2, pp. 133.

Bogliolo, Luigi (1977). "Sulla fondazione tomista della morale," in *Tommaso d'Aquino nel suo settimo centenario: Atti del Congresso Internazionale* (Roma-Napoli 17–24 aprile 1974), V: *L'agire morale* (Naples: Edizione Domenicane Italiane), pp. 107–21.

Boswell, James (1934). *Life of Johnson*, ed. G. B. Hill (Oxford: Clarendon Press).

Brennan, Robert (1941). *Thomistic Psychology: A Philosophic Analysis of the Nature of Man* (New York: Macmillan).

Burton, Robert (1927). *The Anatomy of Melancholy*, ed. Floyd Dell and Paul Jordan-Smith (New York: Tudor Publishing Company).

Buytaert, Eligius M. (1955). Introduction to *Saint John Damascene: De Fide Orthodoxa: Versions of Burgundio and Cerbanus* (St. Bonaventure, New York: The Franciscan Institute).

Byers, Sarah (2003). "Augustine and the Cognitive Cause of Stoic 'Preliminary Passions' (*Propatheiai*)," *Journal of the History of Philosophy* 41, pp. 433–48.

Cajetan, Tommaso de Vio (1889). *Commentaria in primam secundam Summae theologiae*. In Thomas Aquinas (1882–10), VI.

Candler, Peter M. (2006). *Theology, Rhetoric, Manuduction, or Reading Scripture Together on the Path to God* (Grand Rapids: Eerdmans).

Catherine of Siena (1980). *The Dialogue*, tr. S. Noffke, OP (New York: Paulist Press).

Chenu, M. D. (1964). *Toward Understanding Saint Thomas* (Chicago: Henry Regnery).

(1974). "Les passions vertueuses: l'anthropologie de saint Thomas." *Revue Philosophique de Louvain* 72, pp. 11–18.

Chesterton, G. K. (1956). *Saint Thomas Aquinas* (New York: Image Books).

Cicero, Marcus Tullius (1927). *Tusculan Disputations*, ed. J. E. King (Cambridge, Mass., and London: Harvard University Press).

Collingwood, R. G. (1938). *The Principles of Art* (Oxford: Oxford University Press).

(1939). *An Autobiography* (Oxford: Oxford University Press).

(1940). *An Essay on Metaphysics* (Oxford: Clarendon Press).

(1942). *The New Leviathan* (Oxford: Clarendon Press).

(1956). *The Idea of History* (New York: Oxford University Press).

Dante (2003). *Purgatorio*, tr. R. M. Durling (Oxford: Oxford University Press).

D'Arcy, Eric (2006). Introduction to Thomas Aquinas 2006f.

De Lubac, Henri (1987). *Paradoxes of Faith* (San Francisco: Ignatius Press).

Deigh, John (1994). "Cognitivism in the Theory of Emotions," *Ethics* 104, pp. 824–54.

Dixon, Thomas (2003). *From Passions to Emotions: The Creation of a Secular Psychological Category* (Cambridge: Cambridge University Press).

Eschmann, Ignatius, OP (1997). *The Ethics of Saint Thomas Aquinas: Two Courses*, ed. Edward A. Synan (Toronto: Pontifical Institute of Medieval Studies).

Farrell, Walter (1942). *A Companion to the Summa*, II (New York: Sheed & Ward).

Floyd, Shawn D. (1998). "Aquinas on Emotion: A Response to Some Recent Interpretations," *History of Philosophy Quarterly* 15, pp. 161–75.

Francis, St. (1982). *Francis and Clare: The Complete Works*, ed. R. J. Armstrong and I. C. Brady (New York: Paulist Press).

Francis, de Sales (2002). *Introduction to the Devout Life* (New York: Vintage).

Frankfurt, Harry (1971). "Freedom of the Will and the Concept of a Person," *Journal of Philosophy* 67, pp. 5–20.

Fromm, Erich (1956). *The Art of Loving* (New York: Bantam Books).

Galeazzi, Umberto (2004). "Le passioni secondo Tommaso d'Aquino: *De veritate*, q. 26," *Aquinas* 47, pp. 547–70.

Gondreau, Paul (2002). *The Passions of Christ's Soul in the Theology of St. Thomas Aquinas* (Münster: Aschendorff).

Gordon, Robert (1986). "The Passivity of Emotions," *The Philosophical Review* 95, pp. 371–92.

Harak, G. S. (1987). "The Passions, the Virtues, and Agency: Modern Research and Thomistic Reflection," *Logos* 8, pp. 31–44.

Hobbes, Thomas (1991). *Leviathan*, ed. Richard Tuck (Cambridge: Cambridge University Press).

James, Susan (1997). "Passion and Action in Aquinas," in *Passion and Action: The Emotions in Seventeenth-Century Philosophy* (Oxford: Clarendon Press).

Jeffrey, David Lyle (1996). *People of the Book: Christian Identity and Literary Culture* (Grand Rapids: Eerdmans).

John Damascene (1857–66). *De fide orthodoxa*, in *PG* 94.

Johnson, Samuel (1905). *The Lives of the Poets*, III, ed. G. B. Hill (Oxford: Clarendon Press).

Jordan, Mark (1986). "Aquinas's Construction of a Moral Account of the Passions," *Freiburger Zeitschrift für Philosophie und Theologie* 33, pp. 71–97.

(1992a). *The Alleged Aristotelianism of Thomas Aquinas* (Toronto: PIMS).

(1992b). "Rhetorical Form in the Historiography of Philosophy," *New Literary History* 23, pp. 483–504.

(1994). "The *Pars moralis* of the *Summa theologiae* as *Scientia* and as *Ars*," in Ingrid Craemer-Ruegenberg and Andreas Speer, eds., Scientia *und* ars *im Hoch- und Spätmittelalter* (Berlin and New York: Walter de Gruyter), pp. 468–81.

Keats, John (2002). *Selected Letters of John Keats*, ed. G. F. Scott (Cambridge, Mass., and London: Harvard University Press).

Kenny, Anthony (1963). *Action, Emotion and Will* (Atlantic Highlands, N.J.: Humanities Press).

(1993). *Aquinas on Mind* (London: Routledge).

(2004). "Stump's Aquinas," *Philosophical Quarterly* 54, pp. 457–58.

Kierkegaard, Søren (1980). *The Sickness Unto Death*, tr. H. Hong and E. Hong (Princeton: Princeton University Press).

King, Peter (1998). "Aquinas on the Passions," in Scott MacDonald and Eleonore Stump, eds., *Aquinas's Moral Theory: Essays in Honor of Norman Kretzmann* (Ithaca: Cornell University Press), pp. 101–32.

(2002). "Late Scholastic Theories of the Passions: Controversies in the Thomistic Tradition," in Lagerlund and Yrjönsuuri 2002, pp. 229–58.

Klubertanz, George (1952). *The Discursive Power: Sources and Doctrine of the Vis Cogitativa According to St. Thomas Aquinas* (Carthagena, Ohio: Messenger Press).

Knuuttila, Simo (2002). "Medieval Theories of the Passions of the Soul," in Lagerlund and Yrjönsuuri 2002, pp. 49–79.

(2004). *Emotions in Ancient and Medieval Philosophy* (Oxford: Oxford University Press).

Lagerlund, H., and Yrjönsuuri, M., eds. (2002). *Emotions and Choice from Boethius to Descartes* (Boston: Kluwer Academic).

La Rochefoucauld, F. de (1959). *Maxims*, tr. Leonard Tancock (London: Penguin Books).

Larkin, Philip (1988). *Collected Poems* (London: The Marvell Press).

Lazarus, Richard S., and Lazarus, Bernice N. (1996). *Passion and Reason: Making Sense of Our Emotions* (New York: Oxford University Press).

Leget, Carlos (2003). "Martha Nussbaum and Thomas Aquinas on the Emotions," *Theological Studies* 64, pp. 558–81.

Lewis, C. S. (1947). *The Abolition of Man* (New York: Macmillan).

(1960). *The Four Loves* (San Diego: Harcourt Brace Jovanovich).

Loughlin, Stephen (2005). "*Tristitia et Dolor:* Does Aquinas Have a Robust Understanding of Depression?" *Nova et Vetera* 3, pp. 761–83.

Machiavelli, Niccolò (1998). *The Prince*, tr. H. Mansfield (Chicago: University of Chicago Press).

Mackey, Louis (1997). *Peregrinations of the Word: Essays in Medieval Philosophy* (Ann Arbor: University of Michigan Press).

MacIntyre, Alasdair (1990). *Three Rival Versions of Moral Enquiry* (Notre Dame: University of Notre Dame Press).

(2004). Preface to *The Unconscious: A Conceptual Analysis*, rev. edn. (New York and London: Routledge).

Manzanedo, Marcos F. (1987). "El deseo y la aversión según Santo Tomás," *Studium* 27, pp. 189–233.

(1989). "Efectos y propiedades de la delectación," *Studium* 29, pp. 107–39.

(1991). "El dolor y sus causas," *Studium* 31, pp. 63–97.

(1993). "Relaciones y moralidad de la esperanza," *Studium* 33, pp. 389–410.

(1994). "La audacia según Santo Tomás," *Studium* 34, pp. 437–53.

Maritain, Jacques (1932). *Distinguer pour Unir ou Les Degrés du Savoir* (Paris: Desclée de Brouwer).

Marmo, Costantino (1991). "*Hoc autem etsi potest tollerari . . .* Egidio Romano e Tommaso d'Aquino sulle passioni dell'anima," *Documenti e studi sulla tradizione filosofica medievale* 2, pp. 281–315.

Mauro, Letterio (1974). *"Umanità" della passione in Tommaso d'Aquino* (Firenze: Felice Le Monnier).

(1977). "Le passioni nell'antropologia di san Tommaso," in *Tommaso d'Aquino nel suo settimo centenario: Atti del Congresso Internazionale* (Roma-Napoli 17–24 aprile 1974), v: *L'agire morale* (Naples: Edizione Domenicane Italiane), pp. 337–43.

Merton, Thomas (1961). *The New Man* (New York: Farrar, Straus & Giroux).

Meyer, Michel (1991). *Le philosophie et les passions: Esquisse d'une histoire de la nature humaine* (Paris: Le Livre de Poche).

(1994). "Le problème des passions chez saint Thomas d'Aquin," *Revue Internationale de Philosophie* 48, pp. 363–74.

(1995). *Of Problematology*, tr. D. Jamison and A. Hart (Chicago and London: University of Chicago Press).

Michelet, Jules (1859). *L'Amour*, 4th edn. (Paris: L. Hachete et cie).

Migne, J.-P. (1844–55). *Patrologia latina*, 221 vols. (Paris).

(1857–66). *Patrologia graeca*, 161 vols. (Paris).

Miner, Robert (2000). "Non-Aristotelian Prudence in the *Prima secundae* of the *Summa theologiae*," *Thomist* 64, pp. 401–22.

Murphy, Claudia (1999). "Aquinas on Our Responsibility for Our Emotions," *Medieval Philosophy and Theology* 8, pp. 163–205.

Montaigne, Michel de (1930). *Essais*, ed. P. Villey, 3 vols. (Paris: Librairie Félix Alcan).

Nietzsche, Friedrich (1966). *Beyond Good and Evil*, tr. R. J. Hollingdale (London: Penguin Books).

(1967). *On the Genealogy of Morals* and *Ecce Homo*, tr. W. Kaufmann and R. J. Hollingdale (New York: Vintage Books).

(1982). *Daybreak*, tr. R. J. Hollingdale (Cambridge: Cambridge University Press).

Nussbaum, Martha (1990). *Love's Knowledge: Essays on Philosophy and Literature* (New York: Oxford University Press).

(2001). *Upheavals of Thought: The Intelligence of the Emotions* (Cambridge: Cambridge University Press).

Nygren, Anders (1937). *Eros und Agape*, I (Berlin: Gütersloh).

O'Brien, T. C. (1977). "*Sacra Doctrina* Revisited: The Context of Medieval Education," *Thomist* 41, pp. 475–509.

Pascal, Blaise (1966). *Pensées*, tr. A. J. Krailsheimer (London: Penguin Books).

(1976). *Pensées*, ed. L. Brunschvicg (Paris: G. F. Flammarion).

Pasnau, Robert (2002). *Thomas Aquinas on Human Nature* (Cambridge: Cambridge University Press).

Pegis, Anton C. (1955). "St. Thomas and the Unity of Man," in James A. McWilliams, ed., *Progress in Philosophy: Philosophical Studies in Honor of Rev. Doctor Charles A. Hart* (Milwaukee: Bruce Publishing Co.), pp. 153–73.

Pegis, Anton C. (1997). Introduction to *Basic Writings of Saint Thomas Aquinas*, I (Indianapolis: Hackett Publishing).

Pègues, R. P. Thomas (1912). *Commentaire Français Littéral de la Somme Théologique de Saint Thomas d'Aquin*, VII: *Les Passions et les Habitus* (Toulouse and Paris: Imprimerie et librairie Édouard Privat).

Percy, Walker (1960). *The Moviegoer* (New York: Ivy Books).

(1971). *Love in the Ruins* (New York: Farrar, Straus & Giroux).

Pieper, Josef (1991). *Guide to Thomas Aquinas*, tr. Richard and Clara Winston (San Francisco: Ignatius Press).

(1997a). "On Hope," in *Faith, Hope, Love* (San Francisco: Ignatius Press).

(1997b). "On Love," in *Faith, Hope, Love* (San Francisco: Ignatius Press).

Pinckaers, Servais (1990). "Les passions et la morale," *Revue des sciences philosophiques et théologiques* 74, pp. 379–91.

(2005). *The Pinckaers Reader*, ed. J. Berkman and C. Titus (Washington, D. C.: Catholic University of America Press).

Plato (1997). *Complete Works*, ed. John M. Cooper (Indianapolis and Cambridge: Hackett Publishing).

Ramírez, S. M. (1973). *De passionibus animae in I-II Summae Theologiae divi Thomae expositio (qq. XXII–XLVIII)*. Obras completas de Santiago Ramírez, V (Instituto de Filosofía Luis Vives, Madrid).

Ricken, Friedo (1998). "Aristotelische Interpretationem Zum Traktat *De Passionibus Animae* (Summa theologiae I II 22–48) des Thomas von

Aquin," in Martin Thurner, ed., *Die Einheir de Person: Beiträge zur Anthropologie des Mittelalters* (Stuttgart: Kohlhammer), pp. 125–40.

Rieff, Phillip (1973). *Fellow Teachers: Of Culture and Its Second Death* (Chicago: University of Chicago Press).

(2006). *My Life Among the Deathworks* (Charlottesville: University of Virginia Press).

Roberts, Robert C. (1988). "What an Emotion Is: A Sketch," *Philosophical Review* 97, pp. 183–209.

(1992). "Thomas Aquinas on the Morality of Emotions," *History of Philosophy Quarterly* 9, pp. 287–305.

(2003). *Emotions: An Essay in Aid of Moral Psychology* (Cambridge: Cambridge University Press.)

(2004). Review of Robert Solomon, *Not Passion's Slave*, in *Mind* 113, pp. 588–90.

Rorty, Amélie Oksenberg (1984). "Aristotle on the Metaphysical Status of *Pathe*," *Review of Metaphysics* 38, pp. 521–46.

Rosenkrantz, Max (2005). Review of Thomas Dixon, *From Passions to Emotions*, in *Journal of the History of Philosophy* 43, pp. 214–15.

Rousseau, Jean-Jacques (1987). *Discourse on the Origin and Foundations of Inequality Among Men*, tr. D. Cress (Indianapolis and Cambridge, Mass.: Hackett Publishing).

Sayers, Dorothy L. (1936). *Gaudy Night* (New York: HarperCollins).

(1955). *The Comedy of Dante Alighierio: Cantica* II: *Purgatory*, tr. D. L. Sayers with commentary (London: Penguin Books).

Solomon, Robert (1983). *The Passions* (Notre Dame: University of Notre Dame Press).

(1999). Review of Paul Griffith, *What Emotions Really Are*, in *Philosophical Review* 108, pp. 131–4.

(2002). Review of Martha Nussbaum, *Upheavals of Thought*, in *Mind* 111, pp. 897–901.

Spinoza, Benedict de (1994). *A Spinoza Reader*, tr. E. Curley (Princeton: Princeton University Press).

Stagnitta, Antonino (1979). *L'Antropologia in Tommaso D'Aquino* (Naples: Edizione Domenicane Italiane).

Stanislavski, Constantin (1948). *An Actor Prepares*, tr. E. R. Hapgood (New York: Routledge).

Stanovich, Keith (1989). *How to Think Straight About Psychology*, 2nd edn. (Glenview, Ill.: Scott, Foresman & Company).

Strauss, Leo (1952). *On the Political Philosophy of Thomas Hobbes* (Chicago: University of Chicago Press).

(1964). *The City and Man* (Chicago and London: University of Chicago Press).

Stump, Eleonore (2003). *Aquinas* (London and New York: Routledge).

Sweeney, Eileen (1999). "Restructuring Desire: Aquinas, Hobbes and Descartes on the Passions," in Stephen F. Brown, ed., *Meeting of the Minds: The*

Relations between Medieval and Classical Modern European Philosophy. Rencontres de Philosophie Médiévale, VII (Turnhout: Brepols), pp. 215–33.

Terruwe, Anna A., MD, and Baars, Conrad W., MD (1972). *Loving and Curing the Neurotic: A New Look at Emotional Illness* (New Rochelle, N. Y.: Arlington House).

Thomas Aquinas (1882–). *S. Thomae Aquinatis Doctoris Angelici Opera Omnia* (Rome: Commissio Leonina).

(1887–9). *Summa theologica,* 5 vols., ed. X. Faucher (Paris: Lethielleux).

(1947–8). *Summa theologiae,* tr. L. Shapcote (New York: Benzinger).

(1949). *Les Passiones de l'âme,* tr. M. Corvez (Paris: Edition de la Revue des Jeunes).

(1961). *Commentary on the* Metaphysics *of Aristotle,* tr. J. P. Rowan (Chicago: Henry Regnery).

(1993). *Commentary on Aristotle's* Nicomachean Ethics, tr. C. I. Litzinger (Notre Dame: Dumb Ox Books).

(1994–6). *Somme théologique,* tr. A. M. Roguet *et al.* (Paris: Éditions du Cerf).

(1999). *Commentary on Aristotle's* De anima, tr. R. Pasnau (New Haven: Yale University Press).

(2002). *The Treatise on Human Nature,* tr. R. Pasnau (Indianapolis and Cambridge: Hackett Publishing).

(2006a). *Quaestiones disputatae De veritate,* ed. E. Alarcón. Electronically published at www.corpusthomisticum.org.

(2006b). *Sententia libri De anima,* ed. E. Alarcón. Electronically published at www.corpusthomisticum.org.

(2006c). *Sententia libri Ethicorum,* ed. E. Alarcón. Electronically published at www.corpusthomisticum.org.

(2006d). *Sententia libri Metaphysicae,* ed. E. Alarcón. Electronically published at www.corpusthomisticum.org.

(2006e). *Summa theologiae,* ed. E. Alarcón. Electronically published at www.corpusthomisticum.org.

(2006f). *Summa theologiae* (1a2ae QQ22–30), XIX, tr. E. D'Arcy (Cambridge: Cambridge University Press).

(2006g). *Summa theologiae* (1a2ae QQ31–39), XX, tr. E. D'Arcy (Cambridge: Cambridge University Press).

(2006h). *Summa theologiae* (1a2ae QQ40–48), XXI, tr. J. P. Reid (Cambridge: Cambridge University Press).

Torrell, Jean Pierre, OP (1996). *Saint Thomas Aquinas, 1: The Person and His Work,* tr. Robert Royal (Washington, D.C.: Catholic University of America Press).

U2 (1991). *Achtung Baby* (Island Records).

Uffenheimer-Lippens, Elisabeth (2003). "Rationalized Passion and Passionate Rationality: Thomas Aquinas on the Relation between Reason and the Passions," *Review of Metaphysics* 56, pp. 525–58.

Vaught, Carl G. (2003). *The Journey toward God in Augustine's* Confessions, *Books I–VI* (Albany: State University of New York Press).

Vico, Giambattista (1971). *De nostri temporis studiorum ratione*, in P. Cristofolini, ed., *Vico: Opere filosofiche* (Florence: Sansoni).

Vogler, Candace (2002). *Reasonably Vicious* (Cambridge, Mass.: Harvard University Press).

Wadell, Paul (1992). *The Primacy of Love: An Introduction to the Ethics of Thomas Aquinas* (New York: Paulist Press).

Wallace, William A. (1997). *The Modeling of Nature* (Washington, D. C.: Catholic University of America Press).

Weinandy, Thomas (2000). *Does God Suffer?* (Notre Dame: University of Notre Dame Press).

Westberg, Daniel (1996). "Emotion and God: A Reply to Marcel Sarot," *Thomist* 60, pp. 109–21.

White, Kevin (2002). "The Passions of the Soul," in Stephen J. Pope, ed., *Essays on Aquinas's Ethics* (Washington, D. C.: Georgetown University Press), pp. 103–15.

White, Victor (1943). "Thomism and 'Affective Knowledge,'" *Blackfriars* 24, pp. 8–16.

Wilde, Oscar (1999). *De profundis* (Hertfordshire: Wordsworth Editions).

Wilhelmsen, Frederick (1962). *The Metaphysics of Love* (New York: Sheed & Ward).

Williams, Cornelius, OP (1974). "The Hedonism of Aquinas," *Thomist* 38, pp. 257–90.

Wittgenstein, Ludwig (1922). *Tractatus Logico-Philosophicus,* tr. C. K. Ogden (London and New York: Routledge).

   (1953). *Philosophical Investigations*, tr. G. E. M. Anscombe (New York: Macmillan).

Wolfson, H. A. (1935). "The Internal Senses in Latin, Arabic, and Hebrew Philosophical Texts," *Harvard Theological Review* 28, pp. 69–133.

Index

CPSIA information can be obtained
at www.ICGtesting.com
Printed in the USA
LVOW07s1929061216

516069LV00003B/254/P